Sixth Edition

McLaughlin & Kaluzny's
Continuous Quality Improvement in Health Care

Julie K. Johnson, PhD, MSPH
University of North Carolina at Chapel Hill
Chapel Hill, North Carolina

Anna P. Schenck, PhD, MSPH
University of North Carolina at Chapel Hill
Chapel Hill, North Carolina

JONES & BARTLETT LEARNING

World Headquarters
Jones & Bartlett Learning
25 Mall Road
Burlington, MA 01803
978-443-5000
info@jblearning.com
www.jblearning.com

Jones & Bartlett Learning books and products are available through most bookstores and online booksellers. To contact Jones & Bartlett Learning directly, call 800-832-0034, fax 978-443-8000, or visit our website, www.jblearning.com.

Substantial discounts on bulk quantities of Jones & Bartlett Learning publications are available to corporations, professional associations, and other qualified organizations. For details and specific discount information, contact the special sales department at Jones & Bartlett Learning via the above contact information or send an email to specialsales@jblearning.com.

31779-4

Production Credits
Vice President, Innovative Learning and Assessment Solutions: Ada Woo
Senior Director, Content Production and Delivery: Christine Emerton
Director, Product: Melissa Kleeman-Moy
Product Manager: Sophie Fleck Teague
Manager of Content: Carol Brewer Guerrero
Content Manager: Jessica Covert
Content Coordinator: Rachelle Soden
Manager, Intellectual Properties and Content Production: Kristen Rogers
Content Production Manager: Belinda Thresher
Content Production Manager (Digital): Michael Lepera
Senior Intellectual Property Specialist (eBook): Angela Dooley
Senior Product Marketing Manager: Susanne Walker
Director, Product Fulfillment: Aaron McKinzie
Purchasing Manager: Wendy Kilborn
Composition: XBP Global
Project Management: XBP Global
Cover Design: MPS Limited
Text Design: MPS Limited
Manager, Rights and Permissions: Julie Geagan-Chevez
Media Developer: Faith Brosnan
Intellectual Property Specialist: Lisa Passmore
Cover Image (Title Page and Chapter Opener): © Flavio Coelho/Moment/Getty Images
Printing and Binding: The P.A. Hutchison Company

Library of Congress Cataloging-in-Publication Data
Library of Congress Cataloging-in-Publication Data unavailable at time of printing.

LCCN: 2026003593

6048

Printed in the United States of America
30 29 28 27 26   10 9 8 7 6 5 4 3 2 1

The sixth edition of *Continuous Quality Improvement in Health Care* is dedicated to the memory of Arnold D. Kaluzny and Curt P. McLaughlin, the original editors of this book.

Dr. Kaluzny was a remarkable mentor and friend whose immeasurable contributions to health administration, leadership, and the improvement of quality of care shaped the lives of countless students, colleagues, and professionals. Throughout the years, Arnie's influence on each of our careers was ever present. Whether as a professor, advisor, supervisor, or mentor, he was first and foremost a trusted friend.

Dr. McLaughlin's scholarship, vision, and leadership laid a foundation that has guided generations of improvement in healthcare organizations. Curt set a standard of rigor and purpose that continues to inform research, teaching, and practice.

As longtime collaborators, their enduring legacies continue to shape the field of continuous quality improvement in health care. Their final gift to us was entrusting us with stewardship of this text and the responsibility to guide the next generation of learners.

Brief Contents

Contents

Foreword

. . .questions
that have no right
to go away (Whyte, 2007).

This text invites two questions that may "have no right to go away" in our journey toward better health:

1. If we make improving quality, safety, and value an "enterprise-wide effort," what do we need to know and do?
2. If we make improving the "value of the healthcare service contribution to better health" our focus, what do we need to know and do?

Enterprise-Wide Effort?

In response to this question, our attention has been directed at the ways and structures through which leaders lead organizations and the way(s) organizations and their people respond. In the last few decades, in addition to work "inside," we have been encouraged to look outside of the healthcare services sector to organization-wide efforts in automotive, computer, aerospace, and elsewhere, where great gains in quality, safety, and value have been made. We have learned a great deal about our own work: healthcare service as a system, process; system leadership; measurement of outcome; unwanted variation; system failure and unreliability; organization-wide contributions to better health; making improvement part of everyone's job; accountability for better performance; and many other themes.

The *First Edition* of this text was published as we were deeply into these pursuits and learning (McLaughlin & Kaluzny, 1994). Several chapters in this edition of that text honor this question and help identify what might be known and done currently. Their content helps frame important contributions to leader development, selection, and performance assessment. In the short-term, following these chapters can offer today's leaders and organizations real substance in the performance of "leader and organization-wide work" for the improvement of healthcare service.

Value of Healthcare Service Contribution to Better Health?

This question invites focus on the words "service," "value," and "contribution." It suggests that we recognize that we are mainly in the business of making services, that we are invited to attend to the economic value of our efforts, and that we acknowledge that our services are best thought of as a contribution to health. The *Sixth Edition* of this text opened this question.

Service

Victor Fuchs in his early review of the emerging service economy noted that making a service was different from making a product (Fuchs, 1968). Services always required the active participation and insight from two parties: the professional and the beneficiary. Vincent and Elinor Ostrom called that phenomenon "coproduction" (Ostrom & Ostrom, 1977). Osborne, Radnor, and Nasi suggested that a "product-dominant logic" had overtaken a clearer view of the logic involved in making a service (Osborne, Radnor, et al., 2012). Building on these ideas of "service"

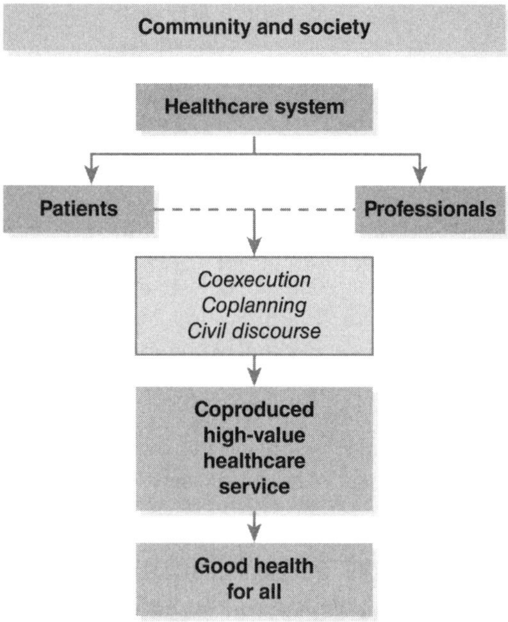

Figure 1 Conceptual Model of Healthcare Services Coproduction

Data from Batalden, M., Batalden, P., Margolis, P., Seid, M., Armstrong, G., Opipari-Arrigan, L., & Hartung, H. (2016). Coproduction of healthcare service. *BMJ quality & safety, 25*(7), 509–517. https://doi.org/10.1136/bmjqs-2015-004315

and how "making a service" might be different from "making a product," Batalden and colleagues offered a description of the coproduction of healthcare service and a model for understanding and use, as illustrated in **Figure 1** (Batalden, Batalden, et al., 2016).

The model invited attention to the interactions of patients and professionals. It suggested that a variety of interactions might be possible, ranging from "civil discourse" to "co-execution." It recognized that these interactions occurred partly within an openly bounded healthcare system and in the context of social and community systems. This variety of interaction depended in part on the knowledge, skill, habits, and willingness to be vulnerable as the parties engaged in the relationships and actions that characterized a healthcare service.

These insights formed the basis of a clearer idea of the interdependent work of two groups of people, some of whom might be named "patients" and some named as "professionals"—though in reality they each brought different expertise to their shared interactions.

If we really mean that healthcare services are "coproduced," new tools that enable visualization and design that reflect the contribution of patients and professionals will be helpful. The measurement of process and result will need to reflect both the implementation and effect of the professionals' science-informed practice (Greenhalgh, 2018) and the methods of addressing and the degree of attainment of the patient's goal.

But not all health professional work seems to fit this service logic. Sometimes the healthcare work seems to better fit "making a product." Helping professionals know when to use which logic—service-making or product-making—will open new approaches to design, as well as professional education and development.

Value

Øystein Fjeldstad has suggested that multiple system architectures might be useful to create value in modern service-making. He includes the development of standardized responses to commonly occurring needs in linked processes (value chains), customized responses to particular needs (value shop), and flexible responses to emergent needs (value network) (Stabell & Fjeldstad, 1998; Fjeldstad, Snow, et al., 2012). Using this typology one can begin to imagine the opportunity to link them in ways that match need and system form. Much more development of these multiple ways of creating value seems likely.

Contribution

This word invites us to remember that a person's health is not easy to "outsource" to a professional. At best, the health professional's coproduced service makes a contribution to further another person's health. Recognizing that the shared work is a contribution to health, invites inquiry into patient need, patient assets, patient supports, patient knowledge and skill, and patient's lived reality as part of the understanding for service coproduction

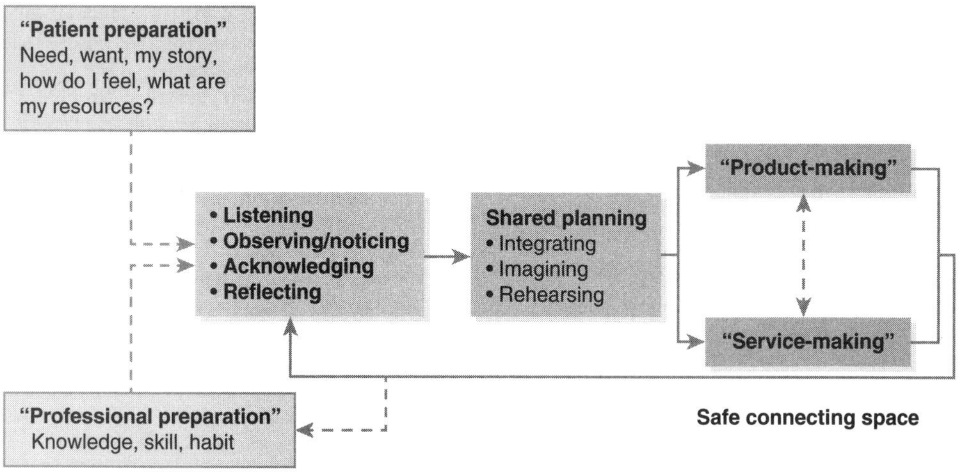

Figure 2 Coproducing Good Health Care

design. A similar inventory of knowledge, skill, habits, capability, and interest of professionals seems in order. Even the professional–patient relationship itself could be explored for its capability in contributing to the process of coproducing a service. Assessments of the role that other complementary resources and services, such as social services, must become even more clear and reliable as we use and integrate them with health-care services for "improved outcomes" (Bradley & Taylor, 2013).

With this edition, the editors point to the future of the second question and have opened this space for readers (Chapter 12). With more attention and as we anticipate continuing application of AI, we've come to see that "Good Health Care" (**Figure 2**) involves attention to the logic, architecture, and science of both "service-like" and "product-like" work.

Each element and each arrow invite our exploration.

In Summary

Both questions seem to have "patiently waited for us" in the poet's words (Whyte, 2007). They both invite strategic thinking and aligned professional action. Both recognize that "knowing" alone is not sufficient. Texts like this can invite knowing and doing, but it is the reader who makes things happen. Enjoy the authors' and editors' words in this text but enjoy their intent in the work of an informed, acting reader even more. Let me close with Mary Oliver's words (Oliver, 2005):

What I Have Learned So Far

Meditation is old and honorable, so why should I not sit, every morning of my life, on the hillside, looking into the shining world? Because, properly attended to, delight, as well as havoc, is suggestion. Can one be passionate about the just, the ideal, the sublime, and the holy, and yet commit to no labor in its cause? I don't think so.

All summations have a beginning, all effect has a story, all kindness begins with the sown seed. Thought buds toward radiance. The gospel of light is the crossroads of—indolence, or action.

Be ignited, or be gone.

Paul Batalden, MD
Active Emeritus Professor
The Dartmouth Institute for Health Policy and Clinical Practice
St. Paul, Minnesota

References

Batalden, M., Batalden, P., Margolis, P., et al., (2016). Coproduction of healthcare service. *BMJ Quality & Safety, 25*(7), 509–517. https://doi.org/10.1136/bmjqs-2015-004315

Bradley, E. H., & Taylor, L. A. (2013). *The American health care paradox: Why spending more is getting us less.* PublicAffairs Press.

Fjeldstad, Ø. D., Snow, C. C., Miles, R. E., & Lettl, C. (2012). The architecture of collaboration. *Strategic Management Journal, 33*(6), 734–750. https://doi.org/10.1002/smj.1968

Fuchs, V. (1968). *The service economy.* National Bureau of Economic Research.

Greenhalgh, T. (2018). *How to implement evidence-based healthcare.* John Wiley & Sons.

Lusch, R. F., & Vargo, S. L. (2014). *Service-dominant logic: Premises, perspectives, possibilities*. Cambridge University Press.

McLaughlin, C. P., & Kaluzny, A. D. (Eds.), (1994). *Continuous quality improvement in health care: Theory, implementation and applications.* Aspen Publishers.

Oliver, M. (2005). What I have learned so far. In M. Oliver (Ed.), *New and selected poems, Vol. 2.* Beacon Press, p. 57.

Osborne, S. P., Radnor, Z., & Nasi, G. (2012). A new theory for public service management? Toward a (public) service-dominant approach. *The American Review of Public Administration, 43*(2), 135–158. https://doi.org/10.1177/0275074012466935

Ostrom, V., & Ostrom, E. (1977). Public goods and public choices. In E. S. Savas (Ed.), *Alternatives for delivering public services: Toward improved performance.* Westview Press, Part 1, 7–44.

Stabell, C. B., & Fjeldstad, Ø. D. (1998). Configuring value for competitive advantage: On chains, shops, and networks. *Strategic Management Journal, 19*(5), 413–437.

Whyte, D. (2007). Sometimes. In D. Whyte (Ed.), *River flow: New & selected poems: 1984–2007.* Many Rivers Press.

Preface

The first edition of *Continuous Quality Improvement in Health Care* was published in 1994. Continuous quality improvement in health care was in its infancy. Paul Batalden had kindly educated us, and others, on his philosophy and groundbreaking efforts at Hospital Corporation of America. The Joint Commission had recently launched the *Agenda for Change*. Within the larger healthcare community there was interest as well as skepticism as to whether manufacturing techniques that were popular and successful were applicable to health care. The obvious need was to explain the basics and provide documentation to illustrate its applicability to healthcare organizations. The *First Edition* provided the basics along with a series of cases to illustrate its relevance to health care.

By the *Second Edition* in 1999, the issues of quality in health care had come of age with the publication of the IOM report *Crossing the Quality Chasm*. Many issues of implementation had become evident and a new key chapter was "CQI, Transformation and the 'Learning' Organization." At the same time the importance of such efforts was recognized by the healthcare version of the National Malcolm Baldrige Quality Award.

The *Third Edition* in 2006 emphasized measurement, especially outcomes measurement, as the use of CQI concepts expanded. It also paid attention to information technology that had the power to enhance implementation and to disseminate results more widely. At the same time the barriers to widespread adoption of the knowledge produced were evident. The new cases on Intermountain Health Care and the American Board of Pediatrics efforts at organizational and professional learning were featured illustrations.

The *Fourth Edition* in 2013, under the leadership of Bill Sollecito and Julie Johnson, aligned with the passage of the Affordable Care Act expanding the insurance coverage to 50 million people and the role of the CMS to assess different delivery models of care. It was a time of great expectations with emphasis on measurement and the movement of these efforts into a number of professional, governmental, and international spheres.

By the time the *Fifth Edition* was published in 2020, elements of the ACA had been dismantled and major segments of the population were at risk of losing insurance coverage. While quality improvement was a well-accepted management tool, issues of institutionalization, measurement, implementation, and adaptation to environments remained challenging.

As the *Sixth Edition* is going to press, the world looks and feels like a different place. The COVID-19 pandemic changed many things in public health, health care, and how people learn. These changes are global. Politically, we have seen opposition to public health measures and a skepticism of science. The need for continuous quality improvement has never been greater.

The past 30 years have taught us a lot about quality improvement, its implementation, challenges, and opportunities in health care. Healthcare quality is not an abstract academic issue. These are real concerns, involving real people. We are all at risk. We know what it is like to observe specialists exhibit mutual hostility at the bedside because one didn't comprehend why the other demanded a prompt weekend consult, or wonder how a case manager can expect an emotionally exhausted family, following an extended and traumatic hospital stay, to select from a list of long-term care facilities without any guidance or insight about the facilities. These experiences change your perspective on quality, quality improvement, and the importance of implementing organizational structures and mechanisms to assure interdisciplinary collaboration and training hospital personnel to effectively manage the transition points in the care continuum.

As we enter an era of an aging population and artificial intelligence, the quality of care at the front line will bring additional challenges and greater opportunities. What Deming, a pioneer in quality improvement, stated 50 years ago remains relevant today—that the problems are with the system. Our methods of quality improvement must encompass these larger, increasingly relevant systems. For the current cohort and future workforce in public health and health care, we need you to carry these ideas forward.

Julie K. Johnson, Chapel Hill, North Carolina
Anna P. Schenck, Chapel Hill, North Carolina

Learning and Teaching Resources

Instructor Resources

Qualified instructors can receive the full suite of Instructor Resources, including the following:

- Slides in PowerPoint format
- Test Bank, including Midterm and Final Exam in LMS-compatible formats
- Image Bank

Student Resources

Each new purchase of the print textbook or Navigate course includes a Navigate eBook with:

- Chapter Review Slides
- Flashcards
- Interactive Glossary

Claire AI™ for Students

Included within the Navigate eBook, Claire AI is an AI-powered study tool that provides students with around-the-clock academic support and personalized guidance. Available at the point of learning, students can access instant, AI-driven assistance through a chat experience leveraging Jones & Bartlett Learning's trusted content to enhance their educational experience.

With Claire AI, learners will have the ability to clarify key content, generate flashcards, create memorable mnemonics, and quiz themselves with unique questions, all within their eBook.

We Value Your Feedback

Do you love this text? Spot an error you'd like to report? Follow this QR code to give us your observations and suggestions for improvement.

Acknowledgments

As we developed the sixth edition of *Continuous Quality Improvement in Health Care*, we reflected on the work of Drs. McLaughlin and Kaluzny. They have inspired us as mentors and as colleagues through the years.

We were also guided by the thought-provoking foreword written by Dr. Paul Batalden where he invited us to ask, "What do we need to know and do?" as we start the journey on improving the quality, safety, and value of health. While this question is intended to guide the reader of the *Sixth Edition*, it is also a relevant starting point for those applying CQI principles into daily work.

We have benefited greatly from the feedback of students who have provided insight and understanding of the importance of making this book a practical teaching tool that addresses the continuing challenges of improving quality and safety of health care in the future. We are most appreciative to our friends and colleagues around the globe who authored chapters. The coordination and integration of the contributing authors was a tremendous undertaking and we were privileged to work with excellent colleagues, who are truly expert practitioners of continuous quality improvement in health care. Dr. William Sollecito, an editor of the *Fourth Edition* and *Fifth Edition* of this text, continued to provide review and encouragement, in addition to co-authoring two chapters.

The production of the book required a team effort at all levels and in multiple locations. We would first like to acknowledge the assistance and guidance of the editorial team at Jones & Bartlett Learning. In Chapel Hill, special appreciation goes to Meaghan Hazelet, of the University of North Carolina Department of Surgery, whose project management skills, creativity, and willingness to support this work kept the project on track.

We appreciate the feedback and guidance we received from the readers of the *Fifth Edition*, which among other things led us to streamline the chapters, and provide more examples of application of CQI concepts.

Finally, we want to acknowledge the support of our families. It was a vital, constant reminder that quality is personal and local.

Julie K. Johnson, Chapel Hill, North Carolina
Anna P. Schenck, Chapel Hill, North Carolina

About the Authors

Julie K. Johnson, PhD, MSPH is currently a Professor of Surgery at the University of North Carolina in Chapel Hill and serves as the Associate Chair of Quality for the Department of Surgery, the Associate Director of the Univiersity of North Carolina (UNC) Surgical Health Services (USHER) center, and the Director of Quality and Implementation, North Carolina Surgical Quality Collaborative (NC SURG). In these roles, Dr. Johnson leads and participates in studies to improve quality and safety of patient care within clinical microsystems.

Dr. Johnson's career interests have involved building a series of collaborative relationships to improve the quality and safety of health care through teaching, research, and clinical improvement. She has a master's degree in public health from the University of North Carolina and a PhD in evaluative clinical sciences from Dartmouth College in Hanover, New Hampshire.

Since completing her PhD in 2000, Dr. Johnson has focused her research on activities related to quality and safety of patient care and qualitative evaluation of clinical microsystems. She has extensive experience using qualitative research methods as part of implementation research studies.

Anna P. Schenck, PhD, MSPH, is Professor Emerita in the Department of Public Health Leadership and Practice at the University of North Carolina (UNC) Gillings School of Global Public Health. Dr. Schenck served as director, then chair for the Department. At UNC, she developed and taught graduate level courses, including a highly rated course in quality improvement enjoyed by hundreds of residential and online students.

Before joining UNC, Dr. Schenck worked with the Quality Improvement Organization (QIO) for North and South Carolina to improve the quality of care provided to Medicare enrollees. During her time with the QIO, she worked on numerous quality improvement initiatives in hospitals, nursing homes, home health agencies, physician offices and community settings. Dr. Schenck also led two national measure development projects, one for colorectal cancer screening and one for hospice care, resulting in quality measures for use in the Medicare program.

Dr. Schenck holds a doctorate in epidemiology from UNC. Her passion is developing methods to use data to improve community health outcomes.

Contributors

Chapter 6

Elizabeth A. Atchison, MHA
University of North Carolina at Chapel Hill
Chapel Hill, North Carolina

Bruce J. Fried, PhD
University of North Carolina at Chapel Hill
Chapel Hill, North Carolina

Madison G. Kutil
University of North Carolina at Chapel Hill
Chapel Hill, North Carolina

Shreyank H. Thakker
University of North Carolina at Chapel Hill
Chapel Hill, North Carolina

Chapter 7

Carley Riley, MD, MPP, MHS
University of Cincinnati
Cincinnati, Ohio

Brita Roy, MD, MPH, MHS
NYU Grossman School of Medicine
New York, New York

Chapter 8

Rachel C. Forcino, PhD, MSc
University of Kansas School of Medicine
Kansas City, Kansas

Chylla Waggoner
University of Kansas Medical Center
Kansas City, Kansas

Chapter 10

Charlotte E. Armstrong
Portland VA Research Foundation
Portland, Oregon

Sara E. Massie, MPH
Population Health Improvement Partners
Morrisville, North Carolina

Greg D. Randolph, MD, MPH
University of North Carolina at Chapel Hill
Chapel Hill, North Carolina

Chapter 11

Steve J. Meurer, MBA, MHS, PhD
Johns Hopkins School of Medicine
Baltimore, Maryland

Reviewers

Terri Gingerich, BSN, RN, MHCA, CPHQ
Valparaiso University

Jan Welch, MSN, RN
Bushnell University

Kathleen Thomas, DHA, MPH
A.T. Still University

Danny A Schieffler, PhD
Sacred Health University

CHAPTER 1

Quality Improvement Is Local and Personal: Your Journey Starts Here

Anna P. Schenck and Julie K. Johnson

CHAPTER OUTLINE

Introduction

Quality touches every aspect of our lives—the food we eat, our educational experiences, the traffic patterns we experience, our health. In short—quality is *local and personal* (Campbell, 2009; Roberts & Sergesketter, 1993). **Continuous quality improvement (CQI)** is something we engage in daily. We visit a new grocery store in search of fresher produce. We use a different study technique, striving for a higher test grade. We change routes on our way home from work in search of a shorter trip. We embark on self-improvement initiatives to increase our physical activity. In each of these examples, while we may not recognize it as such, we are practicing quality improvement. Some of our quality improvement attempts are successful; others are not. The reasons why some quality efforts succeed when others fail may not be clear to us. In this book, we provide a foundation in CQI to enable readers to strengthen their knowledge, skills, and practices, to empower them to make improvements in their personal and professional lives. Our focus will be on healthcare quality, but the approaches and techniques discussed can be applied universally.

Why Study CQI in Health Care?

CQI began with industrial applications and has now spread to many economic sectors, including health care. Yet, despite the evolution and significant progress in the adoption of CQI theory, methods, and applications, the need for continued efforts in quality improvement in health care is great. Medical errors are estimated to be the third leading cause of death in the United States (Makary & Daniel, 2016). Globally, an estimated one in 10 people are harmed by medical care (Slawomirski & Klazinga, 2022). The challenge of how to cross the *quality chasm* (Institute of Medicine [IOM], 2001) in health care clearly remains. Our goal in this book is to provide the reader with tools to address quality concerns across healthcare settings.

Definitions

Quality in Health Care

Definitions of quality vary across sectors of health care. The World Health Organization (WHO) provides a broad-based definition that encompasses global health care as:

> "the extent to which health care services provided to individuals and patient populations improve desired health outcomes." In order to achieve this, health care must be effective, safe, people-centered, timely, equitable, integrated and efficient (WHO, 2009). Each of these goals can be further defined:
>
> **Effective**—Provides services based on scientific knowledge and evidence-based guidelines.
>
> **Safe**—Delivers health care that minimizes risks and harm to service users, including avoiding preventable injuries and reducing medical errors.
>
> **People-centered**—Provides care that takes into account the preferences and aspirations of individual service users and the culture of their community.
>
> **Timely**—Minimizes delays in providing and receiving health care.
>
> **Equitable**—Delivers health care that does not differ in quality according to personal characteristics such as gender, race, ethnicity, geographical location, or socioeconomic status.
>
> **Integrated**—Provides continuity of health services across the life course.
>
> **Efficient**—Delivers health care in a manner that maximizes resource use and avoids waste.

With multiple goals, it should come as no surprise that the desired outcomes can sometimes be in tension or given differential weight across settings. Timely care is of utmost importance in emergency care settings, whereas people-centered care may be more valued in long-term care settings. When working across disciplines and healthcare sectors, it is important to understand how others view quality and which goals of quality are most valued in order to establish a common purpose.

Quality Assurance and Quality Control

Quality assurance (QA) is a closely related concept to, and sometimes confused with, CQI. QA focuses on conformance quality, which is defined as "conforming to specifications; having a product or service that meets predefined standards" (McLaughlin & Kaluzny, 2006, p. 37). QA was the driving goal of early healthcare accreditation processes. However, The Joint Commission (TJC), which accredits thousands of U.S. healthcare entities, and the Public Health Accreditation Board (PHAB), which accredits state, local, and tribal public health agencies, support going beyond conformance quality, and encourage organizations to engage in CQI practices. QA is sometimes included in broader CQI initiatives as a way of defining baseline care, as an interim goal, or as part of the process definition, but CQI is broader in its goals than QA.

A related concept is **quality control (QC)**, which was widely used in the early development of procedures to ensure industrial product quality. Various definitions can be found for this term and in some cases, QC is confused with QA. It is our experience that QC is synonymous with inspection of products or other process outputs with the goal of determining which products should be rejected and/or reworked, often accompanied by counting the number of "defects." These three terms, QA, QC, and CQI, can be seen along a continuum, with QC as a precursor to QA and CQI. An understanding of failures (QC) is needed to inform the development of standards (QA), and an understanding of standards is needed to embark on CQI.

Continuous Quality Improvement (CQI)

CQI in health care has been defined as: "the combined efforts of everyone—health care professionals, patients and their families, researchers, payers, planners and educators—to make changes that will lead to better patient outcomes (health), better system performance (care) and better professional development (learning)" (Batalden & Davidoff, 2007, p. 2).

CQI is a structured organizational process for involving personnel in planning and executing a continuous flow of improvements to provide quality health care that meets or exceeds expectations. CQI usually involves a common set of characteristics, which include the following:

- A link to key elements of the organization's strategic plan
- A quality council made up of the organization's top leadership
- Training programs for personnel
- Mechanisms for selecting improvement opportunities
- Formation of process improvement teams
- Staff support for process analysis and redesign
- Personnel policies that motivate and support staff participation in process improvement
- Application of rigorous scientific method and statistical process control techniques.

CQI is both an approach and a set of activities applied over time. **Localized improvement** occurs when an ad hoc team is created to look at a specific process problem or opportunity. **Organizational learning** occurs when this process is documented and results in the development of policies and procedures, which are then implemented. Examples include the development of protocols, procedures and clinical pathways. **Process reengineering** occurs when organizations invest internal and external resources to make changes, often including the development of information systems, which radically impact key organizational processes. **Evidence-based practice and management** involves the selection of best health and management practices determined by examination of the professional literature and consideration of internal experience.

Evolution of the Quality Movement

To fully understand the foundation of the CQI approaches, and their use in health care, it is helpful to understand the underlying philosophies of the founders of this "movement" and the way in which CQI methodologies have been adapted from industry to health care. What started as a "business solution" to address major weaknesses, including a reputation for poor quality Japan faced in its manufacturing after World War II, has spread beyond manufacturing to encompass both products and services. This proliferation includes multiple industries across the world and, most notably, all sectors of health care. W. Edwards Deming described what happened in Japan as a "miracle that started off with a concussion in 1950." This miracle was the beginning of an evolutionary process whereby the Japanese military was transformed after the war and given a new goal: the reconstruction of Japan. As a result, "Japanese quality and dependability turned upward in 1950 and by 1954 had captured markets the world over" (Deming, 1986, p. 486). Built upon the expertise of Japanese leaders from industry, science, and the military, and with the guidance of Deming, using his own ideas and those of his colleague, Walter Shewhart, this miracle would transform industry not only in Japan, but also in many other countries around the world.

Although Deming and Shewhart both had been advocating a statistical approach to quality for some time, the Japanese were the first to implement these ideas widely. In Japan, the use of these techniques quickly spread to both product and service organizations. Outside Japan, this movement slowly spread to the United States and Europe in the 1960s and 1970s. But its large-scale adoption did not occur until the 1980s in manufacturing, most notably due to competition from the Japanese automobile industry. In fact, the U.S. industry was perceived to be in a state of crisis when these methods began to receive wider acceptance. As Deming surmised, this crisis was due to poor quality that could be traced primarily to the incorrect belief that quality and productivity were incompatible. Deming demonstrated the fallacy of this notion in his landmark book, *Out of the Crisis* (Deming, 1986), thus forming the basis of what is now known as continuous quality improvement.

From this foundation, CQI has evolved exponentially—over time, across the world, and from industrial manufacturing to the provision of services. Deming made enormous contributions to the development of CQI, but he is perhaps best known for the 14-point program of recommendations that he devised for management to improve quality (see **Box 1.1**). His focus was always on processes (rather than organizational structures), on the ever-continuous cycle of improvement, and on the rigorous statistical analysis of objective data. Deming believed management has the final responsibility for quality because employees work in the system and management deals with the system itself. He also felt that most quality problems are management-controlled rather than worker-controlled. These beliefs were the basis for his requirement that CQI be based on an organization-wide commitment, including the important role and example of senior leaders.

Box 1.1 Deming's 14-Point Program

1. Create and publish to all employees a statement of the aims and purposes of the company or other organization. The management must demonstrate constantly their commitment to this statement.
2. Learn the new philosophy, top management, and everybody.
3. Understand the purpose of inspection, for improvement of processes and reduction of cost.
4. End the practice of awarding business on the basis of price tag alone.
5. Improve constantly and forever the system of production and service.
6. Institute training.
7. Teach and institute leadership.
8. Drive out fear. Create trust. Create a climate for innovation.
9. Optimize toward the aims and purposes of the company the efforts of teams, groups, staff areas.
10. Eliminate exhortations for the workforce.
11. a. Eliminate numerical quotas for production. Instead, learn and institute methods for improvement.
    b. Eliminate management by objective.
12. Remove barriers that rob people of pride of workmanship.
13. Encourage education and self-improvement for everyone.
14. Take action to accomplish the transformation.

The quality evolution later crossed fields as diverse as computer science, education, and health care—and within health care, it has evolved to encompass multiple levels and segments of healthcare delivery.

With this evolution, organizations began to recognize the importance of ensuring changes are improvements and improvement processes are ongoing, requiring learning and involvement in the process at all levels, from the individual to the organization level. No longer was management considered the "master of the facts"—rather, the importance and ability of the people in the organization was recognized.

It is worth noting that the evolution of CQI has been responsive to the needs and contexts of the times. Within health care, we have seen similar responsiveness to contexts that have furthered the evolution of CQI (**Figure 1.1**). For example, in response to high hospital mortality during the Crimean War, Florence Nightingale championed the importance of sanitation and hospital conditions for improved patient outcomes. As public health practices became standard practice, and later as advances in medicine provided us with vaccines and antibiotics, scientific methods of CQI, developed by Shewhart, Juran, and Deming, provided us with ways to understand, measure, and improve variation. When the IOM report *To Err is Human* highlighted medical errors, numerous patient safety initiatives using CQI methods were launched (IOM, 2000). More recently, the COVID-19 pandemic highlighted the need for rapid detection and prevention of disease, creating the context for development of new vaccines, new detection methods, and innovative use of data to track the epidemic and assess prevention efforts. The rise in the use of social media during this time has demonstrated both the potential and perils of the new communication horizon.

As you review Figure 1.1, keep in mind that it is a high-level summary of the evolution of CQI. Not every historical event or CQI leader is included. Our intent is to highlight that a constant theme in CQI has been a "call" from the field, and "response" by the scientists. The health and environmental conditions of the future will change and the tools you learn now may evolve as your career advances. New contexts will require new approaches that will build on the scientific foundation that exists today. Your CQI "journey" will continue throughout your career.

The Role of Cross-Disciplinary Thinking in CQI

The growth of quality improvement represents an evolution of both the philosophies and processes that have been studied and improved over the years, through application, review, feedback, and then broader application. Through a fair amount of scrutiny, these approaches have not only stood the test of time but have evolved to address criticisms and have been adapted to meet specialized needs that are unique in some segments, especially in health care. This phenomenon has occurred naturally as a result of cross-disciplinary strategic thinking processes, where learning occurs by focusing not on what makes industries and disciplines different from each other, but rather on what they share in common (Brown, 1999). A good example of this commonality is a focus on adding value to products and services for customers, be they automobile buyers, airline passengers, or hospital patients. As a result, the common strategic elements of CQI have been adopted from diverse industrial applications and then customized to meet the special needs of health care.

One example of the cross-disciplinary/industry phenomenon, which has been given much attention both in scientific journals and in popular media, is the adoption of surgical checklists to prevent errors. The checklist is a very simple but powerful project management and safety tool that has been used in various industries, but it is probably most well-known for its effectiveness in the airline industry. A strong case has been made in scientific literature and in the popular media for greater adoption of checklists in surgery (Haynes et al., 2009) and other medical specialties (Gawande, 2009; Pronovost et al., 2006). The World Health Organization (WHO) provides a sample surgical checklist that can be modified to fit the practice environment (WHO, 2009). The use of checklists also provides a good illustration of some basic CQI principles that have broader implications. These include standardizing processes fostering team communication in recognition of the fact that reliance on memory alone is insufficient.

The checklist is a simple tool, but it is not a magic bullet—instead, it can be an effective means for helping ensure the application of other CQI principles in an overall program of quality assurance and improvement. For example, its use and effectiveness have broad implications about how healthcare teams communicate and share responsibilities; how leadership supports innovations

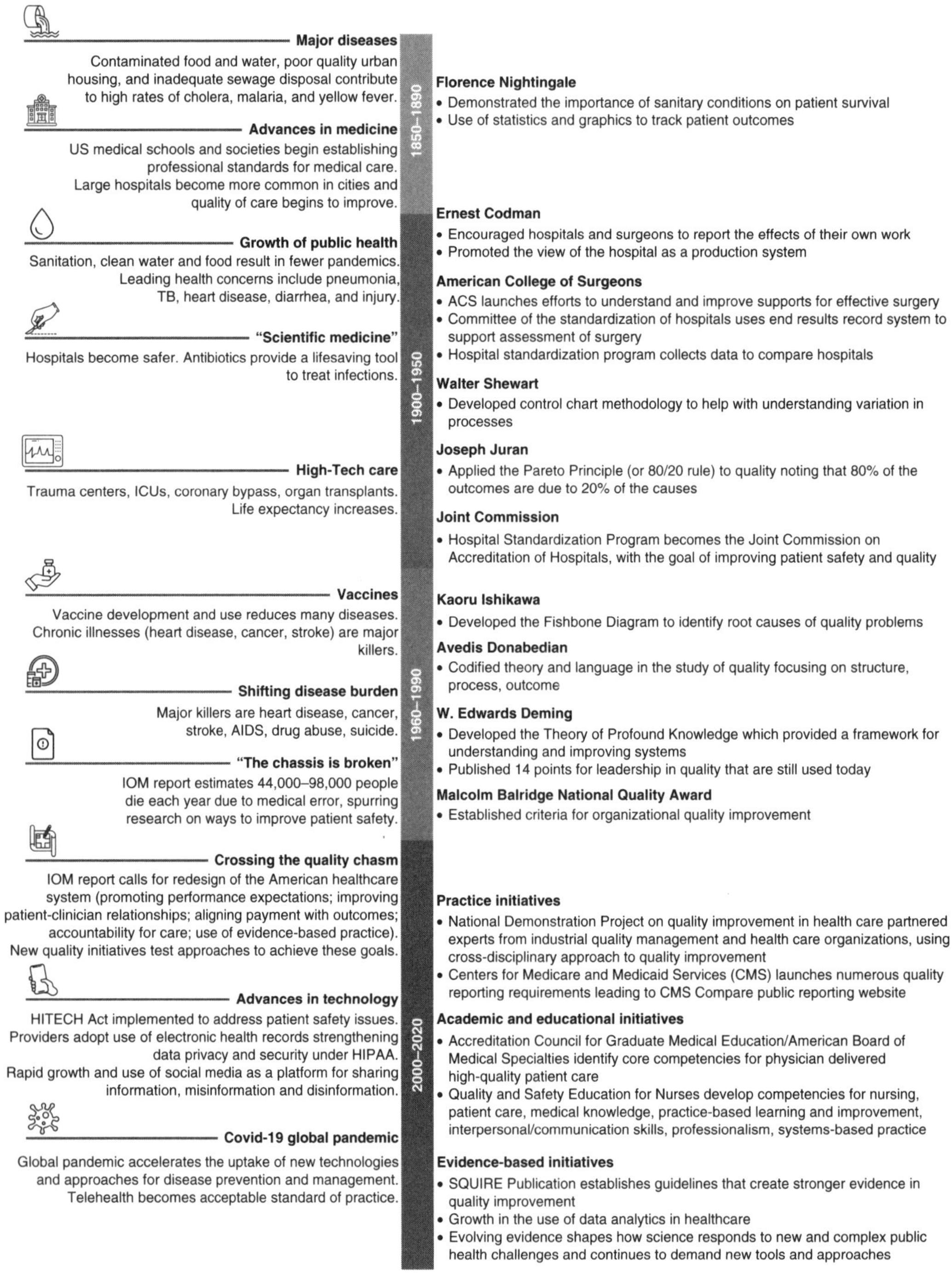

Figure 1.1 Overview of the Evolutionary Context of Quality in Health Care

and change—ultimately a cultural issue; and how to monitor and ensure compliance with CQI initiatives (Avelling et al., 2013; Dixon-Woods & Martin, 2016). Checklists provide an example of the importance of teamwork in CQI (see Chapter 6) and provide an example of a CQI tool (see Chapter 4) as well as an example of the broader issue of culture, leadership, and diffusion of CQI in health care (see Chapter 2).

Growth of CQI in Health Care

Quality, under the rubric of patient safety, suddenly came to dominate the scene following the two significant Institute of Medicine (IOM) reports, *To Err Is Human* (IOM, 2000) and *Crossing the Quality Chasm* (IOM, 2001), which documented the unacceptably high rates of medical errors. The recognition that needless human suffering, loss of life, and wasted resources were related to unnecessary variability in treatment and the lack of implementation of known best practices galvanized professional groups, regulators, and payers into action. Suddenly, quality improvement was acknowledged to be a professional responsibility, a quality-of-care issue rather than a managerial tactic.

In 2002, the National Quality Forum (NQF) developed a consensus list of "never events," which are events that should not occur in a healthcare setting. In 2008, the Centers for Medicare and Medicaid Services (CMS) heightened the importance of medical errors when it adopted a non-reimbursement policy for certain "never events," which are defined as serious, preventable hospital-acquired conditions. The rationale is that hospitals cannot bill CMS for adverse events and complications that are considered never events *because* they are preventable; the goal is to motivate hospitals to accelerate improvement of patient safety. The Joint Commission recommends organizations report "never events" and requires that such events be followed by a root cause analysis to identify factors contributing to the event. NQF has expanded their original list and updated the terminology to call them "serious reportable events" (NQF, 2011). The list is revised periodically to respond to new data, and at time of writing, was in the process of another update (NQF, 2026).

Concern about healthcare quality has increased with mounting evidence of the societal cost of poor-quality care in both lives and dollars (Makary & Daniel, 2016; Shrank et al., 2019). The cost of poor-quality and wasteful care in the United States is estimated to be 25% of total healthcare expenditures (Shrank et al., 2019). The concern about costs has led to a broadening of the definition of quality by introducing the concept of *adding value*, in addition to ensuring the highest quality of care, implying greater accountability and a cost benefit to enhance the decision-making and evaluation aspects of CQI initiatives (Brook, 2010). In the United States, the goals of the Affordable Care Act (ACA) jointly emphasized improvements to access, quality of care, and cost reduction. Although some progress can be attributed to the ACA, for example, in regard to lowering hospital-acquired infections and readmissions—achievement of its long-term goals is still a work in progress (Blumenthal et al., 2015; Somander, 2015).

Current investment and involvement levels are high as evidence has mounted that the variability in clinical processes and the lack of conformance to evidence-based best practices has cost the public dearly. Adverse events are now undergoing scrutiny, and a broad range of quality indicators are being reported, some available on public sites such as the Centers for Medicare and Medicaid Services (CMS) Care Compare sites, where consumers can view quality measures specific to providers of interest (CMS, 2025).

Local and regional variability in health care has long been known to exist, but the translation of that variability into missed opportunities for improved outcomes has been slow in coming. With that veil of secrecy about medical errors lifted, the demands for action and professional responsiveness have become extensive. This sea change goes well beyond concerns about malpractice insurance to issues of clinical governance, professional training, certification, and continuity of care. However, concerns about cost of care continue and need to be considered relative to CQI initiatives and the relationship between cost, quality and value.

The National Academies of Sciences, Engineering, and Medicine (NASEM), formerly known as the IOM, has continued to shine a light on the need for improvements in quality and published a series of reports under the "quality chasm" banner. Their report on global quality health care highlights the burden and costs of poor-quality care, and suggests pathways to improvement (NASEM, 2018). The report also links quality to access, highlighting the fact that achieving the goal of universal access will be a hollow victory if high-quality care is not provided.

An increasingly important innovation in healthcare CQI is a willingness to examine existing healthcare processes and rework these processes collaboratively using state-of-the-art scientific and administrative knowledge and relevant data-gathering and analysis methodologies. Chapter 11 provides insights into the role of data in CQI.

Elements of CQI

CQI is simultaneously two things: a management philosophy and a management method. It is distinguished by the recognition that customer requirements are the key to customer quality and that customer requirements ultimately will change over time because of changes in evidence-based practices and associated changes in education, economics, technology, and culture. Such changes, in turn, require continuous improvements in the administrative and clinical methods that affect the quality of patient care and population health. This dynamic between changing expectations and continuous efforts to meet these expectations is captured in the Japanese word *kaizen*, translated as "continuous improvement" (Imai, 1986). Change is fundamental to the healthcare environment, and the organization's systems must have both the will and the way to master such change effectively.

As healthcare organizations and professions develop their own performance improvement approaches, their management must lead them through a decision process in which activities are initiated, adapted, and then institutionalized. Organizations embark on CQI for a variety of reasons. Many wish to improve their processes to give their customers the quality of care they deserve. Others are driven by pressure from employers and payers, requirements, cost control and competition. Although CQI is initiated for a variety of reasons, it does have distinguishing elements, described as follows.

Philosophical Elements

The philosophical elements are those aspects of CQI that, at a minimum, must be present in order to constitute a CQI effort. They include:

1. Strategic focus—Emphasis on having a vision/mission, values, and objectives that performance improvement processes are designed, prioritized, and implemented to support.
2. Customer focus—The customer can be external or internal to the system—a patient, a payer, a colleague, or someone from another department. User satisfaction then becomes one ultimate test of process and product quality. Consequently, new efforts and new resources must be devoted to ascertaining what the customer wants through the use of consumer surveys, focus groups, interviews, and various other ways of gathering information on customer preferences, expectations, and perceived experiences. Co-production of health services involves working together with customers to improve healthcare quality (Chapter 8).
3. Systems view—CQI is further distinguished by its emphasis on avoiding personal blame. The focus is on managerial and professional processes associated with a specific outcome—that is, the entire production system. The initial assumption is that the process needs to be changed, and the people already involved in that process are needed to help identify how to approach a given problem or opportunity.
4. Data-driven (evidence-based) analysis—Another distinguishing feature of CQI is the

rigorous belief in fact-based learning and decision making. The primary purpose of data and measurement in CQI is learning—how to make system improvements and understand the impact each change we have already made has had on the overall system (Chapter 4).

5. Implementer involvement—Emphasis on involving the owners of all components of the system in seeking a common understanding of its delivery process.
6. Multiple causation—Multiple causation is assumed and the search for answers starts with trying to identify the full set of factors contributing to less-than-optimal system performance.
7. Solution identification—Emphasis on seeking a set of solutions that enhance overall system performance through simultaneous improvements in a number of normally independent functions.
8. Process optimization—Emphasis on optimizing a delivery process to meet customer needs regardless of existing precedents and on implementing the system changes regardless of existing territories and fiefdoms.
9. Continuing improvement—Emphasis on continuing the systems analysis even when a satisfactory solution to the presenting problem is obtained.
10. Organizational learning—Emphasis on organizational learning so that the capacity of the organization to generate process improvement and foster personal growth is enhanced.

Structural Elements

Beyond the philosophical elements, a number of useful structural elements can be used to organize and support the continuous improvement process. Almost all CQI initiatives make intensive use of these structural elements, which reflect the operational aspects of CQI and include:

1. Process improvement teams—Emphasis on forming and empowering teams of employees to deal with existing problems and opportunities (Chapter 6).
2. CQI tools—Use of one or more of the CQI tools so frequently cited in the industrial and health-quality literature: flowcharts, checklists, cause-and-effect diagrams, frequency and Pareto charts, run charts, and control charts (Chapter 4).
3. Parallel organization—Development of a separate management structure to set priorities for and monitor CQI strategy and implementation, usually referred to as a quality council.
4. Organizational leadership—Leadership, at the top levels and throughout the organization, to make the process effective and foster its integration into the institutional fabric of the organization (Chapter 2).
5. Statistical thinking and analysis—Use of statistics, including statistical process control, to identify common vs. special causes of variation in processes and practices (Chapter 4).
6. Customer satisfaction measures—Understanding the importance of measuring customer satisfaction, but also the strengths and weaknesses of available sources of data and survey methodologies in current use (see Chapter 4).
7. Benchmarking—Use of benchmarking to identify best practices in related and unrelated settings to emulate as processes or use as performance targets (Chapter 11).
8. Redesign of processes from scratch—Making sure the end product conforms to customer requirements by using techniques of quality function deployment and/or process reengineering, engaging customers in the process (Chapter 8).

Health Care–Specific Elements

The use of CQI in health care is often described as a major management innovation, but it also resonates with past and ongoing efforts within the health services research community. The healthcare quality movement has its own history, with its own leadership and values that must be understood and respected. Thus, there are a number of additional approaches and techniques in health care that health managers and professionals have successfully added to the philosophical and structural elements associated with CQI, including:

1. Epidemiological and clinical studies, coupled with insurance payment and medical records data, often referred to as the basis of evidence-based practice
2. Involvement of the medical staff governance process, including quality assurance, tissue committees, pharmacy and therapeutics committees, and peer review
3. Use of risk-adjusted outcome measures
4. Use of cost-effectiveness analysis
5. Use of quality assurance data and techniques and risk management data

The Scientific Method of CQI

The philosophical and structural elements of CQI are supported by the scientific method of CQI. We highlight specific CQI tools and approaches that are used extensively in health care: goals and aim statements, the Plan, Do, Study, Act (PDSA) cycle, and the Model for Improvement. We include the Model for Improvement here because of its near-universal use in health care. It should be noted, however, that there are other successful approaches to CQI that combine many of the same elements. Two such approaches—Lean and Six Sigma – are described in Chapter 6.

Goals and Aim Statements

The goals of any CQI program clearly state what will be accomplished as a result of the program. In health care, these goals may be specific to the size and nature of the initiating team or organization and can include:

- Patient Goals
- Project Goals
- Employee Goals
- Program Goals
- Organizational Goals
- Community Goals
- State and National Goals

Goals should be clearly communicated to provide clear direction and envision a new reality; for example, the specific expected outcome to be achieved. There should also be an awareness that in complex systems, such as healthcare delivery, changes to one part of a system may interact or impact other parts. This is an example of systems thinking, a critical component of improvement strategies. Another important characteristic of systems thinking is the concept of tight coupling, which relates to the fact that often in health care "the actions in the system interact strongly with one another" (Sterman, 2000, p. 22). A simple example of this in health care is that changes in program goals or employee goals may lead to unanticipated changes in patient goals and vice versa. Careful thought must be given to systems thinking concepts when planning and evaluating intended improvements. One important tip for setting improvement goals is avoid focusing on one element—pursue several goals at once.

In complex healthcare systems, a useful set of characteristics of goals that provide overall direction for achieving ongoing improvement are those that can be described by the acronym **SMART** (Doran, 1981):

- **S**pecific
  - Provide direction but do not limit improvement
- **M**easurable
  - May need to develop specific measures relevant to each situation
- **A**chievable
  - Perception of what is achievable but should not be limited—otherwise potential for innovation might be limited; allow change as needed, based on feedback
- **R**elevant
  - Perspective and context matter when defining relevance
- **T**ime-bound
  - Continuous process should be the goal, but with a sense of urgency that must be balanced against the possibility of being too limited so as set up the effort to fail

Aims

Before initiating a CQI process, it is important to understand *change* versus *improvement*, and in particular, which changes will lead to improvements, and not all changes lead to improvement. An important way to define these criteria and to tie them into the goals of an organization or team is to start with an effective "aim statement" to guide the improvement process, including collection of appropriate data to assess success, failure or, most important, how to improve further. Briefly, an **aim statement** should answer three questions: for whom, by when, and how much.

An effective aim statement includes six parts:

- Overarching aim
- Importance
- Target of the goal
- Timeframe
- How the goal will be reached
- Specific measurable goals

The aim statement should be as specific as possible to provide unambiguous guidance to those responsible for implementation and to allow a clear assessment of progress on achieving the desired improvement (Langley et al., 2009). One simple example in a public health department is an aim statement to achieve a recommended immunization rate (with the mandate clearly stated as the reason for the goal). It might be stated as follows: *"We aim to improve the health of children in our community by increasing recommended immunizations among children two years of age or younger. Specifically, we aim to increase the percent of children who have 4 doses of the diphtheria-tetanus-acellular pertussis (DTaP) vaccine by age two to 90% by 2030. We will accomplish this through data-targeted outreach to populations identified with low vaccination rates."*

The inclusion of a clearly stated aim/goal is crucial to achieving the desired improvement(s). A feedback loop with repetition (replication or further improvements) after assessment of the impact of changes is central to the effectiveness of the improvement cycle to achieve ongoing changes and improvements to a project, a system, or an entire organization.

PDSA Cycle

A commonly used tool incorporating the feedback loop was first introduced by Walter Shewhart at Bell Laboratories (Shewhart, 1939). Deming (1950) and other scientists continued to evolve the approach into what is now known as the **Plan, Do, Study, Act (PDSA) cycle**, illustrated in **Figure 1.2**. Over time, the abbreviation PDSA was changed by some to PDCA, the "S" for study being changed to "C" for check, as in *checking* what impact an improvement has made on the process being changed. Today the terms are used interchangeably, as we will do throughout this book. Either way, Shewhart's concept has become a very powerful and frequently used quality improvement methodology that has withstood the test of time.

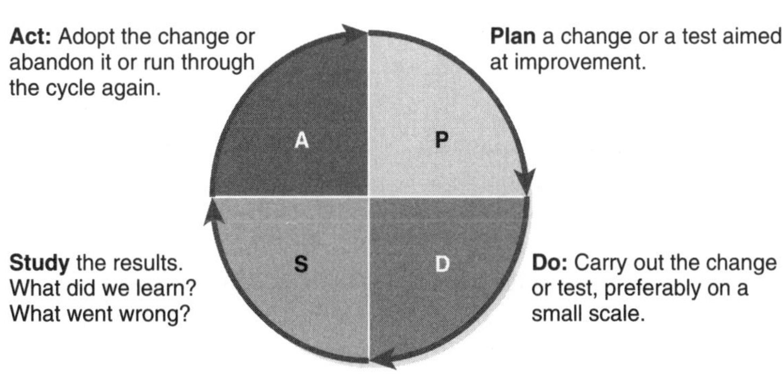

Figure 1.2 Shewhart (PDSA) Cycle

Stated quite simply, PDSA cycles "provide a structure for iterative testing of changes to improve quality of systems. . . . The pragmatic principles of PDSA cycles promote the use of a small-scale iterative approach to test interventions, as this enables rapid assessment and provides flexibility to adapt the change according to feedback to ensure fit-for-purpose solutions are developed" (Taylor et al., 2014, pp. 290–291). The key features of any PDSA application are:

1. The use of repeated iterative cycles
2. Prediction-based test of change (developed in the plan stage)
3. Small-scale testing (build as confidence grows—adapting according to feedback and learning)
4. Use of data over time (to understand the impact of change)
5. Documentation (to support local learning and transferability to other settings) (Taylor et al., 2014, p. 293)

The Model for Improvement

The Model for Improvement (Langley et al., 2009) is a CQI approach commonly used in health care that pulls together the crucial components of CQI—the aims, the PDSA cycle, the use of data and scientific approach, and the continuous, iterative process. The broad applicability of the PDSA cycle in health care can be traced directly to its roots as it was applied by Deming. One of Deming's (1993) major premises was that management needs to undergo a transformation to respond successfully to challenges to organizations and their environments. The way to accomplish that transformation, which must be deliberately learned and incorporated into management, is by pursuing his concept of profound knowledge. Four key elements of his system of profound knowledge directly relate to the steps in implementing PDSA applications: (1) appreciation for a system, (2) knowledge about variation, (3) theory of knowledge, and (4) psychology.

The Deming process is especially useful in health care because professionals already have deep subject matter knowledge as well as a set of values and disciplines that fit the Deming philosophy. Training in Deming methods adds knowledge of how to build a new theory using insights about systems, variation, and psychology, and it focuses on the answers given to the set of basic questions that center around knowing what is to be accomplished. Furthermore, it applies a cyclical process of testing and learning from data whether the change being made is an improvement and what improvements are needed in the future (Batalden & Stoltz, 1993).

Building off the Deming philosophy, and earlier versions of a cyclical model, the use of the Model for Improvement in health care was promoted by Langley and colleagues (2009). It includes a PDSA cycle as its core approach, returning to the traditional "S," emphasizing the importance of *studying* what has been accomplished before making further changes (**Figure 1.3**). Careful study and reflection are points of emphasis made by Berwick (1996), who describes this model as "inductive learning—the growth of knowledge through making changes and then reflecting on the consequences of those changes."

The Model for Improvement addresses three questions (shown in the figure): What are we trying to accomplish? How will we know that a change is an improvement? What change can we make that will result in an improvement? (Langley et al., 2009.) These questions highlight fundamental principles of improvement: understand the need, have measures in place that provide feedback about whether the change is an improvement, and test the change through small PDSA cycles before deciding whether to make the change permanent.

A range of diverse healthcare examples using PDSA cycles are described throughout our book. The wide applicability of these approaches is due directly to the elegance and simplicity of the PDSA methodology. Likewise, the range of applications ties directly to the generalizability of the PDSA cycle.

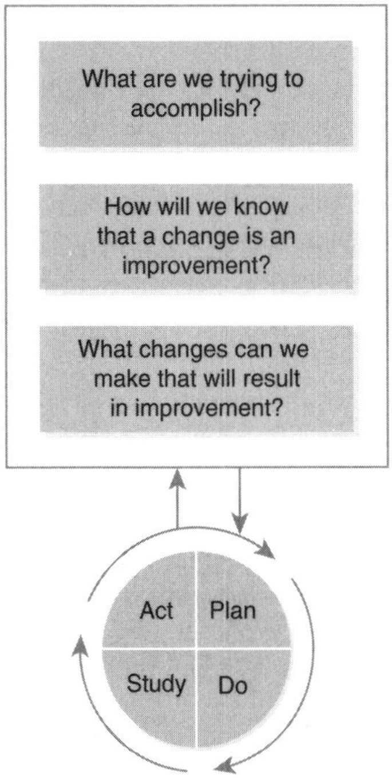

Figure 1.3 Model for Improvement

Reproduced from Langley, G. L., Moen, R. D., Nolan, K. M., Nolan, T. W., Norman, C. L., & Provost, L. P. (2009). The improvement guide: A practical approach to enhancing organizational performance (2nd ed.). Jossey-Bass.

However, with the widespread use of PDSA, there have been some questions raised about how to assess validity and generalizability of specific applications before their results are transferred into clinical practice as new evidence-based methods (Speroff et al., 2004). These questions fall under the broad heading of how to apply critical appraisal criteria to PDSA, and other CQI initiatives, in a manner that is similar to appraisal of clinical research studies that are directed at efficacy and safety of new treatments, drugs, or vaccines. One approach to addressing these questions is to carefully review how well the key features of the PDSA methods (listed previously) have been applied in a specific application; this approach is outlined by Taylor et al. (2014). Included in this approach is Berwick's emphasis on careful study of findings at the "S" stage of each cycle, before acting on those findings (Berwick, 1996).

A useful set of guidelines for strengthening PDSA applications, as well as other CQI initiatives, and which parallel the recommendations of Taylor et al. (2014), are presented by Speroff et al. (2004, p. 36) and start with four core questions:

1. Is the quality improvement study pertinent and relevant?
2. Are the results valid?
3. Are appropriate criteria used to interpret the results?
4. Will the study help you with your practice or organization of care?

These authors also present detailed recommendations for how to address each of these four questions, including how to improve the causal inferences (internal validity) and generalizability (external validity) of PDSA studies (Speroff et al., 2004). Because of the simplicity and consequently the broad usage of PDSA, careful attention should be paid to the guidelines described previously in order to ensure proper use and both internal and external validity of applications of the PDSA methodology.

Similar discussions have also been carried out relative to improving the applicability of other well-known CQI methods and specific results. Recommendations have been presented for greater emphasis on the fidelity of the applications and fuller understanding, and consideration of the context in which project-specific results are obtained before broadly assuming the robustness of their findings. Some CQI methods do not achieve the results that are expected. CQI requires a change which must be implemented. The implementation process, with insights into the context in which the intervention is being implemented, is crucial to the success of the intervention. Integrating implementation science into CQI is seen as the next frontier for CQI (Chapter 3). Care should be exercised before generalizing methods and results to other settings, and we should always be cautious to not assume that a "magic bullet" has been found that will produce improvements in any situation, regardless of context (Dixon-Woods & Martin, 2016).

Conclusion

In this chapter, we have provided an overview of the unique characteristics and building blocks of CQI. Subsequent chapters provide more depth into these topics.

- Chapter 2 describes the conditions organizations need to have success with CQI efforts and overviews actions that can be taken to improve CQI capacity.
- Chapter 3 provides insights into how to integrate CQI improvement and implementation efforts.
- CQI tools and statistical approaches are covered in Chapter 4.
- Chapter 5 provides examples of two popular CQI approaches: Lean and Six Sigma.
- Actions to improve the use of teams can be found in Chapter 6.
- Chapters 7 and 8 respectively address equity and co-production in the healthcare setting.
- Chapter 9 provides a deeper exploration of CQI in patient safety.
- Examples of CQI in public health and community settings are covered in Chapter 10.
- Chapter 11 provides insights into the use of data to view quality at macro levels.
- In Chapter 12, we conclude the book with suggestions for continued learning and thoughts about what is needed for CQI in the future.

People who want to improve health and social care, often called "improvers," have a common set of habits and actions (Lucas, 2016). Questioning whether conditions can be improved is a fundamental step towards becoming an improver. We encourage readers to adopt the CQI journey as "your journey." Approach each chapter in this book with questions about how and where you can apply the information personally and professionally, to improve your environment. We need more "improvers" to make the world a better place.

Key Concepts and Terms

aim statement
continuous quality improvement (CQI)
effective
efficient
equitable
evidence-based practice and management
integrated
localized improvement
organizational learning
people-centered
Plan, Do, Study, Act (PDSA) cycle
process reengineering
quality assurance (QA)
quality control (QC)
safe
timely

References

Aveling, E., McCulloch, P., & Dixon-Woods, M. (2013). A qualitative study comparing experiences of the surgical safety checklist in hospitals in high-income and low-income countries. *British Medical Journal Open, 3*. https://doi.org/10.1136/bmjopoen-2013-003039

Batalden, P. B., & Stoltz, P. K. (1993). A framework for the continual improvement of health care: Building and applying professional and improvement knowledge to test changes in daily work. *The Joint Commission Journal on Quality Improvement, 19*(10), 424–452. https://doi.org/10.1016/s1070-3241(16)30025-6

Batalden, P., & Davidoff, F. (2007). What is "quality improvement" and how can it transform health care? *Quality and Safety in Health Care, 16*(1), 2–3. https://doi.org/10.1136/qshc.2006.022046

Berwick, D. M. (1996). A primer on leading the improvement of systems. *British Medical Journal, 312*, 619–622. https://doi.org/10.1136/bmj.312.7031.619

Blumenthal, D., Abrams, M., & Nuzum, R. (2015). The Affordable Care Act at 5 years. *The New England Journal of Medicine, 372*(25), 2451–2458. https://doi.org/10.1056/NEJMhpr1503614

Brook, R. H. (2010). The end of the quality improvement movement: Long live improving value. *Journal of the American Medical Association, 304*(16), 1831–1832. https://doi.org/10.1001/jama.2010.1555

Brown, M. (1999). *Strategic thinking: Considerations for public health—a personal perspective [Paper presentation].* Symposium on Public Health Leadership, School of Public Health, University of North Carolina at Chapel Hill.

Campbell, D. A. (2009). Quality improvement is local. *Journal of the American College of Surgeons, 209*(1), 141–143. https://doi.org/10.1016/j.jamcollsurg.2009.03.012

Centers for Medicare & Medicaid Services. (n.d.). *Find & compare providers near you.* Retrieved August 14, 2025, from https://www.medicare.gov/care-compare/

Deming, W. E. (1950). *Elementary principles of the statistical control of quality*, JUSE.

Deming, W. E. (1986). *Out of the crisis.* Massachusetts Institute of Technology Center for Advanced Engineering Study.

Deming, W. E. (1993). *The new economics for industry, government, education.* Massachusetts Institute of Technology Center for Advanced Engineering Study.

Dixon-Woods, M., & Martin, G. P. (2016). Does quality improvement improve quality? *Future Hospital Journal, 3*(3), 191–194.

Doran, G. T. (1981). There's a SMART way to write management's goals and objectives. *Journal of Management Review, 70*(11), 35–36.

Gawande, A. (2009). *The checklist manifesto.* Metropolitan Books.

Haynes, A. B., Weiser, T. G., Berry, W. R., Lipsitz, S. R., Breizat, A. H., Dellinger, E. P., ... Safe Surgery Saves Lives Study Group. (2009). A surgical safety checklist to reduce morbidity and mortality in a global population. *The New England Journal of Medicine, 360*, 491–499. https://doi.org/10.1056/NEJMsa0810119

Imai, M. (1986). *Kaizen: The key to Japan's competitive success.* McGraw-Hill Education.

Institute of Medicine (IOM), National Academies of Sciences. (2000). *To err is human: Building a safer health system.* National Academies Press.

Institute of Medicine (IOM), National Academies of Sciences. (2001). *Crossing the quality chasm: A new health paradigm for the 21st century.* National Academies Press.

Langley, G. L., Moen, R. D., Nolan, K. M., Nolan, T. W., Norman, C. L., & Provost, L. P. (2009). *The improvement guide: A practical approach to enhancing organizational performance* (2nd ed.). Jossey-Bass.

Lucas, B. (2016). Getting the improvement habit. *BMJ Quality & Safety, 25*(6), 400–403. https://doi.org/10.1136/bmjqs-2015-005086

Makary, M. A., & Daniel, M. (2016). Medical error—the third leading cause of death in the US. *British Medical Journal, 353.* https://doi.org/10.1136/bmj.i2139

McLaughlin, C. P., & Kaluzny, A. D. (Eds.). (2006). *Continuous quality improvement in health care* (3rd ed.). Jones and Bartlett Publishers.

National Academies of Sciences, Engineering, and Medicine; Health and Medicine Division; Board on Health Care Services; Board on Global Health; Committee on Improving the Quality of Health Care Globally—Summary. (2018, August 28). *Crossing the global quality chasm: Improving health care worldwide.* National Academies Press (US). Retrieved August 14, 2025, from https://www.ncbi.nlm.nih.gov/books/NBK535643

National Quality Forum (NQF). (2011). *Serious Reportable Events In Healthcare—2011 Update: A Consensus Report.* National Quality Forum.

National Quality Forum (NQF). Updating the Serious Reportable Events List. Retrieved January 12, 2026, from https://www.qualityforum.org/en-us/key-initiatives/updating-the-serious-reportable-events-sre-list

Pronovost, P. J., Needham, D., Berenholtz, S., Sinopoli, D., Chu, H., Cosgrove, S., ... Goeschel, C. (2006). An intervention to decrease catheter-related bloodstream infections in the ICU. *The New England Journal of Medicine, 355*(26), 2725–2732.

Roberts, H. V., & Sergesketter, B. F. (1993). *Quality is personal: A foundation for total quality management*, Free Press.

Shewhart, W. A. (1939). *Statistical methods from the viewpoint of quality control.* The Graduate School, The Department of Agriculture.

Shrank, W. H., Rogstad, T. L., & Parekh, N. (2019). Waste in the US health care system: Estimated costs and potential for savings. *JAMA, 322*(15), 1501–1509. http://doi.org/10.1001/jama.2019.13978

Slawomirski, L., & Klazinga, N. (2022). The economics of patient safety: From analysis to action. *OECD Health Working Papers, 145.* https://doi.org/10.1787/761f2da8-en

Somanader, T. (2015, March 25). *4 ways the Affordable Care Act is improving the quality of health care in America.* The White House. Retrieved November 3, 2017, from https://obamawhitehouse.archives.gov/blog/2015/03/25/4-ways-affordable-care-act-improving-quality-health-care-america

Speroff, T., James, B., Nelson, E., Headrick, L. A., & Brommels, M. (2004). Guidelines for appraisal and publication of PDSA quality improvement. *Quality management in health care, 13*(1), 33–39. https://doi.org/10.1097/00019514-200401000-00003

Sterman, J. D. (2000). *Business dynamics: Systems thinking and modeling for a complex world.* Irwin McGraw-Hill.

Taylor, M. J., McNicholas, C., Nicolay, C., Darzi, A., Bell, D., & Reed, J. E. (2014). Systematic review of the application of the plan-do-study-act method to improve quality in healthcare. *BMJ Quality & Safety, 23*, 290–298. https://doi.org/10.1136/bmjqs-2013-001862

World Health Organization. (2009). *Surgical safety checklist.* https://www.who.int/docs/default-source/patient-safety/9789241598590-eng-checklist.pdf

CHAPTER 2

Developing a Culture to Ensure the Application and Diffusion of CQI in Health Care

William A. Sollecito and Julie K. Johnson

CHAPTER OUTLINE

Introduction

Continuous quality improvement (CQI) has gained acceptance within all sectors of health care and across geographic and economic boundaries. It has evolved as a global strategy for improving health care in a variety of settings, spanning a broad number of issues and improving services to a variety of customers ranging from individual patients to communities. The range of applications covers direct patient care in clinic or hospital settings, and also disease prevention and population initiatives—such as HIV, childhood obesity, and influenza vaccination programs, and most recently, to address the COVID-19 pandemic—at the local, national, and international levels. These applications are characterized by continuous, ongoing learning and sharing among disciplines about ways to use CQI philosophies, processes, and tools in a variety of settings. In this chapter, we describe the conditions organizations need to have success with CQI efforts and overviews actions that can be taken to improve CQI capacity.

During the past several decades, progress has been made in understanding and implementing CQI; however, new challenges have arisen and old challenges persist, both prior to and after the COVID-19 pandemic. For example, despite incentives for prevention, significant challenges remain in reducing medical errors; these are addressed further in Chapter 9. In addition, some of the advances in technology, which are intended, at least in part, to facilitate greater adoption of CQI at the system level, have had a negative effect on individual healthcare providers' motivation to implement CQI. These include the more widespread use of electronic health records and electronic patient satisfaction surveys; these are discussed further later in this chapter as well as in Chapter 4 (Bodenheimer & Sinsky, 2014). Also challenging the entire healthcare system for many years but brought into sharper focus during the COVID-19 pandemic is the continuing prevalence of health disparities and the lack of health equity among major population segments in the United States as well as throughout the world (IOM, 2003; Lopez et al., 2021), which is discussed in Chapter 7 and in the introduction of the Quintuple Aim later in this chapter (Itchhaporia, 2021; Nundy et al., 2022). As a result, some important questions remain about the adaptation and diffusion of quality improvement methods, especially in regard to the central role of individual healthcare providers. These include questions such as:

- Why aren't more healthcare providers using CQI tools and processes?
- Why is the gap between knowledge and practice so large?
- Why don't clinical systems incorporate the findings of clinical science or copy the "best known" practices reliably, quickly, and even gratefully into their daily work simply as a matter of course?

Historically, we faced challenges due to the scientific method—for example, the definition of evidence-based practice and how it varied across different areas of health care, with medicine perhaps being the most rigid due to an over-emphasis on randomized, controlled trials. Satterfield et al. (2009) reviewed this issue, noting that the interdisciplinary nature of healthcare research requires a new broader definition of evidence-based practice. This broader model represents a transformation in thinking that might increase the flexibility and the range of methodologies that are used to make scientific decisions, for example, through the greater use of quasi-experimentation, and one effect of this model's adoption might be an increase in CQI initiatives. In particular, the COVID-19 pandemic created a sense of urgency leading to an acceleration of clinical research to prevent and control outbreaks in communities, while treating seriously ill patients. The pandemic also presented new challenges, such as how to overcome resistance to proven public health and medical solutions and communicate important healthcare guidance and eliminate misinformation (Peters, 2022). Other transformations that have occurred include the greater emphasis on translational research and the introduction of implementation research (see Chapter 3).

At the system level in the United States, we see many national examples of policy agendas that support more CQI initiatives. For example, the Affordable Care Act (ACA)—launched in 2010 amid great opposition and, despite its great success, opposition and efforts to dismantle or weaken the legislation that still continues today—provides incentives that could serve as a catalyst for innovation such as those directed at lowering hospital-acquired infections and the implementation of new care models such as "primary medical care homes" (Somander, 2015). Also, since 2011, the National Quality Strategy has been in place in the United States; this initiative, led by the Agency for Healthcare Research and Quality (AHRQ), is a transdisciplinary strategy to improve quality of care (AHRQ, 2017). Another major factor influencing system-wide CQI implementation, especially in public health, has been accreditation initiatives (Amaral & Cuthbertson, 2016). Also noteworthy on a global scale has been progress made to expand CQI at a greater pace in resource-poor, or low and middle income countries (Leatherman et al., 2003).

The remainder of this chapter will address several questions:

- How does complexity science, the science of innovation, and CQI interact to drive improvement?
- What are the factors that contribute to the implementation of CQI across industries and settings?
- What are the factors that have influenced the rate of diffusion and spread of CQI in health care?
- What steps are needed to develop a culture in health care where CQI is the norm?

Complexity and the Science of Innovation

The complexity of the healthcare system is both a challenge and a source of ideas for how to make improvements (Plsek & Greenhalgh, 2001). Health care has been described as a complex adaptive system, a concept that has implications for how to improve the system. For example, the importance of leadership is critical, as are incentives for improvement. As a complex adaptive system, health care can only be designed to a certain extent and cannot be designed around minimizing costs; rather, the focus must be on maximizing value (Rouse, 2008; Spath & Kelly, 2017).

While health care is unique in many ways, one commonality that it has with other complex endeavors is the difficulty surrounding diffusion of innovation, starting with simple resistance to change but also including other more complex factors: for example, the resistance to vaccinations and other preventive measures during and after the COVID-19 pandemic (Peters, 2022). Understanding these issues helps to provide pathways toward greater diffusion of CQI in health care. Greenhalgh et al. (2005) summarized the research and principles that are specific to diffusion of innovation of health services. Their review noted that there is a wide range of literature using a variety of concepts and approaches that describe how to move along the spectrum from the initiation of a concept for change to the spread, diffusion, and institutionalization of innovation.

Diffusion theory is useful in understanding the factors that thwart or support the adoption of CQI in health care. Because of the complexity of health care and the added complexity of CQI, as alluded to earlier in this chapter, there are no simple answers about how to move CQI innovations into the mainstream of health care more quickly and efficiently. Complexity must be considered in understanding innovation. Although there are competing theories about how and why, innovation clearly does happen in "complex zones." There is some evidence that while innovation may not be susceptible to being managed, it is possible to design and control organizational conditions that "enhance the possibility of innovation occurring and spreading" (Greenhalgh et al., 2005, p. 80).

The speed and overall adoption of any change, including CQI, can be influenced by the characteristics of the change and how it is perceived by those responsible for implementation. These characteristics include relative advantage, compatibility, simplicity, trialability, and observability (Rogers, 1995). All of these characteristics relate to changes and improvements in health care, and two are particularly relevant to health care: **compatibility**, which relates to how closely the change ideas align with the existing culture and environment, and **trialability**, which addresses how the changes can be adapted and tested in the new environments in which they are being spread.

A further extension of these change concepts yields the following seven rules for dissemination of innovation in health care, as outlined by Dr. Donald Berwick who founded the Institute for Healthcare Improvement (IHI) more than 30 years ago and has also served as Administrator of the Centers for Medicare and Medicaid Services (CMS) (Berwick, 2003):

1. Find sound innovations.
2. Find and support innovators.
3. Invest in early adopters.
4. Make early-adopter activity observable.
5. Trust and enable reinvention.
6. Create slack for change.
7. Lead by example.

All of these rules are applicable to innovations around CQI; leadership, trust, and reinvention are fundamental. Reinvention has to do with the cross-disciplinary learning concept that has permeated CQI and is responsible for its evolution across industries and across the globe. CQI cannot be a top-down mandate. It must be part of the vision of an organization and accepted by all who must implement CQI, thus requiring trust at all levels, which comes from leadership, teamwork, and Deming's concept of "constancy of purpose." Top leadership must be involved, supporting and communicating the vision for innovation and change; however, participation, buy-in, and support from opinion leaders at all levels within an organization are critical for successful implementation and the process of reinvention. This directly relates to the concept of **organizational culture**; this very simple, commonly used term is a very powerful construct for leading or impeding change. Daft defines it as: "the set of key values, assumptions, understandings and norms that is shared by members of an organization and taught to new members as correct" (2015, p. 429). As we will show later, there are powerful examples of the types of culture that are necessary to ensure ongoing implementation of CQI in health care.

One size will not fit all. As described by Berwick, "To work, changes must be not only adopted locally, but also locally adapted" (2003, p. 1974). Berwick asserts that for this to happen, there must be reinvention. The lesson for us is that it is not only ok to learn from others and adapt changes into our own settings, adaption is necessary.

The checklist tool described by Gawande (2009) is a clear illustration of this process of reinvention and leadership. It was adapted from the airline and other industries, first to intensive care and later to surgery, with trusted leaders in their fields and disseminating their ideas and successes via scientific venues. The systematic review of diffusion of innovation in health services identifies complexity as one of the key elements that is inversely associated with successful diffusion. Quite often, due to the complex nature of healthcare systems, equally complex quality improvement strategies are required, thus lessening their quick and easy adoption. This helps to explain why simpler quality improvement processes, such as the use of PDSA cycles (see Chapter 1), have enjoyed broad success. But other factors may need to be considered to overcome resistance to changes in healthcare procedures and understand how these changes truly lead to improvements (Langley et al., 2009). For example, a prospective study of the attributes of 42 clinical practice recommendations in gynecology (Foy et al., 2002) helps to explain what these factors may be. After review of almost 5,000 patient records, findings indicate two relevant outcomes that explain why there may be unexpected resistance to change. First, recommendations that were compatible with clinician values and did not require changes to fixed routines were associated with greater compliance. Second, initial noncompliance could be reversed after audit and feedback stages were carried out, indicating that perhaps more time will yield greater compliance. This is especially to be considered when evaluating improvements in outcomes (vs. processes), which may require more time and repeated cycles of process changes to take hold and be sustained.

The Business Case for CQI

Healthcare delivery systems are large, decentralized, and complex, yet at their core they involve a fundamental personal relationship between providers and patients. Moreover, if this were not a sufficient challenge, rapid and uncertain changes in the structure and processes of providing and paying for care make measuring the effect of any single management intervention over time very difficult, if not impossible. Although evidence has been accumulated from both controlled trials (Goldberg et al., 1998; Mehta et al., 2000; Solberg, 1993) and survey data (Shortell et al., 1998) on the implementation process and perceived impact, much of the evidence remains anecdotal (Arndt & Bigelow, 1995; Bigelow & Arndt, 1995). Leatherman et al. (2003), for example, argue that the "business case" for quality improvement is yet to be proven, even while evidence mounts for the overall societal and economic benefits:

> A *business case* for a healthcare improvement intervention exists if the entity that invests in the intervention realizes a financial return on its investment in a reasonable time frame, using a reasonable rate of discounting. This may be realized as "bankable dollars" (profit), a reduction in losses for a given program or population or avoided costs. In addition, a *business case* may exist if the investing entity believes that a positive indirect impact on organization function and sustainability will accrue within a reasonable time frame. (p. 18)

These arguments continue; the economic case includes the returns to all the actors, not just the individual investing business unit. The social case, as they define it, is one of measuring benefits, but not requiring positive returns on the investment. That has been the overriding consideration in the battle to control medical variation and medical errors (McGlynn et al., 2003). The business case for quality improvement suffers from the same negative factors as the business case for other preventive healthcare measures—namely, all or part of the benefits accruing to other business units or patients, and delayed impacts that get discounted heavily in the reckoning (Leatherman et al., 2003). The regulatory arguments for quality improvement efforts have generally been justified on the basis of social and economic benefits such as lives saved and overall cost reductions, but these arguments are not necessarily profitable to the investor. These authors also present a whole array of public policy measures that would overcome the barriers to a positive business case and encourage wider and more assertive implementation of quality improvement methods. Clearly, economics alone does not provide an argument strongly for or against the use of CQI, but it does add to the complexity that pervades the wider and more rapid implementation of CQI in health care.

In summary, this brief overview indicates that a strong business case for CQI in health care cannot be made. In 2010, looking back over the previous 40 years, Robert Brook, UCLA Professor of Medicine and Health Services and Distinguished Chair in Health Care Services for the RAND Corporation, observed, "Although there are some examples in the literature to support the concept that better quality of care is less expensive, few studies have produced information that could be generalized across time and institutional settings" (Brook, 2010, p. 1831). Building on the traditional business concepts that have been discussed and in consideration of the limited evidence to support the business case for CQI, a transformation that may support greater diffusion of CQI and the continuing need to bridge the quality chasm is to consider a more value-based approach to CQI in health care. This approach argues for simultaneous goals of higher quality and lower cost, which will only be achieved when there is a reorientation among CQI proponents that includes a thorough understanding of how to achieve a positive return on investment (Brook, 2010). This view is consistent with the Triple Aim of Health Care described by Berwick et al. (2008) and its most recent evolution to the Quintuple Aim (Itchhaporia, 2021; Nundy et al., 2022).

Factors Associated With Successful CQI Implementation

Despite the need for greater diffusion of CQI in health care, much progress has been made, suggesting a broad array of factors that can be associated with successful CQI implementation. The key to greater diffusion is understanding and emphasizing those factors that work while exploring new concepts, such as the value focus described previously. This analysis starts with regulatory (e.g., accreditation) factors and organizational factors such as leadership, organizational culture, and teamwork; and finishes with individual providers' internal/intrinsic motivation, perhaps the most important factor for adoption of innovations and CQI.

Regulatory Agencies and Accreditation

Regulatory mechanisms such as accreditation are key factors that have led to greater diffusion of CQI and will continue to do so in the future as a direct result of mandated measurement and improvement of the quality of care (Amaral & Cuthbertson, 2016; Greenfield & Pawsey, 2020).

In the United States, the efforts of The Joint Commission (TJC) and the Centers for Medicare and Medicaid Services (CMS) have led to the implementation of a series of initiatives that require hospitals to report on quality measures; after a period of strong resistance, routine reporting of key metrics is now commonplace and required for accreditation by TJC; and has been reinforced by provisions in the ACA (Somander, 2015).

Likewise, CMS generates extensive CQI activities and associated reporting of findings via the efforts of quality improvement organizations (QIOs). QIOs represent a clear example of diffusion of CQI in health care as they grew from what they were in 1972 when they were termed professional standards review organizations (PSROs). They continue to play an important role in ensuring the highest quality of care to the millions of beneficiaries covered by Medicare in the United States. (Schenck et al., 2013).

The processes for each of these regulatory mechanisms provide evidence for factors to be considered, as well as lessons learned, regarding further diffusion of CQI in health care. For example, the impact of the measurement requirements has been notable. In a review published by members of TJC, this impact was described as being due to the use of robust, evidence-based measures, which link process performance and patient outcomes (Chassin et al., 2010). Despite extensive documentation of successes in the article, these authors also note the need and define a direction for further improvement, centered on process measurement. They point out that the focus of this measurement process is entirely on hospital care, leaving much to be done relative to ambulatory care. They also note that the measures in place are process measures, not outcome measures. In the spirit of continuous improvement, they offer guidance in improving the measures that are currently in place.

Once again, this program, while not without problems, is a good model for further diffusion of CQI; early resistance to measurement no longer exists, and now the issue is more about finding the most effective measures, with little resistance expected from hospitals and physicians. In the language of diffusion of innovation, TJC has passed the early adoption stage and is now well into the institutionalization stage, at least in the hospital sector, and relative to a subset of process measures. However, despite their optimism about the progress that has been made and the value of their proposed measurement framework, Chassin et al. (2010) close their discussion of these new accountability measures by realistically pointing out that perpetual vigilance is required to review and improve the measurement process via feedback from internal and external customers. So, a partial answer to our question of how to fix what some have called "a broken system" (Swensen et al., 2010) is provided by accreditation, and much has been accomplished, with some guidance from TJC on what to do next. However, these comments are specific to measurement of processes in hospitals, and a more general answer is still needed to truly address the broader healthcare system and its subcomponents.

For example, one recent proposal to supplement the current role of accreditation in ensuring quality of care is specific to promoting equity in cancer care. It recommends that the two primary bodies for cancer care accreditation, the U.S. Commission on Cancer and the National Cancer Institute, broaden accreditation mechanisms to promote greater equity in cancer care by incorporating "equity into their standards across four domains: clinical care, clinical trials, and data collection and reporting" (Erfani et al.,

2024, p.429). Similarly, the leadership of American College of Cardiology has proposed greater adoption of the quintuple aim, which incorporates health equity to achieve improved patient care outcomes and reduced costs (Itchhaporia, 2021). These recommendations may serve as models for other specialties and areas of health care for promoting quality and safety with greater equity and improved economy.

Lateral Linkages

Healthcare organizations are characterized by their many medical specialties, each organized into its own professional fiefdom, and often with different cultures. Specialization is just one response to an information overload in the organization (Galbraith, 1973). By specializing, each unit tends to learn more and more about less and less. One way to offset the effects of this specialization is to provide lateral linkages—coordinators, integrating mechanisms—to get the information moving across the organization as well as up and down the chain of command (Galbraith, 1973; Lawrence & Lorsch, 1967). So far, that has proved very difficult in healthcare institutions. CQI, through its use of interdisciplinary teams and its focus on a broader definition of process and system as it affects customers rather than professional groups, presents one way to establish linkages. The technology of CQI focuses as much on coordination of the change process as on its motivation. In modern medicine, as practiced in the twenty-first century, this coordination and motivation of CQI is bolstered by the need for greater coordination in medical care in general and is therefore quite natural. There is a greater emphasis on interdisciplinary care, which leads to fostering interdependence and, in turn, better teamwork, including greater employee engagement and improvements in the patient experience and the financial performance of practices (Swensen et al., 2010).

Motivational Factors

Several motivational factors contribute to the sustained interest and enthusiasm for healthcare improvement. These factors have an impact on the motivation of the management of the organization and its employees. The first argument for CQI is its direct impact on quality, usually a net gain to the customer/patient and to the employees of the organization, the external and internal customers. The second argument relates to the set of benefits associated with a plan that empowers employees in health care through participation in decision making. These factors represent benefits for employees and management that can be classified as follows.

Internal/Intrinsic Motivation

With the proper internal or **intrinsic motivation**, the vast majority of healthcare workers support the concept of quality care and would like to see improvements and participate in a meaningful quality improvement process. Allowing personnel to work on their own processes, permitting them to "do the right thing," and then rewarding them for that behavior is almost sure to increase intrinsic motivation in employees, if done properly. It is a classic case of empowerment and job enrichment for healthcare workers and follows the principle clearly delineated by Deming about the important role of internal (vs. external) motivation and employee engagement in CQI efforts. It should be noted that internal and intrinsic motivation will be used interchangeably throughout this text, representing the form of motivation that Deming describes as being linked to self-esteem and dignity (1993).

System of Profound Knowledge

It is well known that the system of profound knowledge and the original 14 points of Deming (see Chapter 1) emphasize high levels of trust, empowerment, and especially internal motivation and engagement as important factors associated with implementation of CQI initiatives (Deming, 1986, 1993). This is clearly and succinctly emphasized in Deming's point number 12: "remove barriers that rob people of pride of workmanship" (Deming, 1986, p. 77). In health care, and especially in nursing and medicine, one indication of demotivation and lack of engagement is the increasing rate of burnout and work dissatisfaction initially noted in the first decade of the twenty-first century, although it was also present but perhaps less well documented in earlier years (Shanafelt et al., 2015). A systematic review and meta-analysis reported in *The Lancet* in 2016 described physician burnout as reaching epidemic proportions (West et al., 2016). Burnout, which can be defined as the opposite of engagement, is indicated by emotional exhaustion, depersonalization, and perceived lack of personal accomplishment; and in health care, burnout is manifested by diminished personal well-being and longevity and leads to decreased quality of patient care (Chew et al., 2017). Provider burnout has also been linked to greater patient dissatisfaction and higher costs. Examples that have been cited of lower quality/safety of care resulting from burnout include prescribing inappropriate medications (Bodenheimer & Sinsky, 2014). Reports of physician burnout have been persistent during the second decade of the twenty-first century, as indicated by findings from two large studies, which reported prevalence of at least one symptom of burnout as high as 54.4% in 2014 (Shanafelt et al., 2015) compared to 45.5% in 2011 (Shanafelt et al., 2012). In both studies, the sample sizes consisted of over 3,000 responding physicians; although response rates were in the 20% range, which may compromise the ability these data have to serve as predictors of population parameters, the consistency and large sample size that these findings are based on are indicative of a long-term trend that burnout is persistent and may be worsening over the time period between these two studies. Other studies in the United States and Europe of a range of types of healthcare providers, including nurses and staff as well as physicians, yield similar findings. For example, one provider survey, in 2013, in the United States found that 60% of respondents reported burnout and 34% indicated that they planned to look for another job (Bodenheimer & Sinsky, 2014). A 2015 survey of British physicians reported that 44% of respondents reported very low or low morale, with similar findings for nurses and health care staff (Sikka et al., 2015).

The impact of the COVID-19 pandemic and its ongoing endemic phase have further exacerbated burnout among providers and its impact on quality of care (Kamra et al., 2024). During the pandemic, provider stress increased due to unsafe working conditions and higher workloads. A systematic review and meta-analysis based on 4,732 articles and 170 studies spanning the timeframe of the height of the pandemic, through 2021, yielded direct evidence of physician burnout indicated by increases in job dissatisfaction, regret about career choice and turnover intention and most notably adverse effects on patient safety, quality of care and patient dissatisfaction (Hodkinson et al., 2022). Further evidence of the impact of the pandemic is found throughout the literature during and after the pandemic. For example, a systematic review and meta-analysis spanning the years of the pandemic, through November 2022 that included 57 studies/28,965 participants in 25 countries, found an 18.3 % prevalence of post-traumatic stress syndrome (Kamra et al., 2024). These findings indicate that concern for stress and burnout and their relationship to quality and safety, which had already been of concern for many years needed even greater attention in the pandemic and post-pandemic years. Among the various factors that thwart innovation and CQI implementation, burnout and low morale are often mentioned not only for the sake of encouraging innovation, but more importantly, to improve the health and well-being of healthcare providers. A key question for all in health care and specifically to address the topic of this chapter is how to reverse these trends; how to eliminate factors that may be causally related to burnout and how to identify factors that will increase the rate of innovation and CQI implementation.

From Triple Aim to Quintuple Aim

An important innovative concept that was first introduced in 2008 is the **Triple Aim** of Health Care (Berwick et al., 2008). This innovation broadens the goals and definition of quality health care through the simultaneous pursuit of three aims: "improving the experience of care, improving the health of populations, and reducing the per capita costs of health care" (Berwick et al., 2008, p. 759). Since its introduction, the adoption of the Triple Aim has become a goal of many healthcare providers both nationally and globally and can be viewed as an important innovative step in the ongoing evolution of CQI in health care; it has done so by using a systems optimization perspective and has taken advantage of associated innovations that have facilitated the implementation of systems to pursue the Triple Aim. For example, adoption of the Triple Aim has benefited from improvements in technology, such as the broader overall use and the institutionalization, at least in large hospital systems, of electronic health records. It has also benefited from CQI tools and techniques that have become more widely adopted in recent years such as elimination of waste in healthcare processes via LEAN/Six Sigma, described in Chapter 5.

The introduction of the Triple Aim is an example of innovation in healthcare systems, and the application of a systems approach utilizing synergy derived from the interdependence of the three aims. However, this interdependence requires careful attention to system optimization since changing any one has a direct impact on the other two aims. This important characteristic has direct implications on the further adoption of CQI in health care, which requires that intrinsic motivation for change and improvement is maintained by providers. For example, if cost reductions lead to overburdening busy providers with lower leverage tasks, then they may not be motivated to identify and implement new CQI ideas. The cost-reduction mentality that is described in some business models as "doing more with less" can also lead, in health care, to poorer quality and lower patient satisfaction if tradeoffs are not carefully understood and managed.

Quadruple Aim

Although many healthcare providers have adopted the Triple Aim, others have not been able to do so successfully. One explanation for less than full implementation may be that "practices working toward the Triple Aim may increase physician burnout and thereby reduce their chances of success" (Bodenheimer & Sinsky, 2014, p. 575). A partial explanation for this trend is that some of the very same factors that lead to successful adoption of the Triple Aim may have inadvertently led to burnout and demotivation among some healthcare providers. For example, the widespread increase in utilization of electronic health records, a plus factor for implementing the Triple Aim, has been shown to lead to increases in burnout (Babbott et al., 2014).

Provider burnout and dissatisfaction, the opposite of internal motivation and engagement, may also lead to a reluctance to adopt or lead the development of innovations/CQI initiatives. Because of its possible causative links to burnout, the Triple Aim, while by definition designed to lead to greater CQI implementation and innovation in health care, may inadvertently have the opposite effect, at least in some cases.

To address this conflict in positive and negative effects of pursuing the Triple Aim, one solution that has been widely adopted is to expand the Triple Aim by adding a fourth aim—improving the work life of clinicians and healthcare staff and increasing the experience of joy and meaning in healthcare work (Bodenheimer & Sinsky, 2014; Nundy et al., 2022; Rangachari, 2023; Sikka et al., 2015).

Since its introduction, the **Quadruple Aim** has been widely adopted within health care and perhaps has become even more relevant in response to the exacerbation of burnout and stress, and associated lowering quality of patient care, due to the COVID-19 pandemic. (Hodkinson et al., 2022; Kamra et al., 2024) "The Quadruple Aim has gone from simply being an academic concept to serving as the bedrock for primary health care reform. Notably the Quadruple Aim has provided the basis for rapid proliferation of innovative new models of care delivery, including Accountable Care Organizations (ACOs) and the Patient-Centered Medical Home (PCMH)" (Rangachari, 2023, p. 2239).

Both the Triple Aim and the Quadruple Aim have represented new frameworks for implementation of CQI and since 2014 the Triple Aim and/or the Quadruple Aim have been broadly adopted and is cited frequently by researchers and accrediting bodies. (Nundy et al., 2022).

Furthermore, the Quadruple Aim concepts have also been promoted as a means to improve healthcare practice, leadership, and quality for a broad range of healthcare professions, for example, including nursing (Bowles et al, 2018; Krumwiede et al., 2023) and public health as well (Kovach, 2024).

Quintuple Aim—A Focus on Equity

"Quality improvement without equity is a hollow victory"

Nundy et al., 2022

As with the expansion of the Triple Aim, there has been further impetus to continuously improve by expanding this successful concept, initially by the addition of a fourth aim, to increase intrinsic motivation to achieve ongoing CQI goals. More recently this has led to proposals for a broader framework, the **Quintuple Aim**, that includes a fifth aim, advancing health equity. This aim is intended to be an explicit goal and ensure a long overdue focus on health disparity elimination (Itchhaporia, 2021; Nundy et al., 2022).

Racial and ethnic disparities have long been identified as predictors of (poor) quality of health care received; this recognition of health disparities and the need to improve health equity as a part of the process for implementing healthcare quality improvements in the United States were included in two pioneering reports by the National Academy of Medicine (IOM 2001, 2003). Although there has been some progress towards greater health equity in the 20 years since the National Academy of Medicine reports, it is clear that elimination of health disparities has remained as an important gap in healthcare delivery and CQI initiatives. Closing this gap has become central to the mission of many healthcare organizations. For example, in describing its mission in the future, the President of the American College of Cardiology stated in 2021 that "without understanding the social determinants of health, which drive 70% of health care outcomes, and without a clear path forward to solve for health equity, all attempts to globally transform cardiovascular care will be futile" (Itchhaporia, 2021, p. 2262).

Population health measures, such as infant mortality, provide another perspective on the importance of health equity to achieving the highest levels of access and quality of care in the United States and across the world. In 2003, Dr. Donald Berwick noted: "Americans spend almost 40% more for health care than any other country, yet rank 27th in infant mortality . . . and are less satisfied with their care than the English, Canadians or Germans" (Berwick, 2003, p. 1969). Unfortunately, a review of these trends almost 20 years later, in 2021, indicates a similar pattern, with the United States ranking thirty-third in infant mortality among the 38 countries included in the Organization for Economic Co-operation and Development (OECD), lagging behind other developed countries such as Japan and Norway, which had the best rankings. (America's Health Ranking, 2023). High infant mortality in the United States, which parallels other similar population health indicators, can be linked at least partially but most directly to a lack of healthcare equity among minorities, with clearly evident causes.

"A variety of factors that characterize minority populations, including experiences of racial discrimination, low income and education levels, poor residential environments, lack of medical insurance, and treatment at low-quality hospitals, demonstrate strong correlations with high infant mortality rates. Identifying, acknowledging, and addressing these disparities must be performed before engaging in strategies to mitigate them." (Jang & Lee, 2022, p.1).

During the COVID-19 pandemic, the lack of health equity was an important contributor to poorer outcomes among minorities, in the United States and internationally. Socially marginalized populations experienced worse outcomes overall, not just rates of COVID-19 (Nundy et al., 2022).

The Quintuple Aim would supplement and improve on the Triple and Quadruple Aims by specifying the addition of a fifth aim, health equity, defined as a "state in which everyone has the opportunity to attain their full health potential, and no one is disadvantaged from achieving this potential because of social position or other socially determined circumstances" (National Academies of Sciences, Engineering and Medicine, 2017).

At the patient care level, this fifth aim requires that healthcare practitioners identify specific disparities and design and implement evidence-based interventions to reduce them. Healthcare leaders should incentivize practitioners and provide resources needed to measure and report quality and operational data stratified by relevant social categories (Nundy et al., 2022). The use of sociodemographic and clinical data at the individual and community levels allows for better understanding of the distinct needs of populations served and would help to focus CQI initiatives, especially for those who have been underserved. Additionally, practitioners can play an important role in helping combat implicit bias among clinicians with the goal of improving communication and engagement with patients and ultimately transforming patient experience and health outcomes (Itchhaporia, 2021). Other leadership or legislative steps can include broadening healthcare accreditation standards to incorporate equity (Erfani et al., 2024).

In summary, the concept and effectiveness of the Triple Aim was further improved by the addition of a fourth aim that focuses on the welfare of providers because of the relationship between provider satisfaction and patient satisfaction and overall quality of care, thereby supporting the primary goal of the triple aim, to improve population health. Stated more succinctly, "health care is a relationship between those who provide care and those who seek care, a relationship that can only thrive if it is symbiotic" (Bodenheimer & Sinsky, 2014, p. 575). And this symbiotic relationship, which is at the core of successful CQI implementation, must also include health equity. In the same way that failing to address burnout would make quality improvement unsustainable, i.e., a hollow victory (Nundy et al., 2022).

The addition of health equity will also enhance achievement of the other aims, better experience of care and better health for populations, thereby reducing or eliminating health disparities in communities and strengthening all aims in the Quintuple Aim.

Culture of Excellence

Throughout the evolution of CQI, one of the most important factors associated with successful applications of CQI has been the interaction of leadership, organizational culture, teamwork, and internal motivation. To ensure CQI, the most important role of a leader is transformation (Deming, 1993), which starts with a motivating vision that must be developed, communicated, and embraced by all in the organization, and which in turn leads to high levels of commitment to the vision of change and improvement (Melum & Sinioris, 1993; Tichy & Devanna, 1986). Leaders ensure commitment to the vision by shaping a culture that not only accepts but embraces change (Balestracci, 2009; Schein, 1992). **Figure 2.1** describes the way in which this is accomplished in an organization that is dedicated to CQI and thereby defines a set of factors that are critical to the greater diffusion of CQI in health care.

The type of culture that is needed to succeed in an organization whose goal is to continuously improve can be called a "Culture of Excellence." This framework is similar to a "**Safety Culture**," defined as a culture in which "a commitment to safety permeates all levels of the organization from frontline personnel to executive management" (AHRQ, 2011). Likewise, parallels can be found in a **Culture of Health**, an action model developed by the Robert Wood Johnson Foundation to inform its decisions in awarding grants and develop strategic collaborations. Its goals include creating healthier and more equitable communities and transforming health and healthcare systems (Plough, 2015; Rangachari, 2023).

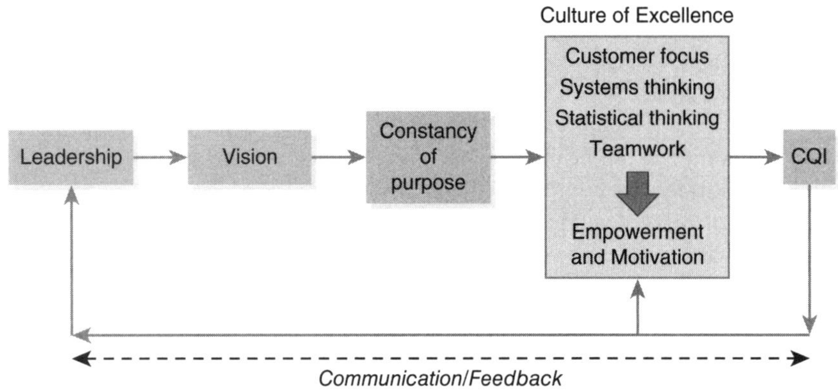

Figure 2.1 A Cultural Framework to Ensure Successful CQI Implementation

In addition to the obvious similarity of all of these frameworks, using the well-known organizational term, culture, is a similar vision focused on quality and safety and an organizational structure characterized by the components listed in Figure 2.1. A commitment to such a vision leads to what Deming called constancy of purpose for all in the organization, referring to a clear sense of where the organization is going or what a system is intended to accomplish (Deming, 1986).

Within and outside of health care there has been an emphasis for many years on the value of culture to ensure and sustain quality and safety. In fact, the use of the phrase **Culture of Excellence** spans many types of organizations; it will be used here to define a set of characteristics of healthcare organizations that ensure the highest quality and safety standards as a way to bundle the concepts exhibited in Figure 2.1 in one concise phrase.

The strength of culture, especially in regard to sustaining quality and safety, is evident in shared assumptions and norms. As the organization evolves, these assumptions and norms are taught to new members. (Daft, 2015). In a Culture of Excellence, thoughts and feelings about mission are directly influenced by finding ways to improve constantly with an operating standard that utilizes the principles of the Quintuple Aim to meet and exceed the safety and quality needs of communities, patients, and providers with an emphasis on equity. With the many changes that are faced every day in health care it is critical that healthcare organizations be prepared to apply a set of actions to not only meet new challenges but to develop new learning and create paradigm shifts that are focused on future improvements.

Underlying the development of a Culture of Excellence is a need for a systems view. A healthcare systems view emphasizes the importance of adding value and the importance of leadership rather than management, influence rather than power, and the alignment of incentives focused on quality rather than quantity of services (Rouse, 2008). A Culture of Excellence embraces this view, is performance oriented, and at a minimum adopts a CQI philosophy (as defined in Chapter 1). It exemplifies the following elements outlined in Figure 2.1:

- *Customer focus:* Emphasizing the importance of both internal and external customers (see Chapter 1). It should be noted here that in defining the population who will ultimately benefit from healthcare innovations and CQI (i.e., the external customer), there may be some discomfort with the generic term "customer," especially among physicians and nurses (Houpt et al., 2015). There should be awareness of this issue, especially when developing a culture to embrace the ideas presented here, but for simplicity and consistency with terminology presented here and in the CQI literature in general, the term *customer* will continue to be used—as

a term that denotes the highest respect for the patients, their families and communities served in health care.
- *Systems thinking:* Maintaining a goal of optimizing the system as a whole and thereby creating synergy (Deming, 1986; Spath & Kelly, 2017).
- *Statistical thinking:* Understanding causes of variation and the importance of learning from measurement; having the ability to use data to make decisions (see Chapter 4 and Balestracci, 2009). In the modern age of healthcare research, which includes "big data" and "analytics," we now have easier access to large amounts of online data. More than ever before statistical thinking must also include the ability to be judicious in choosing the right data at the right time for the specific purpose that is required in a CQI effort.
- *Teamwork:* Teams of peers working together to ensure empowerment, thereby creating the highest levels of motivation to ensure alignment of the organization, the team, and the individual around the CQI vision (see Chapter 6 and Grove, 1995).
- *Motivation and empowerment:* A key component of the Culture of Excellence is its ability to increase empowerment and internal motivation necessary for any successful CQI initiative (Deming, 1986, 1993). Ultimately, this will lead to higher levels of engagement where people are willing to go the extra mile. Involving the employees closer to the front line increases engagement. A Culture of Excellence creates an environment where empowerment, motivation, and engagement are the norm. It should ultimately address the need for "joy in work" by providing a platform for the Quintuple Aim to be achieved, and in a cyclical manner this will in turn further increase the motivation of healthcare providers to be innovative and embrace CQI initiatives.
- *Communication and feedback:* Maintaining open channels of communication and feedback to make adjustments as needed, including modifying the vision to achieve higher levels of quality in a manner consistent with a learning organization (Senge, 1990), including feedback that is fact-based and given with true concern for individuals' organizational success (Balestracci, 2009). Open communication and feedback are key characteristics of the team approach necessary to achieve the goals of CQI (see Chapter 6). It should also be noted that open communication and the collection and feedback of information stratified by relevant social categories in a population is also critical to achieving equity in CQI and health care in general (Nundy et al., 2022).

Leadership and Diffusion

In discussing factors that support the implementation of CQI, the theory of diffusion of innovation clearly supports the important role of leadership in CQI. A capacity for innovation, as described in the literature of organizational psychology, is seen as critically dependent on good leadership; one of the key factors to the implementation and routinization of innovation once adopted is the consultation and active involvement of leaders—and especially leadership by example. Furthermore, organizational leadership is critical to the development of a culture that fosters innovation (Greenhalgh et al., 2005). CQI is a form of change and innovation that also requires cultural change driven by leadership. As Greenhalgh et al. explain, "Leaders within organizations are critical firstly in creating a cultural context that fosters innovation and secondly, establishing organizational strategy, structure, and systems that facilitate innovation" (2005, p. 69). This perspective ties directly back to Deming's point about leadership: leaders must know and understand the processes they are responsible for and lead by example, acting as part of the improvement effort and on the "corrections" required (Deming, 1986). This point was emphasized by Gawande (2009, p. 146) in describing how the initial adoption of surgical checklists was accomplished:

> Using the checklist involved a major cultural change, as well—a shift in authority, responsibility, and expectations

> about care—and the hospitals needed to recognize that. We gambled that their staff would be far more likely to adopt the checklist if they saw their leadership accepting it from the outset.

Leaders at All Levels

Various types of leaders can contribute to (or detract from) the innovation process. Traditional organizational and team leaders are most often associated with CQI initiatives; however, in regard to innovations, the terminology of "leader" can be expanded to include opinion leaders, champions, and boundary spanners.

Opinion leaders represent a broad range of leaders "within the ranks" as well as those at the top level. In clinical settings, opinion leaders have influence on the beliefs and actions of their colleagues, either positive or negative in regard to embracing innovation. Opinion leaders may be experts who are respected for their formal academic authority regarding a particular innovation; their support represents a form of evidence-based knowledge. Opinion leaders may also be peers who are respected for their know-how and understanding of the realities of clinical practice (Greenhalgh et al., 2005).

Unlike opinion leaders, who may support or oppose an innovation, **champions** persistently support new ideas. They may come from the top management of an organization, including technical or business experts. Champions include team and project leaders and others who have perseverance to fight both resistance and/or indifference to promote the acceptance of a new idea or to achieve project goals (Greenhalgh et al., 2005).

Boundary spanners represent a combination of these various types of leaders and are distinguished by the fact that they have influence across organizational and other boundaries (Greenhalgh et al., 2005; Kaluzny et al., 1974). Boundary spanners play an important role in multi-organizational innovations and quality improvement initiatives, such as quality improvement collaboratives (Kilo, 1998; Leape et al., 2000). Each of these types of leaders is found in the adoption of quality improvement initiatives in health care, and often these various types of leaders are found in combination.

Teamwork

CQI in health care is a team game (see Chapter 6). These teams are composed of peers who are highly trained technical experts supporting each other and empowered to take a leadership role as required to meet the needs of customers. Teamwork is one of the most important components of all successful CQI initiatives; team building centers on the ability to create teams of empowered and motivated people who are leaders themselves and who will take the lead as needed to foster change, innovation, and improvement (Byham & Cox, 1998; Grove, 1995; Kotter, 1996). The glue that holds a Culture of Excellence together and that ensures there will be quality at every interface is the link between leadership and teamwork, with leadership exhibited as called for at all levels within a team. As Deming states, "There is no substitute for teamwork and good leaders of teams to bring consistency of effort along with knowledge" (1986, p. 19).

Motivation and Empowerment

Inherent in teamwork is a high level of empowerment of team members, which in turn leads to high levels of motivation. Empowerment implies that levels of authority match levels of responsibility and training. For example, suggestions and interventions can be made to allow improvements and prevent problems or errors. This initiative goes beyond simply allowing team members to speak up; it means ensuring they are comfortable speaking up when something seems wrong (Byham & Cox, 1998; Deming, 1986; Grove, 1995).

Improved motivation is the direct result of transformational leadership and especially its emphasis on empowerment. Motivation and empowerment both will interact to lead to higher quality; but to work, these elements require another aspect of cultural change and associated leadership responsibility—building a culture of trust. This is emphasized in Deming's 14 points, namely point number 8: Drive out fear. Create trust. Create a climate for innovation (see Chapter 1). Deming explains, "No one can put in his best performance unless he feels secure. ... Secure means without fear, not afraid to express ideas, not afraid to ask questions" (1986, p. 59). This ties directly back to the surgical checklist example where use of a checklist implies responsibility to communicate and question each other as part of the checklist process, regardless of the team member's rank. A leader's goal must be to create a culture where people are empowered to do their jobs to the best of their abilities, with trust and a clear understanding of the vision that creates the constancy of purpose needed to achieve the highest quality.

Training is critical to the success of leaders and the ability to achieve constancy of purpose, not only training of employees in the skills required to do their jobs, which removes barriers to motivation, but also training the future leaders of the organization, which creates further motivation. Training of future leaders is one of the most important responsibilities of a leader (Tichy, 1997). And it is a key characteristic of transformational leadership (Gawande, 2009) addresses this issue in describing the process for testing and implementing the surgical safety checklist. Despite the obvious key role of the surgeon, it was decided that the "circulating nurse" on the surgery team would be the one to start the checklist process at the beginning of a surgery. This was done for several reasons, but one of the most important was "to spread responsibility and the power to question" (p. 137).

Examples of Leadership and Teamwork in CQI

The linkage between leadership and teamwork to ensure success in quality improvement in health care has been demonstrated in many instances, including the very successful implementation of quality improvement collaboratives (QICs). QICs represent a form of virtual organizations (Byrne, 1993) the effectiveness of which has been demonstrated in industry for many years. Part of the success of QICs can be tied to this effective team structure. For example, in describing the successful application of a QIC using the IHI Breakthrough series (Kilo, 1998) in 40 U.S. hospitals to reduce adverse drug events, Leape et al. (2000) identify strong leadership and teamwork among their most important success factors: "Success in making significant changes was associated with strong leadership, effective processes, and appropriate choice of intervention. Successful teams were able to define, clearly state, and relentlessly pursue their aims, and then chose practical interventions and moved early into changing a process" (Greenhalgh et al., 2005, p. 165).

In summary, leadership, effective teamwork, and the empowerment of teams, which lead to higher levels of internal motivation, have been critical factors in the evolution of CQI in health care and are directly related to the pace and broad adoption of CQI in health care in recent years. Chapter 6 provides a detailed description of how to build teams and ensure that they operate most effectively to improve quality in health care. Grove (1995) provides examples of how to create an organizational structure that supports multiple teams working in parallel and how to ensure efficiency in doing so.

Sustainability

Important characteristics that can be used to assess the validity of an organizational design or a change model include its resilience and sustainability over time. Also important is sufficient flexibility to permit or even encourage replication in diverse settings. Based on these goals the Culture of Excellence described here will ensure the sustainability of CQI to not only address specific quality and safety problems, but also to instill a level of dedication and understanding among organizational members that quality improvement is everyone's job in health care and that it is a continuous endeavor; some have described it as a "race without a finish line" (Schmidt and Finnegan, 1992). It can be compared to other models within and beyond health care, as well as beyond geographic boundaries.

A traditional model that is used to define a culture of change beyond health care is the eight-stage change model developed by John Kotter (1996). The discussion of leadership, organizational culture, and teamwork presented previously described "what is" the type of culture that is needed to implement successful CQI initiatives; Kotter's model describes "how to" implement major change and also provides guidance on traditional errors to avoid. These two approaches are closely related. There is clear overlap between Kotter's model and the components defined in Figure 2.1 that define the CQI Culture of Excellence. These common elements include vision, empowerment, communication, feedback loops to produce continuous change, and, most important, the critical step of anchoring change in the culture. "Changes in a workgroup, a division or an entire company can come undone, even after years of effort, because the new approaches haven't been anchored firmly in group norms and values". (Kotter, 1996, p. 148).

Kotter's model, which is well known and well tested with widespread application beyond health care, also serves as validation for the basic concepts of the Culture of Excellence framework.

When bundled together, the components described here to define a Culture of Excellence will ensure ongoing CQI in health care and sustainability in the face of expected and unexpected changes and crises.

Change is constant in health care, and one way to prepare for change and continuously improve is to develop a sustainable culture such as the Culture of Excellence. First and foremost, new evidence-based methodologies and critical thinking must be expected and encouraged; also to be expected is new legislation, e.g., the ACA (Somander, 2015) as well as unexpected crises such as the COVID-19 pandemic, including the "surprising" level of resistance to preventive and curative solutions. It is only through anchoring change methodologies in a strong culture that practitioners and communities can remain motivated to work together to face challenges and foster continuous improvement (Peters, 2022).

Examples of Sustainability

There are numerous examples in health care of the impact of culture driving sustainable quality and safety standards. One prominent example of a high quality sustainable culture is the New York-Presbyterian Hospital System (NYP). For many years NYP was widely recognized for having a culture known for quality, safety, and equity. This was clearly demonstrated when facing the high stress levels imposed by the COVID-19 pandemic. It is also an example of a large expanding organization that maintained its culture of quality and safety while increasing its size and population served; in 2021 it was estimated to provide care to over 20 percent of the population of New York City (Brenner, 2022; Georgescu, 2024).

NYP is known for encouraging open communication utilizing formal feedback mechanisms; it exhibits constancy of purpose that is centered on a vision and mission of zero harm for patients and employees, accomplished by building a continuous improvement culture (Georgescu, 2024). The level of staff motivation and engagement during the pandemic was noteworthy and well documented as central to their culture (Brenner, 2022).

An analysis of the characteristics of this distinguished healthcare organization indicates that it uses many of the principles of a Culture of Excellence and a Safety Culture. They also exhibit characteristics of the Quintuple Aim, with a clear focus on equity. (In fact one of the co-authors of one of the seminal publications on the Quintuple Aim that has been cited several times in this chapter is Kedar Mate, MD, who has an appointment at Weill Cornell Medical College, affiliated with NYP).

Any discussion of sustainability of a quality culture must also include the sobering fact that the wrong kind of culture or a change in well-established cultural values and norms, can have a negative impact on quality and/or safety; for example, when expansion is undertaken but is not properly managed, or the leadership or culture of the expanded organization is very different from the previous organization (Frakt, 2015, Levinson, 2024). A critical step in any expansion or growth strategy is to understand the impact on culture;

especially during mergers and acquisitions time and care should be taken to understand cultural differences of all participating entities and make adjustments if necessary, without sacrificing core principles and values.

One example of an organizational/cultural change that resulted in declining quality and safety with some catastrophic results—leading to many lost lives—was in the airline industry in the second decade of the twenty-first century. The airline manufacturing company, Boeing, which had for many years been applauded as an example of high quality and safety standards experienced a significant reversal, leading to two airline crashes in 2018 and 2019 and several other safety incidents that were life threatening, e.g., doors and other parts falling off of airplanes, due to improper installation or poor maintenance of aircrafts. As reported in the popular press the main cause of the lack of sustainability of Boeing's leadership in quality and safety was thought to be purposeful shifts in the culture, away from an "engineering-centric culture" to one that may have become too focused on profit and an aggressive growth strategy. "The answer that pretty much everyone arrived at after these two fatal crashes was the same: Boeing's culture had changed" (Surowiecki, 2024, p. 5). These cultural changes led to ignoring feedback about safety issues from front line staff and a willful disregard of safety regulations, e.g., failing safety audits. In summary, the loss of Boeing's leadership in quality and safety was due to significant changes in their culture. It should be noted that it was not growth per se that caused problems; instead it was a purposeful change in the culture under new leadership that led to quality and safety problems (Georgescu, 2024; Shefrin, 2024; Surowiecki, 2024). It is important to note that at the time of final publication of this chapter Boeing has made organizational changes and is striving to return their culture to where it was several years ago - a difficult task and certainly a work in progress. One quote from the NY Times that describes their more current status (in November, 2025) is as follows: "Boeing is trying to change its culture, but opinions about how that is going remain mixed. In a survey this year, 67 percent of employees said they were proud to work at the company, down from 91 percent in 2013 (Chokshi, 2025).

In summary, dynamic growth is not a problem in itself as long as a quality culture can be maintained. Health care organizations have been undergoing substantial growth in the twenty-first century with one goal being to provide quality health care to larger communities. Once again NYP, which has grown vertically and horizontally (acquiring other hospitals) over the years has maintained a culture of quality, safety, and equity, and a level of resilience that was demonstated most dramatically in combatting the COVID-19 pandemic (Brenner, 2022). On the other hand, Boeing and other organizations that lost sight of their mission during periods of growth present clear warnings for large, expanding healthcare organizations, which are directly relevant here. An important lesson that can be drawn from these examples is that in order to adjust to growth, change, and new challenges, sustainability of quality and safety standards requires shaping and nurturing of a culture with a focus on CQI using principles such as those described for the Culture of Excellence. It is also important to note from these descriptions of poor quality being attributed to cultural defects that in addition to the positive impact of a quality culture, these demonstrations of the negative impact of a poor culture help to validate the construct of culture as influential on quality and safety, good and bad.

Conclusion

Despite the increased use of CQI and a good understanding of the philosophy and processes of CQI, its effectiveness and further adoption in health care remain subjects of ongoing concern. The literature on diffusion of innovation suggests some guidelines to understand factors that influence the adoption of CQI. Understanding the factors that enable or influence adoption of CQI, as well as the factors that present barriers, is particularly important as more countries around the world are utilizing CQI to solve health challenges, including resource-poor countries and as national health initiatives are being modified or introduced around the world, including in the United States.

Among the factors that are gaining greater attention is the emphasis on cost, efficiency, and value. The emphasis on value is directly correlated with concerns about the costs of quality health care and has led to novel concepts such as the Triple Aim of health care—simultaneously focusing on care, health, and cost. At the same time, the critical role of internal motivation, that was emphasized by CQI pioneers, such as W. Edwards Deming, as central to ongoing implementation of CQI, leads to consideration of a fourth aim, improving the motivation and work life of healthcare providers. This consideration has been driven in part by demotivation resulting from increasing rates of burnout that have been reported among healthcare providers, both prior to and since the COVID-19 pandemic. Central to promoting the diffusion of innovation, and in particular CQI, is leadership, vision, and teamwork, resulting in empowerment and motivation of the healthcare workforce.

A most recent expansion of the Quadruple Aim to a Quintuple Aim adds a fifth aim, advancing health equity. This aim is intended to add an explicit and long overdue goal of eliminating health disparities; and to emphasize that quality improvement without health equity is a "hollow victory."

A comprehensive framework for increasing the uptake of CQI and achieving the Quintuple Aim is development of a culture where CQI is embraced as everyone's job. A cultural framework that combines these factors to ensure the continuing adoption and sustainability of CQI in health care, and including the goals of the Quintuple Aim, is a Culture of Excellence; its rationale, components, and sustainability are described in this chapter, with comparisons to other similar cultural frameworks, Culture of Health and the well known Safety Culture.

Key Concepts and Terms

boundary spanners
champions
compatibility
Culture of Excellence
Culture of Health
Intrinsic motivation
Organizational culture
opinion leaders
Quadruple Aim
Quintuple Aim
Safety Culture
trialability
Triple Aim

References

AHRQ Patient Safety Network. (2011). *Glossary: Safety culture.* Agency for Healthcare Research and Quality. Retrieved January 1, 2011, from http://psnet.ahrq.gov

Amaral, A., & Cuthbertson, B. H. (2016). Balancing quality of care and resource utilization in acute care hospitals. *BMJ Quality & Safety, 25*(11), 824. https://doi.org/10.1136/bmjqs-2015-005037

America's Health Rankings (2023). *2023 Annual report.* United Health Foundation. Retrieved October 28, 2025, from http://www.americashealthrankings.org/learn/reports/2023-annual-report/international-comparison

Arndt, M., & Bigelow, B. (1995). The implementation of total quality management in hospitals: How good is the fit? *Health Care Management Reviews, 20*(4), 7–14.

Babbott, S., Manwell, L. B., Brown, R., Montague, E., Williams, E., Schwartz, M., ... Linzer, M. (2014). Electronic medical records and physician stress in primary care: Results of the MEMO Study. *Journal of the American Medical Informatics Association, 21*(el), e100–e106. https://doi.org/10.1136/amiajnl-2013-001875

Balestracci, D. (2009). *Data sanity: A quantum leap to unprecedented results.* Medical Group Management Association.

Batalden, P., & Davidoff, F. (2007). What is "quality improvement" and how can it transform health care? *Quality and Safety in Health Care, 16*(1), 2–3. https://doi.org/10.1136/qshc.2006.022046

Berwick, D. M. (1996). A primer on leading the improvement of systems. *British Medical Journal, 312*(7031), 619–622. https://doi.org/10.1136/bmj.312.7031.619

Berwick, D. M. (2003). Disseminating innovations in health care. *Journal of the American Medical Association, 289*(15), 1969–1975. https://doi.org/10.1001/jama.289.15.1969

Berwick, D. M., Nolan, T. W., & Whittington, J. (2008). The Triple Aim: Care, health, and cost. *Health Affairs, 27*(3), 759–769. https://doi.org/10.1377/hlthaff.27.3.759

Bigelow, B., & Arndt, M. (1995). Total quality management: Field of dreams? *Health Care Management Reviews, 20*(4), 15–25. https://doi.org/10.1097/00004010-199502040-00003

Bodenheimer, T., & Sinsky, C. (2014). From triple to quadruple aim: Care of the patient requires care of the provider. *Annals of Family Medicine, 12*(6), 573–576. https://doi.org/10.1370/afm.1713

Bowles, J., Adams, J., Batcheller, J., Zimmerman, D., & Pappas, S. (2018). The role of the nurse leader in advancing the quadruple aim. *Nurse Leader, 16*(4), 244–248. https://doi.org/10.1016/j.mnl.2018.05.011

Brenner, M. (2022). *The desperate hours—One hospital's fight to save a city on the pandemic's front lines*. Flatiron Books.

Brook, R. H. (2010). The end of the quality improvement movement: Long live improving value. *Journal of the American Medical Association, 304*(16), 1831–1832. https://doi.org/10.1001/jama.2010.1555

Byham, W. C., & Cox, J. (1998). *Zapp! The lightning of empowerment—How to improve quality, productivity, and employee satisfaction*. Fawcett Ballantine, The Ballantine Publishing Group.

Byrne, J. (1993). The virtual corporation. *Business Week, 3304*, 98–102.

Chassin, M. R., Loeb, J. M., Schmaltz, S. P., & Wachter, R. M. (2010). Accountability measures: Using measurement to promote quality improvement. *The New England Journal of Medicine, 363*(7), 683–688. https://doi.org/10.1056/nejmsb1002320

Chew, F. S., Mulcahy, M. J., Porrino, J. A., Mulcahy, H., & Relyea-Chew, A. (2017). Prevalence of burnout among musculoskeletal radiologists. *Skeletal Radiology, 46*(4), 497–506. https://doi.org/10.1007/s00256-017-2578-9

Chokshi, N (2025). *Boeing tackles quality with a 'war on defects'*. New York Times.

Daft, R. L. (2015). *The leadership experience* (6th ed.). Cengage Learning.

Deming, W. E. (1986). *Out of the crisis*. Massachusetts Institute of Technology, Center for Advanced Engineering Study.

Deming, W. E. (1993). *The new economics for industry, government, education*. Massachusetts Institute of Technology, Center for Advanced Engineering Study.

Erfani, P., Uppal, N., & Lam, M. B. (2024). Accreditation standards—An untapped lever for cancer equity. *JAMA Oncology, 10*(4), 429–430. https://doi.org/10.1001/jamaoncol.2023.6811

Foy, R., MacLennan, G., Grimshaw, J., Penney, G., Campbell, M., & Grol, R. (2002). Attributes of clinical recommendations that influence change in practice following audit and feedback. *Journal of Clinical Epidemiology, 55*(7), 717–722. https://doi.org/10.1016/s0895-4356(02)00403-1

Frakt, A. (2015). Hospital consolidation isn't the key to lowering costs and raising quality. *JAMA Forum, 313*(4), 345. https://doi.org/10.1001/jama.2014.17412

Galbraith, J. (1973). *Designing complex organizations*. Addison-Wesley.

Gawande, A. (2009). *The checklist manifesto: How to get things right*. Metropolitan Books.

Georgescu, P. (2024, April 30). Boeing's last chance: Meaningful purpose, powerful culture, enlightened leadership. *Forbes*. https://www.forbes.com/sites/petergeorgescu/2024/04/30/boeings-last-chance-meaningful-purpose-powerful-culture-enlightened-leadership/

Goldberg, H. I., Wagner, E. H., Finh, S. D., Martin, D. P., & Horowitz, C. R. (1998). A randomized controlled trial of CQI teams and academic detailing: Can they alter compliance with guidelines? *The Joint Commission Journal on Quality Improvement, 24*(3), 130–142. https://doi.org/10.1016/S1070-3241(16)30367-4

Greenfield, D., & Pawsey, M. (2020). Health service accreditation: A strategy to promote and improve safety and quality. In J. K. Johnson & W. A. Sollecito (Eds.), *Continuous quality improvement in health care* (5th ed.). Jones & Bartlett Learning.

Greenhalgh, T. E., Robert, G., Bate, P., Macfarlane, F., & Kyriakidou, O. (2005). *Diffusion of innovations in health service organizations: A systematic literature review*. Blackwell Publishing.

Grove, A. S. (1995). *High output management*. Vintage Books.

Gunja, M. Z., Gumas, E. D., & Williams II, R. D. (2023, January 31). U.S. health care from a global perspective, 2022: Accelerating spending, worsening outcomes. *Issue Brief, Commonwealth Fund*. https://doi.org/10.26099/8ejy-yc74

Hodkinson, A., Zhou, A., Johnson, J., Geraghty, K., Riley, R., & Zhou, A. (2022). Associations of physician burnout with career engagement and quality of patient care: Systematic review and meta-analysis. *The British Medical Journal, 378*. https://doi.org/10.1136/bmj-2022-070442

Houpt, J. L., Gilkey, R. W., & Ehringhaus, S. H. (2015). *Learning to lead in the academic medical center—A practical guide*. Springer International Publishing.

Institute of Medicine (IOM). (2000). *To err is human: Building a safer health system*. National Academies Press.

Institute of Medicine (IOM). (2001). *Crossing the quality chasm: A new health paradigm for the 21st century*. National Academies Press.

Institute of Medicine (US) Committee on Understanding and Eliminating Racial and Ethnic Disparities in Health Care, Smedley, B. D., Stith, A. Y., & Nelson, A. R. (Eds.). (2003). *Unequal treatment: Confronting racial and ethnic disparities in health care*. National Academies Press (US). PMID: 25032386.

Itchhaporia, D. (2021). The evolution of the quintuple aim: Health equity, health outcomes, and the economy. *Journal of the American College of Cardiology, 78*(22), 2262–2264. Retrieved November 4, 2024, from https://doi.org/10.1016/j.jacc.2021.10.018

Jang, C. J., & Lee, H. C. (2022). A review of racial disparities in infant mortality in the US. *Children, 9*(2), 257. https://doi.org/10.3390/children9020257

Kaluzny, A., Veney, J. E., & Gentry, J. T. (1974). Innovation of health services: A comparative study of hospitals and health departments. *Milbank Memorial Fund Quarterly: Health & Society, 52*(1), 51–82. https://doi.org/10.2307/3349503

Kamra, M., Dhaliwal, S., & Li, W. (2024). Physician posttraumatic stress disorder during COVID-19: A systematic review and meta-analysis. *JAMA Network Open, 7*(7), e2423316. https://doi.org/10.1001/jamanetworkopen.2024.23316

Kilo, C. M. (1998). A framework for collaborative improvement: Lessons from the Institute for Healthcare Improvement's breakthrough series. *Quality Management in Health Care, 6*(4), 1–13. https://doi.org/10.1097/00019514-199806040-00001

Kotter, J. P. (1996). *Leading change*. Harvard Business School Press.

Kovach, K., (2024). Reshaping the quadruple aim for public health transformation. *JPHMP Direct*. Retrieved September 8, 2024, from https://jphmpdirect.com/reshaping-the-quadruple-aim-for-public-health-transformation/

Krumwiede, K. A., Eardley, D. L., DeBlieck, C. J., & Martin, K. S. (2023). Creating a quadruple aim model for nursing education. *Public Health Nursing, 40*(3), 448–455. https://doi.org/10.1111/phn.13172

Langley, G. J., Moen, R. D., Nolan, K. M., Nolan, T. W., Norman, C. L., & Provost, L. P. (2009). *The improvement guide: A practical approach to enhancing organizational performance* (2nd ed.). Jossey-Bass.

Lawrence, P. R., & Lorsch, J. W. (1967). *Organization and environment*. Harvard University Press.

Leape, L. L., Kabcenell, A. I., Gandhi, T. K., Carver, P., Nolan, T. W., & Berwick, D. M. (2000). Reducing adverse drug events: Lessons from a breakthrough series collaborative. *Joint Commission Journal of Quality Improvement, 26*(6), 321–331. https://doi.org/10.1016/s1070-3241(00)26026-4

Leatherman, S., Berwick, D., Iles, D., Lewin, L. S., Davidoff, F., Nolan, T., & Bisognano, M. (2003). The business case for quality: Case studies and an analysis. *Health Affairs, 22*(2), 17–30. https://doi.org/10.1377/hlthaff.22.2.17

Levinson, Z., Godwin, J., Hulver, S., & Neuman, T. (2024, April 19). *Ten things to know about consolidation in health care provider markets*. Retrieved August 29, 2024, from KFF.org.

Lopez, L., Hart, L. H., & Katz, M. H. (2021). Racial and ethnic health disparities related to COVID-19. *Journal of the American Medical Association, 325*(8), 719–720. https://doi.org/10.1001/jama.2020.26443

McGlynn, E. A., Asch, S. M., & Adams, J. (2003). The quality of health care delivered to adults in the United States. *The New England Journal of Medicine, 348*(26), 2635–2645. https://doi.org/10.1056/nejmsa022615

Mehta, R. H., Das, S., Tsai, T. T., Nolan, E., Kearly, G., & Eagle, K. A. (2000). Quality improvement initiative and its impact on the management of patients with acute myocardial infarction. *Archives of Internal Medicine, 160*(20), 3057–3062. https://doi.org/10.1001/archinte.160.20.3057

Melum, M. M., & Sinioris, M. K. (1992). *Total quality management—The health care pioneers*. American Hospital Publishing.

National Academies of Sciences, Engineering, and Medicine. (2017). *Communities in Action: Pathways to Health Equity*. National Academy of Sciences. Retrieved September 29, 2024.

Nundy, S., Cooper, L. A., & Mate, K. S. (2022). The Quintuple Aim for health care improvement: A new imperative to advance health equity. *Journal of the American Medical Association, 327*(6), 521–522. https://doi.org/10.1001/jama.2021.25181

Peters, M. (2022). Addressing vaccine hesitancy and resistance for COVID-19 vaccines. *International Journal of Nursing Studies, 131*. https://doi.org/10.1016/j.ijnurstu.2022.104241

Plough, A. L. (2015). Building a culture of health: A critical role for public health services and systems research. *American Journal of Public Health, 105*(2), S150–S152. https://doi.org/10.2105/AJPH.2014.302410

Plsek, P., & Greenhalgh, T. (2001). Complexity science: The challenge of complexity in health care. *British Medical Journal, 323*(7313), 625–628. https://doi.org/10.1136/bmj.323.7313.625

Rangachari, P. (2023). The untapped potential of the Quadruple Aim of primary care to foster a culture of health. *International Journal of General Medicine, 16*, 2237–2243. https://doi.org/10.2147/IJGM.S416367

Rogers, E. (1995). *Diffusion of innovations*. Free Press.

Rouse, W. B. (2008). Health care as a complex adaptive system. *Bridge, 38*, 17–25.

Satterfield, J. M., Spring, B., Brownson, R. C., Mullen, E. J., Newhouse, R. P., Walker, B. B., & Whitlock, E. P. (2009). Toward a transdisciplinary model of evidence-based practice. *The Milbank Quarterly, 87*(2), 368–390. https://doi.org/10.1111/j.1468-0009.2009.00561.x

Schenck, A. P., McArdle, J., & Weiser, R. (2013). Quality improvement organizations and continuous quality improvement in Medicare. In W. A. Sollecito & J. K. Johnson (Eds.), *Continuous quality improvement in health care* (4th ed.). Jones & Bartlett Learning.

Schein, E. H. (1992). *Organizational culture and leadership* (2nd ed.). Jossey-Bass.

Schmidt, W., & Finnegan, J. (1992). *The race without a finish line: America's quest for total quality*. Jossey-Bass Publishers.

Senge, P. (1990). *The fifth discipline: The art and practice of the learning organization*. Doubleday.

Shanafelt, T. D., Boone, S., Tan, L., Dyrbye, L. N., Sotile, W., Satele, D., ... Oreskovich, M. R. (2012). Burnout and satisfaction with work-life balance among US physicians relative to the general US population. *Archives of Internal Medicine, 172*(18), 1377–1385. https://doi.org/10.1001/archinternmed.2012.3199

Shanafelt, T. D., Hasan, O., Dyrbye, L. N., Sinsky, C., Satele, D., Sloan, J., & West, C. P. (2015). Changes in burnout and satisfaction with work-life balance in physicians and the general US working population between 2011 and 2014. *Mayo Clinic Proceedings, 90*(12), 1600–1613. https://doi.org/10.1016/j.mayocp.2015.08.023

Shefrin, H. (2024, January 31). *Boeing's weak corporate culture underlies difficulties with 737 MAX 9*. Forbes. Retrieved

Septebmer 17, 2024, from https://www.forbes.com/sites/hershshefrin/2024/01/28/boeings-weak-corporate-culture-underlies-difficulties-with-737-max-9/

Shortell, S. M., Bennett, C. L., & Byck, G. R. (1998). Assessing the impact of continuous quality improvement on clinical practice: What will it take to accelerate progress. *The Milbank Quarterly, 76*(4), 593–624. https://doi.org/10.1111/1468-0009.00107

Sikka, R., Morath, J. M., & Leape, L. (2015). The Quadruple Aim: Care, health, cost, and meaning in work. *BMJ Quality & Safety, 24*(10), 608–610. https://doi.org/10.1136/bmjqs-2015-004160

Solberg, L. (1993). *Improving disease prevention in primary care.* AHCPR Working Paper.

Somanader, T. (2015, March 25). *4 ways the Affordable Care Act is improving the quality of health care in America*. The White House. Retrieved November 3, 2017, from https://obamawhitehouse.archives.gov/blog/2015/03/25/4-ways-affordable-care-act-improving-quality-health-care-america

Spath, P. L., & Kelly, D. L. (2017). *Applying quality management in healthcare: A systems approach* (4th ed.). Health Administration Press.

Surowiecki, J. (2024, January 15). *What's gone wrong at Boeing*. The Atlantic. Retrieved September 17, 2024, from http://www.theatlantic.com/ideas/archive/2024/01/boeing-737-max-corporate-culture/677120

Swensen, S. J., Meyer, G. S., Nelson, E. C., Hunt, G. C. Jr., Pryor, D. B., Weissberg, J. I., . . . Berwick, D. M. (2010). Cottage industry to postindustrial care: The revolution in health care delivery. *The New England Journal of Medicine, 362*(5), e12(1)–e12(4). https://doi.org/10.1056/nejmp0911199

Tichy, N. M., & Devanna, M. A. (1986). *The transformational leader: The key to global competitiveness.* John Wiley and Sons.

Tichy, N. M. (1997). *The leadership engine.* Harper Business.

West, C. P., Dyrbye, L. N., Erwin, P. J., & Shanafelt, T. D. (2016). Interventions to prevent and reduce physician burnout: A systematic review and meta-analysis. *The Lancet, 388*(10057), 2272–2281. https://doi.org/10.1016/s0140-6736(16)31279-x

CHAPTER 3

Integrating Implementation Science Approaches Into Continuous Quality Improvement

Rohit Ramaswamy, Stephanie A. Bogdewic, Susan C. Cronin, Julie K. Johnson, and Lisa R. Hirschhorn

CHAPTER OUTLINE

Introduction

The most consistent challenges to continuous quality improvement (CQI) throughout its evolution in health care have been ensuring the broadest adoption of evidence-based improvements in practice and motivating research into further improvements of processes and outcomes. The challenge of how to maximize adoption of CQI-proven practices is addressed in this chapter through an introduction to implementation science as a methodology to increase the adoption and implementation of innovations and improvements in health care-practice settings. Drawing on its multidisciplinary roots and applications, implementation science represents the next step in the evolution of CQI in health care.

Implementation Science Defined

Implementation is a specified set of activities designed to put into practice, an activity, or program. Even if we know the interventions needed to implement or improve a program, we still need a scientific approach to make sure that these activities are executed in a way that results in their effective use. We also need to learn from this experience to accelerate change more broadly through creating generalizable knowledge.

The field of implementation science explores how best to improve the reach and quality of implementation of interventions and programs that are known to work, typically in health care, public health, behavioral health, education, and other settings where sustainable solutions at scale are difficult to achieve. **Implementation science** has a number of definitions, but it can be understood as the "scientific study of methods to promote the systematic uptake of research findings and other evidence-based practices into routine practice, and, hence, to improve the quality and effectiveness of health services and care … (this) field includes the study of influences on health care professional and organizational behavior." (Eccles and Mittman, 2006) Recognizing the importance of how and where these interventions are implemented, the National Implementation Research Network (NIRN) also defines the field as "the study of factors that influence the full and effective use of innovations in practice" (Blase, Van Dyke, Fixsen, & Wallace Bailey, 2012). In this chapter, we describe the key principles of implementation science and how integrating these principles into improvement strategies can be a valuable step to helping quality improvement (QI) programs achieve their desired results.

While the use of QI methods such as Lean, Six Sigma (see Chapter 5), or the Model for Improvement (introduced in Chapter 1) to improve systems and processes in health care is now well established, there is still much debate about the effectiveness of these methods. For example, a systematic review of Lean methods concluded that there is little evidence to support the claim that Lean leads to improved health care (Moraros, Lemstra, & Nwankwo, 2016). The lack of a systematic approach to implementation is one reason for this conclusion. The most common QI methodologies do not incorporate a systematic approach to the implementation of the improvement solution—a failing that can lead to an incorrect conclusion that the solution is not effective. For example, Six Sigma's Define, Measure, Analyze, Improve, Control (DMAIC) process (**Figure 3.1**) moves directly from the *Improve* step (where improvement solutions are generated and prioritized) to the *Control* step (where the post-improvement process is monitored for stability) without any mention of the context-specific details needed to guide the choice, specification, and implementation of the selected solutions. *The Wall Street Journal* reports

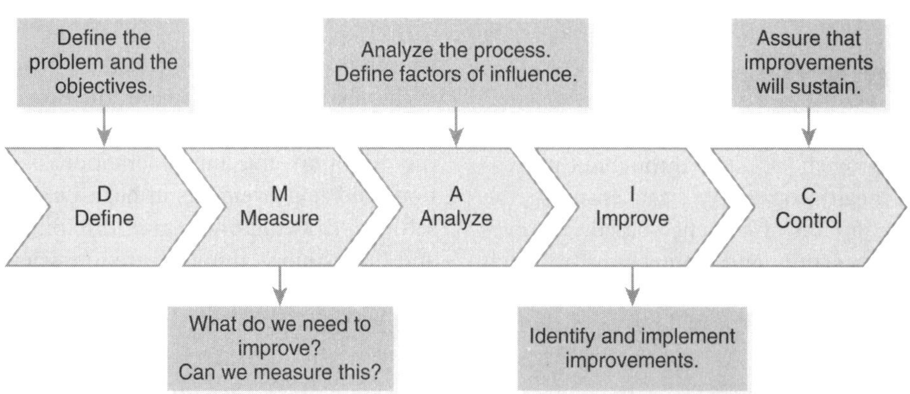

Figure 3.1 Six Sigma DMAIC process

Courtesy of Business Cherub.

that 60% of Six Sigma projects fail to achieve the desired results, because "in the middle stage of an improvement project—when the Six Sigma expert moves on to another project and top management turns its focus to another group of workers—implementation starts to wobble, and teams may find themselves struggling to maintain the gains they achieved early on" (Chakravorty, 2010); these challenges have an explicit impact on the extent to which improvements are sustained long term. The three questions framing the Model for Improvement (**Figure 3.2**) are structured to help teams develop improvement solutions but do not address their implementation and often neglect the broader organizational changes needed for immediate success as well as sustainability of change.

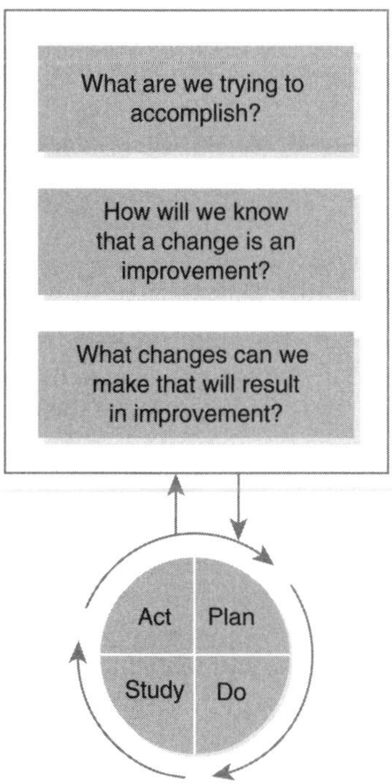

Figure 3.2 Model for Improvement

Reproduced from Langley, G. L., Moen, R. D., Nolan, K. M., Nolan, T. W., Norman, C. L., & Provost, L. P. (2009). *The improvement guide: A practical approach to enhancing organizational performance* (2nd ed.). Jossey-Bass.

In other words, it is not enough to use QI methods rigorously to come up with a solution that works in an individual or across different settings. It is equally important to be rigorous, yet pragmatic, about applying the approaches and tools from implementation science to put these solutions into effective practice and sustain the changes.

The key ingredients needed for interventions to achieve successful outcomes are summarized in **Figure 3.3** (Bertram, Blase, & Fixsen, 2015). Positive outcomes require an intervention (i.e., program, practice, policy, process) that is appropriate to the context, which QI methods can help to develop. But the intervention is just one ingredient. An implementation approach appropriate to the setting and resources and a supportive organizational, policy, or funding environment are needed as well. The multiplicative nature of these "ingredients" means that failure in any of these steps will decrease the chance that desired outcomes are achieved.

Figure 3.4 shows how quality improvement methods and implementation science approaches can work together to achieve effective outcomes in health care and in public health both locally and contributing to the broader learning needed for sustainable and broad change. Systematic improvement methods help to create effective interventions (sometimes referred to as change packages) that fit the local context. Implementation science methods can be used to identify appropriate implementation strategies to ensure effective implementation of the change package.

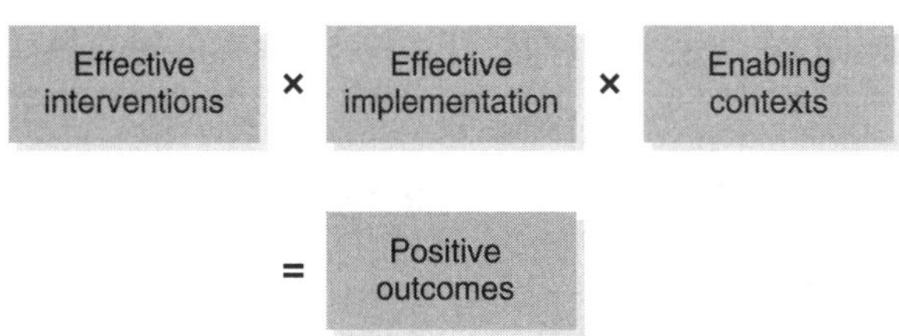

Figure 3.3 Key Ingredients for Achieving Outcomes

Data from National Implementation Research Network.

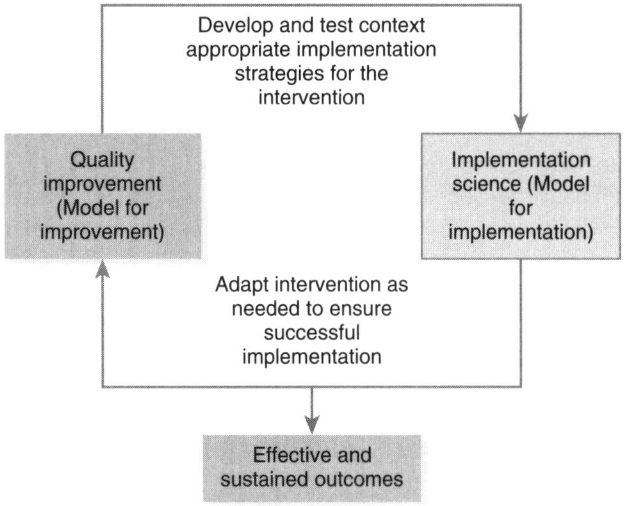

Figure 3.4 Integrating Improvement and Implementation

Integrating Implementation Into QI: The Model for Improvement and Implementation

Incorporating the tools and methods of implementation science in a systematic way requires enhancing the Model for Improvement with implementation steps. We refer to this model, shown in **Figure 3.5**, as the Model for Improvement and Implementation (MFII). This model incorporates three implementation questions into the traditional model for improvement.

The implementation questions begin with **implementation outcomes**, which are the desired results of the implementation of interventions or change ideas arising from QI projects in an organization. Analogous to improvement aims, these outcomes specify the *implementation aims* to ensure quality implementation in a particular setting or context, such as feasibility, fidelity, acceptability, or cost. The second question addresses **implementation determinants**, or factors that may affect the implementation outcomes in that context. And finally, the third question identifies **implementation strategies**, which are implementation interventions to address the determinants that may impede or facilitate the achievement of the implementation—and ultimately the QI—outcomes. The Plan, Do, Study, Act (PDSA) cycles test and refine these strategies so that they fit the implementation context. As a result of this testing, it may become apparent that the change package is inappropriate for the context and may need to be modified or adapted. This will initiate the redesign of the change package and the creation of a new improvement solution. Improvement and implementation are thus intrinsically connected in the joint model.

Implementation Outcomes

The first implementation question of the MFII is intimately connected to the first improvement question, *What are we trying to accomplish?*, because we cannot achieve health improvement goals if improvement interventions are not implemented well. Implementation outcomes are defined as "the effects of deliberate and purposive actions to implement new treatments, practices, and services" (Proctor et al., 2011). In other words, implementation outcomes measure how well the implementation process worked, since the quality of the implementation process affects how well the QI intervention achieves

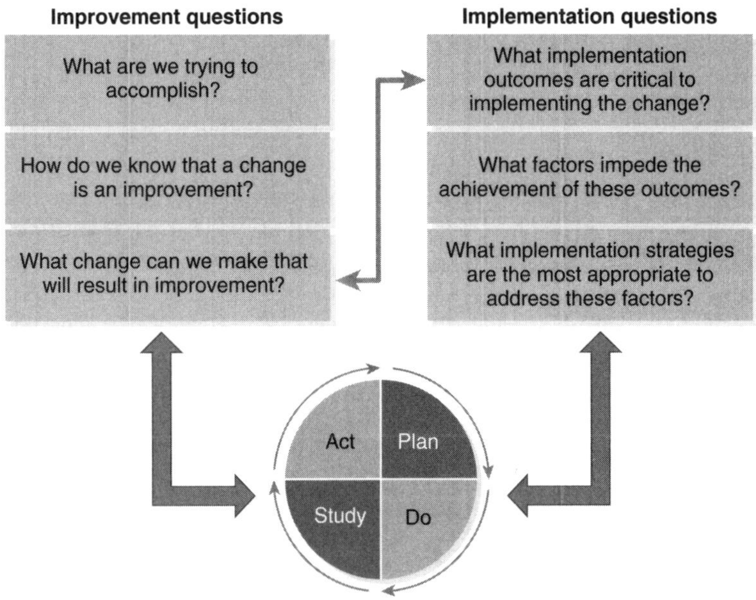

Figure 3.5 The Model for Improvement and Implementation

Data from Langley, G. L., Moen, R. D., Nolan, K. M., Nolan, T. W., Norman, C. L., & Provost, L. P. (2009). *The improvement guide: A practical approach to enhancing organizational performance* (2nd ed.). Jossey-Bass.

the desired health outcomes. There are more than 500 studies offering evidence that the quality of implementation affects health outcomes (Durlak & DuPre, 2008).

Implementation outcomes (listed and defined in **Table 3.1**) are distinct from service outcomes and patient/client outcomes (Proctor et al., 2011). Service outcomes, often referred to as **STEEEP** are safety, timeliness, efficiency, effectiveness, equity, and patient-centeredness. Patient or client outcomes include satisfaction, function, and symptomatolgy.

Table 3.1 Implementation Outcomes and Definitions

Implementation Outcome	Definition
Acceptability	Perception that an intervention is agreeable or satisfactory.
Adoption	Uptake of an intervention by practitioners or providers.
Appropriateness	Fit of an intervention to a particular context or setting.
Cost	Money, resources, time, or effort needed to implement an intervention.
Feasibility	The extent to which organizational resources, motivation, and capabilities can support the implementation of an intervention.
Fidelity	The match between how an intervention is intended to be delivered and how it is actually delivered.
Penetration	The extent to which an intervention reaches the population for whom it is intended.
Sustainability	The extent to which an intervention becomes part of an organization's everyday practice.

Quality improvement project teams can use Table 3.1 to select the implementation outcomes most likely to affect the achievement of their improvement aims. For example, an improvement intervention that relies on fast ambulance services to improve referral processes affecting the timeliness of care may not be feasible or may be too expensive in low-resource settings where ambulance services are not easily available. In this context, **feasibility** and **cost** may be the most important implementation outcomes that affect the ability to improve timeliness of care. In the case of an intervention focusing on improving patient satisfaction by enhanced provider/patient communication, **acceptability** of new communication protocols by providers may be the primary implementation outcome of interest. For a hand-hygiene intervention, **adoption** by clinicians may affect the reduction in health care—associated infection (HCAI) prevalence as well as maintenance over time. In this case, adoption may vary by facility and the adoption rates may be affected by differences in *acceptability* of the intervention and maintenance by the ongoing work and it therefore may be necessary to pay attention to both outcomes.

How should these implementation outcomes be integrated into the work of QI teams? After teams have defined the change package to be implemented as part of the QI initiative, they will consider the implementation questions in the MFII and determine the implementation outcomes that are most relevant to the successful implementation of their change package. They will collect baseline measures for their selected outcomes and set targets for the implementation outcomes that will result in sustained achievement of the improvement outcome. These implementation outcomes could be integrated into the suite of routine process measures that may be used to assess the progress of the initiative.

Implementation outcomes can be measured in a variety of ways. Perceptual measures such as feasibility, acceptability, **appropriateness**, or adoption can be measured through surveys, observation, or semi-structured interviews or routine measurement, depending on the indicators chosen. Some of these measures may be integrated into the data collection plan of the QI project without the need for additional work. For most QI projects, a simple survey with a few questions might suffice. But if more rigor is needed, validated survey instruments exist for these outcomes (Weiner et al., 2017; Roberts, Becker, & Seay, 1997). **Fidelity** can be measured through observations of adherence (Carroll et al., 2007) to a practice or protocol using checklists (Breitenstein et al., 2010). Cost and **penetration** can be measured through reviews of operational documents (e.g., admissions registers or accounting records). Lewis and colleagues (Lewis et al., 2015) identified 104 instruments for measuring one or more implementation outcomes.

Box 3.1 illustrates the use of implementation outcomes in improvement work at a hypothetical hospital. "Mercy Hospital" is a tertiary hospital with a mature QI program. They have been very successful at initiating QI projects but have had trouble making them stick in their organization. Guided by implementation scientists, Mercy Hospital QI teams are beginning to use the MFII to improve their quality of

Box 3.1 Implementing a NICU Transfer Checklist, Part 1

Newborns who are not warmly transported between units are three times more likely to be hypothermic when compared to those warmly transported. Additionally, it is also important that newborns are transferred as quickly as possible between units. The Mercy Hospital QI team looked at recent data and found that newborns are warmly transported from one unit (delivery or theater) to the other (postnatal or NICU) less than 30% of the time. A transport checklist exists to reduce barriers to warmly transporting newborns, but it is often not completed. Currently, the transfer checklist is only being completed during 25% of patient transfers. The Mercy Hospital QI team selects adoption as the implementation outcome of interest and decides to focus efforts on increasing the use of the transfer checklist to 75%. The adoption of the transfer checklist is a necessary precursor to improved patient outcomes.

implementation. Recently, the QI team decided to focus on reducing neonatal morality, noting that neonatal hypothermia is strongly associated with infant deaths. After reviewing their data from a recent a three-month period, they found that 74% of infants admitted to the neonatal intensive care unit (NICU) had hypothermia; among those admitted to the NICU with severe hypothermia, 66% died. The QI team developed an improved process for transporting neonates from the delivery unit or theater into the NICU, and they want to be sure the process checklist is effectively implemented. This is their first project to use the MFII.

Implementation Determinants

The second implementation question in the MFII asks, *What are the factors that facilitate or impede the achievement of the implementation aim?* These are referred to as *implementation determinants* in the implementation science literature. In a comprehensive review of the literature, Durlak and DuPre (2008) identified 23 contextual factors that affect implementation. A partial listing from Durlak is shown in **Table 3.2**.

As shown in Table 3.2, the factors affecting implementation can depend on a variety of characteristics, such as the practitioner, the process, the organization, the program, and the environment. Sorting through these and identifying the factors that are most relevant for a specific QI program in a specific context could be a formidable task. Implementation researchers have developed a variety of frameworks that facilitate a systematic approach. Nilsen (2015) identified 13 "determinant" frameworks in which the "aim is to understand and/or explain influences on implementation outcomes, e.g., predicting outcomes or interpreting outcomes retrospectively." One of the most widely accepted of these is the Consolidated Framework for Implementation Research (Damschroder et al., 2009; Damschroder et al., 2022), commonly referred to as CFIR. The framework, originally developed in 2009 and updated in 2022, has been tested widely in many different contexts. Damschroder et al. (2022) conducted a systematic review and identified 376 published articles that mentioned CFIR in the title or abstract.

Figure 3.6 shows the graphic of the framework, which consists of 48 constructs and 19 subconstructs across 5 domains that are similar to those described in Table 3.2. Extensive documentation to support the use of the framework by practitioners and researchers is available at the CFIR website (cfirguide.org/). Additionally, a brief, 14-item tool exists to support teams

Table 3.2 Selected List of Factors Affecting Implementation

Community-wide or Societal Factors	Practitioner Characteristics	Characteristics of the Program	Factors Related to the Organization Hosting the Program	Factors Specific to the Implementation Process
Scientific theory and research	Perceived need for the program	Compatibility or fit with the local setting	Openness to change and innovation	Successful training
Availability of funding	Perceived benefits of the program	Adaptability (can parts of the program be modified if needed?)	Shared vision and consensus about the program	On-going technical assistance
Policy			Effective leadership	

Data from Durlak, J. A., & DuPre, E. P. (2008). Implementation matters: A review of research on the influence of implementation on program outcomes and the factors affecting implementation. *American Journal of Community Psychology, 41*(3–4), 327–350. doi:10.1007/s10464-008-9165-0

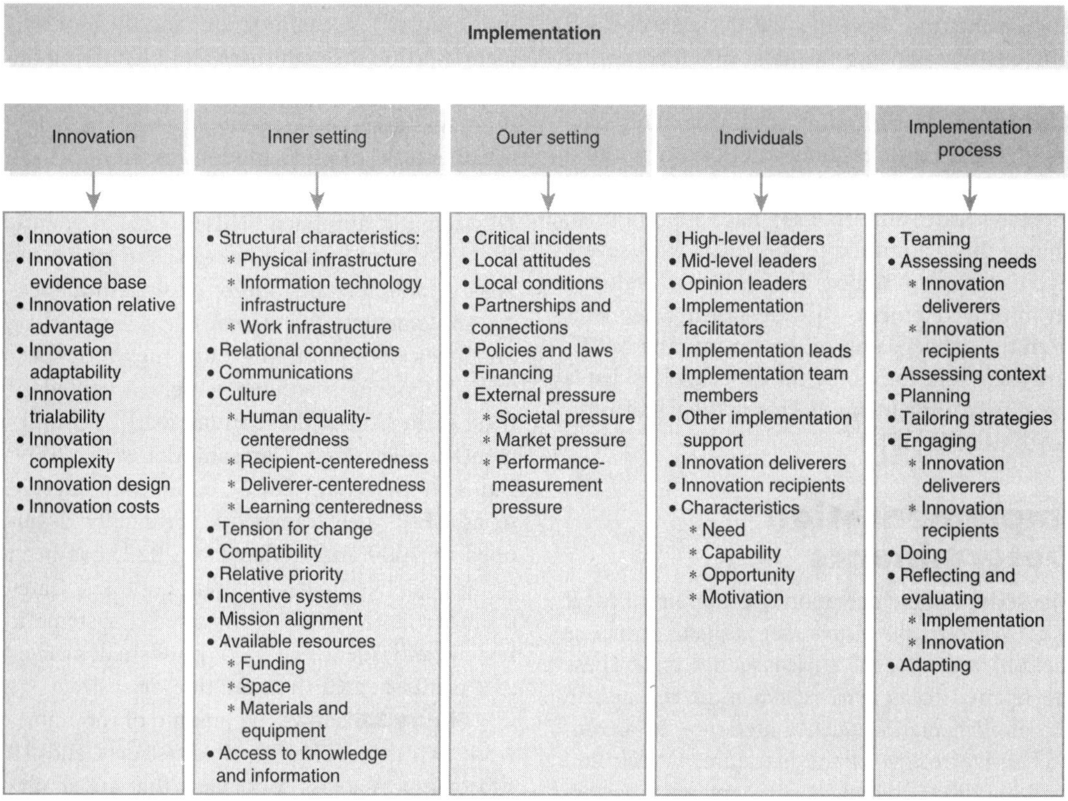

Figure 3.6 Consolidated Framework for Implementation

Data from Damschroder, L. J., Reardon, C. M., Widerquist, M. A. O., Lowery, J. C., & Kilbourne, A. M. (2022). The updated Consolidated Framework for Implementation Research based on user feedback. *Implementation Science, 17*, 75. https://doi.org/10.1186/s13012-022-01245-0

in efforts to identify key barriers and facilitators impacting implementation—the pragmatic context assessment tool (pCAT). To explore how CFIR can be used to identify factors that affect implementation outcomes, **Box 3.2** returns to the hypothetical example of implementing the NICU transfer checklist described earlier.

CFIR was developed to assist implementation researchers, though it is also a useful framework for practitioners. Another set of frameworks oriented primarily toward practitioners is the five Active Implementation Frameworks (AIF) (Blanchard et al., 2017; Metz & Bartley, 2012) created by the National Implementation Research Network (NIRN). Together, these frameworks address all the components needed to realize outcomes through the successful implementation of interventions. The five frameworks are: (1) **usable interventions**, defining the characteristics of interventions that are most suitable for implementation; (2) **implementation stages**, reflecting the process needed to plan and execute implementation of an intervention; (3) **implementation drivers**, which are defined as "key components of capacity and infrastructure that influence a program's success" (Metz & Bartley, 2012); (4) implementation teams to support the implementation; and (5) **improvement cycles** to ensure that the implementation is adapted to local contexts. The frameworks and their definitions are shown in **Figure 3.7**. As with CFIR, extensive resources, training modules, and tools describing the use of these frameworks are available on the NIRN website.

Box 3.2 Implementing a NICU Transfer Checklist, Part 2

Recall that the implementation outcome of interest at Mercy Hospital was the adoption of a NICU transfer checklist among providers. The CFIR domains provide a systematic way of identifying the most important barriers to adoption. With limited resources to assess implementation barriers, the team decided to first deploy the pCAT among staff. To better understand the results of the pCAT and experiences of hospital staff, the QI team conducts a series of semi-structured conversations and clinical observations. By observing how the checklist is being used in real time during transfer situations and asking clinicians probing questions about use of the checklist, the QI team is able to further clarify which determinants are most impacting adoption.

After reviewing the results of the staff survey, interviews, and clinical observations and qualitative data, the team determines that the individuals involved, inner setting (i.e., organizational characteristics), and process are the most important determinants impacting adoption of the transfer checklist. These barriers surfaced at Mercy Hospital include lack of staff familiarity or understanding about the benefits of the checklist, staff perception that the checklist is not an organizational priority, and the lack of a formal process for ensuring the checklist is implemented consistently.

To get a deeper understanding of these determinants, the team could have also used questionnaires to measure organizational readiness for change. Simple, locally developed questionnaires might suffice, but for situations requiring more rigor, several validated instruments are available in the literature, such as the Acceptance of Change Scale (ACS) to measure individual attitudes (Di Fabio & Gori, 2016), or the Organizational Readiness to Implement Change (ORIC) instrument (Shea, Jacobs, Esserman, Bruce, & Weiner, 2014) to assess organizational motivation and capacity for implementation.

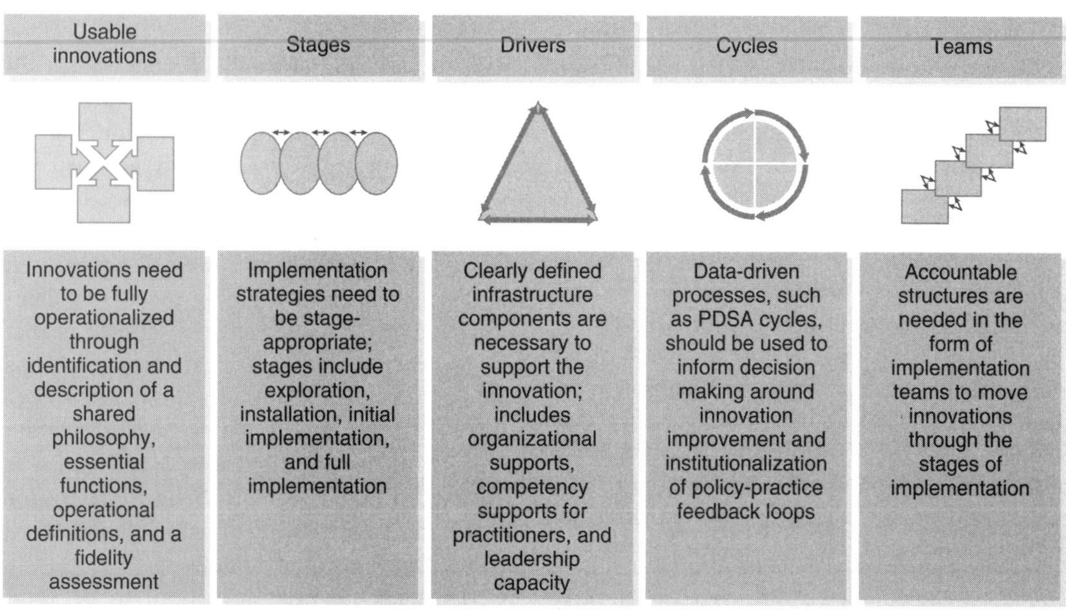

Figure 3.7 Active Implementation Frameworks

Reproduced from Blanchard, C., Livet, M., Ward, C., Sorge, L., Sorensen, T. D., & McClurg, M. R. (2017). The Active Implementation Frameworks: A roadmap for advancing implementation of Comprehensive Medication Management in Primary care. *Research in social & administrative pharmacy: RSAP, 13*(5), 922–929. https://doi.org/10.1016/j.sapharm.2017.05.006

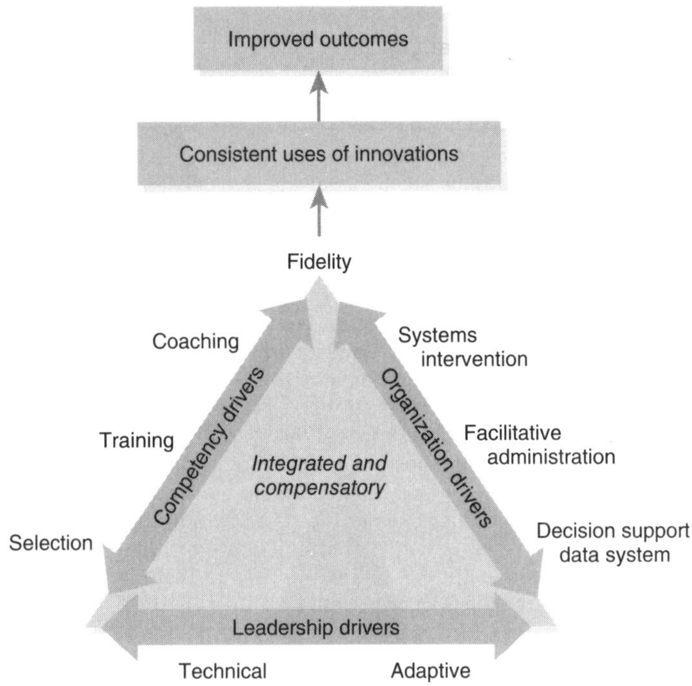

Figure 3.8 Implementation Drivers

Reproduced from Bertram, R. M., Blase, K. A., & Fixsen, D. L. (2015). Improving programs and outcomes. *Research on Social Work Practice, 25*(4), 477–487. doi:10.1177/1049731514537687

Among the five AIFs, the implementation drivers (Bertram et al., 2015) are most directly related to the factors affecting implementation. The drivers are shown in **Figure 3.8** and are categorized into competencies (hiring, training, and support needed to ensure that staff are well equipped to implement), leadership (ensuring that leaders have both the management skills and the ability to adapt to changing implementation environments), and organization (use of data to drive decisions, organizational support for change, and integration of the implementation with other external policy and resource priorities). These drivers can be mapped to the CFIR components of innovation, inner setting, outer setting, individuals involved, and the implementation process.

Implementation Strategies

The third implementation question of the MFII—*What implementation strategies can we use to improve implementation of the chosen intervention?*—addresses the actions that a QI team needs to take to enhance the implementation quality of the QI intervention. Implementation strategies are defined as "methods or techniques used to enhance the adoption, implementation, and **sustainability**" (Powell et al., 2015). Powell and his colleagues used an expert consensus building process to identify 73 discrete implementation strategies that are typically used for implementing programs and practices. (In a further study, these strategies were aggregated into nine categories Waltz et al., 2015), shown in **Table 3.3**. This list is a useful guide for teams seeking to determine approaches to improve the quality of implementation of their QI interventions.

Different strategies may need to be combined depending on the context in which the QI initiative is implemented. Combining tailored implementation strategies into a cohesive package, rather than testing individual strategies

Table 3.3 Implementation Strategies and Key Activities

Strategy Category	Key Activities
Engage consumers	Involve patients and family members to be active participants in the intervention to increase uptake and sustainability
Use evaluative and iterative strategies	Monitor the quality of implementation and use iterative methods (such as PDSA cycles) to improve implementation quality
Provide technical assistance	Use local personnel to provide facilitation and technical assistance to support the implementation
Adapt and tailor to the context	Use data to adapt and modify strategies to the context
Develop stakeholder relationships	Build coalitions, identify local champions, advisory boards and academic partners, train leadership, use early adopters and opinion leaders, capture and share local knowledge, etc.
Train and educate stakeholders	Conduct educational outreach, prepare training materials, train trainers, etc.
Support clinicians (and service providers)	Redesign clinical teams, provide timely data to service providers, develop resource-sharing agreements, develop clinician reminders, etc.
Utilize financial strategies	Provide financial incentives and disincentives (new funding, altered payment schemes, support for innovation, etc.)
Change infrastructure	Change accreditation requirements, liability laws, physical structure and equipment, licensing standards, service sites, etc.

in isolation, enhances the ability to address the multifaceted, context-specific barriers that arise during implementation. While tailored strategies are designed to align with specific determinants or implementation barriers, no single strategy is universally effective across diverse settings. Bundling multiple strategies allows practitioners to address complex barriers to implementation and work to improve implementation outcomes of a given intervention.

Table 3.4 shows how strategies map to implementation outcomes. A similar map between CFIR domains and strategies is shown in **Table 3.5**. Another set of strategies was developed by Michie and is drawn from a distillation of theories related to behavior change (Michie et al., 2013).

To illustrate how Tables 3.3, 3.4, and 3.5 might be used in practice, let us return to the NICU transfer checklist example at Mercy Hospital, shown in **Box 3.3**.

Implementing Well: Using Frameworks for Implementation

Even the best implementation strategies will not be of use unless they are implemented well. Several frameworks for guiding the implementation process exist in the implementation science literature. We will describe three that are useful to practitioners: *Stages of Implementation*, which is one of the AIFs described earlier, the *Quality Implementation Framework*, and the *Interactive Systems Framework for Dissemination and Implementation.*

The NIRN Stages of Implementation framework describes four stages through which the implementation of an intervention takes place (Bertram et al., 2015). The stages are shown in **Figure 3.9**. The *Exploration Stage* overlaps with some of the planning activities mentioned previously to assess organizational readiness for implementation, identify

Table 3.4 Mapping Implementation Outcomes to Strategies

Implementation Outcome	Typical Strategy Categories
Acceptability	Engaging customers, developing stakeholder interrelationships
Appropriateness	Adapting and tailoring, using evaluative and iterative strategies
Adoption	Training and educating stakeholders, providing technical assistance
Feasibility	Supporting clinicians
Fidelity	Providing technical assistance, supporting clinicians
Cost	Changing infrastructure
Penetration	Engaging customers, developing stakeholder relationships
Sustainability	Changing infrastructure, using evaluative and iterative strategies, utilizing financial strategies

Table 3.5 Mapping CFIR Domains to Strategies

CFIR Domain	Typical Strategy Categories
Characteristics of the innovation	Adapting and tailoring
Inner setting	Training and educating stakeholders, providing technical assistance, supporting clinicians
Outer setting	Engaging customers, changing infrastructure, developing stakeholder interrelationships
Individuals involved	Using financial strategies
Implementation process	Using evaluative and iterative strategies

Box 3.3 Implementing a NICU Transfer Checklist, Part 3

Recall that the most relevant implementation outcome for this project was adoption of the NICU transfer checklist and that survey results, interviews, and observations conducted by the QI team identified the individuals involved, the inner settings, and the implementation process as the CFIR domains of interest. Based on Tables 3.4 and 3.5, the QI team may select engaging and educating stakeholders, providing technical assistance, and utilizing audit and feedback as categories from which to create a collection package of implementation strategies. The QI team at Mercy Hospital further refined and operationalized these implementation strategies; Figure 3.6 shows the strategy categories and the detailed strategies that may be used, as defined in Powell (2015). Recall that implementation strategies are often bundled to address complex determinants, and strategies may be effective at addressing more than one barrier to implementation. As shown in Figure 3.4, the selected implementation strategies are tested, refined, and tailored for the implementation context using PDSA cycles. The third column of Table 3.6 describes how this leads to a particular adaptation of the strategy to implement the transfer checklist in the context of Mercy Hospital.

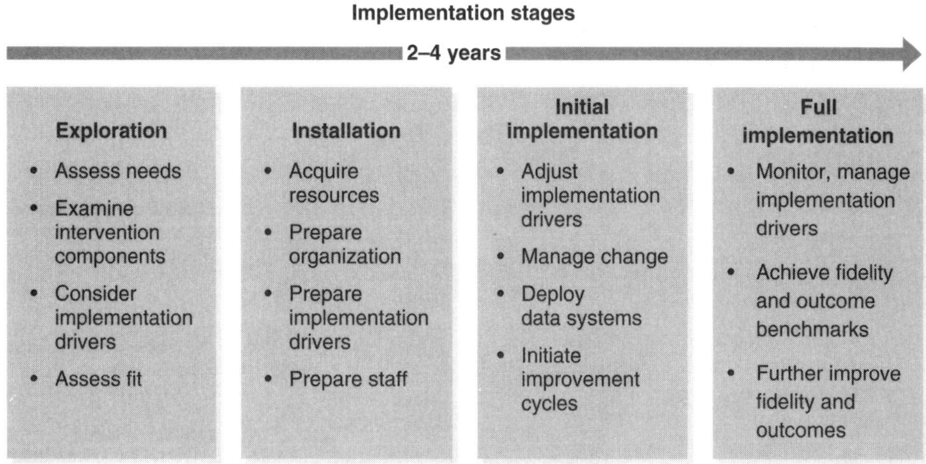

Figure 3.9 Stages of Implementation

Reproduced from Bertram, R. M., Blase, K. A., & Fixsen, D. L. (2015). Improving programs and outcomes. *Research on Social Work Practice, 25*(4), 477–487. doi:10.1177/1049731514537687

key factors affecting implementation, and develop implementation strategies. During the *Installation Stage*, resources for carrying out the implementation strategies are acquired, both for the actual implementation itself and for any technical support that may be required. Training of staff may also take place at this stage. The *Initial Implementation* is where the intervention is implemented for the first time, using the implementation strategies. The strategies themselves may be tested and adapted during this stage, and any changes to the intervention may be considered. During *Full Implementation*, ongoing testing and refinement may take place, but the intervention begins to get embedded in the organization and becomes part of everyday work.

It is important to understand that while the stages are represented as a linear progression, in reality, this is a nonlinear process. The stages overlap with each other, and there may be situations where teams need to conduct small scale tests of change to improve and finalize strategies (e.g., if it is apparent during initial implementation that staff have not been trained adequately or are not motivated, it may be necessary to go back to some of the installation and exploration activities of staff preparation and readiness building).

The Quality Implementation Framework (QIF) is a systematic process to facilitate planning and implementation support (Meyers et al., 2012). The QIF includes four progressive phases, shown in **Figure 3.10**. The first phase involves an assessment of the implementation context; this includes activities such as conducting needs and readiness assessments, assessing context, and building general capacity to implement. The second phase activities are related to creating the structures to support implementation; these may include developing implementation teams or an implementation plan. In the third phase, implementation has begun, and practitioners evaluate the process of implementation, while continuing to adapt and test strategies to improve implementation. Finally, the fourth phase of the QIF focuses on learning from the implementation process, conducting a summative evaluation and considering how best to plan for sustainability.

The Interactive Systems Framework (Scaccia et al., 2015; Wandersman et al., 2008) shown in **Figure 3.11** conceptualizes implementation occurring through interactions between three systems: the *synthesis and translation system*, the *support system*, and the *delivery system*. The synthesis and translation system adapts an intervention (or an implementation strategy) and tailors (translates) it to fit the local context. The support system provides training, coaching, tools, and technical assistance needed for

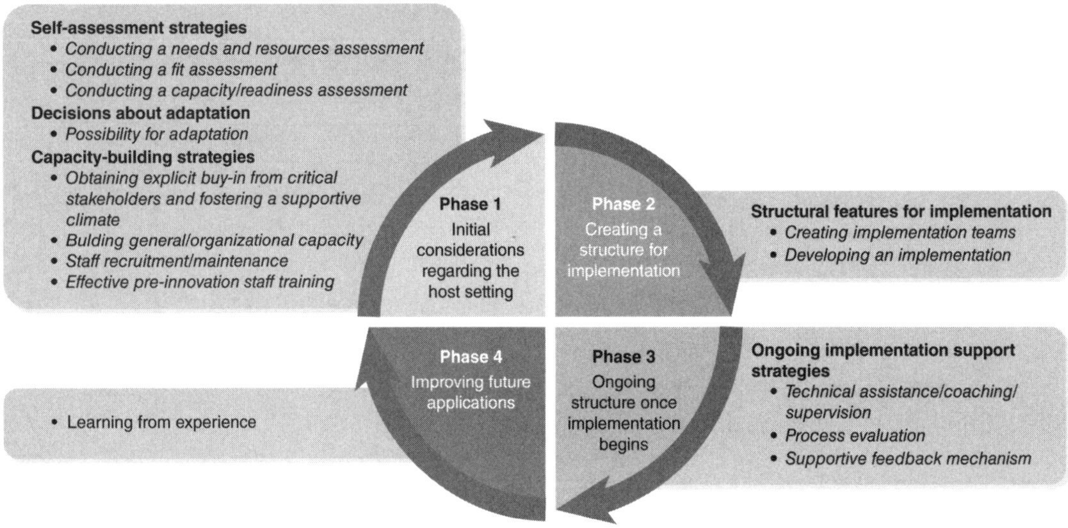

Figure 3.10 Quality Implementation Framework

Reproduced from Meyers, D. C., Durlak, J. A., & Wandersman, A. (2012). The quality implementation framework: A synthesis of critical steps in the implementation process. *American Journal of Community Psychology, 50*(3–4), 462–480.

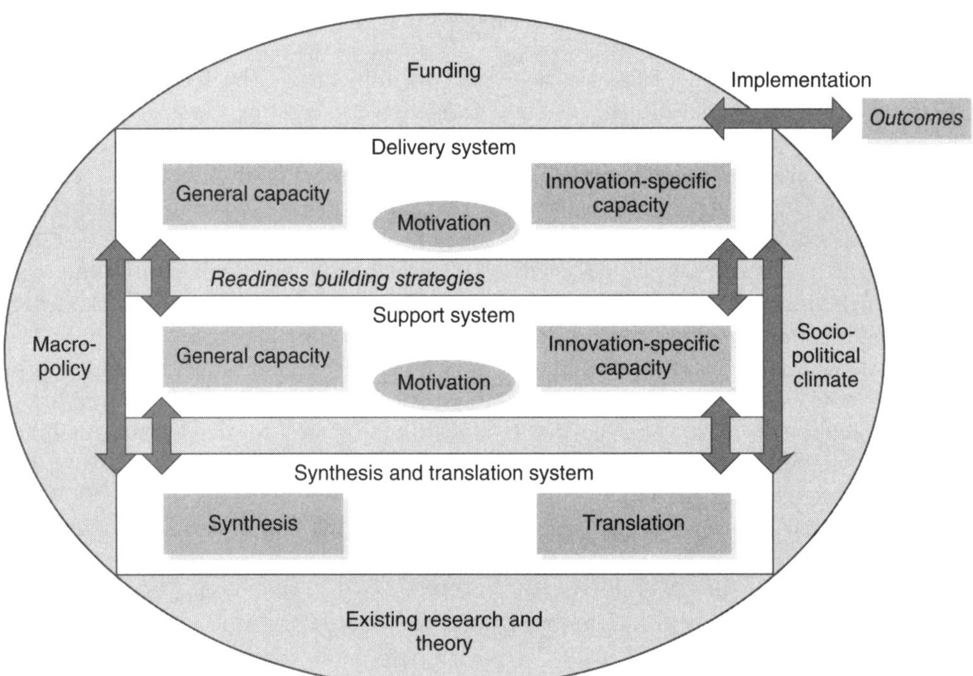

Figure 3.11 Interactive Systems Framework

Reproduced from Scaccia, J. P., Cook, B. S., Lamont, A., Wandersman, A., Castellow, J., Katz, J., & Beidas, R. S. (2015). A practical implementation science heuristic for organizational readiness: R = MC2. *Journal of community psychology, 43*(4), 484–501. https://doi.org/10.1002/jcop.21698

implementation. The delivery system is where the work gets done. According to the framework, successful implementation requires an appropriate implementation strategy, or bundle of strategies, as well as motivation and capacities to both support the implementation and to deliver it in practice. The framework distinguishes between general capacities and innovation-specific capacities. The former relates to overall organizational capabilities and include factors such as leadership, adequate resources, organizational readiness to change and innovate, and effective processes for support and delivery that are needed for the successful implementation of any intervention. The latter refer to knowledge, skills and abilities, and organizational support that are unique to the intervention itself. For example, in the case of a hand-hygiene intervention, this could be knowledge about hand-washing techniques and organizational support for a hand-hygiene program.

How can these frameworks be used in practice to improve the quality of implementation of a QI intervention? As described by Leeman et al., (2017), a collection of selected implementation strategies such as the one shown in **Table 3.6** is nothing more than a list until the strategies can be embedded in the implementation process. For implementation to be successful, different strategies need to be used at different implementation stages and in different systems, and the frameworks provide guidance on how to do this. Let's return to the example of the NICU transfer checklist (**Box 3.4**).

We show how the two frameworks described above can be used to develop an implementation plan based on the strategies in Table 3.6. **Table 3.7** shows the strategies from Table 3.6 organized by implementation stage. **Table 3.8** shows how the Interactive Systems Framework (ISF) may be used for implementation planning.

Using the Quality Implementation Framework (Table 3.8): We can also use the Quality Implementation Framework to develop an implementation plan for the strategies in Table 3.6. The QIF helps to ensure that all phases of the implementation process are considered in a systematic way. As shown in Table 3.8, successful implementation of the transfer checklist requires developing implementation strategies appropriate to the implementation context and training staff to carry out the intervention (Phase 1); selecting enthusiastic staff to serve as implementation champions (Phase 2); providing ongoing technical assistance during active implementation

Table 3.6 Collection of Strategies to Implement a NICU Transfer Checklist

Strategy Category	Discrete Strategy	Adapted Strategy
Developing stakeholder relationships	■ Identifying and preparing champions ■ Organizing clinical implementation team meetings	Select leaders from the physician and nursing staff who are enthusiastic about the transfer checklist to champion the intervention. Use these champions to present updates about the implementation of the checklist at staff meetings.
Training and educating stakeholders	■ Conduct ongoing training	Conduct training sessions to educate staff on the importance of the transfer checklist and its role in improving neonatal outcomes.
Using evaluative and iterative strategies	■ Audit and provide feedback	Regularly provide feedback to staff on transfer checklist adherence and its impact on neonatal outcomes.
Provide interactive assistance	■ Develop a technical assistance system	Provide on-the-job support, mentorship, and guidance to staff on using the transfer checklist.

Box 3.4 Implementing a NICU Transfer Checklist, Part 4

Using the stages of implementation framework (Table 3.7): in the exploration stage, the QI team continues to identify factors that might affect the quality of implementation and develops a package of strategies. In the installation stage, the team may begin conversations with early adopters who might serve as champions, as well as test and refine the messages that these champions should disseminate to other staff. Once the messages have been finalized, the team may test the different methods for dissemination (e.g., face-to-face presentations at staff meetings, informational flyers, video presentations, and so forth). As more staff begin to use the checklist, the champions and other staff members involved in the implementation may organize local seminars and workshops where staff can share their experiences about the implementation process. Over time, as the checklist becomes part of everyday use, staff leaders may monitor its use and continue to provide support for implementation as required and training as new staff enter the system.

Table 3.7 Using the Stages of Implementation Framework for Implementation Planning

Implementation Stage	Implementation Strategy
Exploration	■ Develop implementation strategies.
Installation	■ Select physician and nurse leaders who are enthusiastic about the protocol to champion the intervention. ■ Identify and prepare champions. ■ Use these champions to present updates about the implementation of the checklist at staff meetings. ■ Conduct training sessions to educate staff on the importance of the transfer checklist and its role in improving neonatal outcomes.
Initial Implementation	■ Organize learning sessions where staff from different departments share their experiences with implementation of the checklist. ■ Regularly provide feedback to staff on transfer checklist adherence and its impact on neonatal outcomes.
Full Implementation	■ Provide on-the-job support, mentorship, and guidance to staff on using the transfer checklist. ■ Link implementation and use of the checklist to annual staff performance review.

(Phase 3); and continuously evaluating implementation outcomes and impact (Phase 4). Both the Stages of Implementation framework and the QIF present the same information in slightly different ways, and QI teams can select one or the other, or both, depending on their needs. More specifically, while both frameworks offer a staged-based approach to implementation, the QIF provides an additional level of detail and nuance, serving as a more comprehensive checklist of best practices to optimize implementation quality. The Stages of Implementation framework serves as a useful roadmap for systems or organizations that are navigating the complexity of implementation over time (**Box 3.5**).

Conclusion

The purpose of this chapter is to introduce quality improvement practitioners to some of the key principles, concepts, and tools of implementation

Table 3.8 Using the Quality Implementation Framework for Implementation Planning (Example of the NICU Transfer Checklist)

Implementation Phase	Implementation Strategy
Phase 1 Initial Considerations Regarding the Host Setting	■ Develop implementation strategies. ■ Conduct training sessions to educate staff on the importance of the transfer checklist and its role in improving neonatal outcomes.
Phase 2 Creating a Structure for Implementation	■ Select physician and nurse leaders who are enthusiastic about the checklist to champion the intervention.
Phase 3 Ongoing Structure Once Implementation Begins	■ Use champions to present updates about the implementation of the checklist at staff meetings. ■ Provide on-the-job support, mentorship, and guidance to staff on using the transfer checklist.
Phase 4 Improving Future Applications	■ Continuously evaluate transfer checklist adoption and adherence and its impact on neonatal outcomes.

Box 3.5 Implementing a NICU Transfer Checklist, Part 5

As outlined in Table 3.6, the QI team at Mercy hospital used the Model for Improvement and Implementation to develop and subsequently test and improve, through a series of PDSA cycles, a package of implementation strategies to address barriers to implementation. Although the team observed improvements in the implementation outcomes of interest, they ultimately did not reach the 75% target for adoption of the NICU transfer checklist. The QI team decided to conduct a follow-up evaluation to better understand why the implementation outcome target was not met. After a series of semi-structured conversations with colleagues, the QI team found that although the barriers to implementation, identified through the CFIR, were reduced, the transfer checklist itself remained too long, and it was difficult for providers to complete in the short time available. Given that the remaining barrier was related to the intervention or process itself, the QI team felt it was important to revisit the left side of the Model for Improvement and Implementation; they needed to reconsider the questions related to improvement. The QI team led an effort to redesign the checklist and conduct a series of PDSA cycles to assess acceptability and feasibility of the checklist, which were additional implementation outcomes that needed to be considered. Ultimately, the team was able to craft a checklist that aligned with providers' current capabilities and resources, and their tests indicated improved acceptability.

This highlights the two-way relationship between improvement and implementation shown in Figure 3.5. The MFII can be used to identify barriers and strategies to implement change packages and evidence-based interventions. At the same time, it can also be used to adapt change packages and interventions to make it easier to implement them. In real world settings, "evidence-based" has little value unless it can be put in practice, and while that might require the tools of implementation science, it may also require adaption and new change ideas generated through QI methods. For far too long, QI and implementation science (IS) have existed as separate disciplines within their own silos. In our view, this is a false dichotomy, and one that only serves to impede the adoption and application of important healthcare and public health interventions. Our model presented here seeks to present QI and IS as two sides of the same coin, that together can optimize the generation of new ideas and their implementation in the field.

science and how they can be incorporated and improve the design and impact of their improvement work. Over the years, the fields of quality improvement and implementation science have progressed side by side. QI methods have focused on the development of change packages and interventions with the assumption that someone else will take care of implementation or that implementation is the easy part if the intervention is sound. Implementation science has been concerned with the adaptation and implementation of evidence-based interventions, often without a real understanding of what the intervention is and how it has been developed. As a result, improvement interventions are often poorly implemented, and implementation science has failed to benefit from the wealth of practical knowledge about theories of systems, processes, and variation that are cornerstones of good QI practice. The intent of this chapter is to bridge this gap. QI practitioners, armed with implementation science tools, will be well equipped to realize the old adage, "*What is worth doing is worth doing well.*"

Key Concepts and Terms

acceptability
adoption
appropriateness
cost
feasibility
fidelity
implementation
implementation determinants
implementation drivers
implementation outcomes
implementation science
implementation stages
implementation strategies
improvement cycles
penetration
STEEEP
sustainability
usable interventions

References

Bertram, R. M., Blase, K. A., & Fixsen, D. L. (2015). Improving programs and outcomes. *Research on Social Work Practice, 25*(4), 477–487. https://doi.org/10.1177/1049731514537687

Blanchard, C., Livet, M., Ward, C., Sorge, L., Sorensen, T. D., & McClurg, M. R. (2017). The Active Implementation Frameworks: A roadmap for advancing implementation of comprehensive medication management in primary care. *Research in Social & Administrative Pharmacy, 13*(5), 922–929. https://doi.org/10.1016/j.sapharm.2017.05.006

Blase, K. A., Van Dyke, M., Fixsen, D. L., & Bailey, F. W. (2012). Implementation science: Key concepts, themes, and evidence for practitioners in educational psychology. In B. Kelly & D. Perkins (Eds.), Handbook of implementation science for psychology in education (pp. 13–36). New York, NY: Cambridge University Press.

Breitenstein, S. M., Fogg, L., Garvey, C., Hill, C., Resnick, B., & Gross, D. (2010). Measuring implementation fidelity in a community-based parenting intervention. *Nursing Research, 59*(3), 158–165. https://doi.org/10.1097/NNR.0b013e3181dbb2e2

Carroll, C., Patterson, M., Wood, S., Booth, A., Rick, J., & Balain, S. (2007). A conceptual framework for implementation fidelity. *Implementation Science*, 2, 40. https://doi.org/10.1186/1748-5908-2-40

Chakravorty, S. S. (2010, January 24). Where process-improvement projects go wrong. *The Wall Street Journal*. Retrieved December 28, 2017, from https://www.wsj.com

Damschroder, L. J., Aron, D. C., Keith, R. E., Kirsh, S. R., Alexander, J. A., & Lowery, J. C., (2009). Fostering implementation of health services research findings into practice: A consolidated framework for advancing implementation science. *Implementation Science, 4*(1), 50.

Damschroder, L. J., Reardon, C. M., Widerquist, M. A. O., & Lowery, J. (2022). The updated Consolidated Framework for Implementation Research based on user feedback. *Implementation Science, 17*(1), 75. https://doi.org/10.1186/s13012-022-01245-0

Di Fabio, A., & Gori, A. (2016). Developing a new instrument for assessing acceptance of change. *Frontiers in Psychology, 7*, 802. https://doi.org/10.3389/fpsyg .2016.00802

Durlak, J. A., & DuPre, E. P. (2008). Implementation matters: A review of research on the influence of implementation on program outcomes and the factors affecting implementation. *American Journal of Community Psychology, 41*(3–4), 327–350. https://doi.org/10.1007/s10464-008-9165-0.

Eccles, M.P., Mittman, B.S. Welcome to *Implementation Science*. *Implementation Sci, 1*(1) (2006). https://doi.org/10.1186/1748-5908-1-1

Kirk, M. A., Kelley, C., Yankey, N., Birken, S. A., Abadie, B., & Damschroder, L. (2016). A systematic review of the use of the Consolidated Framework for Implementation Research. *Implementation Science, 11*, 72. https://doi.org/10.1186/s13012-016-0437-z

Leeman, J., Birken, S. A., Powell, B. J., Rohweder, C., & Shea, C. M. (2017). Beyond "implementation strategies": Classifying the full range of strategies used in implementation science and practice. *Implementation Science, 12*(1), 125. https://doi.org/10.1186/s13012-017-0657-x

Lewis, C. C., Fischer, S., Weiner, B. J., Stanick, C., Kim, M., & Martinez, R. G. (2015). Outcomes for implementation science: An enhanced systematic review of instruments using evidence-based rating criteria. *Implementation Science, 10*, 155. https://doi.org/10.1186/s13012-015-0342-x

Metz, A., & Bartley, L. (2012). Active implementation frameworks for program success: How to use implementation science to improve outcomes for children. *Zero to Three Journal, 32*(4), 11–18.

Meyers, D. C., Durlak, J. A., & Wandersman, A. (2012). The quality implementation framework: A synthesis of critical steps in the implementation process. *American Journal of Community Psychology, 50*(3–4), 462–480. https://doi.org/10.1007/s10464-012-9522-x

Michie, S., Richardson, M., Johnston, M., Abraham, C., Francis, J., ... Wood, C. E. (2013). The behavior change technique taxonomy (v1) of 93 hierarchically clustered techniques: Building an international consensus for the reporting of behavior change interventions. *Annals of Behavioral Medicine, 46*(1), 81–95. https://doi.org/10.1007/s12160-013-9486-6

Moraros, J., Lemstra, M., & Nwankwo, C. (2016). Lean interventions in healthcare: Do they actually work? A systematic literature review. *International Journal for Quality in Health Care, 28*(2), 150–165. https://doi.org/10.1093/intqhc/mzv123

Nilsen, P. (2015). Making sense of implementation theories, models and frameworks. *Implementation Science, 10*, 53. https://doi.org/10.1186/s13012-015-0242-0

Powell, B. J., Waltz, T. J., Chinman, M. J., Damschroder, L. J., Smith, J. L., Matthieu, M. M., ... Kirchner, J. E. (2015). A refined compilation of implementation strategies: Results from the Expert Recommendations for Implementing Change (ERIC) project. *Implementation Science, 10*(1), 21. https://doi.org/10.1186/s13012-015-0209-1

Proctor, E., Silmere, H., Raghavan, R., Hovmand, P., Aarons, G., Bunger, A., ... Hensley, M. (2011). Outcomes for implementation research: Conceptual distinctions, measurement challenges, and research agenda. *Administration and Policy in Mental Health, 38*(2), 65–76. https://doi.org/10.1007/s10488-010-0319-7

Roberts, G., Becker, H., & Seay, P. (1997). A process for measuring adoption of innovation within the supports paradigm. *Journal of the Association for Persons with Severe Handicaps, 22*(2), 109–119. https://doi.org/10.1177/154079699702200210

Scaccia, J. P., Cook, B. S., Lamont, A., Wandersman, A., Castellow, J., Katz, J., & Beidas, R. S. (2015). A practical implementation science heuristic for organizational readiness: $R = MC^2$. *Journal of Community Psychology, 43*(4), 484–501. https://doi.org/10.1002/jcop.21698

Shea, C. M., Jacobs, S. R., Esserman, D. A., Bruce, K., & Weiner, B. J. (2014). Organizational readiness for implementing change: A psychometric assessment of a new measure. *Implementation Science, 9*(1). https://doi.org/10.1186/1748-5908-9-7

Waltz, T. J., Powell, B. J., Matthieu, M. M., Damschroder, L. J., Chinman, M. J., Smith, J. L., ... Kirchner, J. E. (2015). Use of concept mapping to characterize relationships among implementation strategies and assess their feasibility and importance: Results from the Expert Recommendations for Implementing Change (ERIC) study. *Implementation Science, 10*, 109. https://doi.org/10.1186/s13012-015-0295-0

Wandersman, A., Duffy, J., Flaspohler, P., Noonan, R., Lubell, K., Stillman, L., ... Saul, J. (2008). Bridging the gap between prevention research and practice: The interactive systems framework for dissemination and implementation. *American Journal of Community Psychology, 41*(3–4), 171–181. https://doi.org/10.1007/s10464-008-9174-z

Weiner, B. J., Lewis, C. C., Stanick, C., Powell, B. J., Dorsey, C. N., Clary, A. S., ... Halko, H. (2017). Psychometric assessment of three newly developed implementation outcome measures. *Implementation Science, 12*(1), 108. https://doi.org/10.1186/s13012-017-0635-3

CHAPTER 4

Using CQI Tools to Measure Variation and Improve Processes

Anna P. Schenck and William A. Sollecito

CHAPTER OUTLINE

Introduction

Continuous quality improvement (CQI) requires knowledge about the behavior of systems and processes, which is most often obtained from data and other sources of information collected for that specific purpose and through the application of tools and techniques that have proven to be effective throughout the evolution of CQI. The use of data and tools is part of the concept of statistical thinking—a key component of both the philosophy and processes of CQI. To make decisions about innovations, especially CQI in health care, we need to improve our knowledge about healthcare process performance. This requires an understanding of the context in which processes behave, asking the right questions, and collecting and analyzing appropriate data. The goal is not simply to analyze data, but to *gain knowledge* by using data to understand processes, sources of variation, and the impact of improvements.

As described in Chapters 1 and 2, CQI requires a systems approach that analyzes assumptions and focuses on customers/patients, processes, and interdependencies based on knowledge. This approach is most efficiently accomplished using stepwise, yet cyclical, procedures that span planning, implementation, and assessment of the impact of the decisions made in identifying and applying changes—including how to determine when a change is needed and whether it leads to an improvement (Langley et al., 2009). Although many different methods can be applied to carry out these steps, CQI efforts in the past have spawned methods that have proven to be robust and efficient when focused on listening to the "voice of the process" underpinned with an understanding of variation (Wheeler, 2000; Wheeler & Chambers, 2010). These methods include a continuous assessment of process performance, including an understanding of sources of variation, followed by decision making based on the application of knowledge about systems and measurements. Over the years, tools have been developed to carry out these steps in the most efficient manner. As with CQI itself, these tools have undergone a continuous improvement process that enhances our learning about how to apply them, and when to introduce new tools. Especially in health care, which itself has undergone an evolutionary process rooted in new knowledge and the greater use of technology, new tools and data sources have been developed to ensure that the "Quintuple Aim" of health care (discussed in Chapter 2) has been met. The Quintuple Aim of health care targets five factors: improving the experience of care, improving the health of populations, reducing the per capita costs of health care while improving the work life of clinicians and healthcare staff, and advancing health equity by modifying conditions so that *everyone* has the opportunity to experience optimal health outcomes (Nundy, Cooper & Mate, 2022). At the heart of these procedures are evidence-based approaches that rely on health information technology to provide high-quality data to ensure correct decisions are made in the efficient application of the "data-to-decision cycle" (McLaughlin & Kibbe, 2013). Greater use of technology to collect and analyze healthcare data presents greater opportunities for both converting data into information or knowledge and applying powerful methodologies for implementing improvement, but also presents challenges to ensure the most appropriate application of tools and techniques to carry out CQI initiatives.

In this chapter, we illustrate the importance of measurement and statistical thinking to quality improvement efforts and highlight the role of variation in quality improvement. We also describe a few fundamental CQI tools that are particularly useful in health care to enhance learning about process changes and facilitate improvement in healthcare processes. Finally, the chapter presents a brief discussion of health information data sources that can be used to carry out CQI initiatives. We include resources for readers who want to dive deeper into the mechanics of the tools introduced here.

Healthcare Systems and Processes

The early work of Donabedian is foundational in understanding healthcare systems and processes (Donabedian, 1980). He described the process of care as a system involving three components—structure, process, and outcomes—with interactions between them influencing care.

A **process** in health care is any action performed along the continuum of care—from scheduling appointments, patient intake or admission, administering tests or medication, and so on—until the defined end of the episode of care is reached. Each of these actions consists of multiple processes. For example, processes that work to ensure the patient gets the right medication include diagnosing the condition, understanding existing medications the patient is taking, selecting the correct medication, dispensing the correct medication, assuring the right dose is administered to the patient, educating the patient about the medication, and the list goes on. Each process has outputs associated with it (e.g., a prescription order, a fulfilled medication order, etc.). Processes take place in a given **structure**, or environment, which influences the process through conditions such as the physical layout of a facility, training of staff, and policies and norms, to name a few. Collectively, the processes performed in the given structure will produce **outcomes**. In CQI, it is important to understand the structure and keep a focus on the outcome. However, much of the work to improve quality is done through process changes. Structural changes may ultimately be needed to achieve the desired outcome, but making structural changes is more likely to lead to improvements when the hard work of understanding and improving processes has been done.

Process Capability

To understand the expected output of a process relative to a particular outcome or quality characteristic, or process capability, the process must be stable. Benefits of a stable process (Deming, 1986) include:

- The process has an identity (capability); it is predictable. Therefore, there is a rational basis for planning.
- Costs and quality are predictable.
- Effects of changes in the process can reliably be assessed with greater speed.

It is important to note that a process being "stable" does not indicate it is satisfactory.

Interpreting Process Requirements and Performance

Variation exists in every process and always will. It is the manager's job to understand variation and continuously improve processes so they meet the needs of the customers who depend upon them. The customer of each process has requirements which specify the level of performance needed. A provider working in the emergency department (ED) would require more rapid turnaround time of laboratory results than a provider working in a primary care office. A 30-minute turnaround time in the ED may be unacceptable, whereas 24 hours may be acceptable for a primary care office. There may also be specific requirements for analyzing the laboratory specimen. Technology used for one type of test may require 30 minutes to be processed, while a different type of test can be completed within seconds. Customer and technical requirements must both be taken into account in order to interpret whether the performance of the process is acceptable or whether the process needs to be improved.

Process requirements may be thought of as the criteria from which the effectiveness of a process may be evaluated from the perspective of those who depend on the process. The requirements function as both inputs to designing a process and outputs from executing a process. It is essential to first identify those who depend on the process, which includes customers, stakeholders, and the market. Brief definitions of each group, using a systems perspective, are provided here:

- **Customer**—A customer is anyone who has expectations regarding a process operation or outputs. In healthcare delivery organizations, the primary customer is the patient, while the community may be the primary customer for a public health agency.
    - Internal customers are those within the organizations and are sometimes thought of as those departments or coworkers "downstream" from the process. In other words, who the customers of a process are depends on the outputs of a process. For example, the recovery room or post-anesthesia care unit may be thought of as a customer of the operating room. Patient care units may be thought of as customers of diagnostic departments (e.g., laboratory, radiology).
    - External customers are those outside the provider organization (e.g., patients,

families, caregivers, payors). Chapter 8 provides an in-depth discussion of customers of healthcare organizations.

- **Stakeholder**—A stakeholder is anyone with an interest in or affected by the work you do. Regulatory bodies such as The Joint Commission (TJC), the National Commission on Quality Assurance (NCQA) and The Centers for Medicare & Medicaid Services (CMS) would be considered stakeholders for hospitals and health insurance companies. Professional societies that define practice standards may also be thought of as stakeholders.
- **Market**—Market refers to the environment in which you operate and do business and may include socioeconomic, demographic, geographic, and competitive considerations.

Once customers, stakeholders, and markets have been identified, it is essential to understand what they require of your services. For example, patients may require access to competent, courteous providers; payers may require a certain level of clinical results delivered in a cost-effective manner; regulatory bodies require compliance; and markets may require a culturally diverse approach to delivering services.

The requirements are vital to determining what services are needed and how the processes comprising the services are designed and improved. These requirements also provide the basis for selecting variables or attributes to measure the process performance from the perspective of the customer.

An example illustrates the link between processes, requirements, and measures. A simplified patient care continuum in a hospital setting might be shown as follows:

$$\text{Admission} \rightarrow \text{Assessment} \rightarrow \text{Care Delivery/Treatment} \rightarrow \text{Discharge}$$

In the admission stage, a hospital requires timely admission and therefore may select measures such as the time it takes to admit patients and patient satisfaction with the timeliness of admission. In the care delivery stage, the hospital pharmacy requires accuracy of prescription administration and may select medication error rate as the measure to track. At the discharge stage, a hospital requires patients and families to receive clear directions for follow-up care; thus it may select the measure of discharge instruction documentation and patient satisfaction with discharge instruction.

It is management's job to ensure that meaningful process specifications, such as plans, goals, budgets, or targets (also referred to as the voice of the customer) and the process performance (also referred to as the voice of the process) are aligned (Carey & Lloyd, 2001; Wheeler, 2000; Wheeler & Chambers, 2010). If the two are not in alignment, the process must be improved.

Identifying the need for a change, understanding *what specific* changes are needed, implementing changes, and assessing whether improvement has occurred are the heart and soul of CQI. Each of these steps has a series of methods and tools that are commonly used in health care, a selection of which is covered in the next sections.

Gaining Knowledge through Measurement

In order to convert data into knowledge and make appropriate decisions about process improvements, critical and statistical thinking is required. This sounds very simple, but in an age of instant access to information and artificial intelligence, it is all too easy to apply statistical methods and focus on results without the necessary step of thinking critically and understanding what our data tell us about the system we are trying to improve. This point was emphasized by Dr. Donald Berwick, among others, when he noted that "We speak here not of measurement for the purpose of judgment (for deciding whether or not to buy, accept, or reject or who to blame) but for the purpose of learning" (Berwick, 1996, p. 621). Not only is this view consistent with the guidelines for improvement spelled out in the earliest applications of CQI—for example, by W. Edwards Deming in his well-known 14 points (1986)—this view is also well understood and espoused in statistical literature (Balestracci, 2009; Langley et al., 2009; Sollecito & Hardison, 2020).

The Critical Role of Understanding Variation

It has long been established that a starting point for any quality improvement effort is understanding variation. It was Shewhart's idea (1931) that statistically controlled variation of processes (also called statistical process control) is the foundation of all empirical CQI activities. Listening to the voice of the process with knowledge of sources of variation will lead to the appropriate actions to take for improvement and is fundamental to CQI (Deming, 1986, 1993; Nolan & Provost, 1990; Nolan, Provost, & Perla, 2016; Wheeler, 2000; Wheeler & Chambers, 2010).

One of the key elements of the system of profound knowledge proposed by Deming (1993) is knowledge about variation and how it interacts with other elements of knowledge to lead to a transformation based on CQI. As quality improvement has evolved over the years from business applications to health care, the concepts related to understanding variation have also been applied specifically to health care with many examples and how the action required for improvement is dependent on this understanding (Carey & Lloyd, 2001; McLaughlin & Kaluzny, 2006; Nelson, Splaine, Batalden, & Plume, 1998).

Variation: What Is It and Why Study It?

Variation is everywhere—a diabetic's glucose level, the waiting time in a physician's office, blood pressure, the balance of trade, the behavior of people, the incidence of cancer, and the price of eggs—all vary over time. In order to understand variation, two definitions are important. **Common causes of variation** are the causes and conditions inherently present that impact every outcome of a process. **Special causes of variation** are not a part of the process all of the time and do not affect every outcome but arise because of specific circumstances (Deming, 1986). For the sake of completeness and clarity, it should also be noted that some authors refer to these two causes in process analysis as **noise** and **signals**, respectively (Wheeler, 2000). The appropriate action for improvement depends upon the correct interpretation of patterns in the variation observed. Is the variation random and attributable to the materials, methods, environment, people, etc. that are common to every outcome, or is there a signal of a trend or another discernable pattern in the data indicating a special cause is present in the process? Variation in a process over time can be measured, analyzed, and displayed in a manner that helps to distinguish its source (i.e., special vs. common cause). The importance of understanding this classification of causes directly relates to predictability of the outcomes of a process, and where special causes of variation are detected, outcomes are not predictable with any reasonable degree of belief (Deming, 1986; Langley et al., 2009; Shewhart, 1931; Wheeler, 2000; Wheeler & Chambers, 2010). This is of critical importance in health care.

Understanding causes of variation and using that knowledge to determine when and how to make process improvements involves the use of tools and procedures designed for these purposes. A key point to remember is that these tools can be used together in a complementary cyclical manner to identify the need for process improvement, decide on what improvements are needed, measure the impact of those changes, and assess what further improvements are needed. For example, the use of process behavior charts may lead to the identification of special causes of variation, which will require process improvement. The specific steps needed to make improvements can be identified through involvement of team members in a brainstorming exercise, analyses, or other CQI approaches. Implementation and measurement of the impact of changes will require methods such as the PDSA cycle described throughout this text followed by use of process behavior charts to assess the need for further improvements. The improvement cycle will then be repeated (Langley et al., 2009).

Nature of Process Variation and Actions for Improvement

A few notes are important to help clarify why understanding variation is vital to CQI. A process is said to be stable and "in statistical control" if only common causes are affecting the outcomes over time. This does not mean that the outcomes are good or bad or that there is no variation. It means that the outcomes are predictable within statistically determined limits. Similarly, an unstable process is a process in which outcomes are affected by both common and special causes, and the outcomes are unpredictable. The appropriate actions for improvement of a process depend upon whether the process is stable or unstable. If the process is unstable, then variation is produced by both common and special causes so the appropriate action for improvement is to investigate and prevent the special causes from happening again. Once the process is stable, then the appropriate action for improvement is to make a change which reduces or removes some of the common causes of variation.

Quality Improvement Methods and Tools

The Plan, Do, Study, Act (PDSA) cycle has broad applicability as a framework in which many other CQI processes can be applied, as emphasized in Chapter 1. Many organizations, including healthcare organizations, have adopted the PDSA cycle or a tailored version of it as their overall framework for CQI (Langley et al., 2009). Improvement begins with plotting a key quality characteristic of a process over time on a run chart or control chart. Then, depending upon the stability of the process, different tools, techniques, and methods may be used to accomplish the purpose of each phase of the PDSA cycle.

There is no one specified point in the CQI process where one needs to use a given method of measurement and analysis. It should be used on a continuous basis. In the context of the PDSA cycle, data and analytical tools may be used throughout the entire cycle. Different tools will be more helpful in different stages of each improvement project, from the initial analysis to monitoring changes already implemented. Reemphasizing the point made earlier in this chapter about using data to learn about improvement, Berwick (1996) notes that it is critical at the studying (S) stage of a PDSA cycle to take the time to reflect and learn about the impact of improvements that have already been made. This should include evaluating whether these changes have actually been improvements and then deciding on what further improvements to make.

There are numerous tools and techniques available to assist managers, clinicians, and organizational teams in improving processes to deliver desired results. These tools include activity network diagrams; affinity diagrams; driver diagrams; box-plots; brainstorming techniques; cause-and-effect diagrams; checklists; check sheets; concentration diagrams; control charts; failure mode and effects analysis (FMEA); flowcharts (process, deployment, top-down, opportunity); force field analysis; frequency charts; histograms; interrelationship digraphs; matrix diagrams; Pareto charts; prioritization matrices; process capability charts; radar charts; run charts; scatter diagrams; Suppliers, Inputs, Process steps, Outputs, Customers (SIPOC) diagrams; time plots; tree diagrams; and workflow diagrams.

While space does not permit detailed description of this entire list of tools, we have selected eight tools for CQI efforts commonly used in health care. The tools we describe in this chapter include:

1. Run charts
2. Process flowcharts
3. Checklists
4. Cause-and-effect diagrams
5. Frequency charts
6. Pareto diagrams
7. Driver diagrams
8. Control charts

This brief list of tools represents examples of types that are useful for understanding a process, assessing, and implementing improvements. As noted earlier, one can visualize a life cycle of the improvement team's efforts where these tools (and others not described here) might be applied sequentially at various project stages.

Run Charts

Run charts are frequently used in health care to better understand process performance. They are relatively straightforward to create, explain and understand, and often provide preliminary insights prior to using control charts, which are more complex (Perla, Provost, & Murray, 2011). Run charts are graphical time series displays of process measurements along with the median value of that measure. The horizontal axis presents a series of time points at which process measures have been collected and the vertical axis represents actual values of some process measure of interest. By definition, in order to calculate a median (the value above and below which 50% of the observations fall) the process measure being plotted should be continuous in scale, e.g., length of stay, time to an event, number of adverse drug events; or if the measure is non-continuous, e.g., dichotomous indications of the occurrence of safety events, convertible to percentages or counts of number of events at each time point. Another important consideration when using run charts is that "the number of data points (subgroups) plotted on the run chart needs to be adequate to detect patterns that may indicate improvement. . .the run chart becomes quite powerful when ten or more data points are available." (Perla, Provost, & Murray, 2013, p. 37)

Important uses of the run chart include:

- Displaying data to make process performance visible
- Determining if changes tested result in improvement
- Determining if we are holding the gains made by our improvement
- Allowing for a temporal (analytic) view of data versus a static (enumerative) view (Perla, Provost, & Murray, 2011, p. 47)

Figure 4.1 presents an example of a simple run chart, illustrating how (primary) data can be displayed to provide knowledge and information about the effect of making a change in procedures leading to a desired result, consistently fewer medication errors. In this hypothetical example a run chart is used to track the number of medication errors before and after a change was made and then to ensure that the improvement held over time. In the case of a planned change that results in an improvement, such as in Figure 4.1, a shift in the process is expected and a new centerline (median) should be computed starting from the time that the process change was introduced. This example illustrates two uses of a run chart: determining if a change led to an improvement and if we are holding the gains made. This also illustrates an important concept about how data and tools can provide feedback based on knowledge of systems and processes to not only make improvements but to provide the motivation for improvement (McLaughlin & Kibbe, 2013).

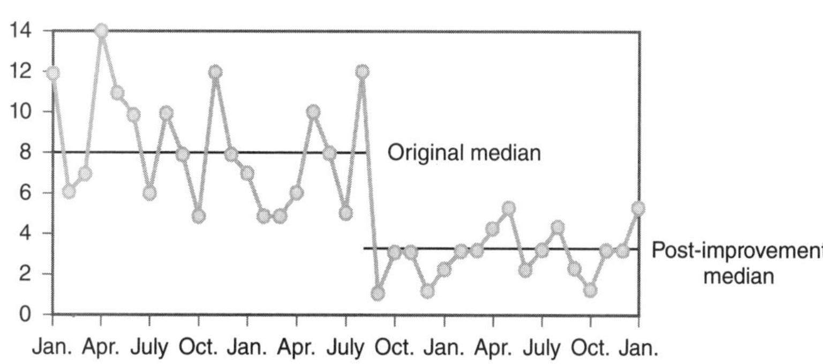

Figure 4.1 Run Chart of Number of Medication Errors

Run charts are also very useful as simple descriptive tools to study variation in processes over time, and to help a CQI team (see Chapter 6) determine whether a process change is needed. Utilizing traditional statistical distribution concepts (e.g., to define a 5% probability of detecting nonrandom patterns in the data), a series of useful rules aid in the interpretation of data variation patterns displayed in run charts. Described in greater detail by various authors (Balestracci, 2009; Langley et al., 2009; Perla, Provost & Murray, 2011), these rules can be summarized as follows:

> Rule 1—Shifts: A series of six or more consecutive points either all above or all below the median. Various authors in the statistical literature commonly define this pattern as a "run"; hence the name, run chart.
>
> Rule 2—Trend: Five or more consecutive points all going up or going down, taking care to only count duplicate consecutive points once.
>
> Rule 3—Number of runs: A non-random pattern is signaled by too few or too many runs or crossings of the median line. Several authors provide tables defining how many runs are to be expected in a random pattern. For example, with 10 points being plotted on a run chart, less than 3 would be the limit for too few runs and greater than 9 would be the limit for too many runs; for 30 data points the lower and upper limits would be 11 and 21 (Perla, Provost & Murray, 2011, p. 49).
>
> Rule 4—Astronomical point: Defined as "one that is obviously, even blatantly different from the rest of the points" (Perla, Provost, & Murray, 2011, p. 48). Care should be taken when such points are observed to not assume they are due to special causes or represent signals, which can only be identified using control charts (to be discussed later). At most, such points should be discussed by team members to understand possible causes of these values and attention should be paid to note whether they are repeated over time.

The presence of data trends in a run chart definitive determination of special or common cause should only be made by reanalyzing the process data using a control chart. Therefore, while run charts represent a very simple and useful tool, especially for monitoring the effectiveness of an improvement effort, as illustrated in Figure 4.1, they also have important limitations and potential abuses for defining special causes.

Also noteworthy is the danger when using run charts of reliance on arbitrary numerical goals which can be counter to our improvement goals (Balestracci, 2009). The run chart is a descriptive tool, not a hypothesis-testing procedure and is best used to describe and ask questions about observed patterns in process data. With these purposes in mind, in our previous discussion of shifts, the definition of the size of a run, 6, should be thought of as a guideline. Some authors throughout the CQI literature use 8 to define the size of a run to be concerned about and although, as Balestracci (2009) and Wheeler (2000) note, there is a statistical basis for choosing the run size of 8, the exact number that defines a run of concern varies somewhat among other authors, e.g., Langley et al. (2009), based on other factors such as the number of time periods in the run chart; i.e., longer runs might be expected due to chance alone when there are larger numbers of time points in the chart (Balestracci, 2009).

The expectation with a run chart is that when a process is "in control," the distribution of observations over time will exhibit a random pattern with 50% of the observations above and below the median. Patterns similar to those described above, such as data shifts, should be described as patterns of non-random variation. In using run charts, the terms special and common cause or stable and unstable should be avoided, reserving those terms for control charts. This is an important limitation of run charts (Perla, Provost, & Murray, 2011). The key takeaway from this discussion is that any non-random pattern of points above and below the median line should warrant further investigation, and more pronounced patterns, based on the rules above, may indicate the need for further analysis via a control chart and should always include a discussion and investigation by the CQI team before deciding on causes or actions.

Further details of how to compute and interpret run charts and their value in healthcare CQI, including their strengths and weaknesses, are presented by Perla, Provost, & Murray (2011, 2013). Most texts on CQI methods in health care/public health describe the construction and interpretation of run charts (Balestracci, 2009; Bialek, Duffy, & Moran, 2009; Langley et al., 2009; Lloyd, 2019; Spath & Kelly, 2017). For an example of how to use run charts, together with control charts and other tools, as part of a Lean management system, see Chapter 5.

Process Flowcharts

As Langley et al. (2009) point out, CQI projects and teams require some of the same kinds of tools commonly used in project management for describing systems and ensuring all steps are carried out in the proper sequence (Chapter 6). Two tools that fall within this definition are the process flowchart and the project checklist. The **flowchart** is one of the most powerful improvement tools for initiating inquiry into a process improvement project. Flowcharts (also called flow diagrams) are pictorial representations of how a process works. Simply put, they trace the steps of a process from start (input) to finish (output). The input may be a specimen in laboratory tests, a specific finding in a medical record, or a patient in a specialty clinic. Flowcharts are used to describe the sequence of actions that must be carried out in order to complete a particular task or set of tasks. In systems thinking terminology the actions performed on inputs are sometimes described as throughput and the entire process that we are studying/improving can be thought of as a system that can be modeled using three major components: input, throughput, and output (Grove, 1995). This is reflective of the Donabedian (1980) model of quality of care based on the inter-relationship of structure, process, and outcome. A flowchart is a first step in describing the details (who, what, when) of each of the components in these system models.

To develop a flowchart, one may proceed as follows:

1. List and define the basic stages of a process.
2. Further define the process, breaking down each stage into specific steps needed to complete the process.
3. Follow the input through the process a number of times to verify the process by observation.
4. Discuss the process with the project team or other employees to clarify the process and include any steps that might be missing (an example of brainstorming).

As the steps of a process are described, they may be documented with simple rectangles or, in some cases, greater complexity can be described using traditional flowcharting shapes to represent different steps or actions. For example, an activity or action step is represented by a rectangle, a decision step by a diamond, a wait or inventory by a triangle, a document by a symbol that looks like a rectangle with a curve at the bottom, a file by a large circle, and the continuation of the flowchart to another sheet of paper by a small circle.

It should be noted that flowcharts may be as simple or as complex as you wish. It is important to agree on what level of detail is suitable for the purpose. For example, very detailed flowcharts may be used in standard operating procedures (SOPs) for highly technical procedures. A high-level flowchart may be used to describe a general overview of how the process is carried out. **Figure 4.2** shows a high-level (simple) flowchart of the medication administration process for the inpatient setting; note that this figure also illustrates different shapes that can be used for different activities. Once the general process is described, more detail may be added, depending on the purpose of the analysis.

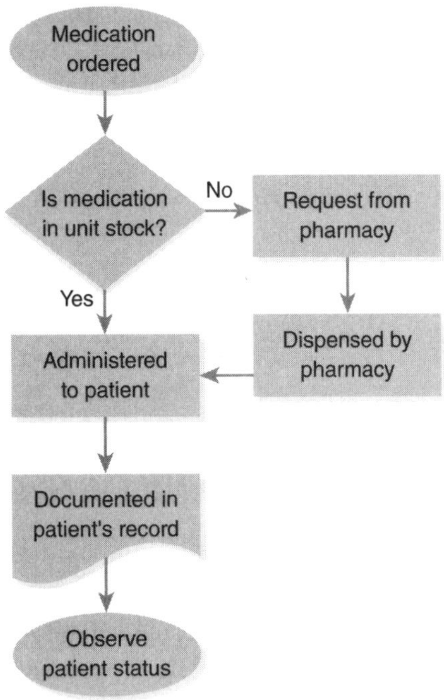

Figure 4.2 Simple Flowchart of Medication Administration Process

Figure 4.3 shows a more detailed flowchart of a similar process. As more detail has been added, the process has evolved from "medication administration" to "medication management" to include additional process stages involving medication inventory management, pharmacy management, and surveillance for adverse drug events. Each step of this process may in turn be mapped with a finer level of detail.

Members of a work team or improvement project team are likely to find that there is no common understanding of how the current process or system works, especially if multiple providers or departments are responsible for carrying out different steps of the process. The development of flowcharts, with input from all team members, allows the team to achieve a common understanding of their work processes and the important customer and supplier relationships internal to the processes. These interdependencies are often the key to sustainable process improvement. With an accurate, shared representation of how the process works, the team is then better able to consider how to improve it.

Once agreement is reached on the representation of the current process, the team may begin to ask questions about that process using the flowchart and guided by a control chart of measurements of process outputs, including:

1. How effective is the process in meeting customer requirements?
2. Are there performance gaps or perceived opportunities for improvement?
3. Have the relevant stages of the process been represented? Are "owners" of each stage represented on the team? If not, what needs to be done to gather their feedback and ideas?
4. What are the inputs required for the process, and where do they come from? Are any inputs constraining the process or not? Which ones?
5. Are there equipment or regulatory constraints forcing this approach?
6. Is this the right problem process to be working on? To continue working on?

The potential benefits of flowcharting are considerable. Staff come to know the process much better. A clear understanding of internal customers and suppliers can be gleaned from the overall process flow. The results can be used as a training aid, especially as new staff join the CQI team. People begin to take ownership of the process by participating in this activity, and most importantly, the possibilities and points in the process for improvement become clear almost immediately. And, in the language of project management, the work breakdown structure, timeline, and budget for an improvement initiative can begin to take shape through careful flowchart development (Project Management Institute, 2021).

Other examples of flowcharts are found throughout this text, including a description of their valuable role in Lean management systems, in Chapter 5, where flowcharts, also denoted as process maps, are used to describe emergency room patient flow and processes.

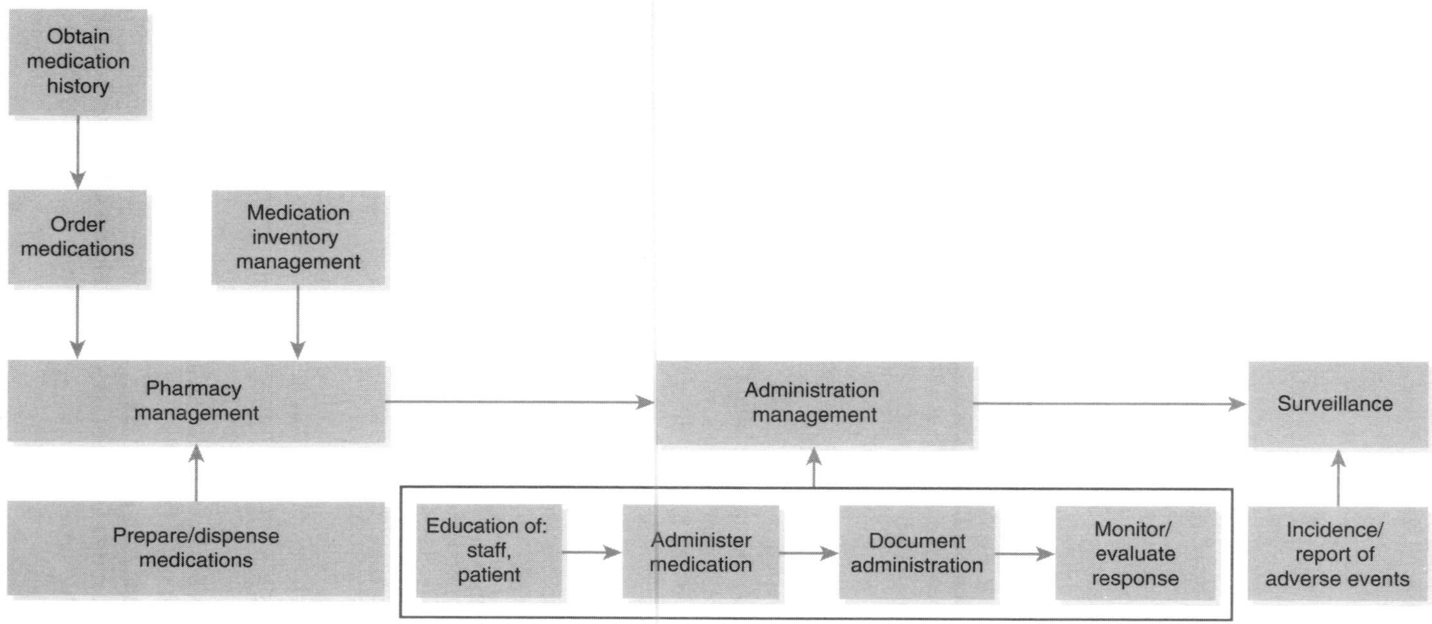

Figure 4.3 Flowchart of Medication Management

Data from Killbridge, P., & Classen, D. (2002). *Surveillance for adverse drug events: History, methods, and current issues* (VHA 2002 Research Series Publication). VHA and First Consulting Group.

Checklists

Although it is neither a statistical tool nor a tool unique to quality improvement, one that is very basic to CQI and project management is the **checklist**. CQI in health care includes as one of its primary goals the prevention of errors (Crosby, 1979), which is an important part of the overall goal of ensuring patient safety, defined as "freedom from accidental or preventable injuries produced by medical care" (AHRQ, 2016). This includes prevention of medical errors and adverse events (outcomes of medical care). (Note that a checklist is different from another CQI tool with a similar name, the check sheet; see Bialek, Duffy, & Moran, 2009).

A checklist can take many forms, but in its simplest form it is a list of process activities, usually in a time-ordered sequence, that must be carried out by various members of a project or CQI team. As each task is completed, a check mark is made next to the item that was completed; in some cases, greater precision is obtained by indicating the date/time that the task was completed or, if multiple team members are involved in the process, the initials of the team member who completed the task may be entered as a way of ensuring accountability. Checklists should be derived from a process flowchart and apply to performing tasks in a stable process. Checklists have been used for many years in other industries, such as the airline industry, and they have long been an important component of the project manager's tool kit in many different industrial and healthcare settings. Their role in improving airline safety is well documented and is an important reason that they have now seen an accelerated evolution into medical care, which has had a greater focus on safety issues in the early part of the twenty-first century (Haynes et al., 2009; Gawande, 2009; Pronovost et al., 2006; Pronovost et al., 2009). Although not without controversy regarding their effectiveness (Bosk et al., 2009), their adoption as part of the medical safety process, to be used in conjunction with other well-established evidence-based practices, continues as we have entered the third decade of this century.

Cause-and-Effect Diagrams

Cause-and-effect diagrams, also called Ishikawa or fishbone diagrams, are one of the most widely used tools of CQI. This tool was developed by Kaoru Ishikawa (University of Tokyo) for use at Kawasaki Steel Works in 1943 to sort and interrelate the common causes of process variation (Ishikawa, 1986). Cause-and-effect diagrams are most useful to begin to identify common causes of variation once the process has been determined to be stable and documented using a process flowchart. However, they are also very useful when special causes have been identified, perhaps via a process behavior chart analysis and the next step is to decide what actions need to be taken to prevent the special cause from recurring. Cause-and-effect diagrams are a schematic means of relating causes of variation to the process output and predictability. It is important to note that not all errors are special causes. Errors can be produced by a process with only common causes of variation present. Therefore, it is critical to determine the type of variation that is present before constructing the cause-and-effect diagram, since the strategy for improvement is different. In either case, the first pass at a cause-and-effect diagram may not be enough to understand the cause-and-effect relationships. Therefore, it may be necessary to stratify cause-and-effect diagrams further to achieve finer gradations of error causes. Increasing the level of detail about causes can help with identifying specific action for improvement.

This tool is especially suited for interactive team situations and is quite useful for focusing a discussion and organizing large amounts of information resulting from a brainstorming session. It can be taught easily and quickly, allowing the group to sort ideas into useful categories for further investigation. The diagram is also referred to as a "fishbone" diagram because the shape resembles the skeleton of a fish.

Figure 4.4 shows the multilayered process of making a fishbone diagram. Step 1 of the diagram shows the identified performance gap or problem at the right and a big arrow leading to it that represents the overall causation. Step 2 involves

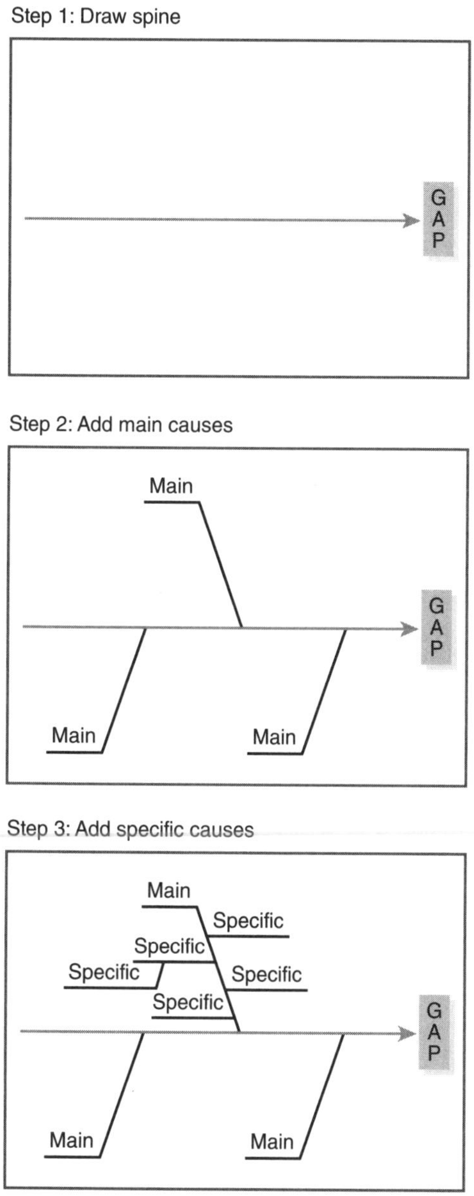

Figure 4.4 Multilayered Process of Developing a Fishbone Diagram

drawing spines from that big arrow to represent main classifications or categories of causes, such as labor, materials, and equipment. Step 3 adds the specific causes along each major spine, which also may occur at multiple levels. Sometimes it is useful to draw the diagram in two stages—one showing the main causes and a separate chart with a spine representing the main cause and its associated levels.

Figure 4.5 illustrates a cause-and-effect diagram that may be used to describe common causes of adverse drug events in a hospital setting. The process outcome is "adverse drug events." The main classifications in this example are people, policies, procedures, and plant and equipment, each showing a variety of levels of causes.

Frequency Charts

In some cases, after a cause-and-effect diagram is generated, data are collected to quantify how often the different causes occur. These data are then presented to the study team and later to others. When measures are based on discrete/attribute data, the simplest display is a **frequency chart**, a diagram of vertical bars representing the frequency of observations in specific categories (Kuebler & Smith, 1976). The bars are arrayed on the *horizontal* (*x*) axis representing discrete events, such as causes identified in a fishbone diagram. The length (height) of the bar against the *vertical* (*y*) axis shows the number of observations falling on that cause or event classification. The frequency chart displays an enumeration of process behavior issues; however, it does not provide any information about process stability. Further analysis using a run chart or control chart is needed to determine whether the process is only producing statistically controlled variation. **Figure 4.6** illustrates a frequency chart of the frequency and causes for the discarding of hospital linens.

Pareto Diagrams

A **Pareto diagram** is a frequency chart with the bars arranged from the longest (most frequent) first on the left and moving successively toward the shortest. The arrangement of the vertical bars gives a visual indication of the relative frequency of the contributing causes of the problem, with each bar representing one cause.

The diagram is named after the seventeenth-century Italian economist, Vilfredo Pareto. When he studied the distribution of wealth, he observed that the majority of the

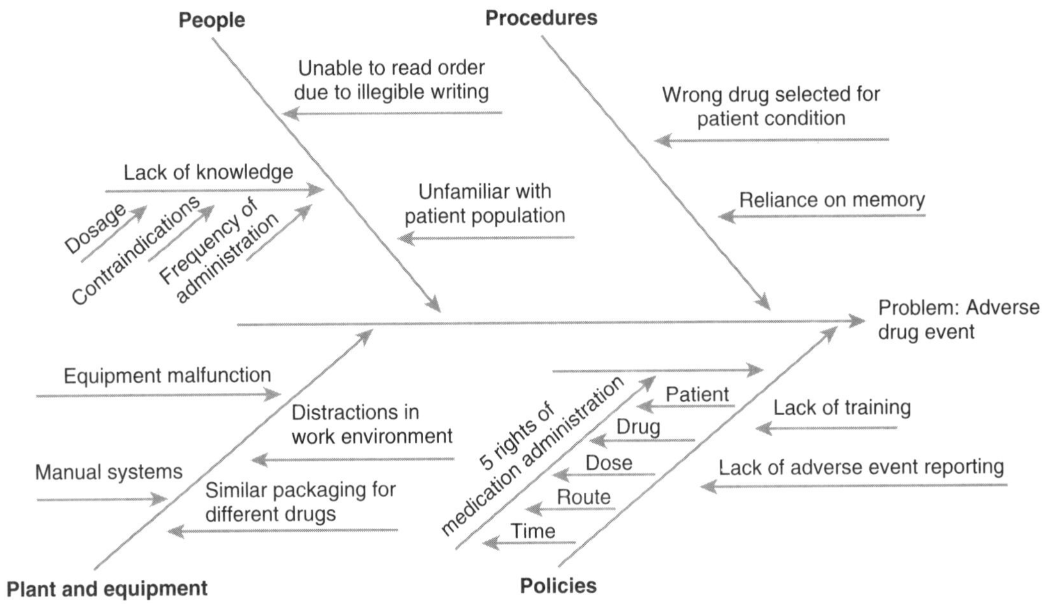

Figure 4.5 Cause-and-Effect Diagram of Adverse Drug Events

wealth had been distributed among a small proportion of the population (Pareto's law). Juran (1988) applied this concept to quality causes, observing that the "vital few" causes account for most of the defects, while others, the "useful many," account for a much smaller proportion of the defects. He noted that these vital few causes are likely to constitute the areas of highest payback to management. Concentrating on the high-volume causes may have the largest potential for reducing process variation once special causes have been eliminated.

On the same Pareto diagram, you can display the cumulative probability distribution incorporating all the proportions of the observations to the left of and including the bar. It is common to display the frequency scale on the left-hand side of the vertical (y) axis and the cumulative percentage

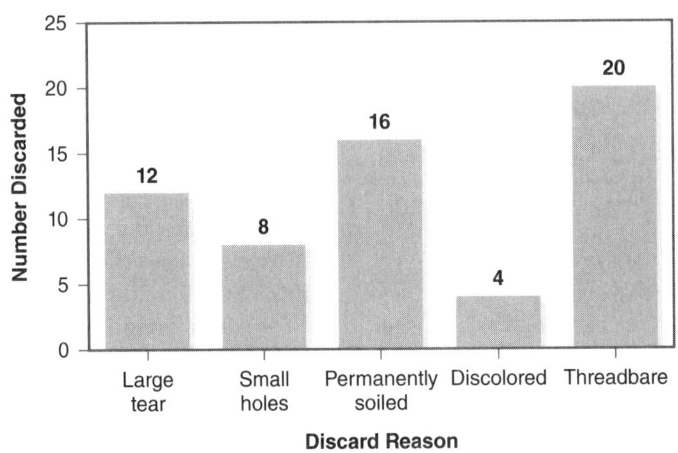

Figure 4.6 Frequency Chart of Linen Discard Causes

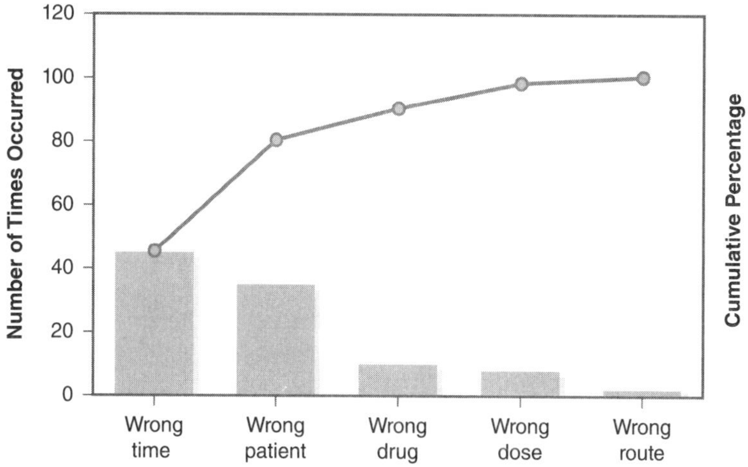

Figure 4.7 Pareto Chart: Cause of Adverse Drug Events

scale on the right-hand edge. Segregating the causes that have large frequencies can help identify potential improvements. However, just because a cause is identified as having the greatest frequency does not necessarily mean it should be worked on first. It must also be tractable and not cost more to change than it is worth. It is likely, however, that the first cause to be studied in detail will be among the left-most group. It is important to remember that even though a cause may not be among the most frequent, if it has a devastating result, such as causing a patient death, it must be addressed in the course of the improvement effort.

Once the cause-and-effect diagram, such as the one in Figure 4.5 which identifies possible causes of adverse drug events, has been described, data would be collected on the frequency of the specific causes. **Figure 4.7** illustrates how a Pareto chart can be developed to analyze the frequency of causes identified in the cause-and-effect diagram. For example, Figure 4.7 displays how often different events contributed to an adverse drug event (ADE). Of 100 ADEs investigated, the Pareto chart shows that "wrong time" occurred most frequently, with "wrong patient" next, and so on.

Driver Diagrams

A **driver diagram** is a useful tool to visualize improvement ideas. Many of the tools discussed thus far are used to understand why something, typically something undesirable, is happening. While a driver diagram can be used in that manner, it is also quite useful once an understanding of causes is established, to organize potential change ideas targeting factors identified as important in the causal chain for achieving improvement. A driver diagram represents a theory of how changes can lead to improvements (Bennett & Provost, 2015; Langley, et al., 2009).

Construction of a driver diagram requires at least four steps. The first is to clearly identify the aim or outcome of interest. The next step is to identify the primary drivers of the outcome, followed by secondary drivers. The primary drivers represent the high-level factors or conditions necessary to achieve the outcome and the secondary factors indicate factors that influence the primary drivers. The final step in the construction of the driver diagram is to list the change ideas.

Figure 4.8 illustrates a driver diagram that might be created to achieve the aim of reducing clinic wait time (an outcome that is presented in the case study provided in this chapter). The clinic aims to reduce the time from when the patient arrives in the clinic to when they are seen by their provider. The clinic staff or CQI team identifies three primary drivers, or factors that influence wait time: front desk procedures, transfer of patients from waiting room to clinic room, and the provider's entering the visit room. For each

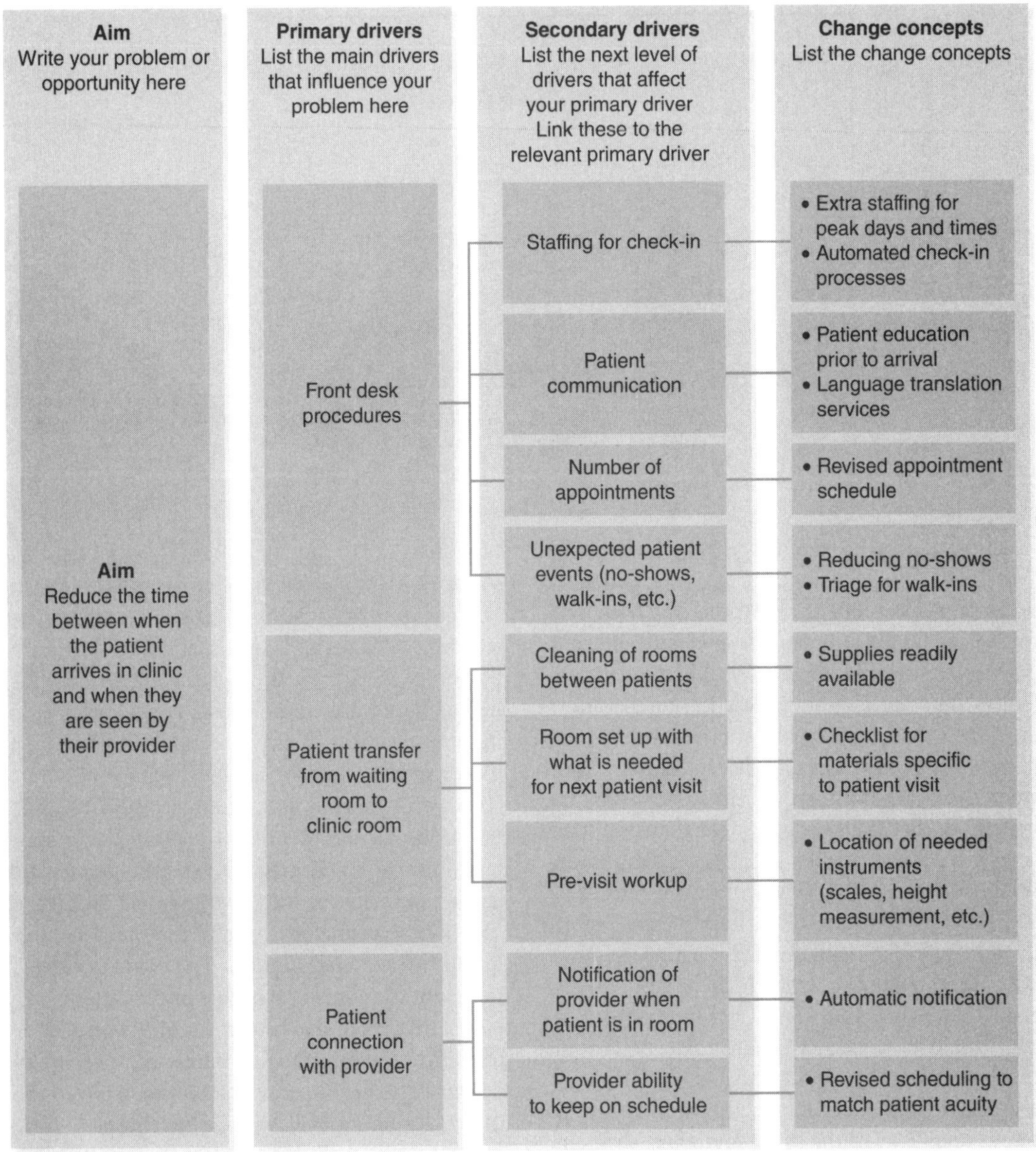

Figure 4.8 Driver Diagram of Clinic Wait Times

primary driver, they identify multiple secondary drivers. In the last column, they list change concepts. The driver diagram presents the CQI team's "theory of change" where the staff proposes ideas they think will improve clinic wait times. If some of the check-in processes were automated, and if language translation services were available, and other ideas shown in the diagram were implemented, they believe the front desk check-in process would be quicker.

Through these examples, one can begin to see how the tools fit together to support CQI and patient safety. Since the Institute of Medicine report *To Err Is Human* (IOM, 2000) was published, the topic of medical errors and adverse events has become a priority area for customers and stakeholders of healthcare organizations. TJC's review process now includes accreditation standards addressing patient safety, medical errors, and adverse events. Various CQI tools, alone and in combination, can be used to address these critical area of concern (see Chapter 9).

Control Charts/Process Behavior Charts

The control chart is arguably the most important CQI tool since it represents a powerful methodology for explaining concepts of process variation and assessing improvement. It was first developed by Shewhart as a methodology for analyzing and understanding process variability and predictability (Shewhart, 1931; Wheeler, 2000; Wheeler & Chambers, 2010). This "tool" has been found to be very useful in many settings and has been called by several names, including Shewhart control charts and most recently, process behavior charts, which is derived from its broad use as a descriptor of process variability. We will use **control chart** and **process behavior chart** interchangeably throughout this chapter and this text.

A control chart is a (time series) plot of process measurements over time, and at first glance, looks similar to a run chart. A control chart, however, includes three statistically computed lines: a center line, an upper control limit, and a lower control limit. The vertical axis of a control chart represents the actual value of the measure we are studying to assess process performance and variability; the horizontal axis represents the time scale over which we have collected process measures. A control chart displays process data in a time series for a fixed timer period. When trying to understand process behavior, this is much more useful than simply analyzing measures of central tendency alone (e.g., an arithmetic average.). In this way, a control chart illustrates and concentrates on the behavior of the underlying process. The upper and lower control limits of a control chart define the Natural Process Limits (i.e., what the process will deliver as long as it continues to operate as consistently as possible), thus describing what Wheeler (2000) defines as the Voice of the Process.

The control chart is the most powerful tool for distinguishing between common and special causes of variation (noise vs. signals, respectively) and predicting future performance of a stable process within a range (Langley et al., 2009). "Points outside the limits are signals—they are opportunities to discover how to improve a process . . . and ask the right questions" (Wheeler, 2000, p. 59). Wheeler also notes that "if you are not pleased with the amount of variation shown by the Natural Process Limits, you must go to work on the system to change the underlying process, rather than setting arbitrary goals, jawboning the workers, or looking for alternative ways of computing limits" (Wheeler, 2000, p. 44). This is accomplished using other CQI tools, such as those previously discussed.

A control chart also provides a comprehensive methodology to observe process changes occurring over time. As with the run chart it serves the equally important purpose of identifying trends in the data to aid in separating noise from signals in a process. A broader description of its usefulness is provided by Wheeler (2000): "Signals of exceptional variation are indicated by points which fall outside the limits or by obvious non-random patterns of variation around the central line". This latter comment is similar to the identification of shifts or trends as indicators of process variation in a run chart. It is recommended that to maximize usefulness of a run chart and a control chart, CQI teams should look not only for values outside the control limits as indicators of special causes of variation, but also "patterns of non-random variation," within the control limits, to guide the CQI team's next decision. These broader interpretations of control chart patterns emphasize the power of the control chart for understanding process behavior.

Further increasing the usefulness of this tool, but also adding some level of confusion, especially to novices in CQI, is that there have been many types of control charts described in the CQI literature over many years. These differ according to their application to various types of data with different measurement scales (Langley et al., 2009):

1. P chart or np chart—Used with classification data/nominal data.
2. C chart or u chart—Used with count data.
3. I chart (X chart/XmR chart), X-bar chart (with R chart or S chart)—Used with continuous data.

Other differences among these charts relate to the number of observations per time point. For example, for continuous data, the X-bar chart is useful when there are multiple observations per time point; and individual, or XmR, charts are used when there is one observation per time point. Before describing details about how to produce control charts, it is useful to review the interpretive concepts that are common to all forms of control charts.

Figure 4.9 shows a series of X-bar charts, including a solid center line (mean, i.e., arithmetic average) and two dashed lines, representing lower and upper control limits. The first chart represents a situation when the data are considered to be stable; the points do not go outside of the control limits and there are no discernable patterns within the limits. This process will continue to produce predictable outcomes within these limits as long as the conditions that produced all of these results continue. The latter is a subject matter judgment, not a statistical one. Improvement will come from changing the process that impacts every output of the process (i.e., the common causes). The second chart shows values outside the control limits; thus, the process is unstable due to special causes of variation. The appropriate action is to investigate the special causes and determine how to remove them. Finally, the third chart describes the situation when there is a discernable pattern within the control limits. In this case, there are too many values in a row below the center line, indicating a pattern of non-random variation and the need for further investigation and discussion, to determine if this is due to a special cause. As with our previous discussion of run charts, the exact definition of how many is too many varies by several factors, including sample size and number of time points. These are discussed by several authors along with other rules that define patterns which may signal special cause variation (Balestracci, 2009; Perla, Provost, & Murray, 2011; Wheeler, 2000).

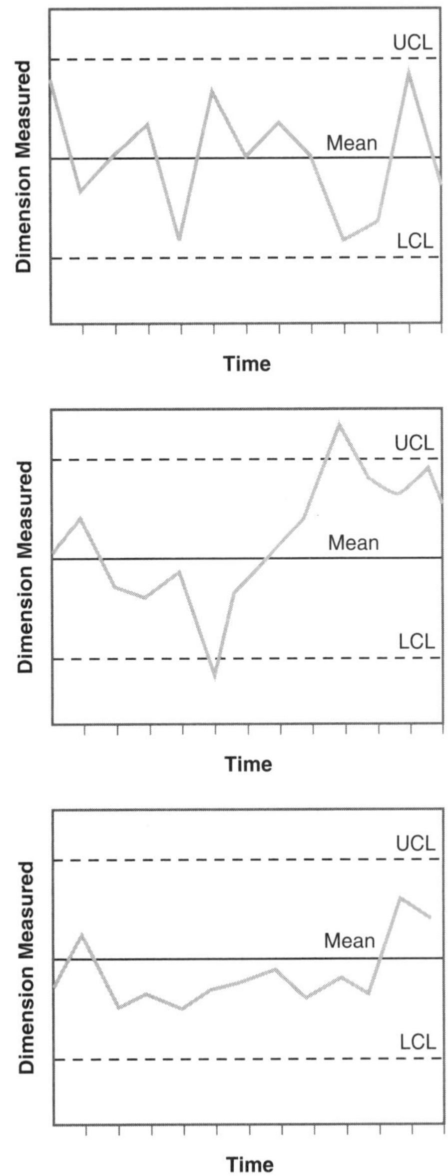

Figure 4.9 Three Examples of Control Charts

The computation of control limits is beyond the scope of this chapter but can be summarized by the statement that control limits provide a "quantitative answer to how much variance will be accepted before a process is investigated" (Ross, 2014, p. 235). Computation of control limits requires knowledge of variability for a process measure, obtained using traditional statistical formulae for measures of variation; either the range or standard deviation of process values in the control chart can be used for various forms of control charts. Ross (2014) provides detailed descriptions of formulae for computation of statistics required for various forms of control charts, including control charts limits, with instructions for how to use Microsoft Excel™ software to carry out these computations.

In addition to measuring process behavior to determine common vs. special causes of variation, control charts are also used to assess the impact of an improvement effort by continuing to plot the process outcomes after a change is made to the process. The change should show up as a special cause signal in the chart and should settle down to a new center line over time unless unplanned special causes impact the process. The process should continue to be monitored and the same diagnostics and actions for improvement as described previously should be employed.

P Charts

The specific type of control chart used depends on two main factors: the measurement scale of the variable of interest and the number of observations at each time point. Similarly, the methodology and formulae used to derive the values represented on the control chart vary depending on the type of chart.

While each type of control chart has utility in the healthcare setting, the P chart is perhaps the most universally applicable. A **P chart** represents a percentage or proportion of patients or events as the variable of interest and is applicable regardless of how many observations are collected at each time point. In health care, we are often interested in whether a specific type of care or process was or was not completed. For example, a hospital may be interested in whether the patient was provided instructions for care at discharge. A P chart could be used to represent the percentage of discharges with evidence of counseling on care at discharge (**Figure 4.10**). Figure 4.10 illustrates common characteristics of a control chart and specifically in this example, a P chart since the vertical axis and the values plotted in the chart are percentages (of patients receiving counseling each month). Time is shown along the horizontal (x) axis; in this case, data are plotted for each month. The vertical (y) axis shows the percentage of patients who were discharged with care instruction (calculated as the count of those with instruction divided by the total number of patients discharged). The solid line in the chart represents the mean of the data included in the chart (42%). The dotted lines represent the upper and lower control limits.

There are several values that fall outside the control limits. Of special concern would be those that fall below the lower limits, indicating that fewer than the expected number of patients had received counseling that month, an indication of a special cause that will require further investigation with the staff and most likely lead to steps to improve the process. The fact that all remaining points are above the lower control limit may indicate that some improvement steps may have occurred. A more detailed description of how to interpret and follow up on findings observed in a control chart can be found in the case study that follows.

This brief overview of control chart concepts also illustrates another factor that may need further clarification for those unfamiliar with control chart analysis. Control limits may take two forms as depicted in Figures 4.9 and 4.10. Control limits may be flat horizontal lines (Figure 4.9) spanning all time points for various types of control charts, including P charts with equal numbers of observations at each time point; alternatively for P charts with values that are based on unequal numbers of observations at each time point, the control limits rise or fall at each time point (Figure 4.10). This difference in shape of control limit lines is a direct result of the formulae used to compute upper and lower control limits, and include sample size at each time point in the

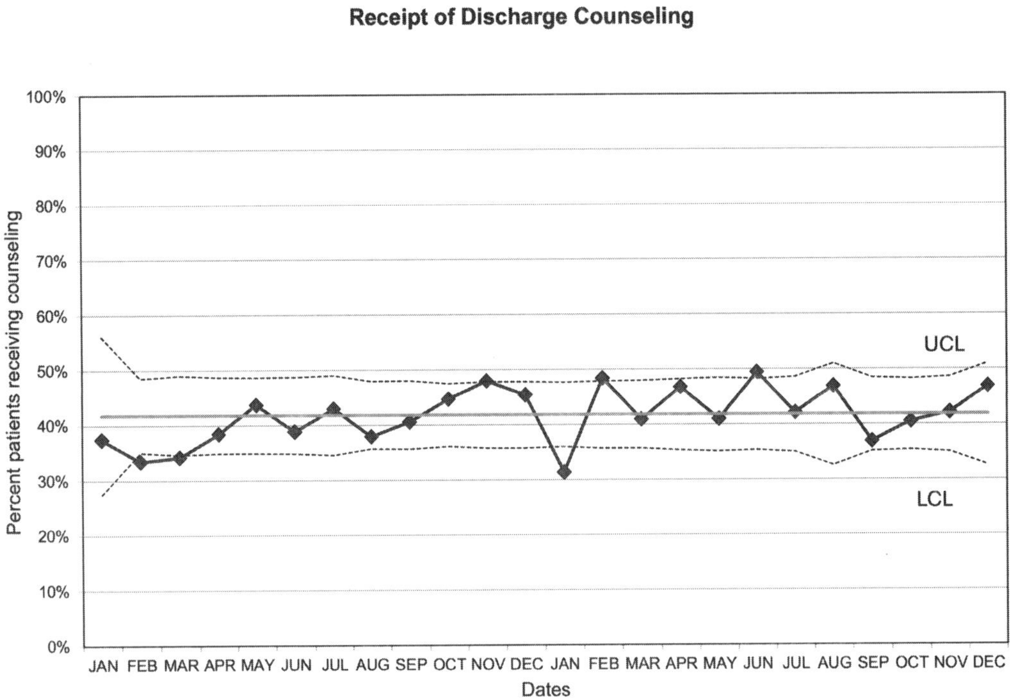

Figure 4.10 P Chart of Hospital Discharge Counseling

formula (Ross, 2014). One other useful point to note about lower control limits is that when the percentage to be analyzed is fairly small, e.g., percentage of patients with serious adverse events, the data may include negative values, in which case the assumed limit of zero is used to represent the lower control limit, since zero would be the lowest achievable value.

Advantages of Time Series Data

Both run and control charts share the common benefit of evaluating system performance over time rather than at a single time point, a major advantage of time series analyses. In this manner, both run charts and control charts analyze behavior of an underlying process or system, rather than individual data points, and are therefore powerful tools for process improvement and to determine if a system is stable or unstable. Both methods allow us to "know when a change has occurred in our process or systems. . . to know about such changes in a timely manner so that we can respond appropriately." (Wheeler, 2000, p. 23).

Run charts have the advantages of simplicity and ease of computation to identify patterns over time and ask questions that will help, with the use of other tools described here, to learn more about process improvement. Control charts add to these advantages but with greater complexity, due to computation of control limits to provide greater process knowledge and separate special from common causes and thereby guide us in taking corrective actions only when necessary.

Applying Concepts

To illustrate the application of the tools presented in this chapter, we have included the following hypothetical case study. This case study illustrates the use of a run chart and a P chart.

Case Study: Reducing Patient Clinic Wait Time

A rural primary care health clinic has struggled with long wait times for patients attending the clinic. A new administrator, with a background in CQI, was recently hired for the clinic. She knows that long waiting times annoy patients and can be symptoms of inefficiency. She has identified this as an important quality of care issue for the clinic.

Some questions to consider in reflecting on this scenario are:

1. What potential process measures might you collect?
2. How might those measures be analyzed to understand what the level of quality is?
3. How would you decide if and when changes in processes are needed?
4. What specific changes could be made and who decides?
5. How would you determine if the changes made were improvements?

These are just a few examples of the kinds of questions that should be asked in applying CQI in this setting. We leave it up to readers of this chapter to discuss these questions and to think of others that might be appropriate. To illustrate the use of tools discussed here, we will focus on the first three questions.

To answer these questions data collection is required. A useful methodology is to collect daily measures and examine them over time. The administrator meets with the staff to decide which measure to track, how to operationally define the measure, and to identify who will be responsible for the measurement. The staff identifies a simple but important measure for clinic quality and patient satisfaction: amount of time, in minutes, between when the patient first arrives and is seen by their provider. This metric not only measures clinic efficiency but can have a direct impact on patient satisfaction. A measurement plan is put in place and the staff is asked to collect data for two weeks. After that time, the administrator plans to meet with staff to review and interpret the data.

The optimal way to monitor and assess variation in the wait times is to use a control chart, which the clinic eventually does. However, the staff is new to CQI, so the administrator begins with the use of a run chart since it is intuitive and more accessible for all to understand. The run chart, using two weeks of data (10 clinic days), is shown in **Figure 4.11**.

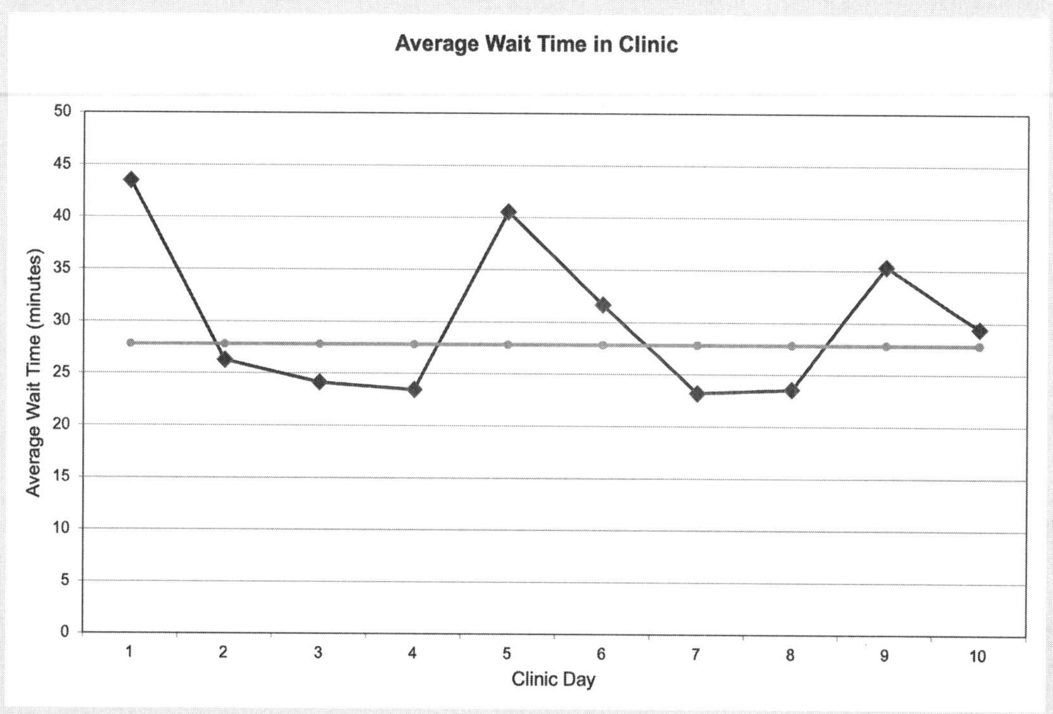

Figure 4.11 Run Chart for Clinic Wait Times

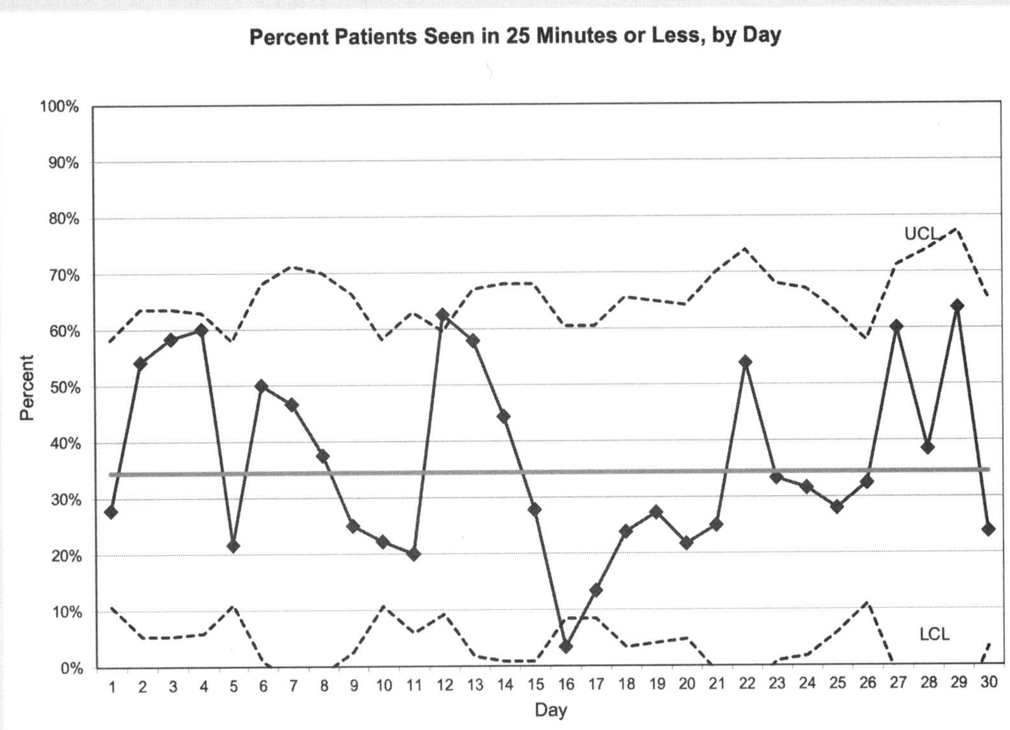

Figure 4.12 Percentage of Patients Seen in 25 Minutes or Less, by Day

During the two-week period, 251 patients were seen. Analyzing the data on a daily basis, as shown in the run chart, median wait time was 28 minutes. The clinic day with the highest average wait time was day 1 (44 minutes). The lowest average wait time was 23 minutes, (on days 4, 7, and 8).

The chart in Figure 4.11 reflects the existing process. The chart indicates variability in wait times by day. It does not indicate any "signals of exceptional or non-random variation" (e.g., a shift or an astronomical point). After the first two weeks of data collection, the clinic administrator shared the data with staff. Given that the process appeared stable, the staff recognized they were seeing common cause variation. Seeing the data helped the staff recognize the length and amount of variation in the wait times and they felt motivated to explore ways to reduce wait times. They decided on a goal of having patients seen by their healthcare provider within 25 minutes of arrival and agreed to continue to collect data on wait times on a daily basis.

The administrator reorganized the data so it could be used in a control chart. She selected a P chart that would represent the percentage of patients each day that were seen within 25 minutes (**Figure 4.12**). For 4 more weeks, the chart was updated daily. The chart showed the process was operating within limits for the first few weeks of data collection. However, from day 15 to 21, the percentage of patients seen within the goal of 25 minutes was below the mean, and at one point (day 16) the percentage of patients seen within 25 minutes was outside of the control limits. With a run (seven consecutive points below the mean) and a value outside the control limits, the staff detected an indication of a process that is "not stable," or to be more precise with our terminology, the observed trend was indicative of a process with signals of non-random variation and required further investigation. The administrator and staff investigated the source of variation and discovered the clinic had been short staffed that week due to an unexpected illness of one of the physicians. The staffing situation represented a "special cause" that explained the pattern of (non-random) variation. Although a special cause does not always indicate a need for an immediate action, this occurrence may be viewed as a signal and in the long term a system modification might be considered. Staff will have illnesses, so a physician back-up process might be worth considering to prevent this problem from reoccurring, and the options for changes could be the subject of future team meetings or other discussions with relevant staff.

Case Analysis

Two important lessons are demonstrated in this case study. First, once data are collected, they can be used in multiple ways, as with the data used in the run chart and P chart. Secondly, when a sequence of low values was noted, a non-random pattern of variability, the pattern was thought to be due to a special cause and an investigation was done to gain knowledge about the cause of the inability to see patients within the goal time. The right questions were asked with input from team members, and in this case the cause was quickly identified. These lessons demonstrate the value of using process behavior charts to monitor and improve processes over time.

In this case study, the source of the non-random variation, a shift below the centerline, was quickly identified by the staff. However, there are often situations when more complex sources must be investigated. While guesses, "executive decisions," and anecdotal information may seem like an easy way to decide on the action to be taken (e.g., blame one of the new staff), the proper way to proceed is to use input from knowledgeable team members and, when necessary, use other CQI tools and techniques to gain knowledge about the cause of this change in wait times. Furthermore, although the process is considered "stable" using the control chart, the staff felt the variation was too high from day to day and agreed to use the tools and techniques such as those described earlier in this chapter (e.g., cause-and-effect diagram), or methods that are described by other authors (e.g., root cause analysis; Ross, 2014) might be appropriate. When a process is stable though not performing at the level needed by the customer, strategies for improvement, such as applying PDSA cycles to test whether changes that are made lead to true improvement (Langley et al., 2009) and using a team approach (see Chapter 6 for more details on the role of teams in CQI), should be applied. These step-wise applications of improvement tools and techniques are always recommended and are especially important to follow when we are analyzing other healthcare processes that are more complex than the simple example presented here. For instance, please see the patient safety examples in Chapter 9.

Other Forms of Control/ Process Behavior Charts

As noted previously, there are other forms of control charts that can also be used to assess process behavior. For example, Chapter 5 presents examples of X-bar charts based on samples of patients to track "door to doctor time" in an emergency department. In a previous edition of this book, a different case study was presented using an XmR control chart (which is applicable to situations where we have only one observation per time point). It is noteworthy that XmR charts can be used as a non-parametric alternative to analyze percentages (Wheeler, 2000), although P charts have the advantage of greater simplicity. Readers interested in using XmR charts for analyzing individual data in CQI are referred to Chapter 4 in the previous edition of this book (Sollecito & Hardison, 2020) as well as other sources (Wheeler, 2000; Wheeler and Chambers, 2010).

Resources for a Deeper Dive in CQI Tools

Combinations of tools, such as flowcharts, Pareto charts, run charts, and control charts, may be used together in a Lean management process analysis/ improvement; an initiative in an emergency room setting is described in Chapter 5. A good description of the many tools that can be applied in health is found in *The Public Health Quality Improvement Handbook* (Bialek, Duffy, & Moran, 2009). Other examples of applications via case studies illustrating these concepts and tools are found in *Implementing Continuous Quality Improvement in Health Care: A Global Casebook* (McLaughlin, Johnson, & Sollecito, 2012). Details of control chart formulae can be found in Ross (2014), Wheeler (2000), or Wheeler & Chambers (2010).

Readers who are interested in the mechanics of CQI analytics and tools are encouraged to explore one of many valuable texts covering that content (e.g., Balestracci, 2009; Carey & Lloyd, 2001; Langley et al., 2009; Lloyd, 2019; Ross, 2014).

When faced with the task of developing specific tools, there are various types of software for developing the tools referenced here, including control charts, e.g., "R" (The R project for statistical computing, 2025) or Microsoft's Excel™; there are also websites that provide tutorials and templates to facilitate the understanding, development, and use of CQI tools (e.g., www.asq.org/quality-resources or www.sqconline.com/about-control-charts). These represent a wide range of easily accessible computing options; however, as with all statistical software, users are urged to study/question findings carefully to understand and gain knowledge from these user-friendly systems before taking actions to change processes.

Sources of Data for CQI

Decisions about process performance and improvements and the application of CQI tools often start by accessing quality data in a stepwise **data-to-decision cycle**. This cycle begins with data that are transformed into information, which facilitates identification of opportunities for improvement and then leads to the transformation of information into knowledge about how to redesign processes (e.g., based on best practices). Ultimately these steps result in decisions and actions to make changes and provide feedback on the need for further improvements (e.g., in a classic PDSA cycle; McLaughlin & Kibbe, 2013). Of course, all decisions should be informed by an understanding of process variation as previously defined.

In defining sources of data for CQI initiatives, it is important to consider timeliness of the data being collected as well as accessibility. Most critical to this process is the quality of the data that are the input to this decision-making cycle. As with any good statistical analysis, data collected for CQI must be of the highest quality and every effort must be taken to ensure this. No matter which tool or procedure is used to perform CQI, its findings will only be as good as the data that it is based on. The age-old acronym GIGO (Garbage In, Garbage Out) must always be kept in mind when deciding on data sources for CQI. It is tempting when starting a data collection effort to collect data in simple format, often simply counting the number of cases an expected standard is met. This may limit your ability to reorganize the data and also to perform data quality checks. For example, in the case study, if staff had collected data by counting the number of patients each day who had a wait of over a given number of minutes, they would not have been able to adjust the data to format it for both run and control charts. Instead, they collected the data in raw format, entering the time of arrival and the time the patient was seen for each patient in an Excel™ sheet, which is a better practice for CQI than collecting data with predetermined limits, which may be appropriate for a quality assurance approach when a standard is known.

Ensuring the highest data quality requires the application of data standards, data management, and quality assurance procedures (Loshin, 2010) to ensure that the information used to make CQI decisions is correct. Also important in ensuring data quality is proper training of team members involved in CQI initiatives (McLaughlin & Kibbe, 2013, p. 343):

> Quality improvement teams are temporary systems whose members may or may not be skilled observers and data recorders. Teams may also have to depend on observers who are not team members. Management must make sure that the appropriate team members are trained to observe and record the relevant events and variables. They also should make sure that all those likely to become involved understand the CQI process and the importance of reliable data. This may also be backed up with validation of those data that are most critical in determining which alternative procedure to adopt.

Two major classifications can be used to describe data that are applicable to most CQI initiatives: primary data and secondary data.

Primary Data

For CQI applications **primary data** can be defined as data that are collected specifically for the purposes of measuring process performance and improvement (i.e., providing information and knowledge about the specific practice setting or other healthcare environment that allows for improvement decisions to be made). The data presented in the case study earlier in this chapter, which were used to develop a run chart and a control chart, provide a good example of how primary data can be collected to provide knowledge and understanding about the need for process improvements. The case study data also illustrate how data can be formatted in different ways to answer different questions.

Sampling Considerations

Primary data analyses can involve collection of all available data for a fixed amount of time, as was done in the case study presented earlier, but quite often, the use of primary data is based on scientific sampling methods. In either case, a clearly defined sampling strategy is a first step.

Any sampling strategy that is used should start with a clear definition of the measures to be selected and the specific sampling methodology that is to be used to select patients or subjects. Two common methodologies in health care are probability (random) sampling and judgement sampling. Also important, especially when process behavior charts involving time-series displays of data are required, is defining how often sample elements will be collected.

Perla, Provost, and Murray (2013, p. 37) present two important concepts, based on the previous work of CQI pioneers, Deming and Shewhart, which provide guidance for sampling in improvement projects:

1. Obtaining just enough data based on past experience to guide our learning in the future.
2. Making full use of subject matter expertise in selecting the most appropriate samples.

Following these guidelines, CQI data are often drawn from judgement or purposive samples. This differs from the types of sampling methods that are used when the goal is to make predictions or derive estimates about large populations, as is the case with probability sampling. Judgement sampling is applicable to CQI when collecting data to measure improvement because such data often come from ongoing processes where we rarely have a fixed population of interest, but instead have a population that is changing over time. In process improvement studies, subject matter experts can be relied upon to choose areas, times of the day, or segments of the population to best represent the process being studied for CQI purposes. (Perla, Provost, & Murray, 2013). When random sampling is being used, for example to measure patient satisfaction, the first step is to carefully identify the **sampling frame**, defined as the source of data for the key elements that are to be analyzed and from which a sample is to be taken in order to make inferences about the larger population of interest, such as the medical care database from the institution whose quality we are assessing. Also critical to successful sampling strategies is careful determination of sample size. Sample size is always important because it plays a role in determining precision of estimates of quality metrics and directly affects study cost estimates (Levy & Lemeshow, 2008).

Also important in probability sampling is estimating the prevalence of the measures being studied:

> Our experience is that the first thing that often happens is that the designers overestimate the prevalence of the phenomenon being studied and hence underestimate the cost of finding enough affected individuals. When the recruitment of participants lags, the perception that the budget is fixed leads to a reduction in those cases surveyed, often jeopardizing what conclusions might be reached. The team must test those prevalence assumptions early on and plan realistically; one of the ways this can be accomplished is through the use of smaller "pilot" studies prior to carrying out the final survey.

> Inter-organizational access to data could make the task of assessing prevalence much easier as well. (McLaughlin & Kibbe, 2013, p. 346).

Whether probability or judgement sampling is used to select primary data, an important data quality concern is consideration of "non-sampling" errors (those that cannot be controlled by traditional sample design and statistical analysis adjustments). One very important example of this type of error that is quite prevalent in healthcare surveys, such as those used to measure patient satisfaction, is non-response (i.e., when the number who respond to a survey is smaller than the number selected to be studied). High levels of non-response can lead to selection bias and under-representation of the patients intended to be surveyed, sometimes also compromising the power of any statistical or process behavior analysis to be carried out based on these data. Quite simply, if a sample of patients is selected, and patients are contacted to provide feedback on patient care they have received, the data derived from such a survey will only be useful if a high response rate is obtained. This fact is true for all types of scientific surveys, but especially health surveys, including those that are used to assess and improve quality of care.

In addition to response rate issues, sample size must also be considered before making decisions related to quality of care. For example, when target sample sizes are not achieved, unacceptably high margins of error may invalidate conclusions based on survey data and especially comparisons over time or between departments or providers (Zusman, 2012). Decisions based on patient survey results also require careful consideration of the limits of the data and possible confounding factors that may influence findings; for example, there have been reports of physicians' employment and income being threatened based on poor satisfaction scores and some assertions that patient satisfaction scoring actually leads to poorer quality of care due to some providers altering medical treatment to influence patient satisfaction scores (Zusman, 2012). These examples underline how important it is to consider both the source of the data being collected in measuring quality and also how the results are used; attention to detail on both extremes—data collection and decision making—is critical.

Despite some criticism of patient satisfaction surveys, their use is increasing, which creates opportunities for continuous improvement. The Centers for Medicare & Medicaid (CMS) includes patient-reported measures in their National Quality Strategy and is continually working to advance standardization and reliability of patient reported measures (CMS, 2025).

The key point to be taken from this discussion is not to demean the efforts of measuring patient satisfaction; but in the same way that process improvement actions should only be taken when there is evidence of special cause variation, the same advice applies to only taking action based on surveys of (patients or providers) when data sources are proven to be reliable and high quality and are sufficient to support the level of decisions to which they are being applied. It is important for those who make use of survey data to carefully consider the basic principles of measurement and understanding variation before taking actions and whenever possible use knowledge gained to improve processes, including survey methodology processes.

Secondary Data

Secondary data are data collected for purposes other than the specific process performance or improvement initiative of interest. With the broad availability of information stored in electronic format, secondary data have become and will continue to be very useful for carrying out CQI initiatives. Secondary data sources that can support CQI include: clinic visit data (e.g., from electronic medical records), data registries (such as vaccine registries), and claims data. One rich source of claims data represents information available as part of the Medicare program, administered by the Centers for Medicare and Medicaid Services (CMS, 2025; McLaughlin & Kibbe, 2013). Although claims data have been frequently criticized for poor quality in the past, through the years, CMS has implemented a number of innovative approaches to drive quality improvement at the national level. These include adopting the use and promoting the development of standard quality measures, public reporting of quality measures, and pay-for-performance efforts to reward physicians for providing better quality care (McLaughlin & Kibbe, 2013). Quality improvement organizations (QIOs) serve as Medicare's primary agents for carrying out quality improvement initiatives using CMS (secondary) data sources (Schenck, McArdle, & Weiser, 2013). Chapter 11 provides examples and discussion of using secondary data to assess quality.

Conclusions

This chapter reviewed the importance of measurement concepts in CQI and presented an introduction to commonly used methods to assess and improve quality of healthcare processes. Most important is understanding variation in process behavior and, in particular, understanding the distinction between special and common causes of variation and how this understanding determines the most appropriate action for improvement. A case study designed to facilitate classroom discussion is provided to illustrate the application of these methodologies.

We have illustrated the effectiveness of plotting data over time as a way to understand process variation, preferably, using a run chart or ideally on a control chart/process behavior chart. Once the appropriate improvement strategy is determined, then the use of CQI tools described here together with other methodologies described in this text (e.g., PDSA) is recommended. A cautionary note that applies to all CQI tools and techniques is a warning that before we assume that a "magic bullet" exists which can be widely applied to guarantee quality, we should take time to carefully understand the context in which a CQI tool or procedure has been developed and understand the limits of its generalizability to other settings (Dixon-Woods & Martin, 2016). Furthermore, while tools are helpful in decision making, they are not a substitute for careful study, as in the sense of the S stage in a PDSA cycle of improvement—always keeping in mind the important goal of learning about the what and how of improvement.

This chapter has not attempted to exhaustively cover the broad range of topics associated with CQI tools and techniques. In addition to the material presented here, readers are urged to consult other resources referred to throughout this chapter as well as other chapters in this text; for example, Chapter 3, which discusses implementation science and Chapter 5, which addresses Lean/Six Sigma methodology.

Key Concepts and Terms

cause-and-effect diagrams
checklist
common causes of variation
control chart
customer
data-to-decision cycle
driver diagram
flowchart
frequency chart
market
noise
outcomes
P chart
Pareto diagram
primary data
process
process behavior chart
run chart
sampling frame
secondary data
signals
special causes of variation
stakeholder
structure

References

Agency for Healthcare Research and Quality (AHRQ). (2016). *Patient safety network–Glossary*. Retrieved May 15, 2025, from https://psnet.ahrq.gov/glossary-0

Balestracci, D. (2009). *Data sanity: A quantum leap to unprecedented results*. Medical Group Management Association.

Bennett, B., & Provost, L. (2015). What's your theory? Driver diagram serves as tool for building and testing theories for improvement. *Quality Progress, 48*(7), 36–43.

Berwick, D. M. (1996). A primer on leading the improvement of systems. *British Medical Journal, 312*(7031), 619–622.

Bialek, R., Duffy, G. L., & Moran, J. W. (2009). *The public health quality improvement handbook*. ASQ Quality Press.

Bosk, C. L., Dixon-Woods, M., Goeschel, C. A., & Pronovost, P. J. (2009). The art of medicine—Reality check for checklists. *The Lancet, 374*(9688), 444–445.

Carey, R. G., & Lloyd, R. C. (2001). *Measuring quality improvement in healthcare: A guide to statistical process control applications*. ASQ Quality Press.

Centers for Medicare and Medicaid Services (CMS). *CMS national quality strategy*. Retrieved May 15, 2025, from https://www.cms.gov/medicare/quality/meaningful-measures-initiative/cms-quality-strategy

Crosby, P. B. (1979). *Quality is free—The art of making quality certain*. Mentor.

Deming, W. E. (1986). *Out of the crisis*. Massachusetts Institute of Technology Center for Advanced Engineering Study.

Deming, W. E. (1993). *The new economics for industry, government, education*. Massachusetts Institute of Technology Center for Advanced Engineering Study.

Dixon-Woods, M., & Martin, G. P. (2016). Does quality improvement improve quality? *Future Healthcare Journal, 3*(3), 191–194.

Donabedian, A. (1980). *Explorations in quality assessment and monitoring: Vol. 1—The definition of quality and approaches to its assessment*. Health Administration Press.

Gawande, A. (2009). *The checklist manifesto*. Metropolitan Books.

Grove, A. S. (1995). *High output management*. Vintage Books.

Haynes, A. B., Weiser, T. G., Berry, W. R., Lipsitz, S. R., Breizat, A. H., Dellinger, E. P., . . . Safe Surgery Saves Lives Study Group. (2009). A surgery safety checklist to reduce morbidity and mortality in a global population. *The New England Journal of Medicine, 360*(5), 491–499.

Institute of Medicine (IOM). (2000). *To err is human: Building a safer health system*. National Academies Press.

Ishikawa, K. (1986). *Guide to quality control* (Asian Productivity Organization, Trans.). Kraus International Publications.

Juran, J. (1988). *Juran on planning for quality*. Free Press.

Kilbridge, P., & Classen, D. (2002). *Surveillance for adverse drug events: History, methods, and current issues*. VHA Research Series. VHA, Inc.

Kuebler, R. R., & Smith, H. (1976). *Statistics: A beginning*. Wiley and Sons.

Langley, G. J., Moen, R. D., Nolan, K. M., Nolan, T. W., Norman, C. L., & Provost, L. P. (2009). *Improvement guide: A practical approach to enhancing organizational performance* (2nd ed.). Jossey-Bass.

Levy, P. S., & Lemeshow, S. (2008). *Sampling of populations: Methods and applications* (4th ed.). Wiley and Sons.

Lloyd, R. C. (2019). *Quality health care: A guide to developing and using indicators* (2nd ed.). Jones & Bartlett Learning.

Loshin, D. L. (2010). *The practitioners' guide to data quality improvement*. Morgan Kaufman OMG Press.

McLaughlin, C. P., Johnson, J. K., & Sollecito, W. A. (2012). *Implementing continuous quality improvement in health care: A global casebook*. Jones & Bartlett Learning.

McLaughlin, C. P., & Kaluzny A. D. (Eds.). (2006). *Continuous quality improvement in health care* (3rd ed.). Jones and Bartlett Publishers.

McLaughlin, C. P., & Kibbe, D. C. (2013). The role of health information technology in quality improvement. In W. A. Sollecito & J. K. Johnson (Eds.), *Continuous quality improvement in health care* (4th ed.). Jones and Bartlett Publishers.

Nelson, E. C., Splaine, M. E., Batalden, P. B., & Plume, S. K. (1998). Building measurement and data collection into medical practice. *Annals of Internal Medicine, 128*(6), 460–466.

Nolan, T. W., & Provost, L. P. (1990). Understanding variation. *Quality Progress, 23*(5), 70–78.

Nolan, T. W., Provost, L. P., & Perla, R. J. (2016). Understanding variation—26 years later. *Quality Progress, 49*(11), 28–37. Retrieved September 17, 2017, from https://healthleadsusa.org

Nundy, S., Cooper, L. A., & Mate, K. S. (2022). The Quintuple Aim for health care improvement: A new imperative to advance health equity. *JAMA, 327*(6), 521–522. Retrieved September 29, 2024, from https://doi.org/10.1001/jama.2021.25181.

Perla, R. J., Provost, L. P., & Murray, S. K. (2011). The run chart: A simple analytical tool for learning from variation in healthcare processes. *BMJ Quality and Safety, 20*(1), 46–51.

Perla, R. J., Provost, L. P., & Murray, S. K. (2013). Sampling considerations for health care improvement. *Quality Management in Health Care, 22*(1), 36–47.

Project Management Institute. (2021). *A guide to the project management body of knowledge (PMBOK guide)* (7th ed.). PMI Publications.

Pronovost, P. J., Goeschel, C. A., Olsen, K. L., Pham, J. C., Miller, M. R., Berenholtz, S. M., . . . Clancy, C. M. (2009). Reducing health care hazards: Lessons from the commercial aviation safety team. *Health Affairs, 28*(Suppl. 1), w479–w489.

Pronovost, P. J., Needham, D., Berenholtz, S., Sinopoli, D., Chu, H., Cosgrove, S., . . . Goeschel, C. (2006). An intervention to reduce catheter-related bloodstream infections in the ICU. *The New England Journal of Medicine, 355*(26), 2725–2732.

Ross, T. K. (2014). *Health care quality management—Tools and applications*. Jossey-Bass.

R. *The R project for statistical computing*. Retrieved May 12, 2025, from https://www.R-project.org

Schenck, A. P., McArdle, J., & Weiser, R. (2013). Quality improvement organizations and continuous quality improvement in Medicare. In W. A. Sollecito & J. K. Johnson (Eds.), *Continuous quality improvement in health care* (4th ed.). Jones and Bartlett Publishers.

Shewhart, W. A. (1931). *Economic control of quality of manufactured product*. D. Van Nostrand Company.

Sollecito, W. A., & Hardison, D. (2020). Understanding variation, tools and data sources for CQI in health care.

In J. K. Johnson & W. A. Sollecito (Eds.), *Continuous quality improvement in health care* (5th ed.). Jones and Bartlett Learning.

Spath, P. L., & Kelly, D. L. (2017). *Applying quality management in healthcare: A systems approach* (4th ed.). Health Administration Press.

SQC Online. (2017). *About control charts*. Retrieved May 15, 2025, from https://www.sqconline.com

Wheeler, D. J. (2000). *Understanding variation: The key to managing chaos*, (2nd ed.). SPC Press.

Wheeler, D. J., & Chambers, D. S. (2010). *Understanding statistical process control* (3rd ed.). SPC Press.

Zusman, E. E. (2012). HCAHPS replaces Press Ganey as quality measure for patient hospital experience. *Neurosurgery, 71*(2), N21–N24. Retrieved August 12, 2017, from https://doi.org/10.1227/01.neu.0000417536.07871.ed

CHAPTER 5

Lean and Six Sigma Management: Building a Foundation for Optimal Patient Care Using Patient Flow Physics

Ed Popovich, Hal Wiggin, and Paul Barach

CHAPTER OUTLINE

Introduction

High-performing healthcare organizations distinguish themselves by relentlessly and continuously improving services and outcomes around what matters most to patients. They achieve this through disciplined process-improvement systems that translate clinical insight into reliable, high-quality care. Continuous Quality Improvement (CQI), Lean Management Systems (LMS), and Lean Six Sigma (LSS) are complementary leadership and improvement philosophies that provide a systematic framework, a set of analytic and operational tools, and a shared way of thinking about how to design, study, and improve clinical work. Together, these approaches enable organizations to improve patient flow, reduce unwarranted variation, and strengthen safety, efficiency, and reliability across care processes. Although LMS and LSS are broadly applicable across health systems—including public health and resource-constrained settings—this chapter focuses primarily on their application in health care delivery organizations in high-income countries.

Lean and Six Sigma Management Defined

Six Sigma, (sigma being the Greek symbol used in statistics to measure variation), utilizes statistical methods to identify and reduce variation in processes (Duffy, Farmer, & Moran, 2009). (See Chapter 4 for a detailed description of types and causes of variability.) Programs and organizations become more manageable and predictable when variation is reduced.

In 1986, when Motorola originated and launched the continuous improvement and innovation effort they called *Six Sigma*, it was an evolution of quality methods that originated in the United States and Japan that were further developed at Motorola. The U.S. and Japanese quality leaders, followed by other companies, learned from each other as they evolved systems of quality management. Ford Motor Company developed mass production systems that Toyota broadened into the Toyota Production System (TPS) through their emphasis on elimination of waste, which they termed *muda*, *muri*, and *mura* (McManus, 2013).

Muda: Wasting Resources

Muda is the waste due to non-value-added activities, which was translated by companies in the United States as elimination of waste in the use of seven resources or in the following practices: transportation, inventory, motion during production, waiting time spent during production, over-processing (by doing more than necessary), over-production (by producing more products or items than needed), and defects, such as producing faulty parts or making mistakes in the process. Often, the focus of the **Lean Management System (LMS)** in health care is reducing *muda*, especially with respect to waiting time experienced by patients, mistakes or "near misses" in patient care, transitions in patient care due to shift changes in staffing, transportation and/or motion in moving patients between care providers or services, and managing inventory of equipment and supplies. Thus, examples of waste in health care include wasted inventory, rework, excess waiting times—whether by patients or staff members who need results of another provider's inputs to make decisions, lost time, errors, or extra work associated with poor processing of information or outdated procedures, and waste from transporting patients unnecessarily (Spath & Kelly, 2017). LMS implements leader standard work, visual controls, and daily accountability (Mann, 2015).

Muri: Overburdening Staff and Equipment

Muri is the waste due to over-burdening the people or equipment in a process, as processes that are balanced are desirable. Less-than-optimal attention paid to *muri* in health care often is evident when physicians and staff feel overwhelmed with the level of effort required for them to provide patient care, document the care provided, address regulatory reporting requirements, attend required meetings, and provide all the support beyond the efforts required for patient care. Burnout is experienced by many physicians and healthcare providers (Hartwell, 2023). Improving the balance of processes is an imperative in reliable patient care delivery.

Mura: Uneven Process Workflow

Mura is the waste due to unevenness in workflow processes. *Mura* is the reason for the development of "just-in-time" production systems so that the process flow is more predictable and consistent. In health care, the desire to "get things off your plate" and send it to the next function in the process is common. In other words, rather than providing each person what is needed at the time it is needed, there is a tendency to batch up work and then send it in "one pile" to the next step downstream in the process. Examples include batch reading of radiology exams rather than reading the exam at the time the patient is present and providing the results for each individual patient as they progress through the patient care process. Morning blood draws in an acute care setting are another example, as the blood is drawn and sent to pathology in batches to do the analyses.

How Six Sigma Originated

Motorola was very much aware of the quality methodology practiced in Japan going back to Deming's seminal contributions in 1950's, including just-in-time processing, *Poka-Yoke* ("fool-proofing processes"), process simplification, and continuous improvement by all staff (Harry, 1988). They observed that efficient and effective process flow through the elimination or reduction of non-value-added processing could not only reduce the number of errors or defects in production, but it also could increase the consistency of performance of the process. Motorola decided to select skilled staff with technical backgrounds and train them in advanced quality, engineering, manufacturing, and statistical methodology, which in turn facilitated their ability to improve or innovate the design of both their products and work processes. Motorola established two improvement goals as part of what they defined as their Total Customer Satisfaction (TCS) strategy:

1. All defects were to be reduced 10-fold every 2 years, which implies a 68% improvement per year. For example, a process yielding a success rate of 90% is expected to perform at a 96.8% success rate at the end of Year 1, and 99% at the end of Year 2. Note that in the 2 years, the failure rate would be expected to drop from 10% to 1%, which is a 10-fold improvement.
2. All core processes must reduce their cycle time (lead time) by 50% within 2 years.

To achieve these goals, Motorola recognized that:

- Variation in process performance can lead to greater defect/error rates. Therefore, a reduction in process variation can induce a lower rate of defects, where a defect was defined as the failure of a process to achieve its goals.
- Speeding up processes requires the elimination of unnecessary (e.g., non-value-added) tasks or steps since simply doing the same steps faster to achieve a 50% reduction in cycle time often will drive more defects while overwhelming workers and which violates the simultaneous goal of a reduction in defect rates.

In 1990, the term "Lean Production" received attention due to the book *The Machine That Changed the World* by James Womack, Daniel Jones, and Daniel Roos. The authors explained that mass production systems emanating from Toyota via Ford and other companies were evolving into a coherent narrative that enabled systems requiring less time for production, less effort from people, lower inventories of supplies, and less capital investment. Remarkably, this new system of work yielded fewer defects, and was able to better mass customization by serving smaller and smaller market sizes at lower costs.

In 1996, Womack & Jones published *Lean Thinking*, which distilled the LMS theory into five principles:

1. The customer defines value.
2. Organizations should identify the value stream in every process and seek to eliminate all wasted steps that do not add value.
3. Organizations should make the product (or, in health care, management of the patient's care) flow through the steps of the value-added process continuously.
4. Organizations require that subsequent steps in the process "pull" products (or patients) from the previous process steps rather than push them forward, causing them to batch up waiting for the next step.

5. Organizations should work to continuously improve, and to reduce steps, time, costs, and the information (data) needed to serve the customer (again, the patient in our case) (Anthony, Palsuk, Gupta, Mishra, & Barach, 2018).

It was not until the later 1990s that LMS evolved into the time-based techniques "Lean," although these methods had already been incorporated into Motorola's two simultaneous goals of the Six Sigma program. The more technical analyses that incorporated variation and defect reduction were called Six Sigma by many, rather than the more encompassing meaning behind Six Sigma as envisioned by Motorola. Motorola viewed what later became called LMS and Six Sigma as separate management activities that were "two sides of the same coin," which they simply called Six Sigma. For example, having fewer steps to accomplish the same process leads to fewer steps to make errors, less variation across the process, and ultimately to better, cheaper, and faster manufacturing processes.

Michael George is one of the people credited with popularizing the term "**Lean Six Sigma**." Acknowledging this "two sides of the same coin," he wrote (George, 2002, p. 7):

> Lean Six Sigma is a methodology that maximizes shareholder value by achieving the fastest rate of customer satisfaction, cost, quality, process speed, and invested capital. The fusion of LMS and Six Sigma is required because:
>
> - LMS cannot bring a process under statistical control.
> - Six Sigma alone cannot dramatically improve process speed or reduce invested capital.

Thomas Jackson and Karen Jones note that organizations cannot incorporate a LMS overnight. More specifically:

> To support lean production, management must build, nurture leaders, and support the logic and machinery that drives lean production. Lean Management is a sophisticated practice built around several key conceptual and physical tools. It is about looking at your organization in an entirely different way, describing its processes with *a new vocabulary*. The process that delivers lean management has been designed, tested, and refined into what we call the lean management system. This system reflects the principles and methodologies of leading international managers and consultants. (Jackson & Jones, 1996, pp. 7–8)

"Lean Six Sigma" (LSS) adoption in health care and public health represents an evolution resulting in part from alliances and interchanges with corporate and government partners, and it promoted the evolution of CQI across several industries (Duffy, Farmer, & Moran, 2009). The combination of LMS and Six Sigma is used in a wide range of healthcare applications, and provides a synergistic methodology for analyzing, and reducing or eliminating waste in healthcare processes.

The following sections of this chapter will define these methodologies in greater detail by describing their use in healthcare settings and, in particular, by illustrating hospital and health system flow applications.

Patient Flow as an Application of LSS

While Lean focuses on eliminating waste, Six Sigma concentrates on reducing variation. Together they form Lean Six Sigma, a powerful approach for improving healthcare operations. Healthcare organizations can develop a strategic and competitive advantage by improving value-added activities (Byrne, 2013, p. xi). Improving process "flow" is one of the primary goals of LSS and continuous quality improvement (CQI). A value stream or process with optimum flow would be analogous to a river that cascades over a cliff and rages through a narrow gorge, flowing downhill with no bends, rocks, or other impediments. This is akin to a clinic with high patient flow and demand that has the right number of highly skilled staff working with patients to meet their care needs using well-designed processes that have minimal waste (Sanchez & Barach, 2012). Staff are led by patient-focused leaders who have access to real-time data to manage with the "right" data, and these leaders empower staff to continuously improve the workplace as they deliver exceptional care.

With the advent of the 21st century, there have been discernable improvements in the efficiency and effectiveness of care in some settings, including broader applications of what has been called the Quintuple Aim of Health Care: improving (1) the experience of care and (2) population health while (3) reducing costs, (4) improving staff wellness, and (5) advancing health equity (Berwick, Nolan, & Whittington, 2008; Bodenheimer T & Sinsky C, 2014; Itchhaporia D, 2021). However, despite this progress, patients still experience unacceptable harm; processes are not as efficient as they could be; and costs continue to rise at alarming rates, while quality issues remain (Wong, Ahmed, Ray, et al., 2021). The key to ensuring CQI in healthcare organizations is changing the organizational culture, as discussed in Chapter 2. Organizations seeking to be efficient and effective in care delivery need to embed a culture that identifies wasteful effort, seeks ways to continually improve existing processes, and designs processes for those that do not currently exist to increase efficiency and effectiveness in meeting their outcomes with no wasted effort. Womack and Jones correctly observe that ". . .patients often discover that the time spent on treatment was a tiny fraction of the time you spent going through the 'process.' Mostly you were sitting and waiting ('patient' is clearly the right word) or moving about to the next step in the diagnosis and treatment. . ." (2003, p. 50).

If waiting is a non-value-adding activity, why do most healthcare facilities incorporate a formal "waiting" room into their care delivery processes? When flow is attained and information, materials, and activity proceed seamlessly through processes without interruption, then optimal experiences can occur. This is more likely to happen if leaders ensure "rules that require the learning of skills, they set up goals, they provide feedback, and they make control possible. They facilitate concentration and involvement by making the activity as distinct as possible from the so-called paramount reality of everyday existence" (Csikszentmihalyi, 1990, p. 72).

This "ideal state" can be approached and accomplished in real terms by integrating the principles that govern patient flow and variation management—we call it **Patient Flow Physics**, a nod to the universality of the physical rules that govern the universe and LMS (Popovich, Wiggin, et al., 2020). This powerful gestalt can greatly increase the achievement of key process core measures in health care. (Readers are also referred to similar concepts related to time management that are illustrated by control chart analyses of a clinic start-up time in Chapter 4.) We begin the discussion with two real-world examples, the first from an emergency department (ED), and the second from an ambulatory screening mammography clinic.

Applying LSS to Patient Flow in a Community Hospital Emergency Department

Previously, one of the authors (EP) was a Vice President for Enterprise Excellence (outside health care, this position is often termed operational excellence leader) at a non-profit private hospital, where he sought to improve both the patient flow in the ED and the women's mammography service lines. The hospital was located in a wealthy south Florida community that supported the hospital through a large foundation. The board was concerned about reports from some wealthy benefactors that the waiting times to see a physician in the ED were too long. EDs are often called the "front door" to the hospital, in that approximately 65% of patients admitted to the hospital arrive via the ED. Long wait times at various times of the day in the ED lead to patient and family dissatisfaction, frustration by staff and the community, and in turn may lead to reducing charitable donations to a hospital foundation.

One of the authors (EP) was involved in the early days of the evolution of LSS at Motorola and had the opportunity to learn about the use of a concept called Factory Physics™. Although

LSS was recognized as a philosophy for process improvement and design, it was in its early days of being utilized by hospital systems. **Factory Physics** describes the "laws" that govern patient process flow much like physics is a science describing the "laws" that govern the forces on physical materials in our world. Factory Physics modeling was used to improve the understanding of patient flow through the ED from the time the physician first encountered the patient until a decision was made as to whether to discharge the patient to go home ("treat-to-street" cycle time) or to admit the patient to the hospital ("doctor-to-decision" cycle time). In addition, the time between when a decision was made until the patient left the ED to go home or was moved to an in-patient room was termed the "decision-to-disposition" cycle time. At a high level, patient demand in the ED was addressed by representing the number of patients presenting to the ED at each hour of the day and at each day of the week, as shown in **Figure 5.1**.

John Tukey introduced the box-and-whiskers plot (aka box plot) as part of his toolkit for exploratory data analysis (Tukey, 1977). The box plot is a compact distributional summary, displaying less detail than a histogram but more compact. Box plots use robust summary statistics and actual data points and are easy to compute and interpret. They are especially useful for comparing distributions across different groups.

Figure 5.1 shows a box plot of patient arrivals to this community hospital ED by the hour of the day. Each box has a median line in the box that represents the 50th percentile (median) number

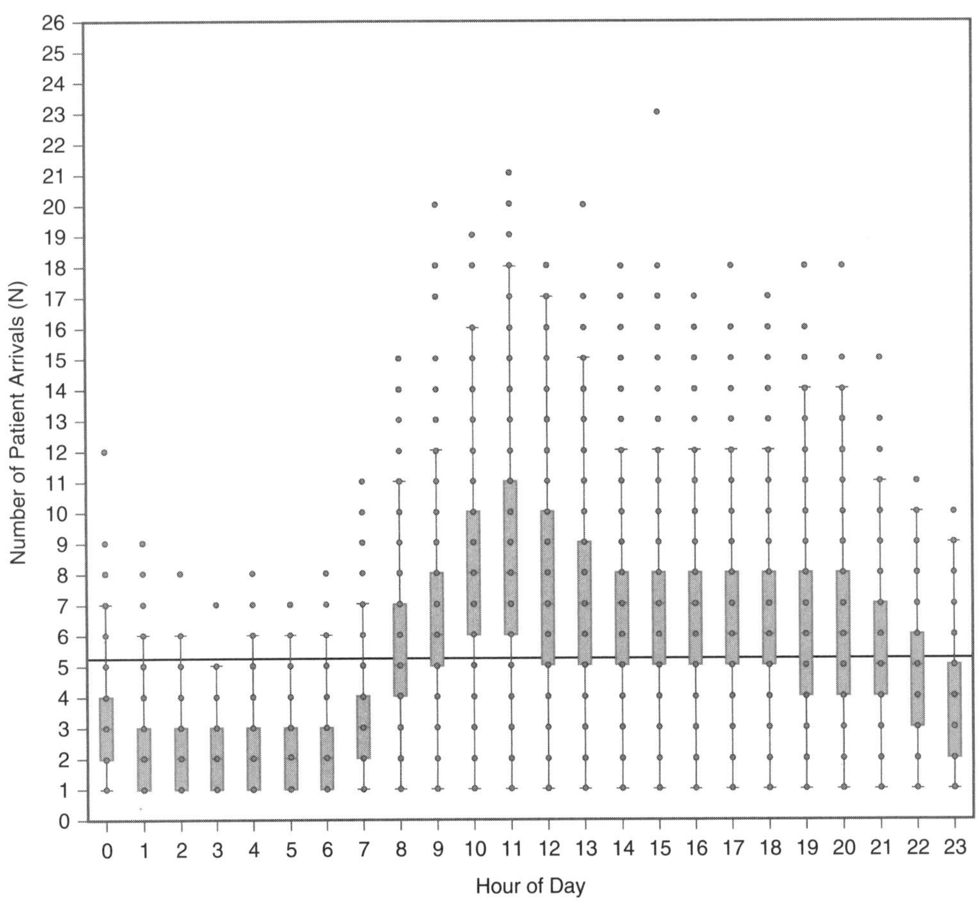

Figure 5.1 Box Plot of Patient Arrivals by Hour of Day

of arrivals for each hour. The bottom of the box represents the 25th percentile, and the top of the box represents the 75th percentile of patient arrivals each hour. The distant points (outliers) outside the box represent the range of patient arrivals each hour, with those points that are larger than the top of the lines extending from each box representing outliers in the number of patient arrivals that seldom occur but were observed.

Distinct, daily patterns in patient arrivals were discovered, i.e., days of the week had hourly arrival patterns that were similar from week to week. Knowing the demand patterns helps a healthcare administrator be better prepared to address the demand. Some of the emerging questions included:

1. How does the demand pattern support management decisions and lead to more effective staffing up- and downstream?
2. What are the optimal levels of staffing to meet patient demand?
3. Does the nature of the demand vary over the course of the day?
4. Are there certain "chief complaints" or issues that are seen more often during a certain time of the day or on particular days of the week?
5. Does the type of staff skills needed differ at various times of the day or on certain days of the week?
6. What should the organization do, if anything, to be prepared to handle the variation and demand outliers, including during mass casualty or pandemic events?

If the organization is only staffed for the median hourly demand, then 50% of the time, the demand will be greater than expected. This can contribute to increased waiting times and dissatisfaction by patients that choose to stay and wait. Delays can also adversely affect clinical outcomes. Of course, some patients may choose to leave and go elsewhere rather than wait, which may lead to increased patient risks, lower facility revenue, and may undermine the organization's community reputation.

Further, the study of time of day, day of week, along with primary clinical issues of patients that were admitted yields information about the patient demands on each floor and unit of the hospital. For example, often hospitals have rules for discharging patients (e.g., all patients going home on a certain day are to be discharged by 2 PM). Unfortunately, the data indicated that the demand for beds within the hospital from patients admitted by the ED did not synchronize with the 2 PM discharge goal. Therefore, some units had patients in beds who were not discharged by 2 PM, although there was a need for these beds to relieve the congestion in the ED. The Patient Flow Physics model predicted the number of beds that were likely to be needed by each unit, stratified by both the day of the week and the time of the day. Knowing the demand requirements for beds in advance allowed each floor to identify the patients most likely to go home each day and determine which patients were likely to be discharged by each hour to meet the bed needs of the ED. Simply put, if the flow out of each unit at least closely approximates the flow into each unit by day of the week and time of day, then there should be less back-up of patients in the ED. In turn, this allows patients to flow smoothly into and out of the ED.

Incorporating process and flow data can facilitate effective handling of patient demand, utilization of resources such as staff skills, and provide rich input as to where process improvements can be applied to reduce waiting time, poor staff utilization, and other wasteful aspects. Applying the Factory Physics principles to healthcare patient flow through the ED led to better-managed patient volume, better provider and staff scheduling, and higher satisfaction among patients and care providers.

Applying LSS to Patient Flow in Community Hospital Mammography Service

The women's mammography service line at the hospital also benefited significantly. At the beginning of the effort, the women who started their diagnostic journey with a self-referral mammography and were diagnosed with cancer would find, on average, that it took 8 weeks to move through the diagnostic journey (e.g., screening, focused mammography views, ultrasound, biopsy, MRI) to treatment, which may include radiation, chemotherapy, and surgery. The journey was reduced to one week or less after detailed assessment of the process and utilization of LSS. The significance of this improvement cannot be understated: The earlier cancer is identified and treatment begun, the greater the chance for improved clinical outcomes, patient satisfaction, and overall quality of life (Viau & Southern, 2007).

The Patient Flow Physics Framework

The Patient Flow Physics framework provides a performance model that describes how items (patients and information) flow through a patient care process. This framework can help improve the control and predictability of healthcare operation service lines. This framework recognizes that all processes consist of:

1. Demand
2. Transformation
3. Inventory

Demand is the rate at which patients present to the patient care organization. *Transformation* is the activity that converts sick patients into healthy ones or, at least, brings wellness from illness or injury. *Inventory* consists of both the supplies used for treating patients and the patients who are waiting for the next stage of their patient care.

Because the healthcare network consists of interconnected elements, one is able to characterize and manage patient flows in three different arenas:

1. Flow *into* the patient care process (e.g., ED or out-patient clinic);
2. Flow *through* the patient care process; and
3. Flow *out* of the patient care process.

Whether the utilization or flow is smooth or chaotic, fast or slow, restricted or unrestricted, depends on a range of factors internal as well as external to the patient care process. Patient flow *into* the ED is a consequence of patient flows from emergency medical services, nursing homes, transfers from other hospitals, direct patient admits (referrals by outside physicians), and walk-in patients. The patterns and sources of patient arrivals are very important because they critically influence the queuing effects on the input side of the ED or, in general, of any patient care process. Queuing theory provides an accurate means of determining the appropriate supply of beds.

Understanding the patterns and sources can often allow better management of demand. For example, EDs can choose to divert patients from emergency medical services to other EDs. Also, EDs are often utilized by outside physicians to directly admit patients to a hospital in-patient setting. Why does this happen? Referring physicians recognize that their patients will have tests associated with admission carried out without delay ("stat" orders) in the ED, meaning they are prioritized and completed as soon as possible, versus the expected delays by going to the ambulatory clinic. Therefore, EDs could better work with outside physicians to schedule direct patient admits for less busy times of the day, thus reducing the demand during peak demand times and improving the hospital's relationships with community providers. For patients that are treated in the ED and are not admitted yet may want follow-up support from the ED (e.g., a patient wanting stiches removed), the ED can either set up an appointment during a typically less busy time in the ED or suggest the best dates/times to the patient for the follow up. In effect, this allows for opportunity to reduce demand in typically busy times in the ED and reduce patient waiting times.

Patients are different in the time and resources required to manage their illnesses. Patient flow through the ED is also a function of ED resource utilization and the variability associated with differences between staff and ED providers. ***Utilization*** of ED providers is of high concern. These providers include physicians (MDs and DOs), physician assistants (PAs), and nurse practitioners (NPs). Another key resource that often serves as a constraint in EDs are the ED beds. Whenever an ED requires each new patient to be seen in an ED bed, patients may be waiting longer to be seen when beds are filled with patients. Some EDs have recognized that having ED beds as a constraint can be overcome through seeing patients in triage areas without beds where they can be assessed and treated rapidly (FitzGerald, Jelinek, Scott, & Gerdtz, 2009).

A three-part series published in 2013–2014 called *Cracking the Code: Fixing the Crowded Emergency Department*, written by Dr. Joseph Guarisco, Chair of Emergency Services at Ochsner Health System in New Orleans, captures many of these ideas. The Ochsner Health System uses qTrack for "quick sorting" of patients, which protects ED beds from being over-utilized. Some ED professionals will invoke the rule of thumb that "vertical patients should remain vertical, while horizontal patients should remain horizontal," meaning that those patients who can walk in are vertical and are often able to be treated while standing or sitting. The patients who arrive via emergency medical transport (EMT) are often in a stretcher and should remain lying on a bed.

Patient flow *out* of the ED is crucial to avoid overly long stays in the ED. The patients who are admitted to the hospital yet are "blocked" from being transported to in-patient units will remain in the ED until an in-patient unit can accept the patient. These patients are referred to as "ED boarded" patients. (Croft, Barach, Bona, et al., 2025). The reason **ED boarding** arises may be due to a lack of transport personnel, unavailability of consulting physicians (consults), and insufficient beds (either in the hospital or perhaps destinations outside of the hospital). Patient flow out of the ED is an issue during winter seasons when demand is greatest; for example, during the winter in Florida, there is often a significant increase in part-time residents and visitors, which may lead to an increase in the in-patient census.

Cycle ***times*** through a care process can depend upon flow through and out of a care process. This, of course, can be influenced by the design of the care process, for example, whether processes are coupled in series or in parallel and whether process steps serve a useful function or exist merely because of physician traditions and organizational legacy.

Patient Flow and the VUT Equation

Patient flow through and out of a patient care process is often the focus of clinical operations. The flow *into* patient care processes is impacted by the demand that operations try to manage. The flow *through* patient care processes is impacted by the utilization of key resources (e.g., staffing levels, providers available, equipment, *and* room availability) to keep patients flowing smoothly through the care processes. The flow *out* of patient care processes is impacted by both internal resources and readiness of resources outside of the current patient care process. For example, it is more difficult to discharge some older patients if there are not enough available beds in skilled nursing facilities (SNF) in the community. Likewise, limited behavioral health program options impact the release of patients needing these services.

In their book *Factory Physics: Foundations of Manufacturing Management*, Hopp & Spearman (2008) provide the "laws that govern process flow" in manufacturing systems. Interestingly, just as the laws of physics are those that define and describe motion and gravity, the principles of process flow can also describe flow in healthcare processes. One of the concepts discussed in the book is the **VUT equation** (**Box 5.1**).

Patient wait times are driven by three fundamental forces in any service system:

- **Variability (V)** – how unpredictable arrivals and service times are
- **Utilization (U)** – how busy the system is
- **Time (T)** – the resulting waiting experienced by patients

Box 5.1 **VUT Equation**

Average Patient Flow Care Time = Variation (V) × Utilization (U) × Process Time (T)

The **VUT equation** captures how these factors interact. As variability or utilization increase, waiting times grow—often dramatically. It is sufficient for our discussion to understand that anything that increases the variation (V), increases resource utilization (U), or operates in processes that are designed to take a long time (T) will lead to increases in average patient flow care time. In other words, to reduce the overall cycle time in the care of patients requires efforts to reduce the variation in the clinical processes, reduce utilization of key resources (e.g., having extra capacity in terms of resources), and optimize the process design to eliminate wasted time.

The following paragraphs describe V, U, and T and provide examples as they relate to patient care and flow.

Variation

Knowledge of process variation is one of the four parts of W. Edwards Deming's System of Profound Knowledge (Deming, 1993, pp. 98–99):

> Variation will always be, between people, in output, in service, and in product. What is the variation trying to tell us about a process, and about the people who work in it? . . . . A process may be in statistical control or it may not be. In the state of statistical control, the variation to expect in the future is predictable. Costs, performance, quality, and quantity are predictable. [Walter] Shewhart called this the stable state. If the process is not stable, then it is unstable. Its performance is not predictable.

Variation is either common or special. **Common cause variation** can be the routine patient census number increases and decreases across hours, days, and seasons. **Special cause variation** is not random, and it can be assigned to special events or circumstances such as with extremely high patient count in an ED due to a major, mass casualty event, new providers such as in July when new trainees arrive or an epidemic such as COVID-19 (Riguzzi C, et al. 2014). It could also be attributed to an increase in medical errors due to new equipment failures.

Causes of variation in data can be detected with control charts, which are run charts (or time-series graphs) that incorporate upper and lower control (sigma) lines (see Chapter 4 and examples later in the chapter) (Johnson, J. & Barach, P., 2010). There are eight universally accepted decision rules that are applied to detect extreme points from the mean, trends, and the unusual patterns that are low probability events. Wheeler (2000) prefers the name *process behavior charts* because it better describes the variation as the "voice of the process." These charts can help distinguish between routine, always occurring "noise" vs. "signals" that are hopefully less frequent indications of some special cause variation. If important, these signals should initiate an investigation of possible influencing factors or root causes. Finally, data and variation can only be understood in the context in which they were collected (Hesselink et al., 2013). More specifically, the analysis must be applied to a specific process; individual or group; period of time; or the use of specific material or equipment. This latter point is critical and often misunderstood.

Control charts must use rational sampling and rational subgrouping to produce valid results (Wheeler, 1995). For example, a study of length of stay over time should include groups of similar patients or lab turn-around times should be based on the same types of laboratory tests. Selection of the time and data must be consistent and based on logic. When data collection is properly conducted, the three sigma limits *and* within-group variation will help identify legitimate process "signals." The goal of rational subgrouping is to identify differences between short- and longer-term process variation at single points in time. The variables that effect variation are random if there were no deliberate changes to the process. Purposeful modifications could include staffing changes, new devices or equipment, such as more bronchoscopes or surgical microscopes, or the introduction of new treatment protocols. If data are regularly collected and analyzed, staff will more likely know "what is different."

Jensen and Mayer (2015) propose the terms natural and artificial variation. Natural variation is commonly occurring and due to chance, bias, or an artifact in data collection. Variation is natural and it is going to happen. It cannot be eliminated but it can be managed. On the other hand, artificial variation "is neither necessary nor random. It is driven by largely unknown, ignored, or unchallenged priorities." It is like the self-inflicted wound of scheduling elective surgeries during busy, prime hours.

We posit that variation can be attributed to:

- Demand for patient flow into the processes
- Differences in patient needs (e.g., presenting problems, ambulatory vs. handicapped, or older vs. younger)
- Differences in how care is delivered by clinical staff
- Reliability of patient care and handoffs to avoid errors, and rework
- Availability of resources internal or outside current patient care processes (e.g., rehabilitation, assisted living or skilled nursing facilities, family support, and in-patient care units)

Hospital leaders work to understand how fluctuations in demand and constraints in key resources affect the movement of patients through care. We have found the following observations about managing variation to be helpful.

(i) Learn the patterns of demand. Although demand of clinical processes can vary significantly from day to day or within a day, there are tools, including run charts, control charts, and box plots, that can lead to a better understanding of demand variation in terms of when it may occur and how much variation during the day it can cause. For example, grocery stores use forecasts to manage inventory along with staffing matched to customer demand. Some stores will provide extra capacity by having enough check-out lanes for each hour in a day for each day of the week. They also call "all baggers" to the front when lines start forming. And just as grocery stores know the customer demand by day of week and hour of day, similarly for EDs, Mondays will look like other Mondays, Tuesdays like other Tuesdays, and so forth. Dr. Dave Eitel, an emergency medicine physician who co-created the Emergency Services Index (ESI) Triage protocols, would often say that he knew when the typical patient was arriving at the ED, but just did not know their name (AHRQ, 2012). Eitel recommended that EDs adopt grocery store practices for forecasting peaks and valleys in demand and adjust capacity accordingly.

(ii) Standardize care for typical patients. Clinical practice variation can be addressed through some form of standardization as discussed later in this chapter in LMS practices. Healthcare systems often use standard order sets to address the 80/20 rule, where 80% of the patients presenting with known conditions can be handled with a basic order set. For example, although patients that visit an ED may be unique, experienced providers will recognize that most of these patients present a similar patient pattern, and standard order sets can be used effectively. "Standard order sets" can be utilized to quickly initiate patient treatments / tests (e.g., blood tests) with less involvement of critical physician resources. The care for these "typical" patients will therefore be more consistent and standardized. The patients presenting with unusual conditions or an unusual manifestation of these conditions can then be addressed with extra attention of medical staff or with different procedures.

(iii) Standardization of activities. An effective way to reduce variation by ensuring that staff perform the same duties in the same preferred ways. Only best practices are standardized so this also increases quality. According to Imai (2012, pp. 54–55), "standards represent the best, easiest, and safest way to do a job." They also preserve organizational knowledge and expertise and facilitate valid measurement of organizational performance. Standards can also help clarify cause and effect relationships and expedite maintenance and improvement.

(iv) Put population data to work. Population health analytics allows tailoring the management approach for various patient demographics and conditions, thus reducing the practice variation and lessening the time needed to address each patient's needs. This knowledge can be readily applied to individual disease management.

(v) Learn from other organizations that have dealt with high variability. High-reliability organizations (HROs) have characteristics that parallel many features of the healthcare environments (i.e., EDs, operating rooms, intensive care units, etc.), including the use of complex technologies, a fast-paced tempo of operations, and a high level of risk, yet they manifest spectacularly low error rates (Sanchez & Barach, 2012). HROs are required to respond to a wide variety of situations under changing environmental conditions in a reliable and consistent way. Examples of HROs include aircraft carriers, nuclear power plants (Apostolakis & Barach, 2003), and firefighting teams. Weick and Sutcliffe (2001) have studied these industries and found that they share an extraordinary capacity to discover and manage unexpected events resulting in exceptional safety and consistent levels of performance despite a fast-changing external environment. HRO methodologies and practices can offer clinical care with greater patient safety, less process rework, improved patient outcomes, and greater patient satisfaction (Oster & Braaten, 2016; Tamuz & Harrison, 2006). Similarly, organizations can learn from other organizations that have found ways to reduce high variability in demand, resource utilization, and improved patient flow processes.

(vi) Create buffers. Buffer management is an effective approach for reducing and mitigating the negative aspects of excessive and/or uncontrolled variation. Buffers are like shock absorbers on cars. Instead of reducing bumps in the road for a car, buffers reduce or dampen the effect of variability when trying to synchronize demand to transformation (Pound, Bell, & Spearman, 2014, p. 51). There are time, capacity, and inventory buffers. Time buffers include waiting times and extra available time that can be used. Capacity buffers are the numbers of staff, beds, and equipment that can be used to treat patients. Inventory buffers can be supplies or patients' waiting for the next step in a process. Buffers must be properly managed, and they cannot be too large. Patients do not like to wait and unused capacity and inventory costs money. The creative use of buffers can greatly reduce patient length of stay. A family practitioner liked to spend extra time with certain patients to socialize. Unfortunately, this usually altered the carefully constructed patient schedule. He did not want to give up this "special" time so it was suggested that he see those patients just before his lunch break or at the end of the day. It proved an effective compromise.

Utilization

Utilization refers to the use of resources. Utilization without any waste or non-value-added activities is an "efficient" process (see the previous *muri* discussion). These resources are more technically referred to as "capacity." Utilization is impacted by:

- Available staffing capacity each hour to handle variation in demand
- Availability of resources such as computer systems, beds/treatment rooms, equipment in imaging/labs, and transportation
- Sufficient availability of inventory such as blood, medications, medical devices including stents/splints, transport equipment, or patients ready for the next procedure
- Financial resources to access services
- The time to complete clinical and administrative activities
- Resources for training and other staff development

This "capacity" must be available across the basic value stream (**Figure 5.2**) and at each step of the microsystem processes.

When the population does not have adequate and effective prevention services, they can develop serious chronic illness conditions that require

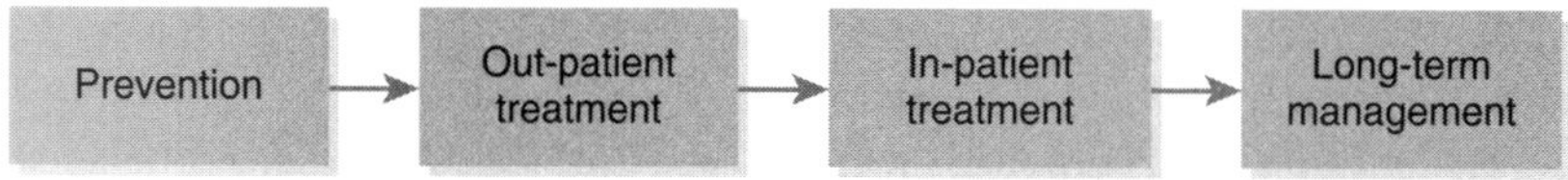

Figure 5.2 Generic High-Level Healthcare Value Stream

secondary or tertiary treatment. Families without health insurance tend to use more expensive ED services because they cannot access ambulatory and out-patient care. A lack of in-patient beds contributes to ED boarding, as does limited availability of SNFs. Inadequate staffing levels add to lengths of stay and decrease the quality of patient care. Both under- and over-utilization of resources can be problematic.

Capacity issues, poor process design, and/or unsatisfactory staff performance contribute to process bottlenecks which are the slowest activity steps. One way to address capacity is to build in "slack" as "a cushion or buffer of actual or potential resources which allows an organization to adapt successfully to internal pressures for adjustment or to external pressures for change in policy as well as to initiate changes in strategy. . ." (Lawson, 2001, pp. 125–131). Slack is uncommitted staff, space, and equipment. It is the antidote for the "myth of 100% efficiency." First, if people are always busy with regular work duties, they have no flexibility or time for reflecting, thinking, planning, training, or improving. (DeMarco, 2001). CQI projects require staff time and resources. Busy staff resent projects being dumped on their already "full plates" (Barach & Kleinman, 2018).

Experienced hospital executives know that ED boarding tends to increase when in-patient bed usage exceeds 80%. The Toyota Production System (TPS) has been the very effective model for many LMS turnaround initiatives in hospitals systems like Virginia Mason (Kenney, 2010). TPS frees up time for quality by empowering workers to "fix" errors when they occur, even if it slows down or stops "the line." They have lower manager- and supervisor-to-staff ratios, which aids in problem solving at the point of care and staff coaching. They also take more time to plan new products and services to "get it right," thus saving significant resources before production and delivery commences.

There are many ways to keep utilization of key resources low:

1. Keeping key resources such as providers and beds in an ED utilized less than 80% of the time allows for better management of demand and enables the system to address more effectively variation in patient flow (see *muri* discussed previously);
2. Understanding variation in demand and patients will allow for better scheduling of people resources (see *mura* discussed previously); and
3. Applying box plots of variation as explained earlier in this chapter allows for determining the 75th percentile of demand and process variation so that adjusting scheduling to meet the demands of the 75th percentile will lessen the impact of overall process demand and minimize flow variation.

Time

Slow and inefficient healthcare processes negatively impact patient satisfaction and can lead to patient harm. Management dictates that "time is money." More importantly, slow treatment can contribute to poor health outcomes. Time includes the activities or tasks within each step and the time spent between steps. Delays can occur during handoffs and transitions (Martins, et al., 2025); departmental or functional group boundaries can also contribute to these "white space" management challenges (Rummler & Brache, 1995).

The cancer screening mammography example discussed earlier in the chapter illustrated the impact that passing time has on the effectiveness of the process. Each step in the diagnostic journey for cancer screening (e.g., initial screening, additional digital imaging, ultrasound, MRI, biopsy, surgical treatment, oncological treatment) may be well-defined and managed. However, the time between steps may be increased due to the unplanned or poorly managed transitions between each step. If an initial screening mammography is completed and no "suspicious" areas of the breast are observed, then the process may stop. If a suspicious area in the mammography is observed, then the provider may either ask the patient to stay longer for additional imaging or, for those providers who do not read the initial imaging in real time while the patient is there, the patient's primary care physician may receive a report indicating more work-up is needed which in turn increases the time between steps in the diagnostic journey of a mammography patient. The patient is contacted and requested to make an appointment for a follow-up visit with either the primary care physician or the mammography center, or both. Therefore, the transition from initial screening imaging and follow-up imaging may have wait times built in that can increase patient anxiety. Furthermore, the delays may allow time for ongoing growth of a cancerous tumor.

In 1915, Gilbreth used time motion studies to show convincingly that the actual time needed to complete a process, such as imaging, reading the results, and determining the next clinical steps, may be short relative to the time spent between steps (Gilbreth & Carey, 2002). Reducing transition time between steps (i.e., eliminating wait time) is often worthwhile in reducing patient anxiety, determining clinical concerns earlier, perhaps reducing the effort needed for treatment if caught earlier, and honoring the patient's personal time. It is not unusual for transition times to be increased for the convenience of the providers, other staff, the facilities in which patients are seen, and to complete documentation consistent with regulatory or compliance requirements. Putting the patient first (beyond merely paying lip service) takes significant effort and may be a challenge to the "way things are done here."

Time is also defined by the process:

- The design of a patient care process can determine the minimal amount of time a patient will enter, flow through, and exit a process if there are no impediments or variation in the process.
- The addition of non-value-added steps in the process only adds time, potentially increases variation, and increases opportunity for errors. For example, in an empty ED, are all patients required to go through a separate step called "triage," or can they immediately proceed directly to being seen by a provider?

We have learned by managing dozens of clinical service line projects that finding ways to reduce the length of time spent in the patient flow care process may require staff to:

1. Eliminate or reduce non-value- added process tasks or steps such as unnecessary waiting times as we documented using process maps (Johnson et al., 2012).
2. Implement LMS (see discussion that follows) to draw staff attention to time spent on identifying and reducing non-value-added process steps.
3. Create value-stream managers that control all the resources needed for their service lines (i.e., ICU patients, hip repairs, etc.). This can reduce the boundary or interface issues. (Barach, P. Risner, P., et al., 2011)

What has not been mentioned is the care facility layout may also contribute to waiting time between process steps if individual care steps are not co-located with previous or subsequent care steps, therefore, requiring time to transition a patient from one care location to another. An understanding of patient care flow can serve to improve the design of new or modified facilities in order to design out non-valued added time in order to enable efficient patient flow (Berry, Crane, Deming & Barach, 2020). Learning from existing processes can serve to avoiding future facility / layout issues that inhibit patient care processes. It is not coincidental that the philosophies and practices of CQI as espoused by Six Sigma, LMS, and LSS, all lead to reducing variation in organizational and physical design processes and overutilization of resources as well as streamlining patient flow care processes, leading to reduced time to care and increased patient satisfaction. In the next part of this chapter, we provide an overview of the principles of LMS.

Lean Management System (LMS)

The VUT equation described above is a simple model to understand, but it is more challenging to implement. LMS models provide for an effective system to optimize process management as suggested by the VUT equation. The active joining of these two models will be discussed later. Specifically, hospital managers and their staff need to direct and set examples about required behaviors to reduce or manage variation, maximize human and equipment utilization, and decrease the process cycle times.

First, a comparison is in order. If a Lean organization is like an automobile, then the engine is similar to the organization's capacity to provide services and the transmission is analogous to an LMS. The transmission sends power to the wheel axle to move the vehicle forward. It also changes gears to better match power and resource demands. An automatic transmission smooths these shifts and helps reduce variation. An organization's LMS coordinates resources and directs them to efficiently satisfy customer work orders (demands). When managers apply the "right" tools, this stimulus and response situation can be virtually seamless.

Management in Lean organizations has "two major functions: maintaining or controlling the existing processes, and improving existing processes" (Charron, Harrington, Voehl, & Wiggin, 2015, p. 1). Hospital performance management occurs through continuous improvement, and emphasizes staff development, socio-technical (belief) systems, and change management. High performing companies are paying increasingly more attention to organizational culture that focuses on reliability and safety (Weick & Roberts, 1993). Hospitals where nurses feel scared to speak up and don't feel respected by physicians for their input, record higher patient mortality (Brubakk, 2021). Organizational goal success can seem entirely random without effective management. On some days, the production might be successful, and on others it will produce near misses and process failures (Barach & Small, 2000). Management and front-line staff will not know when or why either will occur. This is akin to employees starting each day with the important question, "Do I feel lucky?" This mode of operation is very stressful and costly, and one never feels in control of their processes or environment because so much of the output is ruled by chance.

LMS approaches have been successfully applied in hundreds of organizations and two prominent examples in health care are at Virginia Mason and Baylor, Scott & White (BS&W) health systems. A recent book, *The Power of Ideas to Transform Healthcare: Engaging Staff by Building Daily Lean Management Systems* by Steve Hoeft and Robert W. Pryor (2016), thoroughly documents the BS&W Lean journey. The authors credit the successful LMS implementation to the continuous implementation of staff-generated ideas supported by management. Lean management is the vehicle for this staff engagement and the continuous infusion of suggestions supported by staff successfully implemented in both the clinics and administrative activities. The basic principles apply across the board in both healthcare services and manufacturing (Hoeft & Pryor, 2016). A more in-depth treatment can be found in Mann (2015) where he demonstrates the power when attention is devoted to management enabling a robust organizational culture.

The LMS model shown in **Figure 5.3** is adapted from Mann (2015) and is represented as a Venn diagram because there are interconnections and overlaps between the three components. Everything begins with leader standard work, because that is where supervision through executive activities and the standardization of the processes of the other elements are spelled out. For example, how leaders select and maintain the data using visual controls (see the following sections), how their daily accountability (see the following sections) is implemented, and how staff are held to account on a regular and transparent basis.

The three interconnected variables of **leader standard work**, **visual controls**, and **daily accountability** are influenced by the important

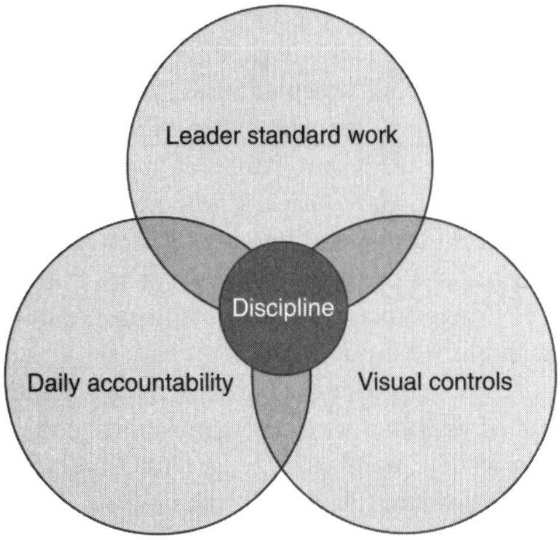

Figure 5.3 Lean Management System Model

factor of discipline. Discipline and stable leadership are needed to ensure that long-term success and flow are maximized at the juncture where important parts of the organizational change model align and need predictability.

The Toyota Production System argues that organizational culture can change through the inculcation of principles delineated in the *Four P Model* (Liker & Ross, 2017, p. 48) and includes:

1. Problem solving for continuous organizational learning and alignment to objectives and plans
2. The experience of people being respected, challenged, engaged, and developed
3. Improvement and stabilization of processes based on customer-defined "value"
4. Philosophy of long-term focus

Staff must be allowed to devote time to completely understand and reflect on their work activities in order to identify waste and standardize best practices ("sense-making") (Barach & Phelps, 2013). To understand variation in one's workflow, one must carefully measure and review multiple data points. Ideally, at least 20 data points are needed for a significant "minimum" trend, but a minimum of seven data points should be used when tracking seasonal changes that are so crucial for healthcare planning (Balestracci, 2015). When more data is available, it is easier to differentiate between common- and special-cause variation patterns.

Lean management is a hands-on activity requiring supervisors and line managers to actively apply these principles on the work floor or "*gemba*." They cannot manage improving their clinical work proceses from their offices while reviewing data or reports and answering emails. This begins with leader standard work.

Leader Standard Work

LMS does not assume that employees, including managers and leaders, know what they are supposed to do. Best practices or standards are clearly spelled out in detail on activity boards to visually track and manage a leader's daily, weekly, and monthly activities, ensuring consistent and efficient performance. Common examples include hand-washing reminders for staff posted outside patients' rooms or graphical safety directions for using dangerous equipment. Many surgical suites post the list of required time outs on a wall for all to view. These best practices are updated as new standards and improvements are made and agreed on.

A lack of standardized work increases variation and can produce very strange data distributions. Variation is a key element in the VUT equation. Different types of patients or procedures require specialized "handling" and will require multiple methods and change-overs, etc. This tends to reduce cycle time. On the other hand, multiple approaches can restrict flow and slow down clinical processes. The following LMS tables (see **Table 5.1**, **Table 5.2**, and **Table 5.3**) have been adapted from *Creating a Lean Culture* (Mann, 2015, pp. 58–59). The three tables are divided to show the frequency of application and levels within the organization. Note that the supervisors or team leaders repeat tasks more frequently than managers or directors. They also do not have the same responsibilities and there is no universal application of this approach across organizations.

Supervisors and managers "go to the **gemba**" or where the work is done on the "shop floor"—or in the clinical context, the operating

Table 5.1 Leader Standard Work for Activities Completed Many Times Each Day*

	Supervisors/Team Leaders	Managers	Directors	Hospital Administrators
	Go to the *gemba* (work floor) to:	Go to the *gemba* (rounds) to:	Communicate with key stakeholders and customers	Communicate with key stakeholders and customers
	Coach employees	Coach employees	Coach employees	Encourage and praise staff
	Remove barriers and help solve problems	Remove barriers and help solve problems	Remove barriers and help solve problems	Remove barriers and help solve problems
	Monitor standard work	Encourage and praise staff	Encourage and praise staff	
	Encourage and praise staff			
	Monitor time and capacity buffers			
	Prevent accidents			

*Data from Mann, D. (2015). Creating a lean culture: Tools to sustain lean conversions, 3rd ed. Boca Raton, FL: CRC Press.

Table 5.2 Leader Standard Work for Activities Completed At Least Once Daily or Every Shift Change*

Frequency	Supervisors/Team Leaders	Managers	Directors	Hospital Administrators
Once daily, every day	Check call-ins Coordinate shift changes Administrative tasks	Monitor and adjust staffing plans Administrative tasks	Administrative tasks	Administrative tasks
	Review performance data from previous day	Review performance data from previous day for all supervisors	Review performance data from previous day for area	Review highest level hospital metrics
	AM review of patient schedule	AM review of patient schedule by type of patient	Review end of day patient totals	Review patient census trends for whole hospital
	AM review of supply inventory		Go to the *gemba* (rounds)	Go to the *gemba* (rounds)
	AM review of repair needs			

(continues)

Table 5.2 Leader Standard Work for Activities Completed At Least Once Daily or Every Shift Change* *(continued)*

Frequency	Supervisors/Team Leaders	Managers	Directors	Hospital Administrators
	Prepare data for huddle boards	Prepare data for huddle boards		
	Huddle with staff for about 10 minutes to: ■ Review performance data ■ Discuss data variation, obstacles, and capacity issues	Huddle with supervisors for about 10 minutes to: ■ Review performance data ■ Discuss common variation, flow, and capacity issues	Huddle with managers for about 10 minutes to: ■ Review performance data ■ Discuss common variation, flow, and capacity issues	Huddle with executive staff for about 10 minutes to: ■ Review performance data ■ Discuss common variation, flow, and capacity issues
	Monitor standard work	Monitor standard work		
	End of shift review of work			
	Follow up on urgent assignments	Follow up on urgent assignments		

*Data from Mann, D. (2015). Creating a lean culture: Tools to sustain lean conversions, 3rd ed. Boca Raton, FL: CRC Press.

room, the intensive care unit, or the ED, many times every day (Imai, 2012). They observe, listen, and question. Staff are encouraged and rewarded to speak up and find simple solutions (*kaizens*) to improve the value work stream. Staff are coached and developed in an apprentice model. Working with staff, managers assist in removing barriers and reducing process variation, capacity restraints, and cycle time. (Sexton et al., 2021).

Table 5.3 Leader Standard Work for Activities Completed Weekly or Less Frequently*

Frequency	Supervisors/Team Leaders	Managers	Directors	Hospital Administrators
Weekly or less frequently	Hold weekly staff meeting for supervisors and team leaders	Hold weekly staff meeting for supervisors	Hold weekly staff meeting for managers	Hold weekly staff meeting for executive staff and directors
	Participate in improvement projects when assigned	Participate in improvement projects when assigned	Champion improvement projects	Champion improvement projects
				Review progress on strategic plan

*Data from Mann, D. (2015). Creating a lean culture: Tools to sustain lean conversions, 3rd ed. Boca Raton, FL: CRC Press.

This direct contact between management and frontline staff builds trust and provides opportunities for learning, data collection, problem identification, and trust building before it might be addressed by middle management. Managers can directly observe how demand, capacity, or time buffers are managed to ensure that patients, transactions, and information are being effectively used. Staff should not be idled because there are not enough patients. Patients should not experience excessively long waiting times because the hospital does not have sufficient staff or equipment, etc. Managers can directly observe staff (and machines) working at a realistically efficient pace or unsustainable breakneck speed. Is there any "slack" or buffer that can be used in positive ways? Finally, the standard work is monitored and modified in the treatment or support areas as different work methods can be a leading cause of process variation.

Many more activities such as staff huddles occur daily and on shift changes in the hospital. These short staff meetings at the beginning of each shift employ a very data-driven approach to planning and problem solving. The key management data are displayed on a wall that is convenient for staff to view during the daily huddles. Staff huddles will be addressed more completely in the Daily Accountability section (later in the chapter).

Staffing levels, equipment, and inventory are checked because those also impact capacity. Supervisors and managers should also briefly review the day's work before going home and especially consider visiting the hospital on weekends where they can help focus on work that can prevent excessive harm on weekends (Shulkin, 2008). Directors and hospital administrators should also go to the *gemba* or "round" at least once a day in one of their many areas or locations (Saposnik, 2007). This helps managers understand the value streams and their regular presence motivates staff to stay focused and continuously improve (Bendavid et al., 2007).

These activities are less frequent but no less important. Note the importance of regular champion meetings to address ongoing improvement needs. These weekly or biweekly staff meetings are longer, sit-down events that communicate important organizational changes, deal with near miss or process failures, etc. Discussions can also be more in-depth, but this is not the time for micromanagement problem solving. That can be assigned to people to handle outside the meeting and report back. Finally, senior leaders need to regularly review strategic plan implementation.

Visual Controls

Visual controls in Lean management should always begin with some type of "as is" value stream or process map. This provides an important context and a reference point for any discussion related to improvement metrics or issues. **Figure 5.4** illustrates an ED process map.

A process map or flowchart is a visual representation of the care or other process that is created with information provided by team members that work in the process. The process mapping exercise can help clinicians clarify through visualization what they "think" they know about their environment and determine what they want to improve in it (Barach & Johnson, 2006). Visualization facilitates the analysis of often very complex activities. The process maps use common flowchart symbols and can describe the current state or baseline, the improved state in transition, and the optimal state (Uramatsu et al., 2024). The exercise helps clinicians make assumptions and expectations explicit and can provide insights into reflections on their current state and, importantly, into how to improve the process of care such as medication infusions or to overcome barriers they perceive to its improvement (Johnson et al., 2012). The numbered steps facilitate a logical sequential discussion and the process efficiency times are a useful ratio for assessing what is value-added time versus non-value-added time activities (Hollingsworth et al., 1998).

An important part of a LMS is "learning to see" what is happening in the value stream or process. The visual display of the right data facilitates this awareness and is crucial because measurement influences behavior. In this approach, the "right" data focuses attention on variation, utilization/capacity, and time (VUT). Clinical microsystems

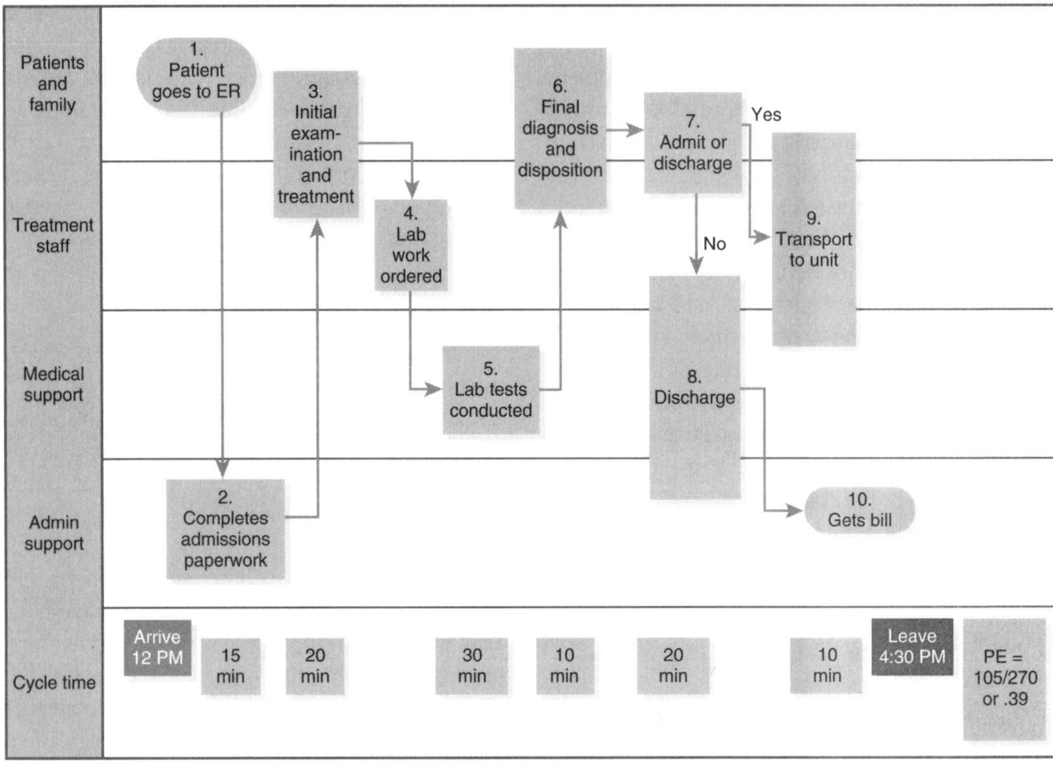

Figure 5.4 Emergency Department Process Map Example

should monitor and analyze no more than four to five key performance indicators (KPIs) because staff focus can easily be distracted and overwhelmed (Mohr, Batalden, & Barach, 2004). Ideal healthcare metrics might include the cycle time, patient wait times, medical errors, scheduling errors, patient volumes, and nurse and provider volumes. The data collected, analyzed, and managed should include important outcomes/outputs (Y's) and the variables that influence (X's) those outcomes.

Every metric selected should include a numerical target which needs to be a "stretch goal" to help motivate improvements. There should be a valid reason for collecting specific data because there is a serious cost associated with those efforts. You may also collect data for the important parts of the clinical process, such as ED times for door-to-doctor, doctor-to-decision, and decision-to-disposition. This enables stratification or the necessary "drilling down" into the datasets to find specific answers to the many important management questions.

It is important that an appropriate sampling plan be developed, as described in Chapter 4 and throughout the CQI evolution, including the earliest work of Deming. Data must be operationally defined to promote both reliability and validity. There are various approaches that can be used to select primary data for CQI processes (Perla, Provost, & Murray, 2013). For many organizations, the management metrics used to understand and manage work processes are often based on averages rather than understanding actual variation in processes (Kim, Spahlinger, Kin, & Billi, 2006). For example, the length of stay (LOS) is often reported as an average length of stay (ALOS) and resource utilization is also reported in averages, etc. This would be adequate if the data did not fluctuate much around the average. As previously stated, patient demand tends to vary hour to hour, day to day, and seasonally, while patient conditions can also markedly differ.

How do we better manage and ultimately improve our healthcare processes? Ideally, the data would be automatically collected by the electronic health record (EHR) or another database aligned throughout the organization. This produces a synergistic effect of added value. "Like magnetism, alignment is a force. It coalesces and focuses an organization and moves it forward" (Labovitz & Rosansky, 1997, p. 6).

The data points need to be collected for every patient or transaction for any desired time period. It should be easily exported into a standard data format that facilitates data analysis. Unfortunately, this is not the current reality in most health organizations, as process data (e.g., waiting time, variation in test and treatment order sets among physicians, real-time utilization of key resources, errors or near-miss causes) are often not tracked or readily available in the IT applications used in clinical processes. Instead, the data tracked in the IT systems are related to activity transactions per patient, such as orders made and fulfilled, tests or procedures applied, and medications administered.

The **huddle board** design template (**Figure 5.5**) was successfully implemented at a large healthcare revenue cycle management organization. Some data examples will follow later. Each team constructed their own board and creative differences were encouraged. It was important to display the current process map for quick reference and context. Finally, each team posted a list of what their successful outcomes would contribute to the next downstream group in the value stream. For example, a chart of the patient recovery staff had time and accuracy goals to expedite coding. This helped employees understand how they contributed to the "big picture." Suneja and Suneja (2010) use the term "Glass Wall" for the same concept.

The top row contains trends for the macro level KPIs that are aligned to the highest level of the organization. Where appropriate, the metrics should include mandated core measures such as patient satisfaction or median length of stay. The run chart shown in **Figure 5.6** is an example of a displayed metric on the huddle board.

A quick glance at the trend reveals nonrandom patterns, including what some authors define as "astronomical" data points (i.e., the two unusually large values at 10:00 AM and 12:00 AM) (Perla, Provost, & Murray, 2011). These variations warrant further analysis using other CQI tools; the analysis methodology and these CQI tools are presented as follows and described further in Chapter 4. This leads to the second row on the huddle board, where "drilldowns" or stratification charts can be displayed. These charts can be tacked under each high-level chart from the first row and can be presented in a chronological "pile" that can be easily explored. Appropriate charts include Pareto charts for medical errors/harm and controls charts for both trended errors and process times

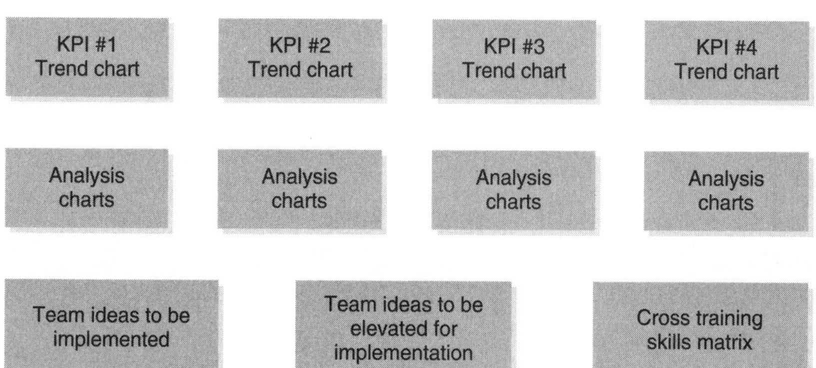

Figure 5.5 Huddle Board Template

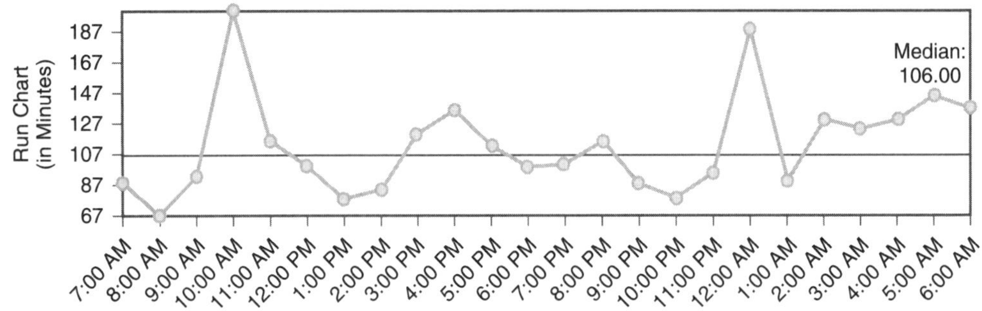

Figure 5.6 Average ED Process Cycle Times for Sampled Patients

(Johnson & Barach, 2017). A typical control chart can be seen in **Figure 5.7**.

The XbarR charts in Figure 5.7 display the means (X-bar) of each sub-group (solid lines). The dashed lines represent different standard deviation levels. In these control charts, four patients were tracked at the beginning of each hour in the initial door-to-doctor phase of an ED redesign process. This is in-between group variation, and there are some obvious special cause outliers and other patterns (see Chapter 4 for further description of special cause variation). The accompanying range (R) chart in Figure 5.7 shows the corresponding within group variation.

Box plots (**Figure 5.8**) are great graphical tools for comparing distributions of variable data such as time passed and costs of care. This graph looks at how much time the ED physicians take from when then they first talk to their patients, to the time when they make their clinical decisions. Box plots provide an interesting perspective on managing this ED variation in care.

A quick glance at Figure 5.8 shows that the physicians labeled #12214, 11288, and 12215 are

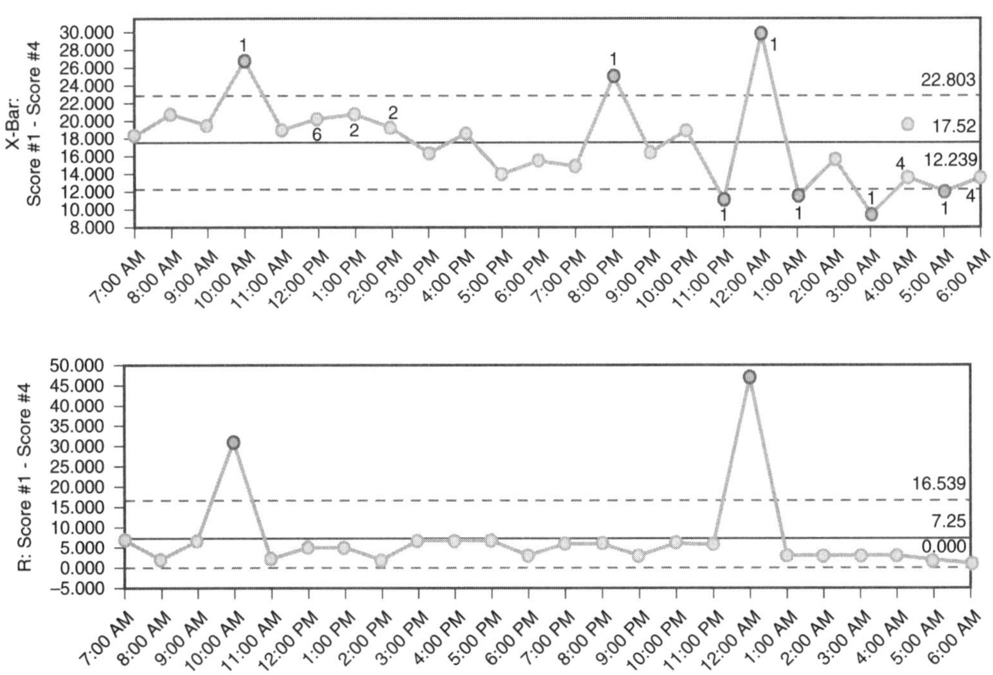

Figure 5.7 XbarR Door-to-Doctor Times for Sampled Patients

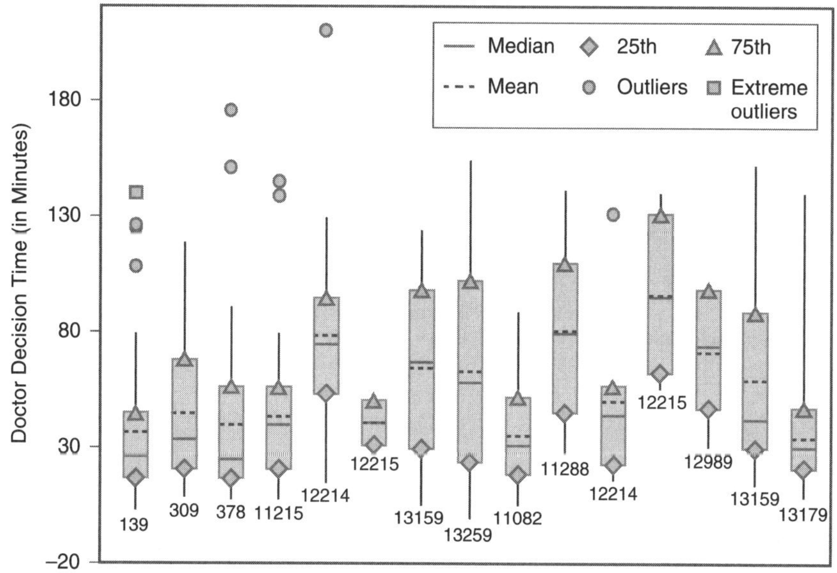

Figure 5.8 Box Plot for Physicians to Assess Their Decision Times

spending relatively more time with their patients than physicians labeled #139, 309, 378, 11215, 11082, 12214, and 13179. The physicians labeled #13159, 13259, and 13179 had a wider range of times to make their decisions. This time data is important because it impacts both utilization (capacity) and process time. It would be important to drill down and compare physician times across common patient type variables such as chief complaints or diagnosis-related groups (DRG).

How can the information in a box plot be used to understand variation (V in the VUT equation)? When comparing between attending ED physicians, patient length of stay (LOS) in the ED can be measured before they are ultimately admitted to an in-patient room at a hospital. If we only compare patients who are admitted with respiratory distress–related issues (e.g., flu, pneumonia), then it is expected that although there may be outliers in LOS, in general the middle 50% of the patients admitted for respiratory reasons by different physicians should be similar. Rather than looking at the exceptions as represented by outliers outside the boxes, we can compare the size of the boxes representing the amount of variation in the middle 50% of the LOS data. It is reasonable to expect similar results between physicians for the middle 50%. If the variation in the LOS for these physicians is quite different, then the natural question is what might be causing the variation in outcomes. The reasons may include physicians ordering more tests and treatments than their colleagues which may result in longer LOS for their patients. Some physicians may either use standard order sets or have a very well-defined process for handling respiratory-challenged patients, hence they are more consistent in their LOS results.

Rather than challenging staff to explain to others the reasons for their variation, it is better to provide staff with the information in a graphical format and let them discuss it among themselves. Having variation data displayed with box plots is useful as it is easy to understand if applied on a regular basis and often sparks vigorous dialogue among providers to understand why variation is occurring and how best to mitigate the causes for the variation.

A Pareto chart (first introduced in Chapter 4) is a powerful tool to help graphically illustrate variation, as illustrated in **Figure 5.9**.

It is obvious in Figure 5.9 that some providers need to sign their charts before the charts can be coded and billed. Missing signatures accounted for 71% of the sampled errors.

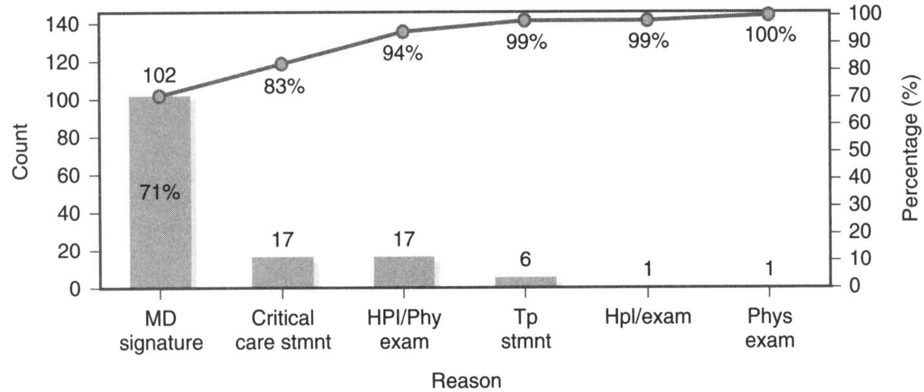

Figure 5.9 Missing Chart Elements from a Coding QA Review

A second level Pareto analysis can drill down to show which providers are the primary offenders. Knowing the "real" times to complete documentation or see patients provides essential information for improving the process.

If "production" is one of the first row KPIs, then pitch charts (**Figure 5.10**) can be used to track work output during specific periods of time against goals. Examples of production might include numbers of tests completed in the

Pitch times	Goal pitch/ cumulative	Actual pitch/ cumulative	Variation pitch/ cumulative	Reason for misses
8–10 AM	20/20	18/18	−2/−2	10 minutes start up meeting. Went over 2 minutes—safety issue
10–12	30/50	30/48	0/−2	
1–3 PM	20/70	15/63	−5/−7	Computers down for 20 minutes
3–5 PM	30/100	27/90	−3/−10	Rework needed
Overtime 5–6 PM	10/100	10/100	0/0	2 staff worked
Totals	100/100			

Figure 5.10 Pitch Chart for RCM Chart Reviews

	Mary	John	James	Susan	William
Skill 1	X		X		
Skill 2	X	X	X		X
Skill 3	X		X	X	X
Skill 4	X	X		X	X
Skill 5	X			X	

Figure 5.11 Staff Skills and Cross-Training Matrix

lab, images read by radiologists, or charts coded during revenue cycle management (RCM).

The chart can also be modified to add an individual worker column. These charts can facilitate demand and capacity planning. This is an example from a revenue cycle management (RCM) analysis but it could be used in any repetitive work environment. Color can be added to highlight good, fair, or bad performance. A simple review of the numerator/denominator differences shows that adjustments need to be made after a quick review. The traffic light colors make it even easier to understand, and "red" really stands out. The colors would be selected based on some standard, agreed-upon levels of performance. Another application for traffic light colors could be for the Centers for Medicare and Medicaid Services (CMS) Five Star Quality Rating System. The 4s and 5s would be green; yellow would be used for 3s and 2s, and 1s would be red. Lighter and darker color shading could also be used for the reds and greens.

The third row of the huddle board is a great place to show capacity and other data such as a training matrix (**Figure 5.11**). This is a simple way to show the most "strategic" skills and which staff members have mastered them. Dates of attainment could be used instead of the Xs.

Another helpful capacity tool is an overlay run chart (**Figure 5.12**). An overlay run chart

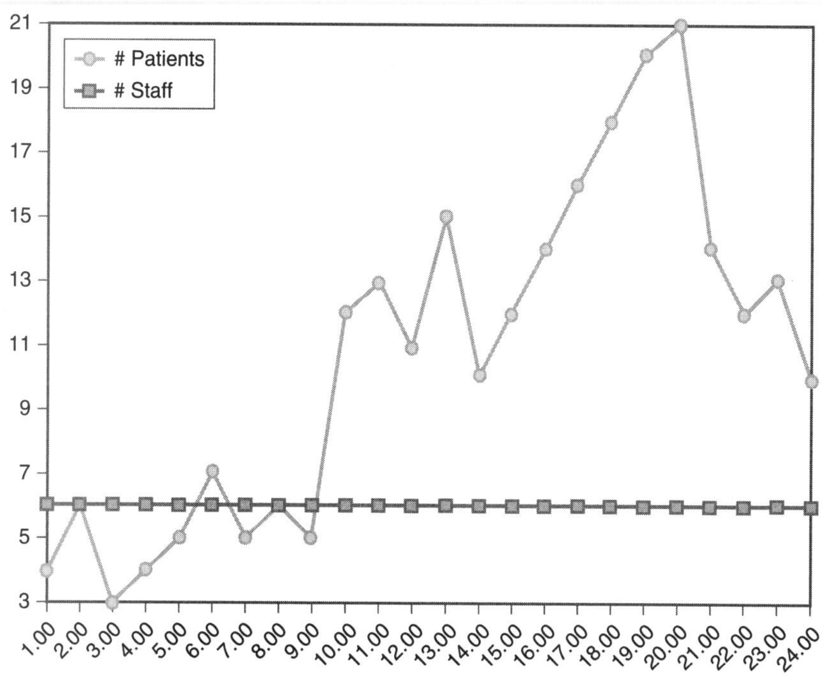

Figure 5.12 Overlay Run Chart for Number of Patients and Staff by Times

Date	Item	Who suggested	Who to implement	Start date	Due date	Status
January 2	Idea 1	Bob	Bob	Jan 2	Jan 3	Successfully completed
January 2	Idea 2	Arif	Arif	Jan 2	Jan 6	In process on schedule
January 3	Idea 3	Sue	Sue	Jan 3	Jan 4	Successfully completed
January 3	Idea 4	Linda	Linda	Jan 3	Jan 5	Successfully completed
January 4	Idea 5	James	James	Jan 4	Jan 10	In process on schedule
January 5	Idea 6	Willie	Willie	Jan 5	Jan 15	In process late

Figure 5.13 Staff Suggestions and Their Implementation

can be used to calculate the demand and capacity, both important aspects of the VUT equation. Managers must successfully juggle patient volume (demand) with staff availability. These two trend lines can easily show what capacity existed during that reporting time period given the varying patient demands. Was there adequate coverage later in the day? What happened to the patient length of stay after 10:00?

Staff suggestions are key to continuous quality improvement and they should be tracked with feedback and feedforward and posted on the activity boards (**Figure 5.13**). The similar companion chart for supervisors can also be maintained and displayed because the staff deserve responses and tracking can increase action.

Traffic light colors make it "easier to see" (unless someone is color blind!). Line graphs could also be used to display this data over time (**Figure 5.14**).

Daily Accountability

Daily accountability is the most interactive part of the LMS model. Management actively engages with staff when they "go to the *gemba*" and during staff huddles (Ben-Tovim et al., 2007). This can also include regular follow-up discussions on clinical improvement projects. *Gemba* walks are at the core of Lean practice. Going to "where the work occurs" is the best place to collect real-time data and show staff that management is attentive to their concerns. This happens when supervisors and managers observe, listen, challenge, and question each other. We want the staff to think and derive the growth and satisfaction that comes from their own problem-solving efforts. We want them to actively "see" what is happening and actively engage their colleagues to look for waste. The simple tool shown in **Table 5.4** can help this exploration.

This list of waste types enables managers to remember what to look for and reminds them to record brief observations and improvement ideas (Fine, Golden, Hannam, & Morra, 2009). Managers should ask the same four questions during *gemba* walks:

1. What are your team's targets or goals today?
2. How well are you meeting these targets (facts)?
3. What is your plan or planned actions to close the performance gaps?
4. How can I help you implement your ideas?

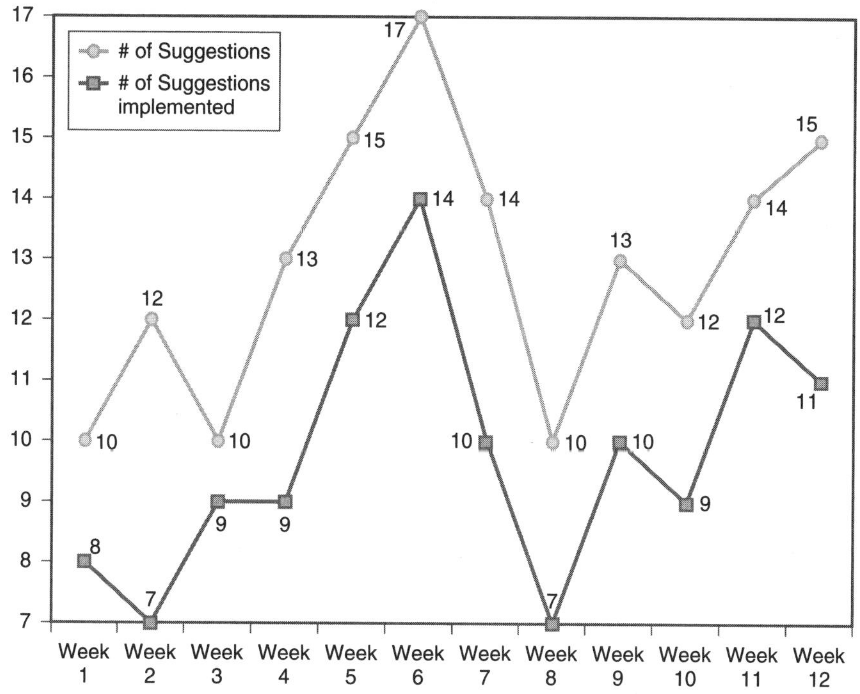

Figure 5.14 Trend Chart for Suggestions Made and Implemented by Staff

The huddle board examples shown in **Figure 5.15** and **Figure 5.16** are the focus of brief, 10- to 15-minute, stand-up meetings that might involve different staff at different levels. They address more than just the exchange of important shift change information or communication "from above." This is an opportunity to briefly review the highlights of KPI data and to focus on both positive and negative variation. Why did that data point increase (or decrease)? What explains the trend? Write comments on the charts, involve staff in these discussions, and have them all take turns leading the huddles. Encourage staff to come back and think about the data. Assignments can be given for later report backs and good facilitation is imperative.

Table 5.4 Waste Walk Tool

Waste	What do you see?	How to Improve
Defects/errors		
Overproduction		
Under-utilizing people		
Motion/transportation		
Transitions		
Over-processing		
Inventory		

Figure 5.15 Huddle Board Example 1

Coaching is another important piece of daily accountability because it is the preferred way to develop staff and improve accountability (Sherrard, Trypuc, & Hudson, 2009). Managers must respect their workers to be effective coaches. This is accomplished by asking staff how something should be done as opposed to just telling them the correct way to complete a task. Coaches model appropriate behaviors and use shaping and modeling to help staff perfect new skills (Stem & Greenberg, 2024). Shaping involves reinforcing each successive approximation until mastery is achieved. Incorrect behaviors are corrected but that can be initiated by asking the worker if the task was completed correctly. If they acknowledge the error, then the follow-up question can be "How would you improve it?"

Figure 5.16 Huddle Board Example 2

Continuing to engage staff and attentively listening to the staff suggestions are the most important output of daily accountability meetings and helps to engage staff while surfacing legitimate concerns. This "sense-making" is a huge part of engendering trust, accountability, and organizational loyalty (Barach & Phelps, 2013). Empowering staff jump-starts creative problem solving. Observing and questioning also facilitates critical thinking. This on-going generation of staff ideas is so important that the number of suggestions made and implemented should be recorded and tracked on the huddle board. Management responses and follow-up should also be posted.

Conclusions

Lean Management Systems (LMS) and Lean Six Sigma (LSS) provide an integrated framework, a set of analytic and improvement tools, and a way of thinking for systematically studying and improving clinical flow, including the identification and reduction of unwarranted process variation. These methodologies are broadly applicable to improving quality, efficiency, and reliability across health care delivery, public health, and other health-related settings.

This chapter illustrates an LSS application using the Patient Flow Physics Framework, demonstrating that effective organizational improvement requires a clear understanding of patient care processes (e.g., through process maps and flow diagrams), the organizational and cultural drivers of variation, the impact of resource utilization on system performance, and the ways in which poor process and organizational design lengthen cycle times and degrade flow.

Improving clinical teamwork is essential to achieving these gains. Indeed, the effectiveness of LMS and LSS depends less on the specific tools used than on how those tools generate insight, engage multidisciplinary teams, and support continuous learning and tracking of patient progress. Ultimately, their purpose is not only to improve processes but also to enable teams to function more effectively in delivering safer, higher-quality care. The importance of teamwork in LMS and LSS as well as other CQI initiatives and methods will be discussed further in Chapter 6.

Key Concepts and Terms

common cause variation
daily accountability
ED boarding
Factory Physics
gemba
huddle board
leader standard work
Lean Management System (LMS)
Lean Six Sigma (LSS)
muda
mura
muri
Patient Flow Physics
Six Sigma
special cause variation
visual controls
VUT equation

References

Agency for Healthcare Research and Quality (AHRQ). (2012). *Emergency Severity Index (ESI): A triage tool for emergency department (AHRQ publication no. 05-0046)*. Retrieved April 27, 2018, from www.ahrq.gov

Antony, J., Palsuk, P., Gupta, S., Mishra, D., & Barach, P. (2018). Six Sigma in healthcare: A systematic review of the literature. *International Journal of Quality & Reliability Management, 35*(5), 1075–1092. https://doi.org/10.1108/IJQRM-02-2017-0027

Apostolakis, G., & Barach, P. (2003). *Lessons learned from nuclear power*. In: M. Hatlie & K. Tavill (Eds.), *Patient safety: International textbook* (pp. 205–225). Aspen.

Balestracci, D. (2015). *Data sanity: A quantum leap to unprecedented results* (2nd ed.). Medical Group Management Association.

Barach, P., & Small, S. D. (2000). Reporting and preventing medical mishaps: Lessons from non-medical near miss reporting systems. *BMJ, 320*, 759. https://doi.org/10.1136/bmj.320.7237.759

Barach, P., & Johnson, J. (2006). Understanding the complexity of redesigning care around the clinical microsystem. *BMJ Quality & Safety in Health Care, 15*(Suppl 1), i10–i16. https://doi.org/10.1136/qshc.2005.015859

Barach, P., & Kleinman, L. (2018). Measuring and improving comprehensive pediatric cardiac care: Learning from continuous quality improvement methods and tools. *Progress in Pediatric Cardiology, 48*, 82–92. https://doi.org/10.1016/j.ppedcard.2018.02.010

Barach, P., & Phelps, G. (2013). Clinical sensemaking: A systematic approach to reduce the impact of normalised deviance in the medical profession. *Journal of the Royal Society of Medicine, 106*(10), 387–390. https://doi.org/10.1177/0141076813505045

Barach, P., Wiggin, H., Risner, P., et al (2011). A perioperative safety and quality change management model and case study: Muda Health. In R. J. Holden, S. J. Karsh, & P. Carayon (Eds.), Handbook of human factors and ergonomics in health care and patient safety (Chapter 15, pp. 315–340). CRC Press / Taylor & Francis. https://doi.org/10.1201/b11335-20

Bendavid, E., Kaganova, Y., Needleman, J., Gruenberg, L., & Weissman, J. S. (2007). Complication rates on weekends and weekdays in US hospitals. *American Journal of Medicine, 120*(5), 422–428. https://doi.org/10.1016/j.amjmed.2006.05.067

Berry LL, Crane J, Deming KA, Barach P. (2020). Using evidence to design cancer care facilities. *Am J Med Qual, 35*(5), 397–404. https://doi.org/10.1177/1062860619897406. Epub 2020 Jan 15. PMID: 31941345.

Berwick, D. M., Nolan, T. W., & Whittington, J. (2008). The triple aim: Care, health, and cost. *Health Affairs, 27*(3), 759–769. https://doi.org/10.1377/hlthaff.27.3.759

Ben-Tovim, D. I., Bassham, J. E., Bolch, D., et al. (2007). Lean thinking across a hospital: Redesigning care at the Flinders Medical Centre. *Australian Health Review, 31*(1), 10–15. https://doi.org/10.1071/AH070010

Bodenheimer, T., & Sinsky, C. (2014). From triple to quadruple aim: Care of the patient requires care of the provider. *Annals of Family Medicine, 12*(6), 573–576. https://doi.org/10.1370/afm.1713. PMID: 25384822; PMCID: PMC4226781.

Brubakk, K., Svendsen, M. V., Deilkås, E. T., Hofoss, D., Barach, P., & Tjomsland, O. (2021). Hospital work environments affect the patient safety climate: A longitudinal follow-up using a logistic regression analysis model. *PLoS One, 16*(10), e0258471. https://doi.org/10.1371/journal.pone.0258471. PMID: 34653217; PMCID: PMC8519418.

Byrne, A. (2013). *The lean turnaround*. McGraw Hill.

Charron, R., Harrington, H. J., Voehl, F., & Wiggin, H. (2015). *The lean management systems handbook*. CRC Press.

Croft, A., Barach P., Bona A., et al. (2025). A novel simulation-based Pediatric Respiratory Distress Educational Curriculum (PReDEC) for emergency medicine residents. *Pediatric Emergency Medicine Journal, 12*(1), 10–19. https://doi.org/10.22470/pemj.2024.01109

Csikszentmihalyi, M. (1990). *Flow: The psychology of optimal experience*. Harper Perennial Modern Classics.

DeMarco, T. (2001). *Slack: Getting past burnout, busywork, and the myth of total efficiency*. Broadway Books.

Deming, W. E. (1993). *The new economics for industry, government, education.* Massachusetts Institute of Technology Center for Advanced Engineering Study.

Duffy, G. L., Farmer, E., & Moran, J. W. (2009). Applying lean six sigma in public health. In R. Bialek, G. L. Duffy & J. W. Moran (Eds.), *The public health quality improvement handbook.* ASQ Quality Press.

Fine, B., Golden, B., Hannam, R., & Morra, D. (2009). Leading Lean: A Canadian healthcare leader's guide. *Healthcare Quarterly, 12*(3), 32–41. https://doi.org/10.12927/hcq.2013.20877

FitzGerald, G., Jelinek, G. A., Scott, D., & Gerdtz, M. F. (2009). Emergency department triage revisited. *Emergency Medicine Journal, 27*(2), 86–92. https://doi.org/10.1136/emj.2009.077081

George, M. L. (2002). *Lean Six Sigma: Combining Six Sigma quality with Lean production speed.* McGraw Hill.

Gilbreth, F. Jr., & Carey, E. G. (2002). *Cheaper by the dozen.* Harper Perennial Modern Classics.

Guarisco, J. (2013). Cracking the code: Fixing the crowded emergency department. *AAEM News, CommonSense*, September/October, 18–20; November/December, 24.

Harry, M. (1988). *The nature of Six Sigma quality*. Motorola University Press.

Hartwell, J. L., Barach, P., Gunter, T. D., et al. (2023). Navigating work-life integration, legal issues, patient safety: Lessons for work-life wellness in academic medicine: Part 1 of 3. *Kansas Journal of Medicine, 16*(2), 153–158. https://doi.org/10.17161/kjm.vol16.19952. PMID: 37377624.

Hesselink, G., Vernooij-Dassen, M., Pijnenborg, L., Barach, P., Gademan, P., Dudzik-Urbaniak, E. European HANDOVER Research Collaborative. (2013). Organizational culture: An important context for addressing and improving hospital to community patient discharge. *Medical Care, 51*(1), 90–98. https://doi.org/10.1097/mlr.0b013e31827632ec

Hoeft, S., & Pryor, R. W. (2016). *The power of ideas to transform healthcare: Engaging staff by building daily lean management systems*. CRC Press.

Hollingsworth, J. C., Chisholm, C. D., Giles, B. K., Cordell, W. H., & Nelson, D. R. (1998). How do physicians and nurses spend their time in the emergency department? *Annals of Emergency Medicine, 31*(1), 87–91. https://doi.org/10.1016/s0196-0644(98)70287-2

Hopp, W. J., & Spearman, M. L. (2008). *Factory physics: Foundations of manufacturing management* (3rd ed.). McGraw-Hill.

Imai, M. (2012). *Gemba kaizen* (2nd ed.). McGraw-Hill.

Itchhaporia, D. (2021). The evolution of the Quintuple Aim: Health equity, health outcomes, and the economy. *Journal of the American College of Cardiology, 78*(22), 2262–2264. https://doi.org/10.1016/j.jacc.2021.10.018. PMID: 34823665; PMCID: PMC8608191.

Jackson, T. L., & Jones, K. R. (1996). *Implementing a lean management system*. Productivity Press.

Jensen, K., & Mayer, T. (2015). *The patient flow advantage*. Fire Starter Publishing.

Johnson, J. & Barach, P. (2010). Quality improvement methods to study and improve the process and outcomes of pediatric cardiac care. *Progress in Pediatric Cardiology, 29*(1), 3–9. https://doi.org/10.1016/j.ppedcard.2010.01.003

Johnson, J., & Barach, P. (2017). Tools and strategies for continuous quality improvement and patient safety. In J. Sanchez, P. Barach, H. Johnson & J. Jacobs (Eds.), *Perioperative patient safety and quality: Principles and practice*. Springer.

Johnson, J., Farnan, J., Barach, P., Hesselink, G., Wollersheim, H., & Pijnenborg, L. . . .HANDOVER Research Collaborative. (2012). Searching for the missing pieces between the hospital and primary care: Mapping the patient process during care transitions. *BMJ Quality & Safety, 21*(Suppl 1), i97–i105. https://doi.org/10.1136/bmjqs-2012-001215

Kenney, C. (2010). *Transforming healthcare: Virginia Mason Medical Center's pursuit of the perfect patient experience*. CRC Press.

Kim, C. S., Spahlinger, D. A., Kin, J. M., & Billi, J. E. (2006). Lean health care: What can hospitals learn from a world-class automaker? *Journal of Hospital Medicine, 1*(3), 191–199. https://doi.org/10.1002/jhm.68

Labovitz, G., & Rosansky, V. (1997). *The power of alignment*. John Wiley & Sons.

Lawson, M. B. (2001). In praise of slack: Time is of the essence. *Academy of Management Perspectives, 15*(3), 125–135. https://doi.org/10.5465/ame.2001.5229658

Liker, J., & Ross, K. (2017). *The Toyota way to service excellence: Lean transformation in service organizations*. McGraw-Hill Education.

Mann, D. (2015). *Creating a lean culture: Tools to sustain lean conversions* (3rd ed.). CRC Press.

Martins, N. R. S., Martinez, E. Z., Simões, C. M., Barach, P. R., & Carmona, M. J. C. (2025). Analyzing and mitigating the risks of patient harm during operating room to intensive care unit patient handoffs. *International Journal for Quality in Health Care, 37*(1), mzae114. https://doi.org/10.1093/intqhc/mzae114. PMID: 39699203; PMCID: PMC11739622.

McManus, W. (2013, May 31). *Muda, muri, mura—Toyota production system guide*. The Official Toyota Blog. Archived at https://web.archive.org/web/20130728145103/http://blog.toyota.co.uk/muda-muri-mura-toyota-production-system

McManus M. L., Long M. C., Cooper A., Litvak E. Queuing theory accurately models the need for critical care resources. (2004) *Anesthesiology, 100*(5):1271-6. doi: 10.1097/00000542-200405000-00032. PMID: 15114227.

Mohr, J., Batalden, P., & Barach, P. (2004). Integrating patient safety into the clinical microsystem. *BMJ Quality and Safety in Healthcare, 13*(Suppl 2), ii34–ii38. https://doi.org/10.1136/qhc.13.suppl_2.ii34

Oster, C. A., & Braaten, J. S. (2016). *High reliability organizations: A healthcare handbook for patient safety & quality*. Sigma Theta Tau International.

Perla, R. J., Provost, L. P., & Murray, S. K. (2011). The run chart: A simple analytical tool for learning from variation in healthcare processes. *BMJ Quality and Safety, 20*(1), 46–51. https://doi.org/10.1136/bmjqs.2009.037895

Perla, R. J., Provost, L. P., & Murray, S. K. (2013). Sampling considerations for health care improvement. *Quality Management in Health Care, 22*(1), 36–47. https://doi.org/10.1097/qmh.0b013e31827deadb

Popovich, E., Wiggin, H., & Barach, P. (2020). The patient flow physics framework. In: J. Johnson & W. Sollecito (Eds.), *McLaughlin and Kaluzny's continuous quality improvement in health care* (5th ed.). Jones & Bartlett Learning.

Pound, E. S., Bell, J. H., & Spearman, M. L. (2014). *Factory physics for managers: How leaders improve performance in a post-Lean Six Sigma world*. McGraw-Hill Education.

Riguzzi C., Hern H. G., Vahidnia F., Herring A., Alter H. (2014) The July effect: Is emergency department length of stay greater at the beginning of the hospital academic year? *West J Emerg Med, 15*(1):88-93. doi: 10.5811/westjem.2013.10.18123. PMID: 24578770; PMCID: PMC3935791.

Rother, M. (2010). *Toyota kata: Managing people for improvement, adaptiveness, and superior results*. Rother & Company LLC.

Rummler, G. A., & Brache, A. P. (1995). *Improving performance: How to manage the white space on the organizational chart* (2nd ed.). Jossey-Bass.

Sanchez, J., & Barach, P. (2012). High reliability organizations and surgical microsystems: Re-engineering surgical care. *Surgical Clinics of North America, 92*(1), 1–14. https://doi.org/10.1016/j.suc.2011.12.005

Saposnik, G., Baibergenova, A., Bayer, N., & Hachinski, V. (2007). Weekends: A dangerous time for having a stroke? *Stroke, 38*(4), 1211–1215. https://doi.org/10.1161/01.str.0000259622.78616.ea

Sexton, J. B., Adair, K. C., Profit, J., et al. (2021). Safety culture and workforce well-being associations with positive leadership walkrounds. *The Joint Commission Journal on Quality and Patient Safety, 47*(7), 403–411. https://doi.org/10.1016/j.jcjq.2021.04.001

Sherrard, H., Trypuc, J., & Hudson, A. (2009). The use of coaching to improve peri-operative efficiencies: The Ontario experience. *Healthcare Quarterly, 12*(1), 48–54. https://doi.org/10.12927/hcq.2009.20348

Shulkin, D. (2008). Like night and day—shedding light on off-hours care. *The New England Journal of Medicine, 358*(20), 2092–2093. https://doi.org/10.1056/nejmp0707144

Spath, P. L., & Kelly, D. L. (2017). *Applying quality management in healthcare: A systems approach* (4th ed.). Health Administration Press.

Stem, J. M., & Greenberg, C. C. (2024). Coaching your faculty and yourself. *Surgery, 175*(4), 1247–1249. https://doi.org/10.1016/j.surg.2023.11.034

Suneja, A., & Suneja, C. (2010). *Lean doctors*. ASQ Quality Press.

Tamuz, M., & Harrison, M. I. (2006). Improving patient safety in hospitals: Contributions of high-reliability theory and normal accident theory. *Health Services Research, 41*(4 Pt 2), 1654–1676. https://doi.org/10.1111/j.1475-6773.2006.00570.x

Tukey, J. W. (1977). *Exploratory data analysis*. Addison-Wesley.

Uramatsu, M., Kimura, N., Kojima, T., Fujisawa, Y., Oto, T., & Barach, P. (2024). Frontline nursing staff's perceptions of intravenous medication administration: The first step toward safer infusion processes—a qualitative study. *BMJ Open Quality, 13*(12), e002809. https://doi.org/10.1136/bmjoq-2024-002809

Viau, M., & Southern, B. (2007). Six sigma and lean concepts, a case study: Patient centered care model for a mammography center, *Journal of Radiology Management, 29*(5), 19–28.

Weick, K. E., & Roberts, K. H. (1993). Collective mind in organizations: Heedful interrelating on flight decks. *Administrative Science Quarterly, 38*(3), 357–381. https://doi.org/10.2307/2393372

Weick, K. E., & Sutcliffe, K. M. (2001). *Managing the unexpected: Assuring high performance in an age of complexity*. John Wiley and Sons, Inc.

Wheeler, D. J. (1995). *Advanced topics in statistical process control*. SPC Press.

Wheeler, D. J. (2000). *Understanding variation: The key to managing chaos* (2nd ed.). SPC Press.

Womack, J. P., & Jones, D. T. (2003). *Lean thinking: Banish waste and create wealth in your corporation (2nd ed.)*. Free Press.

Womack, J. P., Jones, D. T., & Roos, D. (1990). *The machine that changed the world*. Free Press.

Wong A. H., Ahmed R. A., Ray J. M., et al. Supporting the Quadruple Aim using simulation and human factors during COVID-19 care. *Am J Med Qual*. 2021 Mar-Apr 01;36(2):73-83. https://doi:10.1097/01.JMQ.0000735432.16289.d2. PMID: 33830094; PMCID: PMC8030878.

© Flavio Coelho/Moment/Getty Images

CHAPTER 6

Understanding and Improving Team Effectiveness in Quality Improvement

Bruce J. Fried, Elizabeth Atchison, Madison Kutil, and Shreyank H. Thakker

CHAPTER OUTLINE

Introduction

The healthcare industry is of immense scale, with an estimated 83.4% of the U.S. population having at least one healthcare encounter annually (CDC, 2022). In virtually every encounter between patients and providers, collaboration is required among clinicians, administrative staff, patients, and in some cases, other departments, organizations, and family members. The nature of a healthcare team has expanded beyond a team with clear organizational boundaries, but can easily involve individuals in other organizations. Quality and patient safety require dependable teamwork and collaboration within the organization. Our traditional view of a team as having a defined membership with clear lines of accountability and communication is limited and somewhat outdated.

Teams are pervasive in health care and used for virtually every activity carried out in healthcare organizations, including clinical and management-focused activities. While our knowledge of evidence-based practices continues to grow, implementation of best practices has been uneven and fragmented. The development of the field of implementation science, introduced in Chapter 3, has sought to address the challenges of putting evidence into practice (Nilsen, 2015). While there is an array of obstacles to implementation, the application of medical knowledge to clinical service delivery is limited by the effectiveness and efficiency of teams charged with putting knowledge into practice. Similarly, as new management techniques and technologies are developed, including QI methods, successful use of these approaches is dependent upon appropriately staffed and trained teams.

Teams play a critical role in improving the performance of healthcare systems, whether a medical group practice, a hospital inpatient unit, a long-term care facility, or local public health department. Teams are the building blocks of healthcare organizations and are absolutely essential to caring for populations and individual patients, and identifying and successfully resolving quality problems. Teams are not an option but a necessity. As such, it makes great sense to examine these building blocks and see how they can be strengthened.

In this chapter, the concept of team is applied very broadly, and shares characteristics with the concept of microsystems (Nelson et al., 2002), which are also discussed in greater detail, with specific application to patient safety, in Chapter 9. A **microsystem** is one of several subsystems of a larger system that is integral to system performance. This perspective helps us understand how systems operate. When examining the performance of a system, it is essential to examine (among other factors) the effectiveness of each component subsystem, how these subsystems work together (e.g., the nature and adequacy of coordination between a hospital pharmacy and an inpatient unit), and the adequacy of information about system and subsystem performance (e.g., the extent to which the driver of an automobile is provided with information about the automobile's performance).

A health system is composed of many subsystems. In patient care, these may be referred to as clinical microsystems or frontline systems, referring to teams charged with meeting the needs of the patient population. Microsystems provide services that result in positive patient outcomes, provider and patient safety, system efficiency, and patient satisfaction. The effectiveness of a large healthcare system can be no better than the microsystems of which it is composed (Nelson et al., 2002).

Using the terminology of the microsystem, it is apparent how a microsystem is in fact one type of team (Nelson et al., 2002, p. 474):

> A clinical microsystem is a small group of people who work together on a regular basis to provide care to discrete subpopulations of patients. It has clinical and business aims, linked processes, and a shared information environment, and it produces performance outcomes. Microsystems evolve over time and are often embedded in larger organizations. They are complex adaptive systems,

> and as such they must do the primary work associated with core aims, meet the needs of internal staff, and maintain themselves over time as clinical units.

This definition may be applied to other types of teams in health care. The key concepts in relation to teams include:

- People work together toward specific goals.
- They use multiple interconnected processes.
- They produce performance outcomes.
- They have access to information about the team's performance.

In this chapter, we bring together several research traditions on teams. We demonstrate how knowledge of teams informs our understanding of team performance and the important role of teams in QI efforts.

Most of the research on team effectiveness has been carried out in relatively permanent teams with stable membership and opportunities for face-to-face interactions. Traditional approaches to teams support the idea that teams grow and learn as members spend prolonged periods of time together. As teams mature over time, members learn each other's habits, and adapt to members' preferences and needs. However, this is not always the case in health care. Teams may emerge quickly to respond to new situations. Multiple challenges may arise, including working with teams whose membership spans departments, dealing with crisis situations, coping with hierarchical issues which may conflict with team demands, and adapting to new technologies. Some healthcare teams exist for only a short period of time, perhaps as short as a nursing shift. Some teams must organize themselves rapidly, and may not have the luxury of going through extended stages of team maturation. In this chapter, attention is given to traditional as well as temporary teams. Simply put, today's teams do not always fit into traditional team structures and processes, and we need to account for these variations when discussing healthcare teams.

The events in **Case 6.1** illustrate multiple impediments to building a successful, high-performing team. The situation was improved,

Case 6.1: State University Hospital and Donor Services

State Donor Services (SDS) centrally manages the state's organ procurement and donation process. There had been a trend of declining organ availability for transplant, despite efforts to increase awareness and success in registering donors through the Division of Motor Vehicles. To help solve the problem, SDS approached State University Hospital (SUH), one of the biggest sources of and utilizers of donated organs through its organ transplant programs. Initial exploration of the problem quickly indicated a consistent demand for organs, but organ donations at SUH were down, matching the pattern seen by SDS.

Chris Carter, the new administrator for SUH's emergency department, was asked to build a team to solve this problem. The hospital's Chief Operating Officer (COO) told Chris this was a top priority because of the high visibility of the transplant programs, the revenues it brought to the institution, and the fact that the Chairman of Surgery had just threatened to leave the institution if SUH "didn't fix this problem it had obviously created." The COO gave Chris two weeks to assemble a team and develop a solution, which Chris would present at SUH's monthly Executive Committee meeting. Chris asked the COO for advice about team membership and the COO referred him to the Chief Nursing Officer (CNO).

Chris went to the CNO, but the first available meeting time she had was in three days. In the meantime, Chris gathered as much information as possible. On the third day, the CNO's secretary called to cancel the meeting but suggested he talk with the Nursing Division Director for Medicine. She met with Chris that afternoon, and together, they formulated a list of people they thought would be able to address the issue. SUH was a functionally structured organization, so they built a team with nursing directors from each of the transplant services and the emergency department, the Director of Patient Care Services, a clerk, a physician from the emergency room, and the State Medical Examiner—whose office was located at SUH and who was responsible for autopsies—as well as a clerk from his office.

The earliest possible meeting time for this group was in 3 weeks—well beyond the COO's deadline. Nonetheless, Chris set up a meeting with as many team members as possible and met with the others individually. The team would be able to meet only once or twice given the aggressive deadline and members' schedules.

Noting the tight deadline, Chris got right to business when the group met. He told the group his goals and invited an open discussion of each team member's experiences with organ procurement. It quickly became evident several members of the team were too new or too junior to be helpful, with some of Chris's invitees having asked more junior colleagues to be a part of the team in their stead. The Medical Examiner immediately called into question the validity of the group and the authority by which he had been called to the meeting. When Chris told him this was a high-priority project for the COO and CNO—stating only their names and not their titles—the Medical Examiner indignantly replied he had never heard of these people and this was a waste of his time. When Chris clarified their titles, the Medical Examiner became less vocal, but remained indignant. He had been focused on solving a problem of declining autopsies, which placed SUH at risk of violating a state regulation. He was angry to have been diverted from this pressing problem and felt Chris's group would draw organizational focus and energies away from his own needs. His resentment spread to others in the group, which, coupled with their inexperience and a lack of appropriate representation, rendered the meeting—and the group—effectively useless.

In an effort to avoid a public display of this disaster, Chris reported his lack of success to the COO prior to the Executive Committee meeting. The COO realized the impossibility of the goals he had set for Chris and extended the deadline 3 months and also utilized his own authority by agreeing to attend the next team meeting. These two key factors allowed Chris to rebuild a more knowledgeable, representative, and experienced team.

Ultimately, the organ donation problem was traced to a series of new federal regulations and SUH's fragmented approach to processing end-of-life paperwork. In summary, each operational unit had established its own processes for responding to the regulatory requirements, none of which were integrated with the other operational units, thus creating hours of work for the clinical staff, most of whom gave up trying to secure organ donations. Interestingly, the Medical Examiner's problem of a declining autopsy rate was also a result of this same disjointed method of paperwork processing.

however, as senior management became more involved, setting an appropriate timeline, changing membership, and conveying the importance of the team to the organization. As team composition and size were restructured to include the appropriate participants, senior management also granted the team visible and legitimate authority to accomplish its tasks, and an environment of psychological safety (discussed later in this chapter) was created where open communication was encouraged, and individual team members could contribute with no risk of rebuke by others.

The case illustrates how relationship status within teams affects team dynamics and productivity. Relationship status pertains to understanding hierarchy, authority, and the nature of interactions among team members based on their positions and standing within an organization. At first, the Medical Examiner doubted the validity of the team because he was unaware of the authoritative figures present, illustrating how recognition of leadership is vital for building trust and collaboration. The presence of junior and less experienced members further diminished the team's capability, as it lacked essential expertise, resulting in frustration and a diminished sense of legitimacy. Power dynamics and differing priorities, such as the Medical Examiner's emphasis on decreasing autopsies, generated tension and obstructed teamwork within the team. However, after senior management extended the deadline and became more engaged, the team was reorganized with suitable representation, which fostered psychological safety. This environment enabled team members to share their ideas freely, enhancing communication and unity, ultimately leading to the successful identification of the issue at hand. The case underscores how inadequate relationship status can impair performance, but with effective leadership and necessary adjustments, trust and collaboration can be established.

Teams in Health Care

As medical knowledge grows increasingly complex and medical specialties continue to develop around specific focus areas, there is a risk that healthcare organizations will lose their patient-centered orientation. There is a paradox in relation to the adoption of new medical technologies and procedures. On the one hand, increasingly specific diagnostic and treatment procedures imply a narrowing of focus on unique patient characteristics. This is desirable because we all support the discovery and implementation of procedures to improve the sensitivity and specificity of diagnoses and the development of pharmaceuticals, technology, and procedures that treat a disease in a manner specific to the individual and the disease state. However, providing continuing care to a patient requires information from multiple sources and, very often, the involvement of multiple individuals. For example, psychopharmacology has become increasingly specific and sophisticated. However, better utilization of new pharmaceuticals for the benefit of the patient requires psychiatrists understand a patient's social environment, which may require the knowledge base of social workers and others. That is, a team of individuals may be required to ensure home support and respite services are available to caregivers. Thus, the need for patient-centered multispecialty teams becomes ever more important as healthcare providers and organizations specialize and strive to deliver the best and most appropriate care possible.

Healthcare system complexity extends beyond the clinical care arena and into administrative areas. Teams fill an organizational need to help identify and respond to changes brought about by legal and regulatory changes, more complex payer contracts, and increasing accountability and pressure for value.

At the most basic level, clinical healthcare teams are comprised of healthcare providers, including nonclinical personnel from multiple disciplines, focusing on a patient or patient population with similar healthcare needs. Patient-centeredness has extended upward and outward to all aspects of many healthcare organizations. Indeed, the industry has seen a trend away from organizational structures based on functional areas of expertise (e.g., nursing, environmental services, registration, medicine, surgery) and toward functionally integrated organizational structures with clinical care teams based on patient needs (e.g., children's services, women's services, cancer care services). Individual clinical specialists serving on these teams report not only to their disciplinary head (e.g., chief of nursing, chair of medicine), but also to team leaders associated with specific patient-centered service areas. This "dual reporting" format is described in organizational literature as a matrix structure (Grove, 1995). As discussed later in this chapter, dual reporting requirements pose challenges for managing multidisciplinary teams.

While the multidisciplinary team model has been adopted to improve patient-centered health care, teams and supporting organizational structures do not spontaneously form. In fact, reward systems—typically designed around performance of one's particular discipline or function, rather than on an individual's role on teams—often work against team effectiveness. A substantial body of research demonstrates key elements are necessary for teams to perform to their maximum potential (Fried & Edmondson, 2020). If these elements are not addressed, we may see team member and patient dissatisfaction, disjointed care provision, and inefficient and ineffective operations.

High Performance Teams and Quality Improvement

The focus of this chapter is on the critical role of high-performing teams in QI efforts, and on strategies to improve team effectiveness. The value of teams was established in the earliest applications of QI as a way to ensure the multidisciplinary sharing of knowledge (Deming, 1986). In modern health care, teams are critical to success in QI for a number of reasons:

1. Quality problems are often not visible to managers at middle or senior management

levels, but the impact of problems can be experienced by the entire organization, as shown in the organ donation case. Hospital staff nurses, for example, may see repeated examples of poor communication between shifts that result in problems for patients and families, physicians, and other hospital staff. Each occurrence of a problem may be dealt with and resolved in a satisfactory manner; however, in aggregate, these communication problems may become costly in terms of wasted time, reduced quality and patient safety, and lack of continuity of care. Individuals on the front lines are quite frequently aware of systemic problems requiring methodical analysis. One can easily make the case that the farther a person is from the front lines of care, the more removed they are from seeing and addressing problems. Thus, if we wish to identify quality problems and optimal solutions, we need individuals on our teams who are close to the problem and can help uncover root causes.

2. Healthcare organizations accomplish their work through a myriad of processes, which may be flawed, confusing, or inefficient. In some situations, a process itself may be ineffective, while in other cases, a well-designed process may be poorly implemented. For example, what appears theoretically on paper as an accurate flowchart describing patient care may be entirely inaccurate when compared to how the process actually operates. Regardless, much of QI involves process analysis and improvement. Individuals working in dysfunctional processes are often most knowledgeable about process impacts and causes. Therefore, it is essential to have participation from individuals who have the most accurate and detailed understanding of process.
3. Individuals at the front lines often have unique knowledge and insight into organizational problems and are thus in a position to offer effective and feasible suggestions for improvement. It has long been known that individuals at relatively low levels of the organization often acquire considerable knowledge about the organization and are positioned to reduce uncertainty in the organization, and, in some cases, may use this knowledge to acquire power (Crozier, 1964). For example, a receptionist who has worked in a pediatric group practice over several years may have a very clear understanding of why waiting times are unacceptably long at certain times of the day. As a result of that experience, they may have a well-reasoned understanding of how the practice operates and have valuable suggestions about how scheduling and staffing may be altered to help ameliorate the waiting time problem. Note as well that because the receptionist may be considered a "nonprofessional," this person may have never been asked to provide input.
4. Addressing quality problems requires the support of key individuals affected by or having in-depth knowledge of the problem—not simply those at middle or senior management levels. Identifying and proposing solutions to quality problems is central to QI efforts, but unless those involved in solution implementation understand fully the rationale for the effort, implementation may fall short. Those involved in implementing solutions must be involved so they understand the QI strategy and can identify possible obstacles to effective implementation.
5. High-functioning teams empower people by providing opportunities for meaningful participation in problem identification and problem solving. A consequence of empowerment is that people feel greater commitment to the organization and have a stronger sense of ownership. Empowerment promotes a greater willingness to participate in developing and implementing solutions.

As seen in the introductory organ donation case, the well-intentioned manager tasked with solving an institution-wide problem was unable to constitute a team with appropriate members. As a result, the team was frustrated by its inability to achieve its goals. However, one cannot place the blame entirely on the manager. An unrealistic timeline and the absence of initial support by senior management both played a role in the team's failure. Provided with a more appropriate timeline with sufficient authority, the manager built a team comprised of individuals with appropriate experience. This team was able to develop, perform, and reach its goals.

Understanding and Improving the Performance of Quality Improvement Teams

In this section, we present evidence about teams and team management, relate this information to QI teams, and apply case examples to illustrate selective concepts and principles.

Team Tasks and Goals

As a point of departure, all teams have goals and associated tasks. Understanding the fundamental purposes of a team guides other aspects of team development and management, including team composition, decision-making processes, and the types of interdependencies the team has with other entities in the organization. QI teams are, by definition, focused on identifying and analyzing quality and patient safety problems, designing interventions to address these problems, and evaluating the impact of changes. In one form or another, teams complete tasks aligned with the Plan Do Check Act (PDCA) (or PDSA), cycle, which was first introduced in Chapter 1 and is discussed with various applications throughout this book. The clarity of tasks and goals as well as the authority/empowerment of the team to carry out improvement efforts is key to engaging team members.

Although some teams have clear and self-evident goals, QI teams may face ambiguity. The nature of QI itself is a process of discovery; as root causes of problems are uncovered, teams may find team tasks change. For example, a team working in a clinic in a low-income country may be investigating the problem of drug stock-outs. The team may find that a key root cause of the problem is an inconsistent supply chain, which in turn is due to poor communication between clinic staff and a central supply depot. Further, communication problems may also be due to frequent power outages in the clinic. An intervention to reduce stock-outs may therefore require team members with expertise in addressing problems of power supply and connectivity. In this case, the initial composition of the team may be inadequate to address root causes. The team may wish to add a team member from the supply depot to help suggest changes in how and when the clinic communicates with the supply depot. In sum, as underlying problems are identified, team tasks may change.

A common problem facing teams is lack of clarity about the team's authority to implement change. A team's authority may be limited by a range of factors, including organizational politics, intra-organizational dynamics, and environmental changes. What is most important is that teams have a clear understanding of the limits of their authority. It is disheartening and demotivating for team members to believe the team has the authority to implement a change only to face the reality that the team is limited to providing suggestions or recommendations.

Team Characteristics

Team characteristics refer to basic physical and social psychological aspects of a team and include team composition and size, relationships between team members, the impact of status differences among team members, psychological safety, team norms, and the team's stage of development. All of these characteristics potentially affect team effectiveness.

Team Composition and Size

Team composition and size are critically important, and depend upon the nature of the team, its goals, tasks, and perhaps of greatest importance, the types of expertise required. The Institute for Health Improvement (IHI) suggests successful QI teams require four general types of expertise.

A clinical leader is an individual who has authority in the organization to test and implement changes and to overcome implementation problems. A team member with technical expertise has a thorough understanding of the systems and processes of care. A third team member is a subject matter expert and is in a position to drive the project on a day-to-day basis—a project manager of sorts. Finally, a project sponsor is required who has the executive authority to serve as a link with senior management; this individual may or may not be a member of the team on a day-to-day basis (IHI, 2017), but is essential for success.

When deciding upon team composition, one needs to consider the tasks facing the team. For example, if information technology knowledge is needed, it would be helpful to have a team member with this expertise. Team size goes hand-in-hand with team composition. The team must have adequate diversity and expertise to inform all aspects of the team's tasks and goals. Yet the team must not be so large that it poses logistical obstacles (such as difficulty scheduling meetings and reaching consensus) which may threaten the team's ability to follow its timeline.

Team size and composition may vary over time. An individual may join a team for a short period of time to address a specific technical problem. In addition, it is common for members in team meetings to rotate attendance. For example, if the nursing perspective is required, it would be reasonable for different nurses to attend team meetings over time. This type of arrangement is often necessary because of the realities of organizational life; people have multiple commitments and time pressures that may require flexibility in team membership. Furthermore, teams vary in permanence and longevity. While we may think of teams as relatively permanent and stable groups, there are instances where a team must quickly form and work together over a short period of time. Edmondson (2012a) coined the term "teaming" to refer to an organization capable of collaborating and coordinating without the necessary team structures, such as stable team membership. She refers to this capability as "teamwork on the fly." As described by Edmondson, individuals working in hospital emergency departments must work as a team, although each shift may bring different team members who may not have previously worked together. Valentine and Edmondson (2015) use the term "scaffolding" to describe a number of ways in which organizations can support the development and effective operation of temporary or ad hoc teams.

Team Relationships and Status Differences

Because we often learn about quality problems from individuals situated at different levels and units of an organization, a central tenet of QI is participation of a broad array of team members. These include individuals at relatively low levels in the organization without formal authority but with considerable tacit knowledge. In fact, it is often those on the front lines who bring unique perspectives and insights into a situation as seen in **Case 6.2**.

Involving an appropriate range of people is only the first step, however. In any team, people bring with them their roles and status from regular organizational life. Physicians working on a team with nurses bring their higher professional status and authority. The physician–nurse relationship in the organization is "imported" into the team. These preformed relationships and status systems may influence the participation of team members and affect team effectiveness. Individuals from lower status groups are less likely to contribute than those of higher status. They may feel intimidated or may simply feel their input is not valued. For QI teams, such status differences are dysfunctional. To engage all team members and ensure the team can utilize each member's knowledge, QI team leaders need to find a way to moderate status differences.

Recognition of the professional preparation of nurses has contributed to their role in a number of quality initiatives. For example, nurses in California led to improvements in hospital cardiac care by participating in a leadership and innovation program offered through the American Association of Critical-Care Nurses (AACN, 2023).

Team members bring to the team previously formed relationships. We may find two individuals

Case 6.2: Physician and Nurse Discourse at Mercy Hospital

Mercy Hospital is a 300-bed facility serving a largely middle-class suburban population. The hospital is well regarded, largely because of its patient-centered approach. Recently, the hospital transitioned to a collaborative care model aimed at integrating nurses and physicians in developing patient care plans. This model represents a break from its prior approach which saw nurses receiving and carrying out "orders" from physicians. The hope was with medical staff and nurses working together, there would be more interactions with the patient prior to treatment, and patient care would improve. There was hope this new model would decrease nurse turnover as it would put them at professional levels similar to physicians. However, the model highlighted significant challenges that threatened its success.

During a busy morning shift, Nurse Ally was assigned to care for Mr. Scott, a 68-year-old patient with multiple chronic conditions, including diabetes and hypertension, who had been on the ward for almost a week. As the head nurse in charge of his care, she had been closely monitoring Mr. Scott's symptoms and noticed new complaints suggesting a potential heart issue.

While the new collaborative care model urged Nurse Ally to bring her findings to Dr. Williams, a senior physician, she felt he was unwilling to give up his position as head of the team. He made multiple comments regarding the new model as useless and a waste of time. He stated he "has never, and will never, require the suggestion of treatment from someone who did not go to medical school." Ultimately, she chose to document her observations in Mr. Scott's chart, hoping her notes would prompt further investigation.

When Dr. Williams arrived to review Mr. Scott's case, he quickly dismissed Nurse Ally's observations. "His vital signs are stable, and we've already established a care plan. We can't change course without clear evidence," he asserted. While Nurse Ally was adamant that alternative treatment is required for the patient's care and survival, she felt uncomfortable challenging Dr. Williams, worrying her concerns would not be taken seriously and that she might face repercussions for speaking up.

Days later, Mr. Scott's condition deteriorates, leading to a cardiac event that could have been prevented with earlier intervention. The team was now faced with the implications of the missed diagnosis, which contributed to the patient's adverse outcome.

with a history of interpersonal problems serving on the same team. Unfortunately, relationship problems and dysfunctional status differences can dramatically affect the work of a team. It is truly the remarkable team that can dispose of status differences and interpersonal conflicts in the interest of team goals. At the very least, team leaders need to be aware of status differences and the impact of those differences on communication and team effectiveness. One way to avoid the problems of status difference and interpersonal conflict is to have a team leader with sufficient authority and respect act as moderator, encouraging lower status members to participate, keeping higher status members in check, and defusing tension driven by team member conflict.

People who work on QI teams typically have "regular" jobs in the organization, and their participation in improvement efforts requires time away from their normal work. It is therefore important to reduce the amount of time lost to process issues, or activities that are not part of the actual goals and tasks of the team, such as scheduling meetings and managing conflict. Teams may come together amidst great enthusiasm about tackling a difficult problem. However, the work of a team may create frictions and bring to the surface latent conflicts or reignite old disputes. Interprofessional rivalries, which may have been part of the organizational culture for many years, may surface, and leaders should devise strategies to manage and minimize these conflicts.

At Mercy Hospital, differences in status were ultimately detrimental to patient care. First, the new model of collaborative care between physicians and nurses was adopted rapidly with little consideration of already existing relationships. Second, when Nurse Ally attempted to speak up regarding patient treatment she was quickly turned down and ignored. With no one to take her concerns to, the patient ultimately suffered a cardiac event. As a result of high-tension levels and status differences, the collaborative model was not easily implemented. At Mercy Hospital, there was a clear communication breakdown when the lead physician dismissed the nurse's observations and doubts regarding the patient's ongoing treatment and symptoms. This resulted in an environment where crucial information about the patient was not shared effectively, eventually leading to improper and insufficient care. A helpful approach for dealing with communication issues is for the team to have regular interdisciplinary meetings to foster ongoing communication. Meetings would help encourage open dialogue and prevent the tensions described in this case. Communication is not simply a way of improving morale but is central to healthcare quality, and is in fact central to the care model established at Mercy Hospital.

Psychological Safety

Team **psychological safety** is defined as a shared belief that the team is safe for interpersonal risk taking (Edmondson, 1999). A central tenet of QI is the belief people must be forthcoming and honest about quality problems, even where they themselves were responsible for, or shared responsibility for, a quality or patient safety incident. Individuals involved in improvement efforts must feel their suggestions will be heard without fear of intimidation, condescension, or castigation (Deming, 1986). Where people feel safe, there is a greater likelihood of their participating effectively in QI efforts. Furthermore, psychological safety is an important prerequisite for implementing organizational change. Individuals who face the "epidemic of silence," where they do not voice their concerns, usually do so in an attempt to avoid being labeled negatively or damage work relationships (Edmondson, 2020).

The issue of psychological safety is apparent in the Mercy Hospital case. Team collaboration was impacted by the lack of trust and psychological safety. The nurse, feeling hesitant to speak up in front of Dr. Williams, highlights a larger issue of staff not feeling psychologically safe. Quality of care is at risk when team members are unable to express their thoughts or concerns. To foster a more supportive environment, the hospital might consider implementing staff development activities to improve communication and improve the climate of psychological safety. These efforts can establish a space where team members feel comfortable sharing their insights and challenges, ultimately leading to improvements in trust among team members.

As illustrated in the Mercy Hospital case, status differences may be associated with the lack of psychological safety. Where status differences have an oppressive presence, it is unlikely team participants will feel the willingness to participate in discussions of quality. Dr. Williams was adamant there should be no change in the current care model for Mr. Scott, ultimately leading to a cardiac event that could have been avoided. Although concern was voiced prior to the incident, it was never addressed due to prior hierarchical structures being embedded into the culture of the organization.

The absence of psychological safety not only diminished Nurse Ally's confidence but also jeopardized the effectiveness of the collaborative care model. For such a model to thrive, both nurses and physicians need to feel valued and supported in their roles. In the absence of this support, the model cannot operate as intended, putting patient safety at risk. By establishing a setting where psychological safety is prioritized, the hospital can enhance collaboration, avert potential patient safety hazards, and improve the overall effectiveness of the collaborative care model.

Team leaders need to consider questions of psychological safety: Do participants feel safe in making recommendations, participating in discussions, and perhaps of greatest importance, expressing skepticism and disagreement? Leaders must examine their own behavior and assess the extent to which their leadership style and manner of interaction invite participation and promote safety. It is only by creating such a climate that team members will not become subject to "groupthink," a term which describes team members' reluctance to question the dominant view even if their opinions differ (Bang & Frith, 2017).

Team Norms

A team norm is a standard of behavior shared by team members. Norms set expectations and establish standards of behavior and performance. Norms have a strong impact on individuals in organizations, essentially establishing the "rules" under which people function. **Behavioral norms** consist of rules that govern individual behavior and attitudes. In a team context, behavioral norms define how people are expected to behave on a team. These may include expectations about attendance, preparation for team meetings, and the manner in which members communicate with each other during and between team meetings. Norms are different in every team.

In the Sunnyville Hospital case study, **Case 6.3**, we see the interaction between status differences

Case 6.3: Complications at Sunnyville Hospital

Situated in Tampa, Florida, Sunnyville Hospital experienced an emergency trauma case around 11:30 p.m. Thursday night. A male patient in his early twenties arrived after being involved in a severe car accident. He was rushed to the operating room for immediate surgery to address internal bleeding, lacerations, and multiple fractures. As a result of staffing shortages, an ad-hoc team of OR personnel was assembled to manage the case. The team consisted of two travel nurses who had arrived two days prior and were largely unfamiliar with the hospital's trauma protocols; a surgical technician pulled from another department; and a junior resident who had not previously worked under the lead surgeon.

With the patient in critical condition and the team preparing for surgery, there was no time to conduct a pre-op meeting. The travel nurses had not undergone operating room procedures training at this hospital prior to this situation, but were expected to meet the same demands as those that had been hired and trained by the hospital. Furthermore, the lead surgeon was known for his fast-paced and high-demand style, and expected to come into the OR and immediately begin critical care. The surgeon assumed all team members were aware of the hospital's trauma protocols and, therefore, neglected to go over information related to the case.

As the surgery began, the lack of communication between team members became evident. The lead surgeon became frustrated when the nurses struggled to anticipate equipment needs, leading to delay in providing care. Unaccustomed to the surgeon's preferences and the layout of the OR, they were unable to maintain the required pace of work. Fearing reprimand in front of senior staff members, the nurses were reluctant to ask clarifying questions. Unfamiliar with trauma cases of this magnitude, the junior resident was unsure of her role in the operating room and hesitated to take initiative when she saw the situation escalate. To make matters worse, the lead surgeon was occupied managing the case as these issues continued to arise, leading to a lack of delegation to team members. Ultimately, the resident was unable to assist in the operation and spent most of the time assisting the nurses, and was excluded from learning opportunities throughout the procedure.

As the atmosphere within the OR became tense, coordination between team members began to have tangible effects on the patient's condition. Blood transfusions were delayed due to miscommunications about who was responsible for calling the blood bank. Ultimately, the resident, who was familiar with the inner workings of the hospital, put in an emergency call and resolved the problem.

Permanent staff, overwhelmed by the complexity of the procedure and the demands placed on them, failed to step in and assist travel nurses when it became clear they were struggling. The result was a lack of coordination, compounded by dysfunctional communication throughout the surgery. The combination of role ambiguity, poor integration of temporary staff, and ineffective team communication led to a prolonged surgery and increased risk for the patient.

The patient eventually made a recovery in the intensive care unit, but staff were troubled about the manner in which care was provided. A follow-up meeting was called the next day to discuss performance issues and how to improve communication through clarifying team members' roles and responsibilities. Administration worried if future cases were to come through the ER under similar circumstances, similar problems would emerge. As a result, it was decided travel nurses would be briefed on how emergent situations were carried out in the OR, residents would assist the lead surgeon and aid nurses if there was a deficit, and the lead surgeon would state critical case points prior to beginning the procedure.

This case demonstrates the importance of establishing clear norms, communication channels, and support structures—especially when a team is hastily assembled in a high-pressure environment.

and norms. Although there was likely a superficial belief in the desirability of a democratic and participative climate, it was clear behavioral norms emphasized a high regard for hierarchy. For example, nurses were required to produce equipment for the lead surgeon to ensure the procedure proceeded as smoothly as possible. However, due to the unfamiliarity of the OR emergency response team and the lack of role definition, they were unable to efficiently complete their task. Norms about attendance at meetings were non-existent due to the crisis at hand but it was later determined the lead surgeon would provide a briefing and expectations of the case to each team member prior to commencing surgery. Because staff feared being chastised, participation was inhibited, and full discussion of issues was repressed, worsening conditions if there had not been additional attempts at lifesaving procedures.

In contrast to behavioral norms, **performance norms** govern the amount and quality of work expected of team members. In the Sunnyville Hospital case, performance norms were broken, leading to difficulties for the surgical team. The resident was not involved in patient care decisions due to a lack of teaching and instead assisted nurses when efforts fell short of the lead surgeon's needs. While there were expectations about how travel nurses should operate within the hospital system, they had yet to experience an emergency trauma case. Therefore, when they were pulled into the surgical room, they were forced to adapt to new responsibilities which differed from their usual work. This change in work demand was not anticipated, and breaking this performance norm caused additional stress and the inability of the nurses to question authority under an already tense situation.

At Sunnyville Hospital, the lack of defined team norms significantly affected operations. **Team norms**—implied rules or expectations that direct team member interactions—were ambiguous from the beginning, resulting in confusion and frustration in a fast-paced environment.

Initially, the absence of communication norms between the lead surgeon and the rest of the team became evident. The surgeon assumed team members were familiar with his preferences and trauma protocols, but without clear communication guidelines, the travel nurses struggled to keep pace. This illustrates the importance of establishing norms for information sharing, especially in highly stressful and dynamic environments. Defining expectations for when and how to ask questions, delegate tasks, and report concerns would have facilitated a more efficient workflow. Role clarity, another essential norm, was lacking. With poorly defined roles, team members were uncertain about their responsibilities, leading to delays in patient care. Norms specifying individual duties during a procedure would have enabled everyone to participate more effectively, minimizing hesitation and confusion.

Lastly, norms regarding support and adaptability—expectations for assisting team members in challenging situations—were not present. Unfamiliar with the setting, travel nurses struggled without needed assistance from permanent staff. In such situations, norms related to providing support for colleagues were absent. The scenario at Sunnyville highlights the need for proactively establishing team norms, especially concerning communication, role clarity, and mutual support.

Interprofessional Rivalries and Conflict

It is not uncommon for rivalries and conflict to emerge in teams. The important point is how conflicts are resolved. One common source of conflict in health care involves interprofessional conflict. This takes numerous forms, including conflict over "turf," that is, which professional groups have the privilege of providing certain services. Conflict may also be associated with two or more professional groups having different orientations regarding health services delivery. In this section, we provide two examples of interprofessional conflict in health care. In each instance, ineffective management of these conflicts may result in dysfunctional teams and threats to the quality of care.

In anesthesia teams, the relationship between Certified Registered Nurse Anesthetists (CRNAs) and anesthesiologists exemplifies the complexities of status and teamwork in health care. As described earlier, effective teams are characterized by clear role definitions, mutual respect, and communication. The collaboration between CRNAs and anesthesiologists demonstrates the importance of these elements, especially in environments where team members hold different levels of authority. CRNAs and anesthesiologists work closely together to manage anesthesia and ensure patient safety during surgical procedures, particularly through the adoption of techniques such as nerve blocks to reduce opioid use (Schreiber & MacDonald, 2021). However, the status differences between these professionals can introduce challenges in communication and collaboration. This dynamic highlights how status impacts team effectiveness in high-stakes health care settings.

The role of autonomy in CRNA practice is a significant aspect of the team structure in anesthesia care, especially in such states as California where CRNAs are permitted to practice independently without direct supervision from anesthesiologists. Independent practice enables CRNAs to take full responsibility for administering anesthesia, managing pain, and providing perioperative care in both routine and high-pressure situations (Wising et al., 2024). This autonomy can be both an asset and a potential source of tension. While independent practice expands access to care and provides a cost-effective alternative to anesthesiologist-only models, it can challenge traditional hierarchies within healthcare teams. When team roles and responsibilities are clearly defined, even in autonomous or semi-autonomous practice, it promotes smoother collaboration. The ability for CRNAs to work independently underscores the importance of trust and respect within a team structure.

Education plays a critical role in shaping the professional relationship between CRNAs and anesthesiologists. Anesthesiologists are often involved in the preclinical education of CRNAs, providing training in anesthesia management and patient care. This dynamic, as explored by Swerdlow et al., (2020), reinforces hierarchies within the healthcare team. If handled well, this educational relationship can foster mutual respect and contribute to the long-term success of the team. As this chapter emphasizes, team effectiveness is not solely determined by authority but by the ability of all team members to leverage their expertise to achieve shared goals. While anesthesiologists may provide foundational training to CRNAs, it is crucial that this knowledge-sharing is part of a reciprocal learning process that values the contributions of both professionals.

International perspectives on anesthesia team dynamics, such as those explored in Khalafi et al.'s (2023) study in Iran, further illustrate the role of status in team relationships. In hierarchical healthcare settings, communication between anesthesiologists and nurse anesthetists is often affected by differences in perceived authority, leading to challenges in collaboration and decision making. This mirrors the experiences of many healthcare teams in the United States, where rigid status differences can create barriers to effective teamwork. However, when teams focus on clarifying roles and fostering mutual respect, these barriers can be reduced, leading to more efficient and supportive team environments. The Iranian study reinforces the importance of building inclusive team cultures, even in environments where status differences are deeply ingrained.

The relationship between CRNAs and anesthesiologists also brings into focus the broader implications of status within healthcare teams. While collaboration between these professionals is essential for patient care, inherent power dynamics can lead to both positive and negative outcomes. As Wising et al., (2024) note, tensions may arise due to differences in authority, with anesthesiologists sometimes perceiving CRNAs as subordinates rather than equal partners. Yet, when team dynamics are rooted in respect, open communication, and a shared focus on patient outcomes, these tensions can be mitigated.

In the context of dental care, dental therapists are emerging as essential team members who help to address workforce shortages (Yang et al., 2017). Dental therapists are mid-level providers trained to perform preventive and routine restorative procedures, such as fillings, extractions, and patient education. These professionals are crucial in improving access to care, especially in regions like the Yukon-Kuskokwim Delta, where dental therapists have been associated with better oral health outcomes in Alaska Native communities (Chi et al., 2018).

The relationship between dental therapists and dentists is fundamental to delivering comprehensive care. Dentists often assume a supervisory role, delegating routine dental tasks to therapists while concentrating on more complex procedures. Delegation not only allows for a more efficient use of the dental workforce but also enhances patient care by ensuring each professional works at the top of their license. A key aspect of this collaboration is the referral pipeline, wherein dental therapists can manage primary care and refer patients to dentists for more specialized interventions. This system enables continuity of care while optimizing the roles of each team member in meeting patient needs (Barnett et al., 2021).

However, as in other healthcare settings, the dynamics of status and hierarchy can impact the effectiveness of collaboration. The authority of dentists, grounded in their extensive training and experience, may create barriers to communication and teamwork with dental therapists. Just as physicians and nurses can face challenges in interprofessional relationships, dental teams must navigate the complexities of professional hierarchy to foster an inclusive environment. Ensuring dental therapists feel empowered to share their insights and observations is critical for the team's effectiveness.

The evolving dynamics between dental therapists and dentists may lead to a redefined balance in their roles. As dental therapists gain more recognition and expand their scope of practice in the United States, they are likely to become integral to the dental care team, particularly in underserved areas. These changes have the potential to strengthen team cohesion, as trust and collaboration increase with shared responsibilities. The legal and professional status of dental therapists will continue to develop, and their growing role will shape how dental teams operate in the future (Yang et al., 2020).

Team Processes

Team processes refers to the manner in which teams accomplish their work and the factors affecting how they do their work. We discuss communication networks and interaction patterns, stages of team development, decision making, member and team learning, team leadership, rewards, and motivation.

Communication Networks and Interaction Patterns

A key task in any team is the exchange of information. Communication is essential and central to all teams. Communication is also required between the team and the larger external environment, including other teams.

It is critical information be accurately and consistently conveyed. A question is: what is the best method of information exchange and how do we ensure it is carried out effectively and accurately? Information exchange requires responsibilities of both information sender and receiver. This is especially true in teams where exchanges between team members and team leaders do not rely solely on the hierarchy implied by a team structure, but also on the role and expertise of team members. One way to ensure optimal exchange between senders and receivers is to make use of the important concept of **active listening**. Active listening requires drawing out the opinions of fellow team members through open and deliberative stances that are nonjudgmental, and may require asking clarifying questions and other interventions to reduce distortions that prevent mutual understanding.

To ensure communication is carried out in the most effective manner, teams—and especially QI teams—require a communication structure. Communication networks come in several varieties, and each situation demands a different type of structure (Longest & Young, 2006). Where team tasks are simple, it may be most efficient to use a centralized structure in which information passes from the team leader to other team members. Alternatively, information can be passed from the team leader to another team member who passes it down to the next individual. In other teams, one individual assumes the role of network hub and communicates with other members. Information from team members must pass through the hub in order to reach other team members. An all-channel communication structure is dense; communication lines are open and encouraged between all members of the team (Longest & Young, 2006). Such a structure is most useful for complex situations where the work of each team member is interdependent with others' work. In such situations, formal lines of authority are blurred or meaningless.

Quality improvement activities require a rich and dense communication structure. The work of QI teams is complex, and communication lines must be open between all members. For example, an intervention aimed at decreasing waiting time in a clinic requires interaction between clinicians on the team, support staff within the clinic, those involved in data collection, and others. The leader of such a team assumes the important role of ensuring communication networks are open and team members are able to communicate with each other.

Communication between a team and its external environment is also important. As an open system, teams are often dependent upon other individuals and other teams inside or outside the organization. Leaders assume boundary-spanning roles, in which they ensure relationships with critical outside groups are workable (Longest & Young, 2006). This is particularly important in a hospital setting, where a work unit's operations may be highly dependent upon interactions with other units. A QI team may rely on information and resources external to the team and just as communication among team members is critical, so are strong and reliable networks between the team and other units and teams. An isolated team that neglects its external relations is likely to perform poorly because key relationships will not be well managed.

Stages of Team Development

Teams go through various stages, and different tasks and levels of productivity characterize each stage. We can conveniently think of teams going through the stages of forming, storming, norming, and performing. These stages are best viewed as guides, and not rigid expectations. The speed with which teams proceed through these stages varies greatly and some teams never move to the final stage of performing.

A team begins in the forming stage when goals and tasks are established. It is characterized by generally polite behavior among team members, which may mask underlying conflicts. Individuals often do not feel psychologically safe at this time and may be reluctant to contribute and unlikely to disagree. Team members, still unclear about team norms, may stand back until they get a sense of norms and team "rules."

When team members begin to feel more comfortable, there may be a period of mild of severe "storming." Team members may compete for roles, may argue about team goals and processes, or may simply attempt to stake their ground. This type of conflict is normal, and if managed well by the team leader, can result in a resolution of important issues.

If the team resolves its storming stage (which does not always happen), a norming stage emerges in which there is agreement on team norms and expectations. Team member roles are clarified, although these may change during the life of a team.

Following the norming stage is a performing stage in which the team is in the best position to accomplish its goals. Conflicts have mainly been resolved, roles and norms are established, and team time can be spent on the substantive work of the team rather than on process issues.

Teams can function at all stages of their development. However, at earlier stages, teams may suffer from "process loss"—that is, focusing the team's energies and time on team maintenance functions rather than on the substantive work of the team. Teams are most effective when they have matured, meaning they have successfully progressed through the first three stages and are able to focus on team goals and tasks. It is also common for teams to return to earlier stages of development. This may occur for a number of reasons, including new leadership, team membership changes, and team tasks and goals changes.

In **Case 6.4**, Silver Valley Community Hospital organized drive-through COVID-19 testing, involving its nursing, laboratory, IT, and administrative teams. At first, the team functioned effectively, with nurses managing patient flow, lab personnel handling test processing, IT recording information, and administration coordinating the operations through bi-weekly virtual meetings. However, as demand surged, the team

Case 6.4: COVID-19 Testing Under Pressure and Interdepartmental Team Dynamics

Facing a rising number of COVID-19 cases and overwhelming demand from the community, Silver Valley Community Hospital accepted responsibility for facilitating drive-through COVID-19 testing in local parks in the Madison, Wisconsin area. To do so, the hospital mobilized teams consisting of nursing staff, laboratory technicians, information technology (IT) staff, and administrative personnel. Nurses worked on-site to manage patient flow, sample collections, and educate patients. Laboratory technicians were tasked with processing sample tests. IT staff stored and recorded data while administrative staff facilitated communications between the departments through virtual meetings. These allowed for a better understanding of critical information which needed to be conveyed, to avoid delays in providing test results, and communicating new information on practices and procedures as required by the most current information about COVID-19.

While the first few team meetings went smoothly with nurses properly labeling samples and the lab sending out timely test results, the situation deteriorated once testing sites became overwhelmed with an increase in patients. Nurses were concerned about their inability to properly handle the increase in volume while also informing patients of proper care practices. In addition to seeing their roles as outside their normal scope of duties, they felt the laboratory staff were not taking on a fair share of the workload. They insisted the lab take a more active role in test collection processes to alleviate stress on on-site workers.

Laboratory staff, already working extra hours to keep up with the magnitude of test samples, argued they would be unable to adequately support the nursing team without jeopardizing their primary responsibility of distributing test results on an accurate and timely basis. While tensions between staff rose, the overall performance of the drive-through testing system began to decline. Frustration increased and communication broke down, resulting in an increase in sample labeling errors and tracking difficulties, while test turnaround times lengthened, ultimately exacerbating the backlog of unprocessed tests.

Through virtual meetings, administrative staff recognized the negative impact of conflict on team morale and testing effectiveness. They decided the best course of action would be to establish a virtual team meeting focused on team dynamics and workload balance. During this meeting, nurses and laboratory technicians were encouraged to voice their concerns and develop solutions that would assist in relieving some pressure. Administrative staff assisted with this dialogue and with the designation of job roles and expectations.

Ultimately, it was decided additional administrative support would be assigned to drive-through testings to address nurse concerns and assist with sample labeling and tracking. Additionally, IT was mobilized to create QR codes which allowed patients to receive current COVID-19 information; this would help reduce wait times and increase sample collection. Patients with questions that could not be answered through this site were directed to nurses, allowing them to dedicate their primary focus to patient care rather than sample collection. To foster better communication and reduce conflict between departments, cross-departmental check-ins were integrated into the twice-weekly meetings.

These changes reduced mislabeled samples and other problems, allowing laboratory staff to focus their efforts on their primary role, and led to a reduction in turnaround time. After a few weeks, teamwork improved significantly, leading to a restored sense of morale among team members. The successful management of this conflict highlighted the ability of departments to overcome team conflict through communication, adaptability, and the need for clear role definitions.

entered the "storming" stage of development, where conflicts emerged due to stress, increased workload, and miscommunication. Nurses felt inundated with test collection and patient education, while lab staff hesitated to take on extra responsibilities, worried it would interfere with their primary task of processing test results. The collapse in teamwork led to mislabeled samples, a rise in errors, and delays in turnaround times, underscoring the difficulties associated with the storming phase, where team members experience tension and frustration while trying to manage their roles. Both the nursing and laboratory staff experienced stress and, in some instances, burnout, resulting in a drop in critical communication and performance.

Identifying the problem, the administrators organized a special meeting aimed at resolving conflicts and clearly delineating roles, assisting the team in progressing to the "norming" phase. During this meeting, nurses and lab staff expressed their concerns, and solutions were devised to balance workloads without overburdening either department. Support from the administration was provided at testing sites to aid nurses, while IT created a QR code to simplify patient information collection, thereby reducing the workload for nurses. Regular cross-departmental check-ins were introduced to enhance collaboration and avert future conflicts.

These adjustments allowed the team to enter the "performing" stage, characterized by improved communication, well-defined roles, and increased performance levels. Laboratory staff could concentrate on their responsibilities without the issue of mislabeled samples, and nurses were able to prioritize patient care. The resolution of conflict and the clear delegation of tasks enabled the team to successfully navigate the storming phase, emphasizing the significance of effective communication, clarity in roles, and adaptability.

Decision Making

Decision making is a task required of all teams, and the manner in which decisions are made is critical to team success. Teams may reach decisions by consensus or voting, or team members may simply provide advice and leave the final decision to the leader. There is no single, best way for a team to make decisions, and the mode of decision making depends upon the circumstances and goals of the team. The president of a hospital, for example, may charge a team with the task of analyzing an acquisition possibility. The team may return with recommendations and options, but the final decision and accountability for consequences remains with the president. In a multidisciplinary mental health treatment team, it is likely decisions will be based on team consensus, although the team leader may reserve the right to override the team's recommendations. In still other teams, particularly those where there is no single person in a position of formal authority, the team as a whole may make decisions. In such situations, team members should discuss how decisions are to be made—by voting, by working toward consensus and compromise, or perhaps by deferring to the individual most knowledgeable about a particular issue to be decided.

Collaborative decision making may result in better decisions and also be beneficial in resolving conflict and creating a platform to coordinate team tasks (Rosen et al., 2018). Making information available to members enables team members to participate in decision making. Collaborative decision-making support may also be beneficial in resolving conflict and creating a platform to coordinate team tasks (Rosen et al., 2018).

Regardless of how decisions are made, it is critical team members understand their role in decision making. Assuming an advisory rather than decision-making role is acceptable to team members as long as they do not expect to be in the position of making decisions. The decisional authority of the team and that of team members needs to be specific and clear.

Member and Team Learning

A **learning organization** is one that proactively creates, acquires, and transfers knowledge and changes its behavior on the basis of new knowledge and insights. The concept consists of five components: team learning, shared vision, mental models, personal mastery, and systems thinking. The implication of this definition for teams is clear. First, effective teams continuously look for new information to improve their performance, such as new processes or technology. They are open to new ideas and seek them out. They do this by seeking diversity among team members, including people on teams with broad sets of expertise and perspectives, and by ensuring that team members are engaged in continuous training and learning. Effective teams attempt to use new information, ensuring that new knowledge is transferred to the team. Teams may enhance their ability to learn and apply new knowledge through the use of a number of facilitating factors, including scanning the environment for new information; identifying performance gaps within the team; adopting an "experimental mindset" such that team members are open to new approaches; and having leadership supportive of change. Ultimately, a learning organization is consistently open to learning and adapting in order to maintain their relevance under new and changing situations.

Team and organizational learning are key aspects of QI, and are hallmarks of effective QI teams. A QI team is faced not only with solving problems, but also with the responsibility for helping the larger organization transition into a learning organization. Effective QI teams review their own performance and the satisfaction of members and seek to develop strategies and new team management techniques that will enhance their performance. Some teams "debrief" after each meeting to review the progress of their work and the manner in which they worked and seek to learn from this and improve their capabilities.

Team Leadership

Ideally, the leader of a QI team should have thorough knowledge of the organization and the problems being addressed, as well as the authority to implement changes and overcome barriers to implementation. The leader should also have an appreciation of how suggested changes affect other units in the organization as well as authority over all areas affected by proposed changes (Knox L., Brach C., 2015). Finally, the leader should be authorized to allocate space, time, and human resources to the team. These are ideal conditions, but there are times when the team leader is appointed or emerges from group deliberations. Individuals assuming team leader roles may lack some of these characteristics. Absent these qualities, successful teams require support from key people outside of the team who are in positions of authority.

Where team tasks are clear and unambiguous, a top-down leadership style may be justified, although even in such settings, input from team members may be valuable. In essence, the traditional role of a leader in low-uncertainty settings is to see that the job is done and team members communicate and coordinate their work. In the QI area, however, leadership must take on a different look. QI is based on learning and discovery; while the team leader should be very knowledgeable about the issues under examination, no single team member has all of the information to solve or even identify the sources of quality challenges. QI is by definition ambiguous and is largely a problem-solving process. As such, leadership on QI teams is typically collaborative in nature. Team members participate on a QI team because they have expertise relevant to the problem, and should be encouraged to participate actively in identifying problems, analyzing causation, developing interventions, evaluating the impact of change, and so forth.

In an era where uncertainty is the norm, leadership styles are required that emphasize eliciting information from others, information sharing, and using that information to collaboratively design change initiatives. In sum, the need for a participative style of leadership is unavoidable if we hope our teams to be effective. Learning how to use a participative leadership style is not easy, and it is much easier to exercise an autocratic style, although it is doubtful this style will result in positive outcomes. A participative leader does not simply listen to others but encourages and seeks out information from team members and individuals outside of the team.

Material and Nonmaterial Support and Recognition

Regardless of their function, effective teams require both material and nonmaterial resources. Providing resources reflects moral support and encouragement given to a team by the larger organization and, in particular, senior management or other authority. Consider the case of a team established to develop a plan to develop and implement a QI program to improve the ability of the organization to identify individuals with an opiate addiction. This team is given appropriate space and time to meet, where senior managers on occasion voluntarily drop in on team meetings to provide information and support, and where support staff are assigned to the team to assist in its work. Furthermore, while the team is given a specific mandate and set of goals, team members collectively decide on the manner in which it carries out its work. Finally, upon presenting a preliminary report, detailed feedback and questions are provided to the team by relevant stakeholders. In all likelihood, team members will feel valued, and understand how the team's work is contributing to the larger organization and community.

Rewards and Motivation

Related to support and recognition is the need for team and individual rewards. From the perspective of the team, rewards typically include recognition and commendation for the team's work. In QI, team rewards usually consist of the intrinsic satisfaction of overcoming some quality challenge, that is, achieving results. Rewards may also consist of the positive feelings created by a successful team effort. Factors that contribute to team members' intrinsic motivation are of critical importance in QI efforts (Deming, 1994).

In addition to team rewards, individuals on teams need to be rewarded. Participation on teams is sometimes ambiguously defined as something between the person's job and a voluntary effort, that is, it may not be perceived as part of a staff member's "real job." Job descriptions themselves may indicate little about team participation, particularly when team efforts extend beyond one's formally assigned department. Performance appraisals may not include team participation criteria, and compensation and promotion decisions may not take into consideration a staff member's contribution to the work of a team. A team-oriented organization will be more likely to recognize individual contributions on teams by including teamwork in job descriptions, performance appraisal criteria, and incentive compensation programs. Individuals working on teams should receive the message that their participation on teams is important, necessary, and a key part of their jobs.

Organizational Culture

Organizational culture refers to an organization's beliefs, traditions, attitudes, and modes of communication and interaction. An organization can have a single culture, although there are often subcultures within the organization. Among healthcare organizations, for example, we would expect to see cultural differences between a large teaching hospital and a small, rural medical practice. Within an organization, teams themselves can develop their own culture; organizational cultures may include rituals, a specific language, particular modes of communication, and unique systems of rewards and sanctions.

Organizational culture has a number of implications for teams. First, effective teams are usually characterized by a culture that is respectful and supportive of team members, with appropriate levels of empowerment. In a QI team, for example, we would hope to see a culture characterized by interdisciplinary respect, open communication, and a collective spirit. It would be very difficult to imagine a successful QI team that does not share these and other cultural characteristics.

Consider an organization characterized by intense and dysfunctional competition, low staff participation in decision making, and interprofessional rivalries and antagonism. We can consider this type of organization as having a dissonant culture (Fleeger, 1993). Notwithstanding the skills of an effective team leader, can we really expect team members drawn from such an environment to perform effectively on a multidisciplinary team? It is more likely team member attitudes would mirror their attitudes and behaviors outside the team. Team members would likely exhibit distrust, a "them vs. us" norm, and skepticism about their role in decision making.

Alternatively we might expect very different behaviors and attitudes of team members drawn from a positive or consonant culture. We would expect team members to bring with them the very supportive cultural attributes of the larger organization; this would contribute to team growth and performance. We can see how the larger organizational culture can be viewed as a resource: the larger culture can be highly supportive, unsupportive, or destructive to the work of the team.

Although it may be challenging, a team can develop a strong and appropriate culture while enmeshed in an organization with a contrary culture. This is not ideal and requires leadership that can help to build a team culture that promotes team effectiveness.

Cultures are difficult to change, so team leaders and participants must understand the impact of the culture of the larger organization on the work and culture of the team. Team members' negative or dysfunctional attitudes may simply reflect how they are treated in the larger organization. Team leaders should acknowledge the difficulty of leading a participative improvement team within a larger organizational culture that is nonparticipative and autocratic. Staff who work in a rigid, overbearing culture are likely to become skeptical when suddenly asked to participate in decision making, wondering whether their opinions will be valued, and perhaps questioning if there are ulterior motives related to such an opportunity. QI efforts in health care may confront this contradictory culture issue, experiencing the difficulties of introducing a culture that is inconsistent with the dominant organizational culture.

In the case of Silver Valley Community Hospital (Case 6.4), there was an overall shift in culture as well as setting with the COVID-19 pandemic taking precedence and the need for alternative roles and responsibilities. As a result, nurses and laboratory staff felt as though their needs were not being met and became combative, stating opposing parties were not taking on enough of the burden. Ultimately, this was resolved when the administration took note of the change in attitudes and implemented communication procedures between departments.

Looking to the Future: Artificial Intelligence and Teams

Much has been written and discussed about the impact of artificial intelligence (AI) across virtually all segments of society. At this stage in the development and application of AI, we are only at the early stages of understanding its impact. Clearly, there is recognition of its benefits and a growing awareness of its risks. As a "disruptive" set of technologies, AI has the potential to dramatically improve quality and the application of quality improvement methods. However, it also requires a recognition that people and organizations need to adapt to mitigate unforeseen difficulties.

There is no question AI has applications in quality improvement and in the work of QI teams (see Abukhadijah & Nashwan [2024] for discussion of QI and AI). AI clearly will have an impact on the manner in which QI is carried out as well as the manner in which teams accomplish their work. **Case 6.5** focuses on one particular application of AI in health care and includes the remarkable benefits it offers as well as the unknown and potentially negative impacts. As you review the case, consider how its negative impacts could have been avoided or managed. Case questions are included at the conclusion of the case.

Case 6.5: Artificial Intelligence at Sierra Valley Health System

At Sierra Valley Health System, a large academic hospital network in California, leadership implemented an AI-powered documentation tool called MediTech Assist to streamline clinical workflows. Designed to capture doctor–patient conversations in real time, generate medical notes, suggest billing codes, and predict patient outcomes, the tool allowed clinics to take proactive measures, saving time and resources. The promise of MediTech Assist was compelling: physicians, physician assistants, and nurses could spend less time charting during and after shifts, reducing the burden of taking work home. This gave them more personal hours to spend with their families and focus on maintaining work-life balance.

In the early stages, MediTech Assist demonstrated significant potential to enhance team dynamics. Shift changes became smoother, and morale improved as administrative burdens decreased. Technicians once tasked with transcribing notes were reassigned to high-demand areas like outpatient rehabilitation and pharmacy, alleviating strain in overburdened departments. Nurses had more time to engage with patients, improving safety and satisfaction. By streamlining referrals and patient transfers, MediTech Assist fostered greater collaboration between departments, breaking down silos and reinforcing a culture of cooperation.

Additionally, MediTech Assist addressed a critical gap in language accessibility by offering real-time translation tools for non-English-speaking patients. This proved invaluable during emergencies or staff shortages when certified bilingual medical translators were unavailable. While translations required human review for accuracy, the technology bridged communication gaps, improving patient understanding and compliance with care instructions.

MediTech Assist also created new opportunities for teams to bond. The system's ability to simplify referrals and patient transfers between departments encouraged greater interdepartmental collaboration. For example, staff in emergency care worked more seamlessly with outpatient clinics, knowing MediTech Assist had already captured and shared accurate, up-to-date patient information. Silos broke down, strengthening relationships between teams, fostering a hospital-wide culture of cooperation and mutual support.

While MediTech Assist had many benefits, its implementation exposed challenges to psychological safety. For some teams, the tool reduced administrative burdens, creating an environment where collaboration was encouraged, and team members felt more supported. However, for others, the lack of comprehensive training led to hesitation and uncertainty. Some staff members worried voicing concerns about the tool's limitations might reflect poorly on their proficiency with new technology. This fear was exacerbated by the significant investment the hospital made in the AI system's licensing, leaving employees apprehensive that raising issues could be perceived as undermining the system's value.

There was also concern about the system's occasional discrepancies, such as mismatched patient information or inaccurate billing codes. This required staff to fact-check the AI's outputs regularly, which some viewed as an additional task rather than a safeguard. While this verification process ensured accuracy, it also highlighted the necessity of balancing AI efficiency with human oversight.

In some cases, the lack of psychological safety resulted in errors going unchecked, as team members hesitated to challenge the AI's outputs or admit difficulties using the system. Despite these challenges, leadership ultimately recognized the gaps and began taking corrective action, emphasizing feedback was essential for success and encouraging staff to share their experiences without fear of reprimand.

As the benefits of MediTech Assist became more apparent, leadership acknowledged the shortcomings and took corrective action. Additional training sessions and forums for open dialogue were introduced, enabling staff to share feedback and solutions without fear of reprimand. These adjustments helped improve system performance and reinforced leadership's commitment to aligning technology with the hospital's culture of collaboration and patient-centered care. Leadership also emphasized the importance of balancing AI's efficiencies with the irreplaceable human touch in health care. By fostering open communication and addressing gaps in the rollout, they worked to build trust and encourage a more unified adoption of MediTech Assist.

Despite the overall success of MediTech Assist, resistance to the technology persisted among some staff and patients. Some employees were hesitant to fully embrace the AI system, feeling it could never replace their personal judgment or expertise. Similarly, some patients expressed concerns about privacy or felt uncomfortable relying on AI for aspects of their care. These groups required additional reassurance and support to adopt the system more fully.

Leadership addressed these concerns by highlighting success stories where MediTech Assist had improved patient outcomes, such as simplifying referrals, enhancing communication between departments, and bridging language barriers during emergencies. They also acknowledged the necessity of ongoing human oversight to ensure the accuracy of AI outputs. However, fully swaying resistant employees and patients remained a challenge, underscoring the importance of continued efforts to bridge the gap between technology and traditional healthcare practices.

The introduction of MediTech Assist underscored the importance of aligning new technology with the hospital's established culture. Leadership worked to position the tool as a complement to, rather than a replacement for, human expertise. By emphasizing collaboration, communication, and the shared goal of patient-centered care, they aimed to integrate MediTech Assist into the hospital's operations while maintaining its core values.

Though some resistance remained, MediTech Assist ultimately delivered significant benefits, improving efficiency, team collaboration, patient outcomes, and accessibility for non-English-speaking patients. The case highlights the value of proactive leadership, comprehensive training, and a focus on culture in maximizing the potential of new technology in health care.

Discussion Questions

1. Could the problems with MediTech Assist have been anticipated prior to its implementation? If so, how could this have been done?
2. Should Silver Valley Health System have done more to prepare staff for the implementation of MediTech Assist? If so, how might this have been accomplished?
3. How should the health system respond to patient concerns around privacy related to MediTech Assist?
4. In this case, AI was not introduced as an effort to eliminate jobs. Why might employees still be skeptical about the effect of AI on jobs?
5. As a system administrator, how would you address the polarized environment with regard to MediTech Assist?

Conclusion

This chapter describes how quality improvement efforts can be helped or hindered by the manner in which teams are constructed and managed. Beyond quality improvement, we can take it a step further to consider how the entirety of the healthcare world—pharmacies, private clinics, long-term care organizations, hospitals and more—all work together as part of an intersectional and team structure in order to provide quality care to populations.

We have reviewed the importance of teams and effective teamwork in health care and specifically, how teams play a major role in successful implementation of QI efforts. Steps in team development and team processes were reviewed; these include development of balanced team relationships and attention to the impact of status differences on team member engagement. Open communication, feedback, and empowerment are key to team member motivation and team performance. Critical to the success of any team effort is the role of team leaders, who can come from within the team or from traditional leadership positions; also critical to success is developing a team's culture. Finally, ongoing team learning was described as one of the most important aspects of teamwork in CQI; it provides a means for sharing knowledge and improving performance of a team as well as the larger organization in which the team exists.

Key Concepts and Terms

active listening
behavioral norms
learning organization
microsystem
organizational culture
performance norms
psychological safety
team norms

References

Abukhadijah, H. J., & Nashwan, A. J., (2024). Transforming hospital quality improvement through harnessing the power of artificial intelligence. *Global Journal on Quality and Safety in Healthcare, 7*(3), 132–139. https://doi.org/10.36401/JQSH-24-4

American Association of Critical-Care Nurses. (2023, November 9). *Nurse-led initiatives improve cardiac care at California hospitals*. https://www.aacn.org/newsroom/nurse-led-initiatives-improve-cardiac-care-at-california-hospitals

Bang, D., & Frith, C. D. (2017). Making better decisions in groups. *Royal Society Open Science, 4*(8), 170193. https://doi.org/10.1098/rsos.170193. PMID: 28878973; PMCID: PMC5579088.

Barnett, T., Hoang, H., Stuart, J., & Crocombe, L. (2017). The relationship of primary care providers to dental practitioners in rural and remote Australia. *BMC Health Services Research, 17*, 515. https://doi.org/10.1186/s12913-017-2473-z

Centers for Disease Control and Prevention. *–Ambulatory care use and physician office visits*. Retrieved April 15, 2022, at https://www.cdc.gov/nchs/fastats/physician-visits.htm

Chi, D. L., Lenaker, D., Mancl, L., Dunbar, M., & Babb, M. (2018). Dental therapists linked to improved dental outcomes for Alaska Native communities in the Yukon-Kuskokwim Delta. *Journal of Public Health Dentistry, 78*(2), 175–182. https://doi.org/10.1111/jphd.12263. PMID: 29377127; PMCID: PMC6019600.

Crozier, M. (1964). *The bureaucratic phenomenon*. Tavistock.

Deming, W. E. (1986). *Out of the crisis*. Massachusetts Institute of Technology Center for Advanced Engineering Study.

Deming, W. E. (1994). *The new economics for industry, government and education* (2nd ed.). Massachusetts Institute of Technology Center for Advanced Engineering Study.

Edmondson, A. (1999). Psychological safety and learning behavior in work teams. *Administrative Science Quarterly, 44*(2), 350–383. https://doi.org/10.2307/2666999

Edmondson, A. (2012). Teamwork on the fly. *Harvard Business Review, 90*, 72–80.

Edmondson, A. C. (2018). The Fearless organization: Creating psychological safety in the workplace for learning, innovation, and growth. John Wiley & Sons.

Fleeger, M. E. (1993). Assessing organizational culture: A planning strategy. *Nursing Management, 24*(2), 39. https://doi.org/10.1097/00006247-199302000-00009

Fried, B. J., & Edmondson, A. C. (2020). Teams and team effectiveness in health services organizations. In L. Burns, E. Bradley & B. Weiner (Eds.), *Health care management—Organization design and behavior* (7th ed.). Cengage.

Grove, A. S. (1995). *High output management*. Vintage Books.

Institute for Health Improvement. (2017). *Science of improvement: Forming the team*. Accessed 1/20/2026 from https://www.ihi.org/library/model-for-improvement/forming-team

Khalafi, A., Sarvi Sarmeydani, N., & Adarvishi, S. (2023). Workplace health in anesthesia team: A qualitative study in Iran. *Frontiers in Public Health, 11*, 1141447. https://doi.org/10.3389/fpubh.2023.1141447

Knox L., Brach C. Primary Care Practice Facilitation Curriculum (Module 20). AHRQPublication No. 15-0060-EF, Rockville, MD: Agency for Healthcare Research and Quality; September 2015. Retrieved from https://www.ahrq.gov/sites/default/files/wysiwyg/ncepcr/tools/PCMH/pcpf-module-20-creating-qi-teams.pdf

Longest, B. B., & Young, G. T. (2006). Coordination and communication. In S. M. Shortell & A. D. Kaluzny (Eds.), *Health care management — organization design and behavior* (5th ed.). Thompson Delmar Learning.

Nelson, E. C., Batalden, P. B., Huber, T. P., Mohr, J. J., Godfrey, M. M., Headrick, L. A., & Wasson, J. H. (2002). Microsystems in health care: Part 1. Learning from high-performing front-line clinical units. *The Joint Commission Journal of Quality Improvement, 28*(9), 472–493. https://doi.org/10.1016/S1070-3241(02)28051-7

Nilsen, P. (2015). Making sense of implementation theories, models and frameworks. *Implementation Science, 10*, 53. https://doi.org/10.1186/s13012-015-0242-0

Rosen, M. A., DiazGranados, D., Dietz, A. S., Benishek, L. E., Thompson, D., Pronovost, P. J., & Weaver, S. J. (2018). Teamwork in healthcare: Key discoveries enabling safer, high-quality care. *American Psychologist, 73*(4), 433–450. https://doi.org/10.1037/amp0000298

Schreiber, R. S., & MacDonald, M. A. (2010). Keeping vigil over the profession: a grounded theory of the context of nurse anaesthesia practice. *BMC Nursing, 9*, 13.

Swerdlow, B., Osborne-Smith, L., & Berry, D. (2020). Anesthesiologists have an important role in preclinical nurse anesthesia education. *Advances in Medical Education and Practice, 11*, 997–1003. https://doi.org/10.2147/AMEP.S286546. PMID: 33364870; PMCID: PMC7751290.

Valentine, M., & Edmondson, A. C. (2015). Team scaffolds: how mesolevel structures enable role-based coordination in temporary groups. *Organization Science, 26*(2), 405–422. https://doi.org/10.1287/orsc.2014.0947

Wising, J., Ström, M., Hallgren, J., & Rambaree, K. (2024). Certified registered nurse anaesthetists' and critical care registered nurses' perception of knowledge/power in teamwork with anaesthesiologists in Sweden: A mixed-method study. *BMC Nursing, 23*, 7. https://doi.org/10.1186/s12912-023-01677-z

Yang, Y. T., Chen, B., & Wanchek, T. (2017). Dental therapists: A solution to a shortage of dentists in underserved communities? *Public Health Reports, 132*(3), 285–288. https://doi.org/10.1177/0033354917698114. Epub 2017 Mar 22. PMID: 28448769; PMCID: PMC5415248.

CHAPTER 7

Equity in Continuous Quality Improvement

Carley Riley and Brita Roy

CHAPTER OUTLINE

Introduction

The persistence—and recent worsening—of disparities in health outcomes has prompted the exploration of approaches and methods not previously applied to health equity. Providing equitable care may require use of adaptive systems and intentional variation in processes to achieve equal outcomes among subgroups of patients. As such, the use of continuous quality improvement (CQI) has become increasingly recognized for its relevance and utility in efforts to achieve health equity (Green-Rogers et al., 2022; Parsons et al., 2021; Reichman et al., 2021; Schoenthaler et al., 2023; Wyatt et al., 2016). Because CQI can be applied within a wide range of contexts, and CQI approaches tailor interventions to achieve optimal outcomes, it can support a broad expanse of health equity efforts. This chapter will provide definitions, principles, methodological guidance, and multiple real-life examples of CQI strategies to achieve equitable health and healthcare outcomes.

Health Equity Defined

Health equity exists when "everyone has a fair and just opportunity to be as healthy as possible." Achieving and sustaining health equity necessitates "removing obstacles to health such as poverty, discrimination, and their consequences, including powerlessness and lack of access to good jobs with fair pay, quality education and housing, safe environments, and health care" (Braveman et al., 2017).

While health disparity and health inequity are related terms, they are not interchangeable. **Health disparity** signifies difference, whether just or unjust, whereas health inequity indicates differences in health outcomes that are "systematic, avoidable, and unjust" (Wyatt et al., 2016).

For the sake of measurement—an important and meaningful aspect of CQI—health equity results from "reducing and ultimately eliminating disparities in health and its determinants that adversely affect excluded or marginalized groups" (Braveman, 2017). In CQI, disparities in health and in the key drivers of health can be metrics for evaluating progress toward health equity (Braveman et al., 2017).

Social (and political) determinants of health have been defined as the "conditions in which people are born, grow, work, live, and age, and the wider set of forces and systems shaping the conditions of daily life" (U.S. Department of Health and Human Services, 2025; World Health Organization, 2025). This definition notes that "these forces and systems include economic policies and systems, development agendas, social norms, social policies and political systems." Health equity efforts often examine and seek to improve health disparities by sociodemographic characteristics, including race, ethnicity, socioeconomic status, and gender, among others.

To be most effective, individuals contributing to health equity CQI need to understand key terms, such as health equity, health disparity, and social determinants of health.

Health Equity Frameworks and Principles

Over the prior decade, multiple frameworks for achieving health equity have emerged. These include *Achieving Health Equity: A Guide for Health Care Organizations*, *The Rush Equity Framework*, and *The Health Equity Framework*, among others (Ansell et al., 2021; Peterson et al., 2021; Wyatt et al., 2016). Commonalities exist across these frameworks, which ultimately encourage embedding equity in all processes and elements related to health and health production.

Similarly, the pursuit of health equity through CQI ideally entails that equity is incorporated in every aspect of CQI. This principle is recognized in the practices for pursuing equity in a learning health system identified and described in *Learning Health Systems* in 2021 (Parsons et al., 2021). Core practices for the achievement and sustainment of health equity start by establishing the principle that equity is essential, then identifying appropriate measures, ensuring the people most affected by the improvement work are informing and guiding the work (leading from lived experience), co-production, and redistribution of power, among others. Co-production in CQI is presented in detail in Chapter 8, and it is essential to include patients from the group experiencing poor outcomes as part of the data-driven design and implementation teams.

To achieve meaningful, sustainable impact, co-production, with the meaningful inclusion of the people most impacted by the output of the effort, must be implemented in the use of CQI for health equity.

Health Equity Methods

Health equity is both an outcome—a *what*—and a process—a *how*. As a What, health equity is viewed as an outcome to be achieved and sustained. As a How, health equity is the process through which disparities in both health outcomes and their drivers are reduced and eliminated (Braveman et al., 2017). CQI can be applied toward health equity as both a What and a How.

Health Equity as a What

CQI can be applied to reduce and eliminate inequities both in health and healthcare outcomes and in the drivers of those outcomes.

Health Outcomes and Healthcare Utilization

Identifying inequities in outcomes to be improved with CQI requires disaggregation of data by variables that are hypothesized to underly inequities.

These variables often include sociodemographic characteristics, such as race, ethnicity, preferred language, socioeconomic status, insurance status, gender, age, and location of residence, among others. Meaningful disaggregation relies on responsible use of sociodemographic data, a matter that has been receiving increased attention in recent years as the field of health equity seeks to ensure data are used for positive intent and impact.

Historically, the healthcare system has relied upon observed data—data on characteristics such as race and gender assessed by the collector of the data—rather than self-reported data, by which the individual provides the information about their own characteristics. Accuracy and completeness of data on race, ethnicity, preferred language, and gender identity are essential for accurate data disaggregation to inform CQI efforts to improve health equity. As such, many health systems and even states have implemented initiatives to increase rates of self-reported sociodemographic data and improve the accuracy of these data. The "We Ask Because We Care" campaign has been an effective program to collect detailed data on self-identified race, ethnicity, preferred language, and gender identity, and has been implemented at Henry Ford Health System in Detroit, Michigan, UMass Memorial Health in Worcester, Massachussetts, and Yale New Haven Health in New Haven, Connecticut, among others.

To inform health equity CQI, data needs to be disaggregated, ideally by self-reported sociodemographic characteristics, to identify and track inequities in health and healthcare outcomes.

The use of CQI also requires that teams set measurable aims. Early in the application of CQI in health equity efforts, many teams set aims based on closing equity gaps, or eliminating the differences in outcomes that exist between select groups (e.g., inequities in asthma admission rates for Black versus White patients). This practice sets the outcome experienced by the dominant group (often White race, male sex, cis-gender, English speaking, etc.) as the default goal to be achieved by all. This practice is problematic in multiple regards. For one, establishing a goal based on the outcome of the dominant group serves to reinforce the preference for or "betterness" of the dominant group. This frame also sets groups against each other, leading to unproductive tensions, such as concerns that an equity gap may be eliminated by lowering the outcomes of the highest performing group or by trading off outcomes in one group for outcomes in another. Additionally, this approach also assumes that the dominant group is achieving the best possible outcomes, which may not be true. As such, there has been a call for approaches that do not by default reinforce the superiority of the current dominant group and do not trigger othering and 'us versus them' thinking in seeking solutions. As john a. powell et al. (2019) state in the primer, *Targeted Universalism: Policy & Practice*, pubished by the Haas Institute for a Fair and Inclusive Society:

> "There is a hunger for fresh approaches and urgent demand for novel policy methods that can break through our political gridlock, address the problems of our time and create new avenues for thriving individuals and communities. Targeted universalism is an approach that supports the needs of the particular while reminding us that we are all part of the same social fabric."

As a result, the application of targeted universalism in goal and aim setting in health equity CQI efforts is on the rise (powell & Menendian, 2019). In this framework, a universal goal is established based on a "broadly shared recognition of a societal problem and collective aspirations" (powell & Menendian, 2019). For example, a universal goal to reduce or eliminate preventable hospital admissions among children younger than age 18 may be established based on societal norms and national standards (see **Box 7.1**). Subsequently, the team assesses the outcome for the whole population (i.e., rates of preventable readmissions among children for the entire patient population) relative to the universal goal and then identifies groups within the whole population (e.g., rates of preventable readmissions by race) that are performing differently with respect to the goal through disaggregation.

Box 7.1 **Example of Targeted Universalism in CQI Goal Setting**

A population health improvement team at Cincinnati Children's Hospital Medical Center in Cincinnati, Ohio, provides an imperfect example of targeted universalism in CQI goal setting. In their improvement work to lower inequities in hospital admission rates, this team used multiple years of data from their electronic health records to calculate the rate of admission to their hospital for children (18 years old or younger) living in Hamilton County. They then calculated the admission rate for the neighborhoods in the top quartile (lowest rates) and implemented that rate as a global goal for all patient populations to achieve (33.7 per 1,000 population annually). From here, they determined outcomes that would result from 2%, 5%, and 8% improvements in the absolute gap. Admissions per 1,000 population annually and admission counts were subsequently back calculated based on these values (e.g., a 2% improvement in absolute gap is equal to 30 fewer admissions). In addition to neighborhood-level admission rates, this team is looking at hospitalization rates disaggregated by other factors, including patient race. Using these disaggregated data, they could set the goal to reduce the rate for Black youth by 8% relative to their universal goal (see **Table 7.1**). This example is imperfect in that they based their goal on existing data; however, their method avoids the "othering" that occurs when using one subgroup defined by demographic characteristics, such as race, to establish the goal (Unaka et al., 2024).

Table 7.1 **Example of Using Data to Set a Universal Goal**

Time Period	Hospital Admissions	Admissions per 1,000 youth	Absolute Gap per 1,000 youth
Baseline for 25th percentile Neighborhood (Goal)		33.70	
2% Improvement (Min)	−30	57.22	−0.48
5% Improvement (Target)	−72	56.50	−1.20
8% Improvement (Max)	−115	55.78	−1.92

To center equity, a universal target, rather than one based on the experience of a dominant group, should be used when setting a goal for CQI efforts.

Goal setting, as captured in the process of developing a Specific, Measurable, Achievable, Relevant, and Time-Bound (SMART) aim, can also elevate equity, as demonstrated by a recent move toward the use of a *SMART(IE) aim* in healthcare CQI (Bibbs, 2021; Centers for Disease Control and Prevention, 2024). In the new acronym SMARTIE, the 'I' stands for inclusion, prompting the question, "Do you have representation from socially and economically marginalized individuals and groups?" while the 'E' stands for equity, prompting the question, "Did you include an element of justice?" For inclusion, as noted previously, including patients from the group or groups experiencing poor outcomes as part of the data-driven design and implementation team is essential. For equity, identifying and addressing root causes of inequitable health outcomes—and specifying targets to mitigate identified inequities—is a priority.

Health Drivers

Beyond the SMARTIE aim, CQI elements and tools discussed in other chapters may be adapted to support teams in identifying and characterizing inequities in the drivers of health:

- The *key driver diagram* is used to communicate the theory of change in the pursuit of a health equity aim. Including key drivers impacting the health outcome of interest that relate to social determinants of health (community-level factors such as food insecurity), health-related social needs (individual-level factors such as lack of reliable transportation), and/or structural discrimination (systemic factors such as disparities in access to healthcare) embedded in healthcare systems as well as other health-related systems allow the CQI team to explore interventions to address these underlying or associated causes of inequitable health outcomes.

- *Process maps* can be utilized in multiple ways to meaningfully include the perspectives of the people who will be most impacted in CQI. Process maps can be co-produced with people with lived experience of system processes to ensure their perspectives are incorporated into the team's understanding of the processes conducted by people within the healthcare system. Additionally, process maps can be created to capture the processes that people with lived experience themselves must complete to engage with the system. These process maps can elucidate and integrate their perspectives with clinician and staff perspectives and provide essential information and insight for process (and systems) improvement.
- *System failure mode and effect analysis* benefit from the inclusion of people with lived experience of the system, similar to how incorporating their perspective into process maps provides essential information about the "as-is" system. Because of their unique perspectives of the system, patients and the people who interact with and provide direct care for patients are likely to identify failure modes that would not be recognized or prioritized without their inclusion.
- *Pareto charts* can be used to identify the leading factors contributing to the existence of an inequity. Factors related to health-related social needs and social determinants of health should be considered for inclusion. These charts can be leveraged in multiple ways, including for the ranking of factors related to the development and maintenance of an inequity.
- *Fishbone diagrams*, as a tool for conducting a root cause analysis, can support teams in identifying specific drivers of a health or healthcare inequity in a single chart. As with the use of other tools, including people with lived experience can identify factors that would otherwise remain invisible. In using a fishbone diagram for health equity CQI, teams should consider root causes that contribute to differences in care quality and outcomes, not just overall low quality or poor outcomes (Advancing Health Equity, 2022).

To support the use of health equity CQI over the long term, make use of CQI tools that have been adapted to promote equity (e.g., SMARTIE aim) standard practice.

Effectively applying CQI in pursuit of health equity also requires teams to identify and create the relevant partnerships to address the inequities in drivers of outcomes. Partnership formation should be guided by data, quantitative and qualitative, including from patients and frontline staff. These partnerships should collaborate to address inequities in key drivers and should use CQI to track whether their collaborative efforts are leading to improvements over time (**Box 7.2** and **Box 7.3**).

Box 7.2 Medical Legal Partnerships

Medical legal partnerships (MLP) are established to address the health-harming legal needs experienced by low-income individuals and families. MLPs can be based within hospitals, outpatient health centers and clinics, or communities. Created in 2008, the Cincinnati Child Health-Law Partnership (Child HeLP) is a shared initiative among the primary care clinics at Cincinnati Children's and the Legal Aid Society of Greater Cincinnati. To facilitate the identification of problems and patterns, Child HeLP utilizes data-driven CQI methods to co-manage and optimize the partnership and its impact.

Data from Schuh, A. M., Alexander, C., Gasperetti, K., Gorecki, M. C., Cutler, K., Hoffman, C., Kahn, R. S., Okano, C., & Riley, C. L. (2024). A new approach to a wicked problem: Development of a cross-sector community-centered learning network to tackle childhood food inequity. *Frontiers in Public Health, 12*, 1436760. https://doi.org/10.3389/fpubh.2024.1436760

Box 7.3 **CQI and Food Insecurity**

As a potent social determinant of health, food insecurity is a complex societal problem disproportionately impacting households with children and those led by minoritized populations. The negative impacts of food insecurity on health affect individuals and populations across their life course. To tackle food insecurity at a neighborhood level, the System to Achieve Food Equity (SAFE) Learning Network has adapted the learning systems model and its use of CQI in its community-centered, cross-sector efforts in Cincinnati, Ohio. In support of its "Learning to Learn Together" principle, SAFE uses CQI among all network members and provides CQI capability building through direct teaching at monthly stakeholder meetings, coaching by dedicated CQI specialists, and both exposure and formal training during annual summits, learning sessions, and community CQI courses. Its work is guided by a co-created key driver diagram that includes an equity-driven SMART aim and key drivers such as family and community-owned leadership; family-oriented communication and interactions; collaboration among food systems and organizations; data-informed actions and decision making; equitable food policies and systems; and continuous learning and improvement mindset, among others.

Data from Schuh, A. M., Alexander, C., Gasperetti, K., Gorecki, M. C., Cutler, K., Hoffman, C., Kahn, R. S., Okano, C., & Riley, C. L. (2024). A new approach to a wicked problem: Development of a cross-sector community-centered learning network to tackle childhood food inequity. *Frontiers in Public Health, 12*, 1436760. https://doi.org/10.3389/fpubh.2024.1436760

Health Equity as a How

To generate sustainable improvement in health equity, CQI strategies need be applied to addressing disparities in the processes and the attributes of the healthcare system itself that generate health inequities and allow them to persist.

Healthcare Processes

To mitigate inequities in health outcomes, teams must seek to identify the key processes that both lead to and sustain these inequitable outcomes. Teams may then direct their efforts at improving, transforming, and/or dismantling inequity-generating processes using CQI approaches. The New York City (NYC) Department of Health and Mental Hygiene demonstrated use of such a strategy to successfully address racial inequities in COVID-19 hospitalizations during the Omicron wave in NYC; they first traced the cascade of factors that resulted in inequitable COVID-19 hospitalization rates, which informed their roadmap for action that included critical strategies to address structural inequities along the COVID-19 cascade that were directly impacting health outcomes (NYC Health, 2022). Implementation of this roadmap resulted in substantial improvement in COVID-19 vaccination rates, among other processes and outcomes.

Health System

The healthcare system plays multiple important roles in shaping health equity, including not only provider of medical care but also employer, purchaser, investor, partner to other systems, and advocate for public policy (Health Anchor Network, n.d.). Within each role, health systems take concrete actions that may either promote or undermine health equity within their regions (Robert Wood Johnson Foundation, 2022b). Healthcare systems can leverage CQI to address root causes of health inequities within each of these roles. For example, as an employer, a health system can set a target for a percentage of employees hired from the local community and utilize CQI strategies to meet that goal; as a purchaser, health systems can set a target for goods and services procured locally, from minority- and woman-owned businesses, and utilize CQI to meet that goal.

Healthcare institutions can also make systemic changes to identify and address substandard healthcare provided for low income and/or minoritized groups. For example, Rush University in Chicago utilized CQI approaches to improve equitable breast cancer screening and diagnosis among Black women across the care continuum: they updated the technical skills of breast imaging staff, established processes for systematic outreach and follow-up of abnormal screening results, and hired clinical navigators to facilitate follow-up for suspected breast cancers at accredited cancer centers (Pallok, De Maio, & Ansell, 2019). With these efforts, the racial disparity in breast cancer mortality in Chicago has decreased by 20%.

For greatest impact, healthcare institutions can apply CQI in efforts to address causes of health inequity rooted not only in the provision of medical care but also in health care's roles as employer, partner, and advocate (Robert Wood Johnson, 2022a).

Conclusion

CQI provides an overall frame and a set of tools that can be applied and adapted in the pursuit of health equity. Healthcare systems and teams can leverage this frame and these tools to create improvement in the processes, drivers, systems, and outcomes related to health equity.

Key Concepts and Terms

Health disparity
Health equity
Social (and political) determinants of health

References

Advancing Health Equity. (2022, December 23). *Diagnose root causes: Fishbone diagram instructions.* https://advancinghealthequity.org/wp-content/uploads/2023/01/Diagnose-Root-Causes.Fishbone-Diagram-Instruction.12.23.22-.pdf

Ansell, D. A., Oliver-Hightower, D., Goodman, L. J., Lateef, O. B., & Johnson, T. J. (2021). Health equity as a system strategy: The Rush University Medical Center framework. *NEJM Catalyst Innovations in Care Delivery, 2*(5). https://doi.org/10.1056/CAT.20.0674

Bibbs, M. *Be a SMARTIE: An equity-forward approach to goal setting.* The Alford Group. Accessed February 5, 2026. https://alford.com/be-a-smartie-an-equity-forward-approach-to-goal-setting/

Braveman, P., Arkin, E., Orleans, T., Proctor, D., & Plough, A. (2017). *What is health equity? And what difference does a definition make?* Robert Wood Johnson Foundation.

Braveman, P. (2017, June 22). A new definition of health equity to guide future efforts and measure progress. *Health Affairs Forefront.* https://www.healthaffairs.org/content/forefront/new-definition-health-equity-guide-future-efforts-and-measure-progress

Centers for Disease Control and Prevention. (2024). *From SMART to SMARTIE objectives.* U.S. Department of Health & Human Services. https://www.cdc.gov/comprehensive-cancer-control/?CDC_AAref_Val=https://www.cdc.gov/cancer/ncccp/pdf/smartie-objectives-508.pdf

Green-Rogers, Y., Carpenter, C., Leicht, C., Miller, S., Phillips, C., Rudlang-Perman, K., Hickenbottom, A., Moore, E., Santos, C., & Day, A. G. (2022). *Applying race equity strategies throughout the continuous quality improvement (CQI) process.* Chapin Hall at the University of Chicago; Casey Family Programs; ICF; Capacity Building Center for States; James Bell Associates; University of South Florida. https://www.chapinhall.org/project/new-guide-puts-equity-at-the-center-of-research-evaluation-and-cqi-processes/

Healthcare Anchor Network. https://healthcareanchor.network/

NYC Health. (2022, March 2). *Racial inequities in COVID-19 hospitalizations during the omicron wave in NYC.* https://www.nyc.gov/assets/doh/downloads/pdf/covid/black-hospitalizations-omicron-wave.pdf

Pallok, K., De Maio, F., & Ansell, D. A. (2019). Structural racism—A 60-year-old black woman with breast cancer. *The New England Journal of Medicine, 380*(16), 1489–1493. https://doi.org/10.1056/NEJMp1811499

Parsons, A., Unaka, N. I., Stewart, C., Foster, J., Perez, V., Jones, N. Y., Kahn, R., Beck, A. F., & Riley, C. (2021). Seven practices for pursuing equity through learning health systems: Notes from the field. *Learning Health Systems,* 5(3), e10279. https://doi.org/10.1002/lrh2.10279

Peterson, A., Charles, V., Yeung, D., & Coyle, K. (2021). The Health Equity Framework: A Science- and Justice-Based Model for Public Health Researchers and Practitioners. *Health Promotion Practice, 22*(6), 741–746. https://doi.org/10.1177/1524839920950730

powell, j., Menendian, S., & Ake, W. (2019). *Targeted universalism: Policy & practice.* Haas Institute, University of California, Berkeley. https://belonging.berkeley.edu/sites/default/files/targeted_universalism_primer.pdf

Robert Wood Johnson Foundation. *Raising the bar: Healthcare's transforming role.* (2022a). *Framework in practice: Bright spots.* https://rtbhealthcare.org/wp-content/uploads/2022/07/RWJF-RTB-Report-2022-BRIGHT-SPOTS-FINAL-060622.pdf

Robert Wood Johnson Foundation. (2022b). *Raising the bar: Healthcare's transforming role—Executive summary*. https://rtbhealthcare.org/wp-content/uploads/2022/07/RWJF-RTB-FULL-REPORT-060622.pdf

Reichman, V., Brachio, S. S., Madu, C. R., Montoya-Williams, D., & Peña, M. M. (2021). *Using rising tides to lift all boats: Equity-focused quality improvement as a tool to reduce neonatal health disparities. Seminars in Fetal & Neonatal Medicine, 26*(1), 101198. https://doi.org/10.1016/j.siny.2021.101198

Schoenthaler, A., Francois, F., Cho, I., & Ogedegbe, G. (2023). Roadmap for embedding health equity research into learning health systems. *BMJ Leader, 7*(4), 261–265. https://doi.org/10.1136/leader-2022-000720

Unaka, N., Kahn, R. S., Spitznagel, T., Henize, A. W., Carlson, D., Michael, J., Quinonez, E., Anderson, J., Beck, A. F., & Cincinnati Children's Health Equity Network Study Group (2024). An institutional approach to equity and improvement in child health outcomes. *Pediatrics, 154*(2), e2023064994. https://doi.org/10.1542/peds.2023-064994

U.S. Department of Health and Human Services, Office of Disease Prevention and Health Promotion. *Social determinants of health.* Retrieved December 31, 2024, from https://health.gov/healthypeople/objectives-and-data/social-determinants-health

World Health Organization. (2025). *Social determinants of health*. World Health Organization. https://www.who.int/teams/social-determinants-of-health

Wyatt, R., Laderman, M., Botwinick, L., Mate, K., & Whittington, J. (2016). *Achieving health equity: A guide for health care organizations*. IHI White Paper. Institute for Healthcare Improvement. Available at https://www.ihi.org/library/white-papers/achieving-health-equity-guide-health-care-organizations

CHAPTER 8

Coproducing Health: Using Service-Dominant Logic to Improve the Value of Health Services

Rachel C. Forcino and Chylla Waggoner

CHAPTER OUTLINE

Introduction

Coproduction of health has been defined as "the interdependent work of [health service] users and [health] professionals who are creating, designing, producing, delivering, assessing, and evaluating the relationships and actions that contribute to the health of individuals and populations" (Batalden et al., 2016). This interdependent work of service users and professionals is a defining feature of all services. In this chapter, we begin by exploring the core differences between goods and services in the healthcare economy and how that difference drives how we think about the interaction and relationship between clinicians and patients. We then discuss several ways in which services can be configured to create value and we provide examples from the healthcare context. Next, we describe the coproduction process by which all services are created; then we narrow our focus to the healthcare context. Finally, we share examples of tools and other resources that can support health service users and health professionals to more effectively engage in coproduction.

Differentiating Goods and Services

Services are different from goods (Batalden, 2018). While goods are tangible outputs, services are structured as intangible processes (Osborne et al., 2013; Vargo & Lusch, 2008). A service is created through the joint contributions of the professional(s) specializing in the service and the beneficiary or user(s) of the service—leading services to be produced and consumed at the same time. This simultaneous production and consumption of a service is one of its defining features (Alford, 2014). In contrast, goods are produced, sold, and consumed separately, at different times and often by different parties (Osborne et al., 2013). For example, chefs independently create and follow recipes to prepare meals (goods), which restaurant patrons purchase and then consume. Meanwhile, patrons engage with the restaurant's waitstaff as they create the overall dining experience together (service) (See **Table 8.1**).

Vargo & Lusch (2008) describe a "service-dominant logic" that optimizes the creation of services, in contrast to a "goods-dominant logic" that optimizes the creation of goods (**Figure 8.1**). **Goods-dominant logic** is a way of thinking where goods are "the primary focus of economic exchange" and services are "either a restricted type of (intangible) good" or "an add-on that enhances the value of a good." Alternatively, **service-dominant logic** considers services "without reference to goods" and "identifies service as the primary focus of exchange activity."

Through the lens of service-dominant logic, healthcare services are viewed as processes. However, when applying goods-dominant logic, healthcare services appear only as units of output (Vargo & Lusch, 2008). Joiner & Lusch (2016) explain that goods-dominant logic in healthcare service is about nouns, including hospital rooms, medications, medical devices, medical images, laboratory tests, doctors, nurses, and electronic health records. While these nouns can make important contributions to the health and wellbeing of a health service user, accumulation of these outputs is not the goal of a patient seeking health services. Conversely, Joiner & Lusch (2016) argue that service-dominant logic in healthcare is about verbs, including healing, caring, monitoring, facilitating, stewarding, and learning. These service-dominant verbs better illustrate the goal of health service users; that is, to experience a process that contributes to overall health and wellbeing (Batalden, 2018).

Healthcare Value Configurations

Value is a key consideration when we are talking about coproduction. High-value health care contributes to the health and wellbeing of people and populations while making efficient use of required resources. Service-dominant logic recognizes the

Table 8.1 Comparison: Key Features of Goods and Services

	Goods	Services
Nature:	Tangible	Intangible
Value is contributed through:	Outcome	Experience, Outcome
Type of production process:	Manufacturing, Farming, or Extracting	Coproducing
Typical roles of the user:	Purchaser, Consumer	Purchaser, Coproducer, Consumer
Examples:	Medications, Medical devices	Treatment planning, Counseling

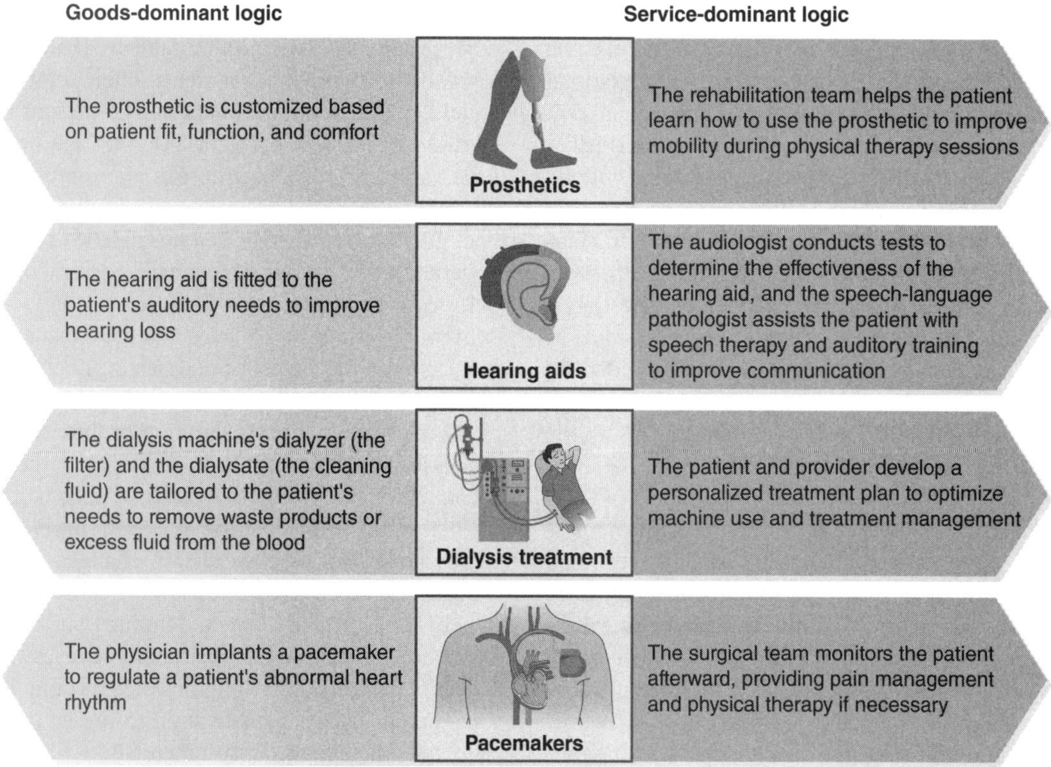

Figure 8.1 Health Care as a Good and Healthcare as a Service

critical role of service users in the service production process. Explicitly recognizing service users' contributions to the production of health services improves both outcomes (i.e., better health and wellbeing) and efficiency (i.e., making use of all relevant inputs), thereby improving the value of the contribution that health services can make toward health (Batalden, 2018).

High-value health care can look different across different clinical contexts. Variation in a specific patient's needs, or in the available resources and technologies available to meet a need, drive corresponding differences in how we optimally configure the processes that make up health services.

Some healthcare services are configured as **value chains**, where inputs are sequentially linked into predictable outputs through standardized, repeatable processes (Stabell & Fjeldstad, 1998). In the healthcare context, value chains position the patient as the owner of a health problem who "yields to a standardized treatment process," the professional as an expert designer and technician of the standardized process, and a healthcare leader as responsible for managing the system and "making resources available for [its] improvement" (Fjeldstad et al., 2020). Many surgical procedures are configured as value chains given the role of the patient in yielding to a standardized treatment process, the role of the professional as a technician carrying out that standardized and repeatable process, and the predictable outcomes that follow this type of standardized treatment process. Also, much of the work of quality improvement and the tools that we describe elsewhere in the book lend themselves to improving the value chain through improving the steps in the process.

Other healthcare services require more interaction between the service user and professional. In a **value shop**, the patient is the owner of a health problem who provides information and takes prescribed actions. The professional is then an expert consultant who mobilizes resources in support of solving the patient's problem, and the healthcare leader is responsible for designing, building, and maintaining an organization that not only allows but facilitates this process (Fjeldstad et al., 2020). The process of managing chronic conditions like heart failure is configured as a value shop, given the role of the patient in sharing information about their symptoms, lifestyle, and personal capacity for carrying out prescribed actions paired with the role of the professional as a consultant who uses information provided by the patient to match resources (e.g., medications, medical devices, lifestyle modifications) to the patient's needs and capacity to use them.

People with health-related problems can also derive value outside the formal healthcare system. Modern technology and its unprecedented opportunities for interpersonal connection have facilitated the growth of **value networks**, where patients can simultaneously act as owners of health problems, resources for the care of those health problems, and facilitators of networks that provide value to people with health problems. Recognizing the existence of this type of network, health professionals can then connect service users to these networks while continuing to contribute their knowledge and professional expertise in support of solving patients' health problems (Fjeldstad et al., 2020). Online communities of people with lived experience of the same chronic condition who share information and experiences are examples of value networks (e.g., PatientsLikeMe communities) (PatientsLikeMe, 2025). Health systems often support patients with complex and chronic conditions in addition to discrete problems. Despite the need for a value shop approach to many chronic conditions, we tend to over-rely on the value chain configuration. This leads to a mismatch between patients' problems and the services designed to help solve those problems. For example, services supporting complex diabetes mellitus management often occur in very brief meetings between a patient and a health professional lasting as few as 15 minutes. The short duration of these visits makes it difficult to shift the focus from superficial recommendations to more interactive negotiation of plans for implementing medication, blood sugar monitoring, and/or dietary changes given an individual patient's resources and constraints. Where services take a goods-dominant structure by prioritizing 15-minute visit increments as the object of exchange, they often cannot account for a patient's capacity or motivation to follow standardized therapeutic recommendations issued by health professionals—like medication dosage, blood sugar monitoring routines, dietary restrictions, etc. Given these limitations, the misapplication of a value chain configuration will not reliably lead to improved diabetes management (**Figure 8.2**). Alternatively, a value shop could prioritize active engagement between patient and professional to determine how to tailor blood

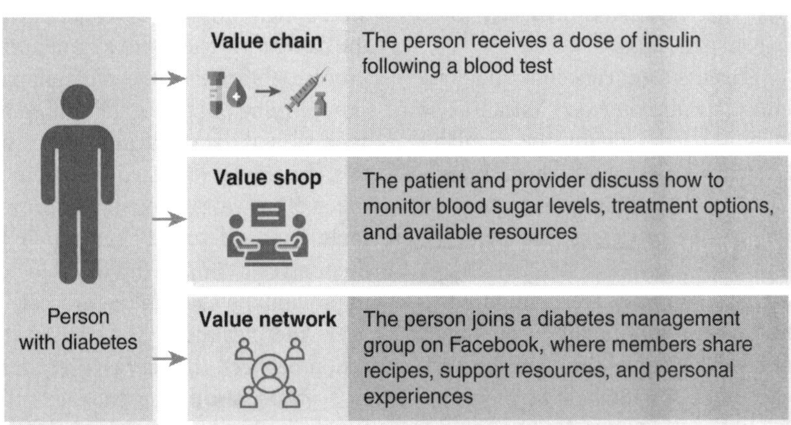

Figure 8.2 Value Configurations in Diabetes Management

sugar monitoring in a way that works for that particular patient, while a value network could connect the person with diabetes to peers who can, for example, recommend recipes or meal plans that use easily-accessible ingredients and/or approachable cooking techniques. These different value configurations often work together to best support a given patient and/or health issue. That is, a person will likely engage with all of these configurations as they navigate the healthcare system.

Phases of Healthcare Quality Improvement

Despite its role in mismatches between specific healthcare services and their configuration/design, goods-dominant logic has made important contributions to healthcare quality improvement. Batalden & Foster (2021) identify three consecutive and additive phases of healthcare quality improvement beginning in the early twentieth century: **Quality 1.0** focuses on standardization and accreditation through the implementation of minimum quality thresholds; **Quality 2.0** involves organization-wide efforts to improve quality through systems science; and **Quality 3.0** emphasizes the coproduction of healthcare services between patients and health professionals (**Table 8.2**).

While the Quality 1.0 standardization and Quality 2.0 systems science approaches to healthcare quality improvement relied heavily upon goods-dominant ways of thinking (e.g., Lean manufacturing), they were critical steps toward safe healthcare systems that offer the capacity needed to ensure widespread access to health services. However, the value of many health services is maximized by applying a service-dominant logic focused on the process in addition to the output. This logic emphasizes both the professional and the beneficiary as critical contributors to service production. To illustrate, economist Victor Fuchs noted as early as 1968 that "in the doctor's office, the quality of the medical history the patient gives may influence significantly the productivity of the doctor" (Fuchs & Leveson 1968).

The Coproduction Concept

Political economist Elinor Ostrom and colleagues (1978) began describing these joint contributions to service production as service *coproduction* in the 1970s. This group of scholars identified numerous examples of services where users contribute as much, if not more, than the professionals who are often thought to drive the production process, including: (1) education; (2) community safety; and (3) fire loss prevention. They explain that while "students can supply much of their own education in the absence of teacher inputs, [. . .] teachers can supply little education without inputs from students." Similarly, they argue that "police have very little capacity to affect community safety and security without citizen input" like securing personal property and making police reports. As a further example, "protection from fire loss is more of a result of household precautions"—e.g., turning off the stove before leaving the house—"than of inputs from regular fire service producers" (Parks et al., 1981). **Figure 8.3** depicts these varied inputs into service coproduction. Following from this premise of

Table 8.2 Approaches to Healthcare Quality Improvement (adapted from Batalden & Foster, 2021)

Quality 1.0	Quality 2.0	Quality 3.0
Establishing minimum thresholds for good, safe healthcare service	Achieving optimal disease management through enterprise-wide systems	Improving the contribution that healthcare service makes to health through coproduction

Data from Batalden, P., & Foster, T. (2021). From assurance to coproduction: A century of improving the quality of health-care service. *International Journal for Quality in Health Care, 33*(Supplement_2), ii10–ii14.

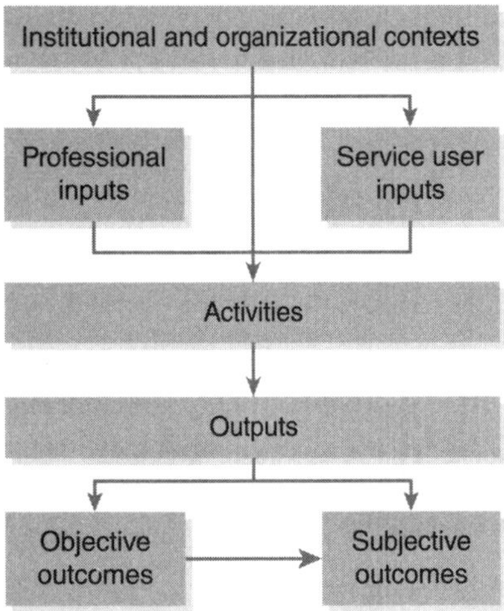

Figure 8.3 Process of Service Coproduction

Data from Ostrom, E., Parks, R. B., Whitaker, G. P., & Percy, S. L. (1978). The public service production process: A framework for analyzing police services. *Policy Studies Journal, 7*(s1), 381.

service user contributions to service production, Osborne and colleagues highlight the fact that service coproduction "is not simply about user satisfaction"—it instead directly influences outcomes (Osborne et al., 2013).

Healthcare Service Coproduction

In the early 21st century, there was growing recognition across the healthcare sector of persistent gaps in quality. The Institute of Medicine published *Crossing the Quality Chasm* in 2001, identifying a mismatch between the care provided by health service organizations and "the care we should receive." Healthcare resources were being used at unprecedented rates, with healthcare spending at an all-time high—but without corresponding improvements in health and wellbeing. To better characterize "the care we should receive," efforts to apply service-dominant logic to the healthcare sector intensified (Dunston et al., 2009; Butler & Greenhalgh, 2010; Sabadosa & Batalden, 2014). Drawing on these emerging applications in clinical settings, Batalden and colleagues (2016) defined coproduction of healthcare service and proposed a corresponding conceptual model (**Figure 8.4**). This model depicts patients and professionals interacting to coproduce healthcare services while simultaneously

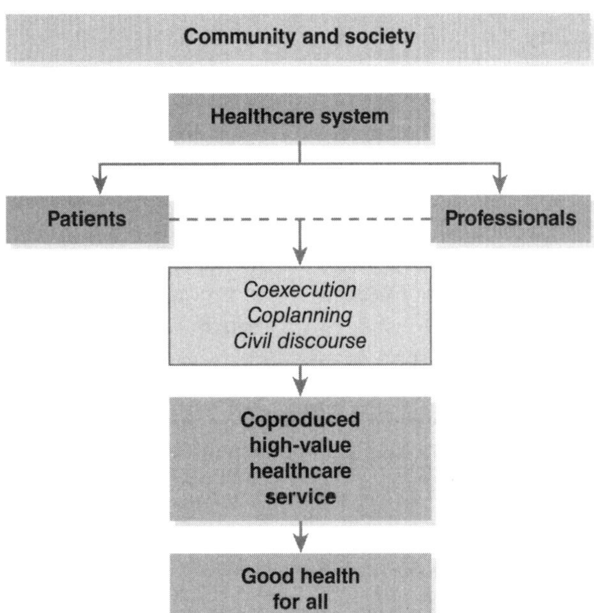

Figure 8.4 Model of Healthcare Service Coproduction

Data from Batalden, M., Batalden, P., Margolis, P., Seid, M., Armstrong, G., Opipari-Arrigan, L., & Hartung, H. (2016). Coproduction of healthcare service. *BMJ quality & safety, 25*(7), 509–517. https://doi.org/10.1136/bmjqs-2015-004315

operating in broader contexts, including healthcare role (patient, professional), healthcare system, community, and society.

Supporting Healthcare Service Coproduction

Organizations experience a variety of drivers to design and implement their services according to service-dominant logic. Alford identifies "fear of sanctions, material self-interest, intrinsic rewards, sociality, and normative appeals" as "the key drivers of coproductive behavior" in service organizations (Alford, 2014). In light of these varied drivers, many tools and frameworks exist to support health service organizations in improving coproduction processes. We describe several of these tools and frameworks below.

Patient and Public Involvement (PPI)

This overarching approach to the design and implementation of health services involves service users in organizational decision-making (Baumann et al., 2022). These activities can range from *consultation* with patients and the public (e.g., through a Patient and Family Advisory Council providing consultation to organizational leadership) to *partnership* (e.g., patients included on the organization's board of directors) to *full control* by people whose primary association with the healthcare organization is in the role of a patient or lay member of the public (Charles & DeMaio, 1993).

Co-Design

This approach to service design involves partnership between health professionals and service users over a period of time as they plan a change to services or operations together. Experience-based co-design involves a further focus on the holistic experiences of service users rather than distilling those experiences into more superficial user views, attitudes, and perceptions. This experience focus requires an in-depth understanding of "how the interface between the user and service is shaped," and a deliberate prioritization of the service's safety and functionality in addition to its sensory appeal (Bate & Robert, 2006).

Training and Self-Assessment

Training both health service users and health professionals and promoting self-assessment facilitates effective coproduction of health services. Related tools include:

- *Coproduction cycle.* Elwyn and colleagues describe coproduction at the point of care as comprising four steps: (1) Co-assessment; (2) Co-decision; (3) Co-design; and (4) Co-delivery. The **co-assessment** step addresses the patient's current health status, whether prior treatments were effective, and if any changes are needed. The **co-decision** step determines next steps based on the patient's goals, generally involving a comparison of options to facilitate "informed and preference-based choices." **Co-design** creates a treatment or management plan that fits the patient's goals, context, and capabilities while minimizing treatment burden. Finally, **co-delivery** prompts service users and health professionals to reflect on both how the patient can contribute to their care and how a healthcare professional or clinical team can support the patient (Elwyn et al., 2020).
- *Case-based scenarios.* Oriented toward health professional training, Johnson and colleagues created a coproduction curriculum that aims to help health professionals understand and integrate four aspects of health services. These include (1) "the lived reality of the persons sometimes known as 'patients'," (2) the 'as-is' systems that guide health services, (3) scientific knowledge of "disease biology, the illness experience, and the effectiveness of services that are available to inform practice," and (4) "the lived reality of the professional." (Johnson et al, 2021). Within this curriculum, case-based scenarios promote reflection and experiential learning. **Table 8.3** presents an example case-based scenario.

Table 8.3 Case-Based Scenario Example (from Johnson et al., 2021)

Scenario	Hillary is in her late 30s and has a complex medical history, particularly for someone so young. She had leukemia at 19, was diagnosed with congestive heart failure (CHF) at 25, and had two strokes and gastric bypass surgery. As a result of her strokes, she slurs her words and sometimes finds herself unable to express herself verbally like she did before her strokes. Hillary also feels like she is sometimes treated how older people are treated and thinks people don't understand her health problems and may feel uncomfortable if she talks about her health. She manages her health conditions moderately well and has a system for taking her medications but gets confused with more complicated medication regimens. She finds her health problems very frustrating but spoke to her doctor about her frustration and he compared bodies to cars in that they require maintenance; Hillary found this comparison helpful in adjusting her thinking. Hillary lives alone in the Minneapolis area, although she has a tight-knit family and her parents and siblings live in Minneapolis, too. Her family moved to Minnesota from Mississippi when she was 12. She is the oldest child with no children of her own, so she takes on more of a parental role with her siblings and thinks she has to be "the glue to keep it [her family] together." She often provides financial assistance to her family members. Even with her health complications, she holds a union job working with numbers and is independent. Hillary has a moderately active social life that seems to mostly revolve around her church. She attends services every Sunday and also goes to church functions whenever they're offered. She credits her faith with getting her through her health challenges. She enjoys traveling because "you don't know when's the next time you're going to see this stuff." Hillary also enjoys cooking and reading, but struggles to concentrate on reading after her strokes. She doesn't have the energy now but hopes to eventually be able to volunteer with older people.
Exercise	Based on what you now know about Hillary, what are her top needs? 1. ____________________ 2. ____________________ 3. ____________________ 4. ____________________

Reproduced from Johnson, J. K., Batalden, P., Foster, T., Arvidsson, C., Batalden, M., Forcino, R., et al., (2021). A starter's guide to learning and teaching how to coproduce healthcare services. *International Journal for Quality in Health Care, 33* (Suppl_2), ii55–ii62. https://doi.org/10.1093/intqhc/mzab131

- *Self-assessment resources for coproduction in clinical care and quality improvement.* Arguing that changes within clinical encounters and microsystems will result in broader change in organizational policy and strategy, Batalden and colleagues created a template to support health professionals and service users in assessing whether "a coproduced experience that creates value for both the provider and the receiver of care has been achieved" in a clinical encounter (Batalden et al., 2023). Several domains and related questions comprise the template as summarized below:
  - Situation: What is known about the context of the care setting?
  - Lived reality of the person sometimes known as "patient": What is known about the person when "sick, not sick," as well as the available resources?
  - "As is" system to be navigated: What can be expected about access to the care that is needed, the process of care, reliability of the processes?
  - Knowledge of the condition: What is known about the disease?
  - Knowledge of the experience of having the condition, illness: What is the experience of people with this disease?
  - Knowledge of the design, improvement of the service: How can this service be

improved to minimize the burden of illness?
    - Lived reality of the person sometimes known as 'professional': What do we know about the care team?
    - Reflection on the process: So what, now what? What have we learned, what will we do differently?
- Oliver and colleagues similarly created a self-assessment guide for quality improvement teams to assess the value contributed through coproduction improvement efforts (Oliver et al., 2021). These questions build on the "chain, shop, value" architecture and could be used on their own or in conjunction with the Batalden domains on coproduction presented above:
    - Who are the patients and how do they interact with professionals?
    - How do (standardized) linked processes work to meet the needs of this population? (Value chain activities.)
    - What "custom" work occurs to meet the particular needs of this population? (Value shop activities.)
    - How are networks of relevant people used to meet the current and emerging needs of this population? (Value network activities.)
    - What systems outside of the usual specialized work systems are accessed regularly to meet the needs of this population?
    - How do leaders develop the full spectrum of system modes (chain, shop, and network) and facilitate the ongoing match between patient need and best system mode to meet that need?

Measurement

The availability of valid and reliable measures of service output and outcomes that follow a service-dominant logic is limited but growing. In the absence of high-quality, service-oriented measures, a tempting solution is to default to goods-dominant measures that reflect tangible and quantifiable units of output. Reflecting on this problem in 1972, Ostrom suggested that "we need [. . .] other measures of output which indicate the level of output received by citizens"—rather than relying on goods-dominant measures such as the number of clinical encounters attended, hospitalizations recorded, medications prescribed, etc. (Ostrom, 1972). Nearly 50 years later, Elwyn and colleagues reiterated this need by describing coproduction as "when users define quality" (Elwyn et al., 2020).

To fill this gap in measures of health service coproduction, Elwyn created and Batalden & Foster highlight three brief questions asked of health service users following a clinical encounter: (1) How much effort was made to help you understand your health issues? (2) How much effort was made to listen to what matters most to you about your health issues? (3) How much effort was made to include what matters most to you in choosing what to do next? (Batalden & Foster, 2021; Elwin et al., 2013). A recent literature review of health service coproduction described outcomes like patients' health status and the acceptability of clinical interventions (Nordin et al., 2023). Further measurement of user experiences and outcomes should be tailored to the clinical context and focused on both the objective and subjective outcomes of health services (Figure 8.1).

Conclusion

In this chapter, we reviewed the differences between goods and services according to their key features, as well as through the lenses of goods-dominant logic and service-dominant logic. While goods are tangible outputs that are made by professionals and subsequently consumed by users, services are intangible processes that are created and consumed at the same time through the interdependent efforts of both service users and professionals. This defining feature of services is known as coproduction. Training health service users and health professionals in effective ways of working together to coproduce health services is an emerging focus of healthcare quality improvement efforts. This chapter reviews resources that are available to support and facilitate effective coproduction among service users and health professionals.

Key Concepts and Terms

Co-assessment
Co-decision
Co-delivery
Co-design
Coproduction
Goods-dominant logic
Quality 1.0
Quality 2.0
Quality 3.0
Service-dominant logic
Value chains
Value networks
Value shop

References

Alford, J. (2014). The multiple facets of co-production: Building on the work of Elinor Ostrom. *Public Management Review, 16*(3), 299–316. https://doi.org/10.1080/14719037.2013.806578

Batalden, M., Batalden, P., Margolis, P., Seid, M., Armstrong, G., Opipari-Arrigan, L., & Hartung, H. (2016). Coproduction of healthcare service. *BMJ Quality & Safety, 25*(7), 509–517. https://doi.org/10.1136/bmjqs-2015-004315

Batalden, P. (2018). Getting more health from healthcare: Quality improvement must acknowledge patient coproduction—an essay by Paul Batalden. *British Medical Journal, 362*, k3617. https://doi.org/10.1136/bmj.k3617

Batalden, P., & Foster, T. (2021). From assurance to coproduction: A century of improving the quality of health-care service. *International Journal for Quality in Health Care, 33*(Supplement_2), ii10–ii14. https://doi.org/10.1093/intqhc/mzab059

Batalden, P., Lachman, P., von Plessen, C., Johnson, J. K., & García-Elorrio, E. (2023). Coproduction of healthcare services—From concept to implementation. *International Journal for Quality in Health Care*. https://doi.org/10.1093/intqhc/mzad083

Bate, P., & Robert, G. (2006). Experience-based design: From redesigning the system around the patient to co-designing services with the patient. *Quality & Safety in Health Care, 15*(5), 307–310. https://doi.org/10.1136/qshc.2005.016527

Baumann, L. A., Reinhold, A. K., & Brütt, A. L. (2022). Public and patient involvement in health policy decision-making on the health system level—A scoping review. *Health Policy, 126*(10), 1023–1038.

Butler, C., & Greenhalgh, T. (2010). What is already known about involving users in service transformation? T. Greenhalgh, C. Humphrey, & F. Woodard (Eds.), *User involvement in health care*. Wiley-Blackwell.

Charles, C., & DeMaio, S. (1993). Lay participation in health care decision making: A conceptual framework. *Journal of Health Politics, Policy and Law, 18*(4), 881–904. https://doi.org/10.1215/03616878-18-4-881

Dunston, R., Lee, A., Boud, D., Brodie, P., & Chiarella, M. (2009). Co-production and health system reform: From re-imagining to re-making. *Australian Journal of Public Administration, 68*(1), 39–52. https://doi.org/10.1111/j.1467-8500.2008.00608.x

Elwyn, G., Barr, P. J., Grande, S. W., Thompson, R., Walsh, T., & Ozanne, E. M. (2013). Developing CollaboRATE: A fast and frugal patient-reported measure of shared decision making in clinical encounters. *Patient Education and Counseling, 93*(1), 102–107. https://doi.org/10.1016/j.pec.2013.05.009

Elwyn, G., Nelson, E., Hager, A., & Price, A. (2020). Coproduction: When users define quality. *BMJ Quality & Safety, 29*(9), 711–716. https://doi.org/10.1136/bmjqs-2019-009830

Fjeldstad, Ø. D., Johnson, J. K., Margolis, P. A., Seid, M., Höglund, P., & Batalden, P. B. (2020). Networked health care: Rethinking value creation in learning health care systems. *Learning Health Systems, 4*(2), e10212. https://doi.org/10.1002/lrh2.10212

Fuchs, V. R., & Leveson, I. F. (1968). *The service economy*. National Bureau of Economic Research.

Institute of Medicine, Committee on Quality of Health Care in America. (2001). *Crossing the quality chasm: A new health system for the 21st century*. National Academies Press.

Johnson, J. K., Batalden, P., Foster, T., Arvidsson, C., Batalden, M., Forcino, R., & Gäre, B. A. (2021). A starter's guide to learning and teaching how to coproduce healthcare services. *International Journal for Quality in Health Care, 33*(Supplement_2), ii55–ii62. https://doi.org/10.1093/intqhc/mzab131

Joiner, K., & Lusch, R. (2016). Evolving to a new service-dominant logic for health care. *Innovation and Entrepreneurship in Health, 25*. https://doi.org/10.2147/IEH.S93473

Nordin, A., Kjellstrom, S., Robert, G., Masterson, D., & Areskoug Josefsson, K. (2023). Measurement and outcomes of co-production in health and social care: A systematic review of empirical studies. *BMJ Open, 13*(9), e073808. https://doi.org/10.1136/bmjopen-2023-073808

Oliver, B. J., Forcino, R. C., & Batalden, P. B. (2021). Initial development of a self-assessment approach for coproduction value creation by an international community of practice. *International Journal of Quality in Health Care, 33*(Supplement_2), ii48–ii54. https://doi.org/10.1093/intqhc/mzab077

Osborne, S. P., Radnor, Z., & Nasi, G. (2013). A new theory for public service management? Toward a (public) service-dominant approach. *The American Review of Public Administration, 43*(2), 135–158. https://doi.org/10.1177/0275074012466935

Ostrom, E. (1972). Metropolitan reform: Propositions derived from two traditions. *Social Science Quarterly, 53*(3), 474–493. http://www.jstor.org/stable/42860228

Ostrom, E., Parks, R. B., Whitaker, G. P., & Percy, S. L. (1978). The public service production process: A framework for analyzing police services. *Policy Studies Journal, 7*(s1), 381. https://doi.org/10.1111/j.1541-0072.1978.tb01782.x

Parks, R. B., Baker, P. C., Kiser, L., Oakerson, R., Ostrom, E., Ostrom, V., et al., (1981). Consumers as coproducers of public services: Some economic and institutional considerations. *Policy Studies Journal, 9*(7), 1001–1011. https://doi.org/10.1111/j.1541-0072.1981.tb01208.x

PatientsLikeMe. (n.d.). *PatientsLikeMe*. Retrieved April 14, 2025, from https://www.patientslikeme.com/

Sabadosa, K. A., & Batalden, P. B. (2014). The interdependent roles of patients, families and professionals in cystic fibrosis: A system for the coproduction of healthcare and its improvement. *BMJ Quality & Safety, 23*(Suppl 1), i90–i94. https://doi.org/10.1136/bmjqs-2013-002782

Stabell, C. B., & Fjeldstad, Ø. D. (1998). Configuring value for competitive advantage: On chains, shops, and networks. *Strategic Management Journal, 19*(5), 413–437. https://doi.org/10.1002/(SICI)1097-0266(199805)19:5%3C413::AID-SMJ946%3E3.0.CO;2-C

Vargo, S. L., & Lusch, R. F. (2008). Service-dominant logic: Continuing the evolution. *Journal of the Academy of Marketing Science, 36*(1), 1–10. https://doi.org/10.1007/s11747-007-0069-6

CHAPTER 9

Assessing Patient Risks and Preventing Harm in the Clinical Microsystem

Paul Barach and Julie K. Johnson

CHAPTER OUTLINE

Introduction

The framework of healthcare delivery is shifting rapidly. Capital budgets and operational efficiency are critical in this time of shrinking reimbursement, increasing share of risk, and evolving models of care delivery. Modern medical care is complex, expensive, and at times dangerous. In the United States, over 250,000 patients who receive medical care each year will experience an adverse event with over 100,000 patients dying from the care that they received (Anderson & Abrahamson, 2017; Stewart et al., 2016). Vulnerable patients are at greater risk for adverse events (Piccardi et al., 2018). Globally, it is estimated that approximately 10% of patients have been affected by at least one adverse event (Schwendimann et al., 2018; Skelly et al, 2023). Furthermore, it is estimated that 43.5% of harmful events are preventable (de Vries et al., 2008; Landrigan et al., 2010). Medical error has been estimated as the third-leading cause of death, following heart disease and cancer (Makary & Daniel, 2016; Rodziewicz et al, 2024). The rates reported vary depending on the methods used in the studies as well as the levels of underreporting; however, what is clear is that there is an urgent need to improve our healthcare systems dramatically. Most significantly, the study of patient safety has identified the need to rethink and redesign better systems—ones that respect the work of frontline providers and are co-produced with patients—and to prevent errors from causing patient harm (Barach & Phelps, 2013; Batalden et al., 2016). From all perspectives—patients' and providers' as well as the healthcare system's—the current level of avoidable harm is unacceptable and financially ruinous.

The goal of this chapter is to discuss, in actionable language, how best to develop reliability and resilience in healthcare systems while embedding a "vision of zero" to avoid patient harm and support health workforce physical and emotional injury reductions and health improvements. Achieving this vision requires a risk management strategy that includes: (1) *identifying risk*—finding out what is going wrong; (2) *analyzing risk*—collecting data and using appropriate methods to understand what it means; and (3) *controlling risk*—devising and implementing strategies to better detect, manage, and prevent the problems that produce harm (Dickson, 1995).

This chapter begins with the background and definitions of risk management. We discuss the universal ingredients of individual adverse events, organizational incidents, and human errors. We then discuss models of risk management, focusing on how to address the barriers to creating an effective culture of safety, including supporting a culture of reporting events and meaningful staff engagement, and we present strategies for applying concepts to clinical microsystem settings. The chapter concludes with a discussion on the role of disclosure of adverse events as part of a comprehensive risk management strategy.

Quality Risk Management—Background and Definitions

Quality is commonly measured by whether a product or service is safe, timely, effective, efficient, equitable, and patient-centered (IOM, 2001). Traditionally, risk has been seen as exposure to events that may threaten or damage the organization (Walshe, 2001). Essentially, **risk** is the chance of something happening that will have an impact on key elements. It can be measured in terms of consequences and likelihoods. The task of **risk management**, therefore, becomes balancing the costs and consequences of risks against the costs of risk reduction. The goal in clinical risk management in complex social technical organizations where social and technical components are deeply intertwined, creating emergent behaviors and requiring holistic approaches to management, should be to improve care and protect patients from harm; however, a perverse incentive for the organization as well as for those who work within the organization is that risk management may become a financially driven exercise that is at odds with the clinical mission of the organization (Small & Barach, 2002; Vincent, 1997). **Clinical risk management**, such as in addressing the risks of patients from physicians in training learning to do invasive procedures safely, is the culture, process, and structures that are directed toward the effective management of potential opportunities and adverse events (Warm, 2021). We measure risk in terms of the likelihood and consequences of something going wrong, which is in contrast to how we measure **quality** (i.e., the extent to which a service or product achieves a desired result or outcome). Our goal as health system managers and clinical leaders is to introduce as low as reasonably achievable (ALARA) a clinical management approach to increase safety margins, and help assess and reduce bedside risks.

There is substantial evidence that the majority of harm caused by health care is avoidable and the result of systemic problems rather than poor performance or negligence by individual providers (Seiden, 2003). The past few decades have seen an increase in proposed or operative legislation, including a near-miss reporting system, changes in mandated reporting systems, and the creation of state agencies dedicated to the coordination of patient safety research and implementation of change (AHRQ, 2016). There is clear policy guidance and a compelling ethical basis for the disclosure of adverse events to patients and their families (Cantor et al., 2005). Mechanisms have been developed to involve all stakeholders—the government, healthcare professionals, administrators and planners, providers, and consumers—in ongoing, effective consultation, communication, and cultural change. Healthcare organizations should develop clear policies to support disclosure and should create supportive environments that enable clinicians to meet their ethical obligations to disclose adverse events to patients and families. These cultural and regulatory devices help engender more trust, which is an essential element in developing and sustaining a culture of safety.

Accidents

Research in managing risk has focused on the culture and structure of the organization. Perrow (1984) advanced the Normal Accidents Theory, which describes accidents as inevitable in complex, tightly coupled systems such as chemical plants and nuclear power plants (Perrow, 1984). These accidents occur irrespective of the skill and intentions of the designers and operators; hence, they are normal and difficult to prevent. Perrow further argues that as the system gets more complex, it becomes opaque to its users and designers, so that people are less likely to recognize and fear potential adverse occurrences. There are three universal ingredients of system accidents:

1. *All human beings, regardless of their skills, abilities, and specialist training, make fallible decisions and commit unsafe acts.* This human propensity for committing errors and violating safety procedures can be moderated by selection, training, well-designed equipment, and good management, but it can never be entirely eliminated.
2. *All man-made systems possess latent failures to some degree.* This is true no matter how well designed, constructed, operated, and maintained a system may be. These unseen failures are analogous to resident pathogens in the human body that combine with local triggering factors (e.g., life stress, toxic chemicals) to overcome the immune system and produce disease. Adverse events such as cancers and heart attacks in well-defended systems do not arise from single causes but from multifactorial hits that overwhelm the system's natural defenses. The adverse conjunction of such factors, each necessary but insufficient alone to breach the defenses, are behind the majority of adverse events.
3. *All human endeavors involve some measure of risk.* In many cases, the local hazards are well understood and can be guarded against by a variety of technical or procedural countermeasures. No one, however, can foresee all the possible adverse scenarios, so there will always be defects in this protective armor.

These three ubiquitous accident ingredients reveal something important about the nature of making health care safer (Bernstein, 1996). We can mitigate the risks of adverse events by process improvement, standardization, and an in-depth understanding of the safety degradations in systems, but we cannot prevent all risk. Embracing this uncertainty and implementing the training and curriculum to cope with it, as opposed to focusing solely on minimizing it, is essential in high-risk, highly coupled industries. Industries characterized by high risk and high coupling such as nuclear power, aviation, and health are those where potential failures can have severe consequences (high risk) and where various components or systems are intricately linked and dependent on each other (high coupling). A failure in one part of a highly coupled system can trigger a cascade of failures throughout the entire system. The principle of making the risk to patients as low as reasonably achievable (a goal sometimes referenced using the acronym "ALARA"), adapted from the nuclear industry, can help protect patients by increasing safety margins. (Barach et al., 2021).

Outside health care, the most obvious impetus for the renewed interest in human error and the impacts of the organizational dynamics has been the growing concern over the terrible costs of human errors that led to disasters. Examples include the Tenerife runway collision in 1977

(540 fatalities), the Three Mile Island nuclear disaster in 1979, the Bhopal methyl isocyanate tragedy in 1984, the Challenger space shuttle accident in 1986 (Vaughn, 1996), the Chernobyl nuclear disaster in 1986 (Reason, 1997), and the Deepwater Horizon disaster in 2010 (Ingersoll, Locke, & Reavis, 2012). There is nothing new about tragic accidents caused by human errors, but in the past, the injurious consequences were usually confined to the immediate vicinity of the disaster. Today, the nature and scale of highly coupled, potentially hazardous technologies in society and hospitals means that human errors by frontline nurses can have adverse effects far beyond the confines of the individual provider and patient settings. (Uramatsu et al., 2024) For example, the *Pseudomonas aeruginosa* contamination of a single damaged bronchoscope potentially infected dozens of patients (DiazGranados et al., 2009). Over time, there has been a noticeable spirit of *glasnost* (openness) within the medical profession concerning the role played by human error in causing medical adverse events (Millenson, 1997).

The Organizational Accident

Systems have been designed and redesigned with a wide variety of technical and procedural safeguards (e.g., operating rooms, airlines), yet they are still subject to accidents and adverse events (e.g., fire in the operating room, wrong-patient procedure, drug errors). These types of accidents and adverse events have been termed **organizational accidents** (Perrow, 1984; Reason, 1997). Organizational accidents are mishaps that arise not from single errors or isolated component breakdowns, but from the insidious changes in resilience due to an accumulation of failures occurring mainly within the managerial and organizational spheres. Such latent failures may subsequently combine with active failures and local triggering factors by errant but well-meaning providers to penetrate or bypass the system defenses. In his classic study of surgical teams, *Forgive and Remember*, Bosk (1979) demonstrates how the underlying culture acts to acculturate newcomers, encourage normalized deviance, and suppress external views for change while enabling substandard practices to go unchecked (Vaughn, 1999). Systemic flaws set up good people to fail. People often find ways of getting around processes that seem to be unnecessary or that impede the workflow. This accumulated acceptance of cutting corners or making work-arounds poses a great danger to health care over time. By *deviance*, we mean organizational behaviors that deviate from normative standards or professional expectations (e.g., low handwashing compliance before patient contact, minimal consultant oversight of hospital care on weekends, suppressing information about poor care, and so forth). Once a professional group normalizes a deviant organizational practice, it is no longer viewed as an aberrant act that elicits an exceptional response; instead, it becomes a routine activity that is commonly anticipated and frequently used (Weick, 2009). A permissive ethical climate, an emphasis on financial goals at all costs, and an opportunity to act amorally or immorally, all can contribute to managerial and clinician decisions to initiate deviance (Barach & Phelps, 2013).

The etiology of an organizational accident can be divided into five phases (Perrow, 1984):

1. Organizational processes giving rise to latent failures;
2. Conditions that produce errors and violations within workplaces (e.g., operating room, pharmacy, intensive care unit);
3. The commission of errors and violations by "**sharp end**" individuals (the "sharp end" refers to the personnel or parts of the healthcare system in direct contact with patients. In contrast, the "**blunt end**" refers to the many layers of the healthcare system that affect the individuals at the sharp end. These colloquial terms are more formally known as "active errors," which occur at the point of contact between a human and some aspect of a larger system, and "latent errors," which are the less apparent failures of the organization);
4. The breaching of defenses or safeguards;
5. Outcomes that vary from a "free lesson" to a catastrophe.

Viewed from this perspective, the unsafe acts of a physician in direct contact with the patient are the end result of a long chain of events that originate higher up in the organization. One of the basic principles of error management is that the transitory mental states associated with error production—momentary inattention, distraction, preoccupation, forgetting—are the least-manageable links in the error chain because they are both unintended and largely unpredictable (Hollnagel, Woods, & Leveson, 2006). These errors have their cognitive origins in highly adaptive mental processes (Sagan, 1993). Such states can strike healthcare providers at any time, leading to slips, forgetfulness, and inattention. The system must be designed with in-depth defenses to mitigate the impact of these momentary lapses in awareness and to maintain the integrity of patient care.

Human Error and Performance Limitations

Although there was virtually no research in the field of safety in medicine and healthcare delivery until the mid-1980s, in other fields, such as aviation, road and rail travel, nuclear power, and chemical processing, safety science and human factor principles have been applied to understand, prevent, and mitigate the associated adverse events (e.g., crashes, spills, and contaminations). The study of human error and of the organizational culture and climate, as well as intensive crash investigations, have been well developed for several decades in these arenas (Rasmussen, 1990; Sagan, 1993). The presumption of the non-linear and increasing risks in health care, associated with an apparent rise in the rate of litigation in the 1980s and attributable to the media's amplified attention to the subject, has brought medical adverse events to the attention of both clinicians and the general public (Kasperson et al., 1988).

In parallel with these developments, researchers from several disciplines have developed increasingly sophisticated methods for analyzing all incidents (Turner & Pidgeon, 1997). Theories of error and accident causation have evolved and are applicable across many human activities, including health care (Reason, 1997). These developments have led to a much broader understanding of accident causation, with less focus on the individual who commits an error at the "sharp end" of the incident and more on preexisting organizational and system factors that provide the context under which errors and patient harm can occur (Cassin & Barach, 2012). An important consequence of this has been the realization that rigorous and innovative techniques of accident analysis may reveal deep-rooted, latent, and unsafe features of organizations. James Reason's "Swiss cheese" model captures these relationships very well (Reason, 1990). Understanding and predicting performance in complex settings requires a detailed understanding of the setting, the regulatory environment, and the human factors and organizational culture that shape and influence this performance.

Models of Risk Management

Risk management deals with the fact that adverse events, however rare, do continue to occur. Furthermore, risk management as a concept means that we should never ignore the possibility or significance of rare, unpredictable events. Using a creative analogy, Nassim Nicholas Taleb (2010) argues that before Europeans discovered Australia, there was no reason to believe that swans could be any color but white. However, when they discovered Australia, they found black swans. Black swans remind us that things do occur that we cannot possibly predict. Taleb continues the analogy to say that a "black swan" is an event with three properties: (1) the probability is low based on past knowledge, (2) the impact of the occurrence is massive, and (3) it is subject to hindsight bias; that is, people do not see it coming, but after its occurrence, everyone recognized that it was likely to happen.

In general, risk management models take into consideration the probability of an event

		Probability		
		Low	**Medium**	**High**
Impact	**Significant**	Considerable management required	Substantial management and monitoring of risks	Extensive management crucial
	Moderate	May accept risks but monitor them	Management effort worthwhile	Management effort required
	Limited/minor	Accept risks	Accept but monitor risks	Manage and monitor risks

Figure 9.1 Risk Management Model

occurring, which is then multiplied by the potential impact of the event. **Figure 9.1** illustrates a simple risk management model that considers the probability of an event (low, medium, or high) and the impact of the consequences (limited/minor, moderate, or significant). Assigning an event in one of the cells is not an exact science, but the matrix offers a guideline to an appropriate organizational response to the risk. The individual unit or organization would need to determine how to translate each cell into action (e.g., what is required for "extensive management" of events with a significant negative impact and high likelihood of occurring).

Engineering a Culture of Safety

How do we create an organizational climate in health care that fosters safety? What are the ingredients and key values of a safety culture? While national cultures arise largely out of shared norms and values, an organizational culture is shaped mainly by shared practices. And practices can be shaped by the implementation and enforcement of rules. **Culture** can be defined as the collection of individual and group values, attitudes, and practices that guide the behavior of group members (Helmreich & Merritt, 2001). Acquiring a safety culture is a process of organizational learning that recognizes the inevitability of error and proactively seeks to identify latent threats. Characteristics of a strong safety culture include (Pronovost et al., 2003):

1. A commitment of the leadership to discuss and learn from errors
2. Communications founded on mutual trust and respect
3. Shared perceptions of the importance of safety
4. Encouragement and practice of teamwork
5. Incorporation of nonpunitive systems for reporting and analyzing adverse events

Striving for a safety culture is a process of collective learning. When the usual reaction to an adverse incident is to write another procedure and to provide more training, the system will not become more resistant to future organizational accidents. In fact, these actions may deflect the blame from the organization as a whole. There is a long tradition in medicine of examining past practices to understand how things might have been done differently. However, morbidity and mortality conferences, grand rounds, and peer reviews share many of the same shortcomings, such as a lack of human factors and systems thinking, a narrow focus on individual performance that excludes analysis of the contributory team factors and larger social issues, retrospective bias (a tendency to search for errors as opposed to the myriad system causes of error induction), and a lack of multidisciplinary integration into the organization-wide culture (Cassin & Barach, 2017).

If clinicians at the sharp end are not empowered by managerial leadership to be honest and reflective on their practice, rules and regulations will have a limited impact on enabling safer outcomes. Healthcare administrators need to understand the fundamental dynamics that lead to adverse events. Employing tools such as root cause analysis and failure mode and effects analysis can help clinicians and others better understand how adverse events occur, but only if done in an open and safe manner (Dekker, 2004). Collecting and learning from near-misses is essential. Definitions vary somewhat, but we define a near-miss as any error that had the potential to cause an adverse outcome but did not result in patient harm (Barach & Small, 2000). It is indistinguishable from a full-fledged adverse event in all but outcome (March, Sproull, & Tamuz, 2003). Near-misses offer powerful reminders of system hazards and retard the process of forgetting to be afraid of adverse events. A comprehensive effort to record and analyze near-miss data in health care has, however, lagged behind other industries (e.g., aviation, nuclear power industry) (Small & Barach, 2002). Vital but underappreciated studies suggest that near-misses are quite common. In a classic study, Heinreich (1941) estimated there are approximately 100 near-misses for every adverse event resulting in patient harm.

A focus on learning from near-misses offers several advantages (Barach & Small, 2000):

1. **Near-misses** occur 3–300 times more often than adverse events, enabling quantitative analysis.
2. There are fewer barriers to data collection, allowing analysis of interrelations of small failures.
3. Recovery strategies can be studied to enhance proactive interventions and to deemphasize the culture of blame.
4. Hindsight bias is more effectively reduced.

If near-misses and adverse events are inevitable, how do we learn from them once they occur? The next section discusses an approach for learning from events using the clinical microsystems framework.

Applying Risk Management Concepts to Improving Quality and Safety Within the Clinical Microsystem

The clinical microsystem as a unit of research, analysis, and practice is an important level at which to focus patient safety interventions. A **clinical microsystem** has been defined as a small team of providers and staff providing care for a defined population of patients (Mohr, 2000; Mohr & Batalden, 2002; Mohr, Batalden, & Barach, 2004). Most patients and caregivers meet and work at this system level, and it is here that real changes in patient care can (and must) be made. Errors and failure occur within the microsystem, and ultimately it is the well-functioning microsystem that can prevent or mitigate errors and failure to avoid causing patient harm. Safety is a property of the clinical microsystem that can be achieved only through a systematic application of a broad array of process, equipment, organization, supervision, training, simulation, and teamwork changes. The scenario included in **Exhibit 9.1** illustrates a patient safety event in an academic clinical microsystem and how the resulting analysis enables a microsystem to learn from the event. Throughout the story, as told from the perspective of a senior resident physician in pediatrics, there are many process and system failures that contributed to the patient harm.

Many methods are available to explore the causal system at work (Dekker, 2002; Reason, 1995; Vincent, 2003; Vincent, Taylor-Adams, & Stanhope, 1998), and they all suggest the importance of holding the entire causal system in our analytic frame, not just seeking a "root" cause. One method that we have found to be useful for systematically looking at patient safety events builds on William Haddon's (1972) seminal framework on injury epidemiology (Mohr et al., 2003). Haddon, as the first Director of the National Highway Safety Bureau (1966–1969), is credited with a paradigm change in the prevention of road traffic deaths and injuries moving from an "accidental"

EXHIBIT 9.1 Patient Safety Scenario—Interview with a Third-Year Pediatrics Resident

Resident: I had a patient who was very ill. He was 12 years old and was completely healthy up until 3 months ago, and since then has been in our hospital and two other hospitals pretty much the entire time. He has been in respiratory failure, he's had mechanical ventilation (including oscillation), he's been in renal failure, he's had a number of ministrokes, and when I came on service he was having diarrhea—3 to 5 L/day—and we still didn't know what was going on with him. We thought that an abdominal CT would be helpful, and it needed to be infused.

He was a very anxious child. Understandably, it's hard for the nurses, and for me, and for his mother to deal with. He thought of it as pain, but it was anxiety, and it responded well to anxiolytics.

When I came in that morning, it hadn't been passed along to nursing that he was supposed to go to CT that morning. I heard the charge nurse getting the report from the night nurse. I said, "You know that he is supposed to go for a CT today." She was already upset because they were very short staffed. She heard me and then said that she was not only the charge nurse, but also taking care of two patients, and one had to go to CT. She went off to the main unit to talk to someone. Then she paged me and said, "If you want this child to have a scan, you have to go with him." I said, "OK." Nurses are the ones who usually go. But it didn't seem to be beyond my abilities . . .at the time.

So, I took the child for his CT and his mom came with us. We gave him extra Ativan on the way there, because whenever he had a procedure he was extra anxious. When we got there, they weren't ready. We had lost our spot from the morning. My patient got more and more anxious and was actually yelling at the techs, "Hurry up!" We went into the room. He was about 5 or 6 hours late for his study, and we had given him contrast enterally. The techs were concerned that he didn't have enough anymore and wanted to give him more through his G-tube. I said, "That sounds fine." And they mixed it up and gave it to me to give through his G-tube. I went to his side and—not registering that it was his central line—I unhooked his central line, not only taking off the cap but unhooking something, and I pushed 70 cc of the gastrografin in. As soon as I had finished the second syringe I realized I was using the wrong tube. I said, "Oh no!" Mom was right there and said, "What?" I said, "I put the stuff in the wrong tube. He looks OK. I'll be right back, I have to call somebody."

I clamped off his intravenous line and I called my attending and the radiologist. My attending said that he was on his way down. The radiologist was over by the time I had hung up the phone. My patient was stable the whole time. We figured out what was in the gastrografin that could potentially cause harm. We decided to cancel the study. . . .I sent the gastrografin—the extra stuff in the tubes—for a culture just in case he grew some kind of infection and then we would be able to treat it and match it with what I had pushed into the line. I filled out an incident report. I called my chiefs and told them. . . .They said, "It's OK. He's fine, right?" I said, "Yes." They came up later in the evening just to be supportive. They said, "It's OK. It's OK to make a mistake."

Interviewer: What was your attending's response?

Resident: The attending that I had called when I made the mistake said, "I'm sorry that you were in that situation. You shouldn't have been put in that situation." Another attending the next day was telling people, "Well, you know what happened yesterday," as if it were the only thing going on for this patient.

I thought it was embarrassing that he was just passing on this little tidbit of information as if it would explain everything that was going on. As opposed to saying, "Yes, an error was made, it is something that we are taking into account." And he told me to pay more attention to the patient. Yes, I made the mistake, but hands-down, I still—and always did—know that patient better than he did. I just thought that was mean and not fair. And the only other thing I thought was not good was the next morning when I was prerounding, some of the nurses were whispering, and I just assumed that was what they were whispering about. I walked up to them and said, "I'm the one who did it. I made a mistake. How is he doing?" I tried to answer any questions they had and move on.

Interviewer: How did the nurses respond when you said that you made a mistake?

Resident: The nurse that had sent me down with him told me, "It's OK, don't worry about it." The others just listened politely and didn't say anything.

Interviewer: How did the mother respond to you the next day?

Resident: The next day, I felt really bad. I felt very incompetent. I was feeling very awkward being the leader of this child's care—because I am still at a loss for his diagnosis. And after the event, when the grandma found out—she was very angry. I apologized to the mom, and I thought it would be overdoing it to keep saying, "I am so sorry." So, the next day, I went into the room and said to the mom, "You need to have confidence in the person taking care of your son. If my mistake undermines that at all, you don't have to have me as your son's doctor, and I can arrange it so that you can have whoever you want." She said, "No. No, it's fine. We want you as his doctor." Then we just moved on with the care plan. That felt good. And that felt appropriate. I couldn't just walk into the room and act like nothing had happened. I needed her to give me the power to be their doctor. So, I just went and asked for it.

or "pre-scientific" approach to an etiologic one focused on root causes of the car crash. Haddon was interested in the broader issues of injury and system failures that result from the transfer of energy in such ways that inanimate or animate objects are damaged. According to Haddon (1970), there are a number of strategies for reducing losses:

- Prevent the marshaling of the energy.
- Reduce the amount of energy marshaled.
- Prevent the release of the energy.
- Modify the rate or spatial distribution of release of the energy.
- Separate in time and space the energy being released and the susceptible structure.
- Use a physical barrier to separate the energy and the susceptible structure.
- Modify the contact surface or structure with which people can come in contact.
- Strengthen the structure that might be damaged by the energy transfer.
- When injury does occur, rapidly detect it and counter its continuation and extension.
- When injury does occur, take all necessary reparative and rehabilitative steps.

All these strategies have a logical sequence that is related to the three essential phases of a vehicular crash relating to pre-crash, crash, and post-crash.

Haddon developed a 3 × 3 matrix with factors related to an auto injury (human, vehicle and equipment, and environment) heading the columns and phases of the event (pre-crash, crash, and post-crash) heading the rows. **Figure 9.2** demonstrates how the Haddon Matrix has been adapted and applied to analyze an auto accident (Haddon, 1972). The use of the matrix focuses the analysis on the interrelationships between the factors and

		Factors		
		Human	Vehicle	Environment
Phases	Preinjury	Alcohol intoxication	Braking capacity of motor vehicles	Visibility of hazards
	Injury	Resistance to energy insults	Sharp or pointed edges and surfaces	Flammable building materials
	Postinjury	Hemorrhage	Rapidity of energy reduction	Emergency medical response

Figure 9.2 Haddon Matrix Used to Analyze Auto Accidents

Data from Haddon, W., Jr. (1972). A logical framework for categorizing highway safety phenomena and activity. *The Journal of trauma, 12*(3), 193–207. https://doi.org/10.1097/00005373-197203000-00002

phases. A mix of countermeasures derived from Haddon's strategies is necessary to minimize injury and loss. Furthermore, the countermeasures can be designed for each phase, similar to designing mechanisms to prevent patient harm. This approach confirms what we know about adverse events in complex healthcare environments—it takes a variety of strategies to prevent and/or mitigate patient harm. Understanding injury in its larger context helps us recognize the basic nature of "unsafe" systems and the important work of humans to mitigate the inherent hazards (Dekker, 2002).

We can also use the Haddon Matrix to guide the analysis of patient safety adverse events. Adapting this tool from injury epidemiology to patient safety, we have revised the matrix to include phases labeled *pre-event*, *event*, and *post-event* instead of *pre-crash, crash, and post-crash*. The revised factors, *patient–family*, *health care professional*, *system*, and *environment*, replace *human*, *vehicle and equipment*, and *environment*. Note that we have added a fourth factor, *system*, to refer to the processes and systems that are in place for the microsystem to function. This addition recognizes the significant contributions that systems and teams make toward harm and error in the microsystem.

"Environment" refers to the context (enablers and barriers) that the microsystem exists within. **Figure 9.3** shows a completed matrix using the

Phases	Factors: Patient/family	Factors: Health care professional	Factors: System	Factors: Environment
Pre-event	• Consent (process, timing) • Anxiety • Patient lines • Mother's presence	• Not familiar with procedure • Lack of MD–RN communication • Focus on anxiety and not on procedure • Assumed roles, made assumptions • Arrogance/respect	• Several lines in patient • Silos	• Nurse shortage • Scheduling delays • Manufacturing (performance shaping factors, human factors) • Lack of process for risk analysis
Event	• Anxiety (patient's and parent's) • No shared expectations • No active participation	• Fatigue • Aware of limitations • Training	• Work hours • Protocols • Standardization • Double-checking	• Work hours for residents • Rushed • No other clinician
Post-event	• Lack of explanation • Disclosure • Who should talk to family?	• Guilt • Lack of confidence • Loss of face	• Lack of understanding of errors/systems • Lack of supportive environment for resident • Incidence report morbidity and mortality • Analysis of event	• Regulatory

Figure 9.3 Completed Patient Safety Matrix

Phases		Factors		
		Patient/family	Health care professional	Systems/environment
Phases	Pre-event	• Orientation to the process (process mapping)	• Probablistic risk assessment • Scenario building • Hazard analysis • Checklists	• Failure modes effects analysis • Human factors engineering
Phases	Event	• Interview	• Crew resource management • Checklists	• Root cause analysis
Phases	Post-event	• Interview • Focus group interviews	• Microsystem analysis • Morbidity and mortality conference	• Root cause analysis • Artifact analysis

Figure 9.4 Patient Safety Matrix with Tools for Assessing Risk and Analyzing Events

pediatric case. The next step in learning from errors and adverse events is to develop and execute countermeasures to address the issues in each cell of the matrix. **Figure 9.4** provides a list of tools that would be appropriate to assess each "cell" of the matrix as part of a microsystems risk assessment framework.

Microsystems and Macrosystems

Healthcare organizations are composed of multiple, differentiated, variably autonomous microsystems. These interdependent small systems exhibit loose and tight coupling (Weick & Sutcliffe, 2001). Several assumptions are made about the relationships between these microsystems and the macrosystem (Nelson et al., 2002):

1. Bigger systems (macrosystems) are made of smaller systems.
2. These smaller systems (microsystems) produce quality, safety, and cost outcomes at the front line of care.
3. Ultimately, the outcomes from macrosystems can be no better than the microsystems of which they are formed.

These assumptions suggest that it is necessary to intervene within each microsystem in the organization if the organization as a whole wants to improve. A microsystem cannot function independently from the other microsystems it regularly works with or its macrosystem. From the macrosystem perspective, senior leaders can enable an overall patient safety focus with clear, visible values, expectations, and recognition of "deeds well done." They can set direction by clearly expecting that each microsystem will align its mission, vision, and strategies with the organization's mission, vision, and strategies. Senior leadership can offer each microsystem the flexibility needed to achieve its mission and ensure the creation of strategies, systems, and methods for achieving excellence in health care, thereby stimulating innovation and building knowledge and capabilities. Finally, senior leaders can pay careful attention to the questions they ask as they nurture meaningful work and hold the microsystem's leadership accountable to achieve the strategic mission of providing safer care.

Table 9.1 builds on the research of high-performing microsystems (Mohr, 2000; Mohr & Batalden, 2002; Mohr, Batalden, & Barach, 2004) and provides specific actions that can be further explored to apply patient safety concepts to understanding the impacts and performance of clinical microsystems. It also provides linkages to the

Table 9.1 Linkage of Microsystem Characteristics to Patient Safety

Microsystem Characteristics	What This Means for Patient Safety
1. Leadership	■ Define the safety vision of the organization ■ Identify the existing constraints within the organization ■ Allocate resources for plan development, implementation, and ongoing monitoring and evaluation ■ Build in microsystems participation and input to plan development ■ Align organizational quality and safety goals ■ Engage the board of trustees in ongoing conversations about the organizational progress toward achieving safety goals ■ Recognition for prompt truth-telling about errors or hazards ■ Certification of helpful changes to improve safety
2. Organizational support	■ Work with clinical microsystems to identify patient safety issues and make relevant local changes ■ Put the necessary resources and tools in the hands of individuals
3. Staff focus	■ Assess current safety culture ■ Identify the gap between current culture and safety vision ■ Plan cultural interventions ■ Conduct periodic assessments of culture ■ Celebrate examples of desired behavior, for example, acknowledgment of an error
4. Education and training	■ Develop patient safety curriculum ■ Provide training and education of key clinical and management leadership ■ Develop a core of people with patient safety skills who can work across microsystems as a resource
5. Interdependence of the care team	■ Build PDSA* cycles into debriefings ■ Use daily huddles to debrief and to celebrate identifying errors ■ *PDSA: Plan, Do, Study, Act
6. Patient focus	■ Establish patient and family partnerships ■ Support disclosure and truth around medical error
7. Community and market focus	■ Analyze safety issues in community, and partner with external groups to reduce risk to population
8. Performance results	■ Develop key safety measures ■ Create feedback mechanisms to share results with microsystems
9. Process improvement	■ Identify patient safety priorities based on assessment of key safety measures ■ Address the work that will be required at the microsystem level
10. Information and information technology	■ Enhance error-reporting systems ■ Build safety concepts into information flow (e.g., checklists, reminder systems)

macrosystem's ongoing organization-centered and issue-centered quality efforts, which can either support or conflict with this approach. **Box 9.1** provides a set of accountability questions that senior leaders should ask as they work to improve the safety and quality of the organization.

Box 9.1 Questions Senior Leaders Should Ask About Patient Safety

- What information do we have about errors and patient harm?
- What is the patient safety plan?
- How will the plan be implemented at the organizational level and at the microsystem level?
- What type of infrastructure is needed to support implementation?
- What is the best way to communicate the plan to the individual microsystems?
- How can we foster reporting—telling the truth—about errors?
- How will we empower microsystem staff to make suggestions for improving safety?
- What training will staff need?
- Who are the key stakeholders?
- How can we build linkages to the key stakeholders?
- What stories can we tell that relate the importance of patient safety?
- How will we recognize and celebrate progress?

Promoting Systems' Resilience Across and Between the Microsystems

Microsystems usually coexist with multiple other microsystems within the organization. Patients are aware of the gaps and handoffs between microsystems as they navigate the healthcare system, such as when they transfer from inpatient care back into the community (Rattray, 2021). Patients are aware of the challenges of "synthesizing" knowledge across the various microsystems they encounter. Models developed by Zimmerman and Hayday (1999) for understanding and supporting work on the relationships across microsystems offer insights into the generative work of interdependence. Understanding the dynamics of effective organizational relationships can be helpful in thinking about how to foster honest and transparent relationships between microsystems within the same organization and across differing organizations. These cross-microsystem relationships are fundamentally related to improving handoffs, but this inquiry can also provide opportunities for learning about systemic problems within the institution and interventions to improve quality and safety (Cassin & Barach, 2017; Groene et al., 2012). An effective collaborative relationship is based on the underlying assumption that collaboration is a more effective approach to achieve a goal than multiple individual efforts (Toccafondi et al., 2012).

Weick suggests that leaders today need to develop groups that are also respectful of the interactions that hold the group together (Weick, 1993, 1995). Resilient groups have respectful interactions that are founded on three major elements (Weick, 1996):

1. *Trust*—a willingness to base beliefs and actions on the reports of others
2. *Honesty*—reporting so that others may use one's observations in developing and enhancing their own beliefs
3. *Self-respect*—integrating one's perceptions and beliefs with the reports of others without depreciating them or oneself

Further, four aspects of the relationship can help generate creative responses to the diagnosed challenges facing entities needing to work better together (Zimmerman & Hayday, 1999):

1. The separateness or differences of the two microsystems
2. The talking–listening–tuning opportunities that the two microsystems have
3. The action opportunities that the two entities have
4. The reasons they have to work together

Balanced attention to each of these aspects enables creative work.

The conditions also must be present for relationships to develop across organizations (Kaluzny, 1985). For voluntary interactions—which may be quite different than those mandated by an external power—several conditions must be met. There must be an internal need for resources, a commitment to an external problem, and the opportunity to change. In addition, there must be a consensus regarding both the external problem(s) facing the organizations and the specific goals and services for developing a joint effort. The Institute of Medicine report *To Err is Human* (IOM, 2000) brought patient safety to the forefront of the agenda and set the stage for discussing specific goals and strategies for achieving those goals.

Mitchell and Shortell (2000) provide a synthesis of the literature on the success of community health partnerships that suggests several factors can influence the success of interorganizational relationships. These factors are:

- Context
- Strategic intent
- Resource base
- Membership heterogeneity
- Coordination of skills
- Response to accountability

Context refers to the environment in which the partnership exists—the internal and external stakeholders, their historical relationships and influence, the presence or absence of human and financial resources, the political environment, public sentiments, and the current challenges facing the community. Strategic intent—a similar concept to a consensus on the external problem(s) facing the organizations—refers to the reasons the interorganizational relationship is formed. A diversified resource base helps ensure that the collaborative is able to pursue the strategic intent without getting sidetracked by pursuing the goals of a single funding agency. Membership heterogeneity refers to the balance of the participating members in regard to the number and types of participants. Informal as well as formal communication mechanisms ensure that the collaborators meet their own goals and are held accountable to demonstrate their progress internally and externally.

Role of Risk Management and Patient Disclosure

When patients seek medical care, they entrust their health to us. Healthcare providers have a responsibility or "fiduciary duty" to act in the best interests of the patient (Kraman & Hamm, 1999). Properly assessing the type of procedure planned (e.g., invasive vs. noninvasive), patient risk factors, type of drug to use (e.g., hypnotic vs. analgesic), and type of team and level of support are all critical. When assessing the level of risk of the procedure, we should ask, *What are the desired clinical effects? How quickly are effects desired? What is the desired duration of effects? And are there any adverse "other" clinical effects?*

Injured patients and their families want to know the causes of their bad outcomes, especially if the adverse event was caused by an error (Studdert, Mello, & Brenna, 2004). The most important factor in the decision to file lawsuits is not merely negligence but ineffective communication between patients and provider after the harm is recognized (Wu et al., 1997). Malpractice suits often result when an unexpected adverse outcome is met with no effort to apologize, with a lack of empathy from physicians and the care team and a perceived or actual withholding of essential information (Barach, 2005; Wu et al., 1997).

Studies consistently show that healthcare providers are understandably reticent about discussing errors, believing they have no appropriate assurance of legal protection (LeBlang & King, 1984). This reticence, in turn, impedes systemic and programmatic efforts to prevent medical errors. A growing initiative in health care has been to encourage open and frank discussion with patients and their families after an adverse event; this initiative has met with salutary effects. The lack of evidence that disclosure adversely impacts claims, case resolution, and patient and family perceptions is changing organizational practices.

Evidence from the University of Michigan supports that an aggressive disclosure policy (Clinton & Obama, 2006) with three components can be effective: (1) acknowledge cases in which a patient was hurt because of medical error and compensate these patients quickly and fairly, (2) aggressively defend cases that the hospital considers to be without merit, and (3) study all adverse events to determine how procedures and systems can be improved.

Disclosing an adverse event should occur when the adverse event (1) has a perceptible effect on the patient that was not discussed in advance as a known risk, (2) necessitates a change in the patient's care, (3) potentially poses an important risk to the patient's future health, even if that risk is extremely small, and (4) involves providing a treatment or procedure without the patient's consent (Cantor et al., 2005). From an ethical perspective, the disclosure process should begin at the time of discussing the consent form and interventions with the patients (Barach & Cantor, 2007).

Conclusions

There is a clear need to improve the safety of care, as patients still suffer harm from medical care at alarmingly high rates. The healthcare system has begun to approach patient safety in a more systematic way, but we continue to tolerate an extraordinary level of risk and preventable harm. What actions should healthcare leaders do to improve safety—how might they go about changing the culture and creating trust? The most advanced healthcare organizations acknowledge that they are on a journey to achieving high reliability and need to address four essential building blocks: (1) a culture devoted to quality; (2) responsibility and accountability of staff; (3) optimizing and standardizing processes; and (4) constant measurement of performance.

Strong leadership is needed to change organizational cultures to achieve a vision of zero tolerance of preventable harm. The application of safety science and reliability principles, methods, and analytical tools in the health sector promises the development of a coherent bundle of interrelated strategies for change. Reliability principles—which include methods of evaluating, calculating, and improving the overall reliability of a complex system—have been used effectively in industries such as manufacturing to improve both safety and the rate at which a system consistently produces appropriate outcomes.

Much organizational and leadership work is needed to change the mental models of clinicians and providers toward a system-based change. The traditional approach within medicine and health care was to emphasize the individual's responsibility for errors and to encourage the belief that the way to eliminate adverse events was for individual clinicians to perfect their practices. This simplistic approach fails to address the important and complex systematic flaws that contribute to the genesis of adverse events, and also perpetuates a myth of infallibility that is a disservice to both clinicians and their patients. The focus on the actions of individuals as the sole cause of adverse events inevitably results in continued system failures, resulting in the injury and death of patients and the tendency for clinicians to blame themselves for this harm. The efforts of the innumerable government bodies around the world to align external financial, regulatory, and educational incentives are beginning to have an impact on clinicians' and providers' interest in embracing the safety themes described in this chapter.

Cultural and process changes require profound alterations in management thinking, staff empowerment, and communications skills within and across disciplines. Attributing errors to system failures does not absolve clinicians of their duty of care or their fiduciary duty to act in the best interests of their patients. In fact, acknowledging system failures adds to that duty a responsibility to admit errors, investigate them collaboratively, and participate in redesign for a safer system.

Key Concepts and Terms

Blunt end
Clinical microsystem
Clinical risk management
Culture
Near-miss
Organizational accidents
Quality
Risk
Risk management
Sharp end

References

Agency for Healthcare Research and Quality (AHRQ). (2016). *Patient safety and quality improvement act of 2005—HHS guidance regarding patient safety work product and providers' external obligations (May 2016)*. Department of Health and Human Services. https://pso.ahrq.gov/resources/hhs-guidance

Anderson, J. G., & Abrahamson, K. (2017). Your health care may kill you: Medical errors. *Studies in Health Technology Informatics, 234*, 13–17.

Barach, P. (2005). The unintended consequences of Florida medical liability legislation. *Perspectives on patient safety*. Retrieved from https://psnet.ahrq.gov/psnet-collection/perspectives

Barach, P., Ahmed, R., Nadel, E. S., Hafferty, F., & Philibert, I. (2021). COVID-19 and medical education: A four-part model to assess risks, benefits, and institutional obligations during a global pandemic. *Mayo Clinic Proceedings, 96*(1), 20–28. https://doi.org/10.1016/j.mayocp.2020.10.017. Epub 2020 Oct 23. PMID: 33413818; PMCID: PMC7584423.

Barach, P., & Cantor, M. (2007). Adverse event disclosure: Benefits and drawbacks for patients and clinicians. In S. Clarke & J. Oakley (Eds.), *Informed consent and clinician accountability: The ethics of report cards on surgeon performance*. Cambridge University Press.

Barach, P., & Phelps, G. (2013). Clinical sensemaking: A systematic approach to reduce the impact of normalised deviance in the medical profession. *Journal of the Royal Society of Medicine, 106*(10), 387–390. https://doi.org/10.1177/0141076813505045

Barach, P., & Small, S. (2000). Reporting and preventing medical mishaps: Lessons from non-medical near miss reporting systems. *British Medical Journal, 320*(7237), 759–763. https://doi.org/10.1136/bmj.320.7237.759

Batalden, M., Batalden, P., Margolis, P., Seid, M., Armstrong, G., Opipari-Arrigan, L., & Hartung, H. (2016). Coproduction of healthcare service. *BMJ Quality & Safety, 25*(7), 509–517. https://doi.org/10.1136/bmjqs-2015-004315. Epub 2015 Sep 16. PMID: 26376674; PMCID: PMC4941163.

Bernstein, P. (1996). *Against the gods. The remarkable story of risk*. Wiley.

Bosk, C. (1979). *Forgive and remember: Managing medical failure*. University of Chicago Press.

Cantor, M. D., Barach, P., Derse, A., et al. (2005). Disclosing adverse events to patients. *The Joint Commission Journal of Quality & Patient Safety, 31*(1), 5–12. https://doi.org/10.1016/s1553-7250(05)31002-6

Cassin, B. R., & Barach, P. R. (2012). Making sense of root cause analysis investigations of surgery-related adverse events. *Surgical Clinics of North America, 92*(1), 101–115. https://doi.org/10.1016/j.suc.2011.12.008. PMID: 22269264.

Cassin, B., & Barach, P. (2017). How not to run an incident investigation. In J. Sanchez, P. Barach, H. Johnson & J. Jacobs (Eds.), *Perioperative patient safety and quality: Principles and practice*. Springer.

Clinton, H. R., & Obama, B. (2006). Making patient safety the centerpiece of medical liability reform. *The New England Journal of Medicine, 354*(21), 2205–2208. https://doi.org/10.1056/nejmp068100

Dekker, S. (2002). *The field guide to human error investigations*. Ashgate Publishing Limited.

Dekker, S. (2004). *Ten questions about human error: A new view of human factors and system safety*. Erlbaum.

de Vries, E., Ramrattan, M., Smorenburg, S. M., et al. (2008). The incidence and nature of in-hospital adverse events: A systematic review. *Quality & Safety in Health Care, 17*(3), 216–223. https://doi.org/10.1136/qshc.2007.023622

DiazGranados, C. A., Jones, M. Y., Kongphet-Tran, T., White, N., Shapiro, M., Wang, Y. F., Ray, S. M., & Blumberg, H. M. (2009). Outbreak of *Pseudomonas aeruginosa* infection associated with contamination of a flexible bronchoscope. *Infection Control & Hospital Epidemiology, 30*(6), 550–555. https://doi.org/10.1086/597235

Dickson, G. (1995). Principles of risk management. *Quality Healthcare, 4*(2), 75–79. https://doi.org/10.1136/qshc.4.2.75

Groene, R. O., Orrego, C., Suñol, R., Barach, P., & Groene, O. (2012). "It's like two worlds apart": An analysis of vulnerable patient handover practices at discharge from hospital. *BMJ Quality & Safety, 21*(Suppl 1), i67–i75. https://doi.org/10.1136/bmjqs-2012-001174

Haddon, W. (1970). On the escape of tigers: An ecologic note. *American Journal of Public Health, 60*(12), 2229–2234. https://doi.org/10.2105/ajph.60.12.2229-b

Haddon, W. (1972). A logical framework for categorizing highway safety phenomena and activity. *Journal of Trauma, 12*(3), 193–207. https://doi.org/10.1097/00005373-197203000-00002

Heinreich, H. (1941). *Industrial accident prevention*. McGraw-Hill.

Helmreich, R., & Merritt, A. (2001). *Culture at work in aviation and medicine*. Ashgate.

Hollnagel, E., Woods, D. D., & Leveson, N. (Eds.). (2006). *Resilience engineering: Concepts and precepts*. Ashgate.

Ingersoll, C., Locke, R. M., & Reavis, C. (2012). *BP and the Deepwater Horizon disaster of 2010*. MIT Sloan School of Management: Ethics, Values and Voice Module 10–110, Rev. April 3, 2012. Retrieved from https://mitsloan.mit.edu/teaching-resources-library/bp-and-deepwater-horizon-disaster-2010

Institute of Medicine (IOM). (2000). *To err is human: Building a safer health system*. National Academies Press.

Institute of Medicine (IOM). (2001). *Crossing the quality chasm: A new health system for the 21st century*. National Academies Press.

Kaluzny, A. (1985). Design and management of disciplinary and interdisciplinary groups in health services: Review and critique. *Medical Care Reviews, 42*(1), 77–112. https://doi.org/10.1177/107755878504200105

Kasperson, R., Renn, O., Slovic, P., Brown, H., Emel, J., Goble, R., Kasperson J. X., & Ratick, S. (1988). Social amplification of risk: A conceptual framework. *Risk Analysis, 8*(2), 177–187. https://doi.org/10.1111/j.1539-6924.1988.tb01168.x

Kraman, S. S., & Hamm, G. (1999). Risk management: Extreme honesty may be the best policy. *Annals of Internal Medicine, 131*(12), 963–967. https://doi.org/10.7326/0003-4819-131-12-199912210-00010

Landrigan, C. P., Parry, G. J., Bones, C. B., et al. (2010). Temporal trends in rates of patient harm resulting from medical care. *The New England Journal of Medicine, 363*(22), 2124–2134. https://doi.org/10.1056/nejmsa1004404

LeBlang, T., & King, J. L. (1984). Tort liability for nondisclosure: The physician's legal obligations to disclose patient illness and injury. *Dickinson Law Review, 89*, 1–18.

Makary, M. A., & Daniel, M. (2016). Medical error—the third leading cause of death in the US. *British Medical Journal, 353*, i2139. https://doi.org/10.1136/bmj.i2139

March, J., Sproull, L., & Tamuz, M. (2003). Learning from samples of one or fewer. *Quality & Safety in Health Care, 12*(6), 465–472. https://doi.org/10.1136/qhc.12.6.465

Millenson, M. (1997). *Demanding medical excellence: Doctors and accountability in the information age*. The University of Chicago Press.

Mitchell, S. M., & Shortell, S. M. (2000). The governance and management of effective community health partnerships. *The Milbank Quarterly, 78*(2), 241–289. https://doi.org/10.1111/1468-0009.00170

Mohr, J. (2000). *Forming, operating, and improving microsystems of care*. Center for the Evaluative Clinical Sciences, Dartmouth College.

Mohr, J., Barach, P., Cravero, J. P., Blike, G. T., Godfrey, M. M., Batalden, P. B., & Nelson, E. C. (2003). Microsystems in health care: Part 6. Designing patient safety into the microsystem. *The Joint Commission Journal of Quality & Safety, 29*(8), 401–408. https://doi.org/10.1016/S1549-3741(03)29048-1

Mohr, J., & Batalden, P. (2002). Improving safety at the front lines: The role of clinical microsystems. *BMJ Quality & Safety, 11*(1), 45–50. https://doi.org/10.1136/qhc.11.1.45

Mohr, J., Batalden, P., & Barach, P. (2004). Integrating patient safety into the clinical microsystem. *BMJ Quality & Safety, 13*(2), ii34–ii38. https://doi.org/10.1136/qshc.2003.009571

Nelson, E., Batalden, P., Huber, T. P., Mohr, J., Godfrey, M. M., Headrick, L. A., & Wasson, J. H. (2002). Microsystems in health care: Part 1. Learning from high-performing front-line clinical units. *The Joint Commission Journal of Quality Improvement, 28*(9), 472–493. https://doi.org/10.1016/S1070-3241(02)28051-7

Perrow, C. (1984). *Normal accidents: Living with high-risk technologies*. Basic Books.

Piccardi, C., Detollenaere, J., Vanden Bussche, P., & Willems, S. (2018). Social disparities in patient safety in primary care: A systematic review. *International Journal for Equity in Health, 17*(1), 114.

Pronovost, P., Weast, B., Holzmueller, C. G., Rosenstein, B. J., Kidwell, R. P., Haller, K. B., . . . Rubin, H. R. (2003). Evaluation of the culture of safety: Survey of clinicians and managers in an academic medical center. *Quality & Safety in Health Care, 12*(6), 405–410. https://doi.org/10.1136/qhc.12.6.405

Rattray, N. A., Flanagan, M. E., Militello, L. G., Barach, P., & Frankel, R. M. (2021). The art of effective handoff communication among medical and surgery residents. *Journal of Cognitive Engineering and Decision Making, 15*(2–3), 66–82. https://doi.org/10.1177/15553434211018296

Rasmussen, J. (1990). The role of error in organizing behaviour. *Ergonomics, 33*(10–11), 1185–1199. https://doi.org/10.1080/00140139008925325

Reason, J. (1990). *Human error*. Cambridge University Press.

Reason, J. (1995). Understanding adverse events: The human factor. In C. Vincent (Ed.), *Clinical risk management: Enhancing patient safety* (pp. 31–54). BMJ Publications.

Reason, J. (1997). *Managing the risks of organizational accidents*. Ashgate.

Rodziewicz, T. L., Houseman, B., Vaqar, S., & Hipskind, J. (2024). *Medical error reduction and prevention*. Updated February 12, 2024. In: *StatPearls* [Internet]. StatPearls Publishing. Available from https://www.ncbi.nlm.nih.gov/books/NBK499956/

Sagan, S. D. (1993). *The limits of safety*. Princeton University Press.

Schwendimann, R., Blatter, C., Dhaini, S., Simon, M., & Ausserhofer, D. (2018). The occurrence, types, consequences and preventability of in-hospital adverse events—A scoping review. *BMC Health Services Research, 18*(1), 521.

Seiden, S., & Barach, P. (2003). The risk management handbook for health professionals. Risk Management, 5, 59–61. https://doi.org/10.1057/palgrave.rm.8240158

Skelly, C. L., Cassagnol, M., & Munakomi, S. Adverse Events. [Updated 2025 Aug 2]. In: *StatPearls [Internet]*. StatPearls. https://www.ncbi.nlm.nih.gov/books/NBK558963/

Small, D., & Barach, P. (2002). Patient safety and health policy: A history and review. *Hematology/Oncology Clinics of North America, 16*(6), 1463–1482. https://doi.org/10.1016/s0889-8588(02)00066-7

Stewart, K., Choudry, M. I., & Buckingham, R. (2016). Learning from hospital mortality. *Clinical Medicine (London), 16*(6), 530–534. https://doi.org/10.7861/clinmedicine.16-6-530

Studdert, D. M., Mello, M. M., & Brenna, T. A. (2004). Medical malpractice. *The New England Journal of Medicine, 350*(3), 283–292. https://doi.org/10.1056/nejmhpr035470

Taleb, N. N. (2010). *The black swan: The impact of the highly improbable*. Random House.

Toccafondi, G., Albolino, S., Tartaglia, R., Guidi, S., Molisso, A., Venneri, F., et al. (2012). The collaborative communication model for patient handover at the interface between high-acuity and low-acuity care. *BMJ Quality & Safety, 21*(Suppl 1), i58–i66. https://doi.org/10.1136/bmjqs-2012-001178

Turner, B., & Pidgeon, N. (1997). *Man-made disasters*. Butterworth and Heinemann.

Uramatsu, M., Kimura, N., Kojima, T., Fujisawa, Y., Oto, T., & Barach, P. (2024). Frontline nursing staff's perceptions of intravenous medication administration: The first step toward safer infusion processes—A qualitative study. *BMJ Open Quality, 13*(2), e002809. https://doi.org/10.1136/bmjoq-2024-002809. PMID: 38942437; PMCID: PMC11216072.

Vaughan, D. (1996). *The Challenger launch decision: Risky technology, culture, and deviance at NASA*. University of Chicago Press.

Vaughan, D. (1999). The dark side of organizations: Mistake, misconduct, and disaster. *Annual Review of Sociology, 25*(1), 271–305. https://doi.org/10.1146/annurev.soc.25.1.271

Vincent, C. (1997). Risk, safety, and the dark side of quality. *British Medical Journal, 314*(7097), 1775–1776. https://doi.org/10.1136/bmj.314.7097.1775

Vincent, C. (2003). Understanding and responding to adverse events [see comment]. *The New England Journal of Medicine, 348*(11), 1051–1056. https://doi.org/10.1056/nejmhpr020760

Vincent, C., Taylor-Adams, S., & Stanhope, N. (1998). Framework for analysing risk and safety in clinical medicine. *British Medical Journal, 316*(7138), 1154–1157. https://doi.org/10.1136/bmj.316.7138.1154

Walshe, K. (2001). The development of clinical risk management. In C. Vincent (Ed.), *Clinical risk management: Enhancing patient safety*. BMJ Books.

Warm, E. J., Ahmad, Y., Kinnear, B., Kelleher, M., Sall, D., Wells, A., & Barach, P. (2021). A dynamic risk management approach for reducing harm from invasive bedside procedures performed during residency. *Academic Medicine, 96*(9), 1268–1275. https://doi.org/10.1097/ACM.0000000000004066. PMID: 3373512.

Weick, K. E. (1993). The collapse of sensemaking in organizations: The Mann Gulch disaster. *Administrative Science Quarterly, 38*(4), 628–652. https://doi.org/10.2307/2393339

Weick, K. E. (1995). *Sensemaking in organizations*. Sage.

Weick, K. E. (1996). Prepare your organization to fight fires. *Harvard Business Review, 74*(3), 143–148.

Weick, K. E. (2009). Emergent change as a universal in organizations. In K. E. Weick (Ed.), *Making sense of the organization* (Vol. 2). Wiley.

Weick, K., & Sutcliffe, K. (2001). *Managing the unexpected: Assuring high performance in an age of complexity*. University of Michigan Business School.

Wu, A. W., Cavanaugh, T. A., McPhee, S. J., Lo, B., & Micco, G. P. (1997). To tell the truth: Ethical and practical issues in disclosing medical mistakes to patients. *Journal of General Internal Medicine, 12*(12), 770–775. https://doi.org/10.1046/j.1525-1497.1997.07163.x

Zimmerman, B., & Hayday, B. (1999). A board's journey into complexity science. *Group Decision & Negotiating, 8*, 281–303.

CHAPTER 10

Continuous Quality Improvement in Public Health Organizations

Sara E. Massie, Charlotte E. Armstrong, and Greg D. Randolph

CHAPTER OUTLINE

Introduction

International health statistics demonstrate the United States trails other developed nations in many public health indicators. Furthermore, although the United States ranks by far the highest among 38 OECD nations in terms of health expenditures, the country has a lower life expectancy, higher avoidable mortality rates, and a higher prevalence of diabetes than the OECD average (OECD, 2023). With rankings such as these, it is evident we need to improve public health services and outcomes in the United States.

Historically, there has been significant variation in how public health and its scope are defined, and these differences still persist today. While the United States emphasizes prevention, health promotion, and community-level interventions, other nations often include a broader range of clinical services within public health, including preventive screening, vaccination programs, and other health services, depending on the structure of their healthcare system and approach to managing health. This variation reflects the different ways in which public health responsibilities are understood and organized across countries, contributing to the ongoing debate over what constitutes the essential services of public health in the United States.

Over the past three decades, U.S. public health organizations have increasingly undertaken a variety of efforts to ensure and improve the quality of their services. In recent years, accreditation has become part of a national focus to advance the quality and performance of public health. At the same time, public health agencies have been implementing quality improvement (QI) using proven methods, such as the Model for Improvement, Lean, and Plan, Do, Study, Act (PDSA) cycles described throughout this text and elsewhere (Deming, 2000; Langley et al., 2009; Smith et al., 2012). Efforts such as these indicate that U.S. public health is moving beyond a series of projects and tools toward adopting continuous quality improvement (CQI) as a means of achieving a public health system that is effective, efficient, and in step with other industrialized nations around the world.

Chapter Objectives

In this chapter, we provide an overview of the adoption and institutionalization of CQI in public health organizations. We begin by providing a brief history of CQI in U.S. public health, then we describe current efforts to promote CQI, and, finally, explore the opportunities, challenges, and progress of public health organizations. Throughout the chapter, we provide relevant international examples of CQI in public health as well. We conclude with a case study of how a public health agency applied QI methods and tools, leading toward institutionalizing CQI.

Key Terms

Public health has been defined as "the science and art of preventing disease, prolonging life and promoting health through the organized efforts and informed choices of society, organizations, public and private communities and individuals" (Winslow, 1920). In public health, **quality** has been defined as "the degree to which policies, programs, services, and research for the population increase the desired health outcomes and conditions in which the population can be healthy" (U.S. DHHS, 2008, p. 2). **Quality assurance** involves systematically monitoring and evaluating the performance of an organization or its programs to ensure it meets established standards. **Quality improvement** (QI) uses formal methods and tools to redesign systems to meet customers' needs by testing and implementing ideas from evidence-based strategies, frontline staff, and customers. It is described as a "distinct management process and set of tools and techniques that are coordinated to ensure that departments consistently meet their communities' health needs and strive to improve the health status of their populations" (Riley et al., 2010, p. 5).

Continuous quality improvement (CQI) in public health organizations involves creating a structured infrastructure and culture that engages staff in ongoing improvements to meet or exceed community expectations. It includes linking to the organization's strategic plan, having a quality council with top leadership, providing QI training for staff, prioritizing projects, and supporting staff involvement. While an organization committed to CQI may have both quality improvement and quality assurance processes, the predominant focus is on continuous improvement. Public health organizations sometimes use the term "**performance management**" interchangeably with CQI (PHAB, 2022).

History of Actions to Promote CQI in Public Health

Early Foundations and Initial Efforts

In 1988, an Institute of Medicine (IOM) report, *The Future of Public Health*, declared that the United States "has lost sight of its public health goals and has allowed the system of public health to fall into disarray" (p. 1). In response, public health experts and analysts began promoting a variety of methods and frameworks to reform and enhance the system. By the mid-1990s, key organizations—the IOM, the Centers for Disease Control and Prevention (CDC), the American Public Health Association, and the National Association of County and City Health Officials (NACCHO)—adopted the 10 Essential Public Health Services framework. This framework outlined the key public health activities that all communities should undertake (CDC, 2024b). (Note: the original framework was revised in 2020 to center equity in the framework (Sellers et al., 2021); see more later). Building on this framework, the National Public Health Performance Standards Program developed three assessment tools to help state and local public health agencies identify performance gaps and guide QI efforts (CDC, 2024a).

During this time of standards development, the Turning Point initiative, jointly funded by the Robert Wood Johnson Foundation (RWJF) and the W. K. Kellogg Foundation, aimed to revamp U.S. public health systems into more community-based and collaborative organizations working to prevent disease and injury, protect the public from threats to their health, and promote healthy behaviors (Turning Point, 2006). Directed by NACCHO, Turning Point emphasized the use of performance standards in conjunction with measurement and reporting as well as the institution of QI methods to manage change and achieve quality.

Expanding Frameworks and Institutionalization

Over time, public health organizations became increasingly interested in standardizing and ensuring quality public health services, which led to a focus on national public health accreditation (Stone & Davis, 2012). In late 2004, the RWJF formed the Exploring Accreditation Steering Committee to develop recommendations for implementing a voluntary national accreditation program, and, in 2005, launched the Multi-State Learning Collaborative (MLC) to assess the feasibility of this accreditation and gather data on existing accreditation practices (Beitsch et al., 2006; Russo, 2007). The MLC's early phases involved grants to states to enhance performance assessments and by 2008, the initiative expanded to include 16 states preparing for national accreditation, support for the Public Health Accreditation Board (PHAB) in developing the national voluntary accreditation program, and QI mini-collaboratives targeting public health processes (e.g., developing a community health profile) and outcomes in specific topic areas (e.g., tobacco, immunizations) (Gillen et al., 2010; Joly et al., 2010).

Also in 2008, the U.S. Department of Health and Human Services (U.S. DHHS) released the Consensus Statement on Quality in the Public Health System. This statement defined quality as "the degree to which policies, programs, services, and research for the population increase the desired health outcomes and conditions in which the population can be healthy" and identified nine quality aims: population-centered, equitable, proactive, health promoting, risk reducing, vigilant, transparent, effective, and efficient (Honoré et al., 2011; U.S. DHHS, 2008). DHHS subsequently charged the IOM with developing quality measures for Healthy People 2020's leading health indicators (IOM, 2013).

Building on these efforts, as well as the experience of existing state accreditation programs like those in Illinois, Michigan, Missouri, and North Carolina (Riley et al., 2012), PHAB was established in 2007 to manage and promote a national voluntary accreditation program for state, local, territorial, and tribal public health departments. Additionally, PHAB has added accreditation programs for military health departments in 2019 and vital records and health statistics departments in 2018 (PHAB, 2024a). Traditionally, accreditation in public health and other areas of health care has focused on meeting external standards set by experts, primarily serving as a quality assurance strategy. In some industries, such efforts have not been particularly successful or popular; of note, they are often unpopular with workers because of the focus on human error, rather than systems, as the source of most problems. In contrast, Bender and Halverson (2010) highlight how PHAB's approach differs: "Unlike some health-related agencies and services that are accredited or otherwise regulated, the PHAB board of directors has set the public health accreditation work solidly on the cornerstone of CQI. In other words, accreditation is a means to an end, not an end unto itself" (p. 80).

As of August 2024, PHAB has accredited 446 health departments in the United States (42 state, 393 local, 6 tribal, and 5 military health departments) (PHAB, 2024b). Its focus on CQI has helped drive widespread adoption of CQI practices. Nevertheless, it is important to keep in mind there are 2,309 local public health agencies in the United States; thus there is much more progress to be made at the local level (Office of Disease Prevention and Health Promotion, n.d.). In 2022, PHAB added a new program called Pathways Recognition designed for health departments that are not currently ready or able to complete full accreditation, but desire to make meaningful progress towards accreditation in the future. The Pathways Recognition program is centered on assessing the foundational capabilities of health departments (described in more detail later), which includes performance management/CQI (PHAB, 2024c).

PHAB's requirements, including a focus on performance management and an annual reporting process wherein accredited health departments must report their QI and performance management activities, foster the institutionalization of CQI. Indeed, evaluation data from PHAB reveals that 92% of PHAB participants agree or strongly agree that the PHAB accreditation process led to a "strong QI culture." Further, focus groups revealed that PHAB accreditation changed CQI use in their health department from periodic to more institutionalized (Kronstadt et al., 2016). A recent qualitative study focused specifically on the experiences of small local health departments, which often struggle with organizational changes like accreditation and CQI, showed a similar positive effect of the accreditation process on the adoption and institutionalization of QI and performance management/CQI (Fifolt et al., 2024).

For more information on CQI training, technical assistance, and other capacity-building public health resources, see **Table 10.1**.

COVID-19 Pandemic Impact

The COVID-19 pandemic significantly underscored the importance of robust public health systems and their role in ensuring the health of communities worldwide (Filip et al., 2022). Even as public health accreditation frameworks evolved to improve organizational capabilities, the pandemic shone a spotlight on the vulnerabilities within the public health system. Critical gaps were revealed, including in preparedness and response, and the underfunding of public health infrastructure as well as its limited resources (Orr et al., 2023; Trust for America's Health, 2024). On top of the misinformation and disinformation that was circulated (Ferreira Caceres et al., 2022), management of the pandemic was often portrayed in the media as ineffective. In addition to the system vulnerabilities, the pandemic highlighted health disparities and showed how marginalized communities faced disproportionate effects in infection rate and economic consequences (Raine et al., 2020). This global crisis increased calls for integrating equity into public health strategies and increasing focus on ways to address social determinants

Table 10.1 Several Key Organizations and Resources That Support CQI in Public Health

National Network of Public Health Institutes http://www.nnphi.org	**Public Health Improvement Training** Search "Public Health Improvement Training" on the NNPHI homepage for more information. **Open Forum: Next Generation** Search "Open Forum: Next Generation" on the NNPHI homepage for more information.
Population Health Improvement Partners https://www.improve partners.org/	**CQI eLearning** Visit the homepage and select "Toolbox" then "QI Video & Tools" from the navigation menu to view the online modules, tools, and templates or search @improvementpartners on YouTube.
Public Health Foundation http://www.phf.org	**Performance Improvement Services** Search for "Performance Improvement Services" on the PHF homepage to learn more.
Association of State and Territorial Health Officials http://astho.org	**Quality Improvement Plan Toolkit** Search for "Quality Improvement Plan Toolkit" on the ASTHO homepage to learn more.

of health across the entire population (Moore et al., 2022). Other system vulnerabilities include outdated data management and tracking systems that impeded real-time understanding of the crisis and created barriers to deploying an effective response (Layden et al., 2024).

Because of the global nature of the pandemic, we saw firsthand the importance of international cooperation and preparedness and how interconnected the world is when faced with global health crises. We will need a collaborative international response to mitigate future risks.

Recent Developments in Public Health CQI

Public Health Infrastructure Grant

The Public Health Infrastructure Grant (PHIG), made available by CDC in 2022, was a critical federal response to the evolving needs of the public health system, particularly in the wake of the COVID-19 pandemic. The 5-year, $5 billion program aims to address significant underfunding of state, local, territorial, and tribal health departments and enhance their ability to manage public health threats (CDC, 2024c). An estimated $4.01 billion has been committed to 107 state, territory, and large city health departments across all 50 states, using a funding formula that considers population size and community resilience (CDC, 2024c). Three national partners, ASTHO, National Network of Public Health Institutes (NNPHI), and PHAB, are providing training and technical assistance to the health departments, facilitating coordination and communication across the initiative, and evaluating the program. This structure ensures that public health departments are equipped to address pressing public health challenges and improve overall infrastructure.

PHIG's three key strategies include workforce development, foundational capabilities, and data modernization. The workforce strategy focuses on hiring, training, and retaining skilled public health professionals to fill existing gaps and address emerging needs. Foundational capabilities, one of which is performance management/CQI, aim to improve organizational systems, processes, and policies as shown in the Foundational Public Health Services framework (**Figure 10.1**). This framework identifies the

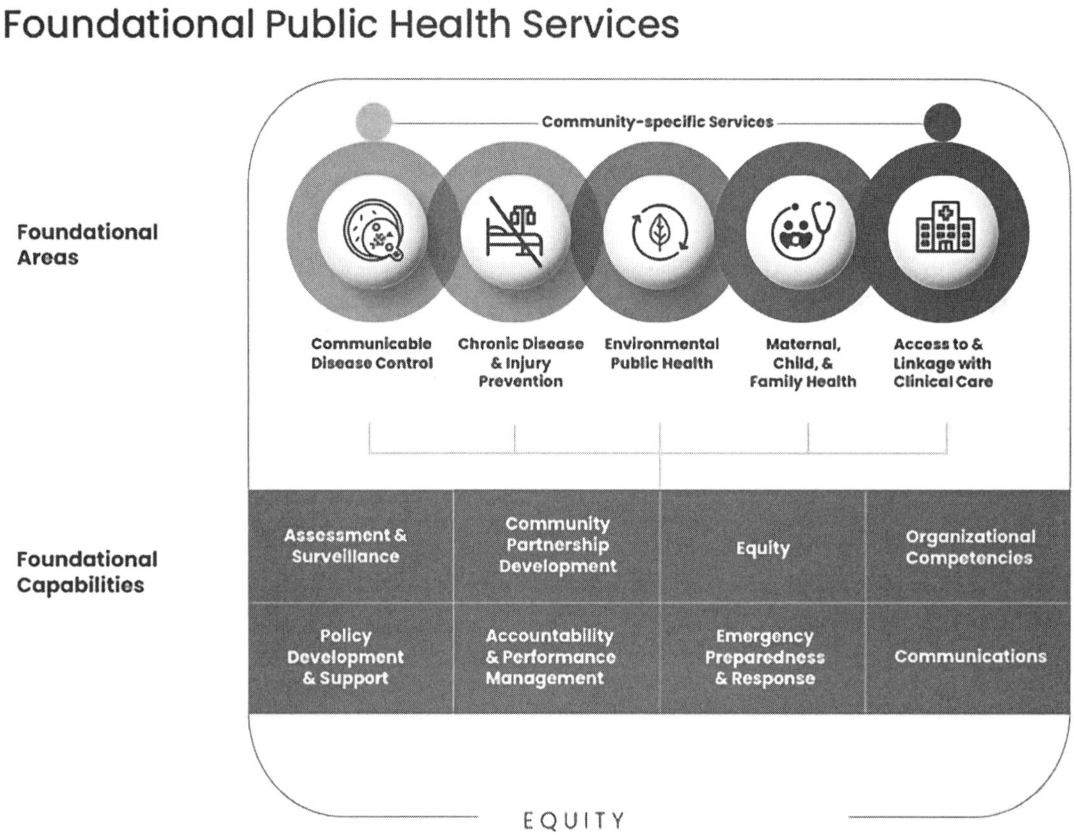

Figure 10.1 Foundational Public Health Services

Reproduced from Public Health Accreditation Board. *Foundational Public Health Services*. https://phaboard.org/center-for-innovation/public-health-frameworks/the-foundational-public-health-services/? Published February 2022.

Note: This framework identifies core functions and capabilities essential for governmental public health agencies to protect and improve the health of their communities. It emphasizes key services like disease control, disease and injury prevention, and access to clinical care, along with capabilities such as partnership development, communications, and surveillance, which together support comprehensive public health efforts.

"skills, programs, and activities that must be available in state and local health departments everywhere for the health system to work anywhere." (PHAB, 2024d). The foundational capabilities are considered necessary for public health departments to carry out the 10 Essential Public Health Services (see **Figure 10.2** and further discussion later in this chapter). Data modernization focuses on upgrading technology and improving data systems to better support disease detection, prevention, and response. By addressing these core strategies, PHIG intends to create a more robust public health infrastructure capable of delivering comprehensive services and improving health outcomes across the nation.

Evidence-Based Strategies and Programs

To improve public health, the field has to generate, and effectively apply, evidence-based strategies, interventions, and programs, while avoiding investment in those that have uncertain benefit or have been proven to have no effect (other than in research and evaluation activities). Fortunately, there are numerous evidence-based strategies, interventions, and programs for improving health and preventing disease in communities are available and catalogued in free online resources, such as those as shown in **Table 10.2**. See the box on international evidence-based strategies for examples.

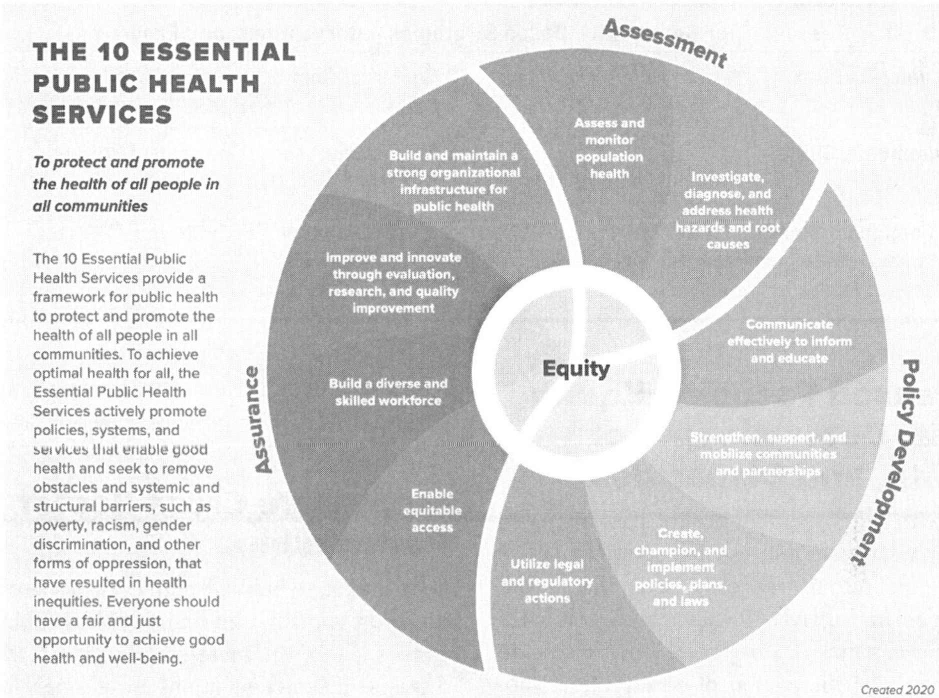

Figure 10.2 The 10 Essential Public Health Services

Framework: 10 Essential Public Health Services Futures Initiative Task Force. *10 Essential Public Health Services.* September 9, 2020. https://phaboard.org/wp-content/uploads/EPHS-Graphic-Image.png

Note: The 10 Essential Public Health Services provide a framework for public health practice, emphasizing the core functions of assessment, policy development, and assurance. These services aim to "protect and promote the health of all people in all communities" (PHAB, 2024f).

International Evidence-Based Strategies: The USAID Applying Science to Strengthen and Improve Systems Project

The USAID Applying Science to Strengthen and Improve Systems (ASSIST) Project, which operated from 2012 to 2020, aimed to support health systems in 46 countries by implementing QI methods. ASSIST developed tailored programs to improve maternal and child health, HIV treatment, malaria management, and other population health challenges, by strengthening service delivery, workforce performance, and community linkages to healthcare facilities. Improvement teams used tools such as flowcharts, system modeling, fishbone diagrams, five whys, Pareto charts, and time series charts. The project demonstrated that when local workers are engaged in improving care processes, they are able to apply QI approaches effectively, leading to measurable improvements in service quality (USAID ASSIST Project, 2020a).

ASSIST achieved several significant milestones, including simplifying QI processes through user-friendly manuals and tools, which led to faster implementation. A compilation of the improvement methods and tools used during the project is available in the Improvement Methods Toolkit, which includes tips and tools for learning improvement, tools for analyzing a system or process, tools for developing and selecting solutions, and tools for presenting data (USAID ASSIST Project, 2020b).

In addition, the project demonstrated the cost-effectiveness of QI interventions, strengthening health systems, and embedding QI principles into national policies and frameworks. By integrating QI strategies with broader health system–strengthening efforts, ASSIST linked improvements at the facility level to policy and resource allocation, ultimately institutionalizing CQI (USAID ASSIST Project 2020a). The tools and resources developed by ASSIST are expected to continue benefiting health programs and workers in the years to come.

Table 10.2 Resources for Community-Based Strategies, Interventions, and Programs

Community Tool Box https://ctb.ku.edu/en	Center for Community Health and Development at the University of Kansas
The Community Guide http://www.thecommunityguide.org/index.html	Centers for Disease Control and Prevention
Rural Community Health Toolkit https://www.ruralhealthinfo.org/toolkits/rural-toolkit/2/program-models	Rural Health Information Hub

Increased Focus on Equity, Social Determinants of Health, and Disparities

In recent years, public health has increased its emphasis on equity, social determinants of health, and disparities, recognizing that health outcomes are highly influenced by factors such as socioeconomic status, race, and access to resources. The integration of equity into established frameworks, such as the Foundational Public Health Services (Figure 10.1) and the revised 10 Essential Public Health Services (Figure 10.2), reflects a shift towards addressing these systemic issues. These frameworks now explicitly incorporate equity considerations, guiding public health practitioners to identify and mitigate barriers that disproportionately affect groups of people in communities. This evolution not only aims to improve health outcomes, but also fosters a more inclusive approach that prioritizes the needs of those who have historically faced inequities (Sellers et al., 2021).

Moreover, the focus on equity is closely tied to the principles of CQI in public health. By systematically evaluating programs and policies through an equity lens, public health agencies can better identify gaps in service delivery and areas for improvement. This iterative process encourages the adoption of best practices that address disparities, ultimately leading to more effective and equitable health interventions. As public health evolves, the commitment to equity will help enhance community well-being and ensure that all individuals have the opportunity to achieve their highest possible level of health.

Innovative Cross-Sector Partnerships

Local and state public health agencies alone cannot address many important public health problems, such as the increasing burden of chronic diseases. Effective solutions increasingly require coalitions involving public–private and other innovative partnerships. These partnerships can be an excellent way to leverage limited public health resources and increase impact.

One major opportunity for innovative partnerships is the 2014 changes in IRS requirements of nonprofit hospitals (78% of U.S. hospitals) through the Affordable Care Act (ACA), which mandates that they conduct a Community Health Needs Assessment (CHNA) every 3 years and collaborate with their local health department to do so, including developing strategies to address the priorities (James, 2016). An excellent example of this type of collaboration in action is Western North Carolina (WNC) Healthy Impact (2024). This partnership involves hospitals, public health agencies, and regional partners aiming to improve community health across 16 counties. The initiative focuses on standardizing data collection, developing collaborative plans, and implementing evidence-based practices.

Private foundations have been another major force driving innovative partnerships. The RWJF Culture of Health initiative is a well-known

International Innovative Partnerships: Making Every Baby Count Initiative

The Making Every Baby Count Initiatives (MEBCI), part 1.0 (2015 to 2017) and part 2.0 (2020 to 2024), are innovative partnership projects that were formed in response to stagnating neonatal mortality rates in Ghana (Kybele, 2024). These initiatives were conducted collaboratively by the Ghana Health Service (GHS) and a number of non-governmental organizations, including Kybele, the Children's Investment Fund Foundation, PATH, the African Population and Health Research Center, the University of Manitoba, and the AYA Collective. Together, these organizations aimed to improve the quality of newborn care provided around the time of birth using a multi-pronged approach to build health worker capacity in resuscitation, essential newborn care, and infection prevention (Chinbuah, 2020). The current iteration, MEBCI 2.0, has expanded upon the successes of the project, and, to date, has created and deployed 10 clinical and operational modules and trained 2,867 participants, engaging 89% of targeted clinicians across target facilities. The initiative has also supported 61 QI projects initiated and led by facilities based on identified gaps, providing essential medical equipment and the necessary training for healthcare providers. These QI projects are led by experienced coaches, who guide QI teams as they implement plan-do-study-act (PDSA) cycles, create project charters, and develop data management systems, among other things. In coordination with GHS, MEBCI 2.0 has spearheaded the development of 15 advanced clinical care forms for integration into the national electronic medical record system and developed a dashboard for facilities to use. Another significant success of the program is the development and approval of Ghana's first national guidelines on advanced newborn care (Kybele, 2024).

national example, as is Healthy People, Healthy Carolinas, funded by The Duke Endowment, a private foundation focused on improving health and well-being in North Carolina and South Carolina communities. This partnership focuses on strengthening and supporting local coalitions and implementing evidence-based interventions to improve nutrition, physical activity, and chronic disease. The initiative has involved 33 community coalitions serving 39 counties, reaching an estimated 3.5 million people across the two states since its inception in 2015 (Population Health Improvement Partners, 2024).

A new U.S. initiative at the intersection of public health and health care, the Common Health Coalition, was established in 2023 to use "lessons from the COVID-19 pandemic to strengthen the relationships between health care organizations and public health systems to help ensure that our health system is ready today to confront the public health emergencies of tomorrow" (Common Health Coalition, 2024). This initiative emphasizes the need for ongoing collaboration between public health and medicine, a partnership essential to addressing complex health challenges, yet one that has historically faced challenges in the United States due to differing systems, priorities, and approaches. The six commitments of the coalition include (1) establish and codify collaboration, (2) more easily get staff where and when they are needed, (3) share data in real time to advance equitable outcomes, (4) expand electronic disease reporting, (5) standardize readiness across the healthcare system, and (6) advance existing federal efforts. Critical partners in the initiative include its founding organizations (AHIP, the Alliance of Community Health Plans, American Hospital Association, American Medical Association, and Kaiser Permanente) as well as a growing list of public health organizations, such as NNPHI, ASTHO, the Public Health Institute, healthcare providers, county health departments, nonprofit organizations, and academic institutions, all working collaboratively to improve community health outcomes.

Making Every Baby Count is an international initiative that illustrates the value of partnerships in CQI, as described in the box on international partnerships.

Financing of Public Health Organizations

In many states and territories, governmental public health agencies have been under substantial financial strain. In fact, the CDC's budget, nearly three-fourths of which funds public health in state and local communities, has only increased by a total of 4% in the past decade, despite the pandemic highlighting the inadequate investment in public health systems (Trust for America's Health, 2024). New and innovative approaches to financing local and state public health agencies are greatly needed and could help improve the population's health as governmental funding remains tight. For instance, public health organizations could benefit from testing and adapting financial approaches that have been successful in other industries, such as business process improvement. Indeed, after experiencing tremendous barriers to using the sudden influx of new dollars to combat the COVID-19 pandemic, many state and territory health departments are increasingly applying QI to their business processes, such as grants management, contracting and procurement. For example, the U.S. Virgin Islands has streamlined its federal grants management through a cross-agency QI effort that combines basic QI training for key staff who focus on addressing bottlenecks, creating standardized procedures and workflows, and utilizing checklists and templates (Sullivan, 2022).

CQI relates to these financial challenges in at least three ways. First, implementing CQI should help reduce overall costs while increasing quality, just as it has in many other industries and organizations (Spear & Bowen, 1999). Reducing costs and inefficiencies can help increase capacity and allow for a greater focus on population health improvement. Indeed, the CDC and other U.S. DHHS agencies routinely tie incorporation of CQI into their grants to state and local public health agencies and programs. Second, although the PHIG is a step in the right direction, if the financing of public health services remains primarily focused on funding specific services and programs rather than infrastructure and other more flexible mechanisms, then public health agencies will likely have difficulty investing in the infrastructure needed for CQI. Finally, and perhaps most importantly, we believe the increasing focus on value (higher quality at a lower cost) in the ongoing healthcare transformation in the United States, which is largely driven by the need to control the rapid increases in healthcare costs, can drive health systems to have a greater focus on improving the health of the populations they serve. Indeed, value-based payment models are gaining momentum in the United States, increasing to approximately 40% of healthcare payments in 2021 (HCPLAN, 2022). An unhealthy population will have much higher healthcare costs, thus opening the door for innovative funding models between public health and healthcare entities (for example, in accountable care organizations) as they strive for the mutually beneficial goal of improving the health of a population to create higher healthcare value. Unfortunately, to date, there have not been any major value-based payment collaborations involving public health departments (P. Bernet, personal communication, September 27, 2024).

High Rates of Staff and Leadership Turnover in Public Health Departments

A recent study showed that almost half of all employees in state and local public health departments in the United States left their jobs between 2017 and 2021, a period of time before and during the pandemic (Leider et al., 2023). Furthermore, turnover of health department leadership is also remarkably high. For example, the average tenure of state health officers is now less than 3 years, down from 7 years in the 1990s (Menachemi et al., 2020). Extremely high rates of staff turnover, especially turnover among leaders and managers, are and will continue to be a threat to building and maintaining effective CQI infrastructure and efforts. Additionally, turnover threatens the quality and effectiveness of QI efforts by draining public health organizations of vital institutional knowledge.

Case 10.1: Institutionalization of Continuous Quality Improvement

CQI in a Local Public Health Agency: Macon County, North Carolina

After becoming accredited through North Carolina's Local Health Department Accreditation Program (https://nclhdaccreditation.unc.edu/), Macon County Public Health began to focus on changing its quality culture. They established a QI council and part-time position for a quality program manager and began to implement a QI program. Over the course of two years, they trained staff and leadership in QI tools and ethods, including Lean.

During this time, staff members completed small QI projects, which helped them apply the concepts they were learning and secure buy-in throughout the organization. After staff were trained and had completed a few successful small-scale projects, the health department began focusing on "projects that would have a greater impact on the organization's overall performance, improve patient/customer service outcomes, and achieve demonstrable cost savings." One such project aimed to improve the appointment scheduling process by seeing all patients within 72 hours of requesting an appointment, while also improving patient and staff satisfaction. The team participated in a rapid cycle improvement event (or, *kaizen* event) that involved using Lean and Plan-Do-Study-Act cycles, performing a *gemba* walk (direct observation of the work), creating workflow diagrams and detailed process maps, and generating and testing change ideas. Soon after, the clinics were scheduling patients for visits in less than 72 hours. Their no-show rates decreased, visit numbers increased, staff downtime decreased, and both patient and staff satisfaction increased.

Leveraging this success, the health department began to spread QI initiatives to other areas of the organization and focused on projects related to the client feedback process, child health visit flow, and vaccine storage and management, among others. To keep staff informed of the organization's QI work, as well as foster ongoing staff engagement, the health department keeps an electronic directory of their work (including project aim statements, meeting notes, process maps and flow diagrams, as well as other team-related communication) and highlights activities and results in the hallways of their organization. They also reinvest cost savings from the projects into other vital activities of the health department. Overall, the health department's CQI efforts have led to organizational efficiency as well as improved care and patient experience (Bruckner, See, & Randolph, 2013).

Applying Concepts

This case (**Case 10.1**) presents an example of a local public health agency that adopted and institutionalized CQI. As you read through the case, refer to the NACCHO Roadmap to a Culture of Quality Improvement (NACCHO, 2020)—which includes the following key elements: Leadership Commitment, Quality Improvement Infrastructure, Employee Empowerment, Customer Focus, Teamwork and Collaboration, and Continuous Process Improvement—and consider these questions:

- According to the NACCHO Roadmap, which elements of a CQI culture are present and which appear to be lacking?
- What could the organization do to address elements that appear to be lacking?
- What are three additional steps the organization could take to ensure sustainability of their CQI efforts?

Conclusion

The need to improve the public's health in the United States remains urgent. Although public health organizations are still early in the process of institutionalizing CQI compared to organizations in many other industries, they have made remarkable progress and adoption in the last two decades, particularly due to the support of accreditation. In this chapter, numerous factors are presented to explain the growth of CQI in public health and, most importantly, the substantial progress made towards institutionalization of CQI. Continuing to use accreditation efforts to promote CQI and learning from the successes and challenges in health care and other industries will help accelerate widespread adoption and institutionalization of CQI. Public health organizations that adopt CQI to help employees work as a team, address gaps in performance by analyzing and redesigning processes, and encourage innovation to meet the needs of communities, hold the promise for a healthier future, both in the United States and throughout the world.

Key Concepts and Terms

Continuous quality improvement
Public health
Quality
Quality assurance
Quality improvement

References

Beitsch, L. M., Thielen, L., Mays, G., Brewer, R. A., Kimbrell, J., Chang, C., . . . Landrum, L. B. (2006). The multistate learning collaborative, states as laboratories: Informing the national public health accreditation dialogue. *Journal of Public Health Management & Practice, 12*(3), 217–231.

Bender, K., & Halverson, P. K. (2010). Quality improvement and accreditation: What might it look like? *Journal of Public Health Management & Practice, 16*(1), 79–82.

Bruckner, J., See, C. H., & Randolph, G. D. (2013). Case study: Quality improvement in the Macon County Health Department. *North Carolina Medical Journal, 74*(2), 138–139.

Centers for Disease Control and Prevention (CDC). (2024a). *National Public Health Performance Standards*. Retrieved October 31, 2024, from https://www.cdc.gov/public-health-gateway/php/about/national-public-health-performance-standards.html

Centers for Disease Control and Prevention (CDC). (2024b). *Original Essential Public Health Services Framework*. Retrieved October 30, 2024, from https://www.cdc.gov/public-health-gateway/php/about/original-essential-public-health-services-framework.html

Centers for Disease Control and Prevention (CDC). (2024c). *Public Health Infrastructure Grant*. Retrieved October 30, 2024, from https://www.cdc.gov/infrastructure-phig/about/index.html

Chinbuah, M. A., Taylor, M., Serpa, M., Mazia, G., Cofie, P. K., Kwarah, W., Dawson, S., Nelson, B. D., & Engmann, C. (2020). Scaling up Ghana's national newborn care initiative: Integrating "Helping Babies Breathe" (HBB), "Essential Care for Every Baby" (ECEB), and newborn "Infection Prevention" (IP) trainings. *BMC Health Services Research, 20*(1), 739. https://doi.org/10.1186/s12913-020-05225-2

Common Health Coalition. (2024). *Together for public health*. Retrieved October 30, 2024, from https://commonhealthcoalition.org/

Deming, W. E. (2000). *The new economics for industry, government, and education* (2nd ed.). MIT Press.

Ferreira Caceres, M. M., Sosa, J. P., Lawrence, J. A., Sestacovschi, C., Tidd-Johnson, A., Rasool, M. H. U., Gadamidi, V. K., Ozair, S., Pandav, K., Cuevas-Lou, C., Parrish, M., Rodriguez, I., & Fernandez, J. P. (2022). The impact of misinformation on the COVID-19 pandemic. *AIMS Public Health, 9*(2), 262–277. https://doi.org/10.3934/publichealth.2022018

Fifolt, M., Allen, P., Crenshaw, A., Erwin, P. C., Lang, B., Thomas, A. B., & Brownson, R. C. (2024). Using national public health accreditation to explore quality improvement and performance management in small local health departments. *Journal of Public Health Management and Practice, 31*(2), 183–189. https://doi.org/10.1097/PHH.0000000000002062

Filip, R., Gheorghita Puscaselu, R., Anchidin-Norocel, L., Dimian, M., & Savage, W. K. (2022). Global challenges to public health care systems during the COVID-19 pandemic: A review of pandemic measures and problems. *Journal of Personalized Medicine, 12*(8), 1295. https://doi.org/10.3390/jpm12081295

Gillen, S. M., McKeever, J., Edwards, K. F., & Thielen, L. (2010). Promoting quality improvement and achieving measurable change: The lead states initiative. *Journal of Public Health Management & Practice, 16*(1), 55–60. https://doi.org/10.1097/PHH.0b013e3181bedb5d

Health Care Payment Learning and Action Network (HCPLAN). (2022). *2022 APM measurement infographic—Health Care Payment Learning & Action Network*. Retrieved October 30, 2024, from https://hcp-lan.org/apm-measurement-effort/2022-apm/2022-infographic/

Honoré, P., Wright, D., Berwick, D. W., Clancy, C. M., Lee, P., Nowinski, J., & Koh, H. K. (2011). Creating a framework for getting quality into the public health system. *Health Affairs (Millwood), 30*(4), 737–745. https://doi.org/10.1377/hlthaff.2011.0129

Institute of Medicine (IOM). (1988). *The future of public health*. National Academies Press.

Institute of Medicine (IOM). (2013). *Toward quality measures for population health and the leading health indicators*. The National Academies Press.

James, J. (2016, February 25). *Health policy brief: Nonprofit hospitals' community benefit requirements. Health Affairs/RWJF Policy Brief*. https://www.healthaffairs.org/do/10.1377/hpb20160225.954803/full/healthpolicybrief_153.pdf

Joly, B. M., Shaler, G., Booth, M., Conway, A., & Mittal, P. (2010). Evaluating the multi-state learning collaborative. *Journal of Public Health Management & Practice, 16*(1), 61–66. https://doi.org/10.1097/PHH.0b013e3181bedcdc

Kronstadt, J., Meit, M., Siegfried, A., Nicolaus, T., Bender, K., & Corso, L. (2016). Evaluating the impact of national public health department accreditation—United States, 2016. *Morbidity and Mortality Weekly Report, 65*(31), 803–806.

Kybele. (2024). *MEBCI 2.0*. Retrieved October 30, 2024, from: https://kybeleworldwide.org/our-work/mebci/

Langley, G. L., Moen, R. D., Nolan, K. M., Nolan, T. W., Norman, C. L., & Provost, L. P. (2009). *The improvement guide: A practical approach to enhancing organizational performance*. Jossey-Bass.

Layden, J. E., Swain, M. J., Brennan, N., & Tripathi, M. (2024). Plugging public health data into the health IT ecosystem to protect national health. *NEJM Catalyst Innovations in Care Delivery, 5*(8), CAT.24.0129. https://doi.org/10.1056/CAT.24.0129

Leider, J. P., Castrucci, B. C., Robins, M., Hare Bork, R., Fraser, M. R., Savoia, E., Piltch-Loeb, R., & Koh, H. K. (2023). The exodus of state and local public health employees: Separations started before and continued throughout COVID-19. https://doi.org/10.1377/hlthaff.2022.01251

Menachemi, N., Danielson, E. C., Tilson, H. A., Yeager, V. A., Sellers, K., & Halverson, P. K. (2020). Tenure and turnover among state health officials from the SHO-CASE survey: Correlates and consequences of changing leadership. *Journal of Public Health Management and Practice, 26*(1), 23–31. https://doi.org/10.1097/phh.0000000000000991

Moore, J. T., Luna-Pinto, C., Cox, H., Razi, S., St Louis, M. E., Ricaldi, J. N., & Liburd, L. (2022). Promoting health equity during the COVID-19 pandemic, United States. *Bulletin of the World Health Organization, 100*(2), 171–173. https://doi.org/10.2471/BLT.21.286074

National Association of County & City Health Organizations (NACCHO). (2020). *Roadmap to a culture of quality improvement*. Retrieved October 3, 2024, from http://qiroadmap.org

Office of Disease Prevention and Health Promotion. (n.d.). *Accredited health department list*. Retrieved February 25, 2025, from https://odphp.health.gov/healthypeople/objectives-and-data/data-sources-and-methods/data-sources/accredited-health-department-list

Organisation for Economic Co-Operation and Development (OECD). (2023). *Health at a glance 2023: OECD indicators*. OECD Publishing. https://doi.org/10.1787/7a7afb35-en

Orr, J. M., Leider, J. P., Kuehnert, P., & Bekemeier, B. (2023). COVID-19 revealed shortcomings of the US public health system and the need to strengthen funding and accountability. *Health Affairs (Project Hope)*, 42(3), 374–382. https://doi.org/10.1377/hlthaff.2022.01234

Population Health Improvement Partners. (2024). *Healthy People, Healthy Carolinas (HPHC)*. Retrieved October 30, 2024, from https://improvepartners.org/initiatives-projects/past-2/current/healthy-carolinas/

Public Health Accreditation Board (PHAB). (2022). *PHAB acronyms & glossary of terms*. (Version 2022). Retrieved October 30, 2024, from https://phaboard.org/wp-content/uploads/2019/01/Acronyms-and-Glossary-of-Terms.pdf

Public Health Accreditation Board (PHAB). (2024a). *Accreditation & recognition*. Retrieved October 30, 2024, from https://phaboard.org/accreditation-recognition/

Public Health Accreditation Board (PHAB). (2024b). *Accreditation Activity Map*. Retrieved from https://phaboard.org/wp-content/uploads/Accreditation-Activity-Map.pdf

Public Health Accreditation Board (PHAB). (2024c). *Accreditation & Recognition*. Retrieved October 30, 2024, from https://phaboard.org/accreditation-recognition/pathways-recognition-program/

Public Health Accreditation Board (PHAB). (2024d). *PHAB transformation frameworks*. Retrieved October 30, 2024, from https://phaboard.org/center-for-innovation/21st-century-learning-community/transformation-frameworks/

Public Health Accreditation Board (PHAB). (2024e). *The foundational public health services*. Retrieved October 30, 2024, from https://phaboard.org/center-for-innovation/public-health-frameworks/the-foundational-public-health-services/

Public Health Accreditation Board (PHAB). (2024f). *The 10 Essential Public Health Services*. Retrieved October 30, 2024, from https://phaboard.org/center-for-innovation/public-health-frameworks/the-10-essential-public-health-services/

Raine, S., Liu, A., Mintz, J., Wahood, W., Huntley, K., & Haffizulla, F. (2020). Racial and ethnic disparities in COVID-19 outcomes: Social determination of health. *International Journal of Environmental Research and Public Health, 17*(21), 8115. https://doi.org/10.3390/ijerph17218115

Riley, W. J., Moran, J. W., Corso, L. C., Beitsch, L. M., Bialek, R., & Cofsky, A. (2010). Defining quality improvement in public health. *Journal of Public Health Management & Practice, 16*(1), 5–7. https://doi.org/10.1097/phh.0b013e3181bedb49

Riley, W. J., Bender, K., & Lownik, E. (2012). Public health department accreditation implementation: Transforming public health department performance. *American Journal of Public Health, 102*(2), 237–242. https://doi.org/10.2105/AJPH.2011.300375

Russo, P. (2007). Accreditation of public health agencies: A means, not an end. *Journal of Public Health Management & Practice, 13*(4), 329–331. https://doi.org/10.1097/01.phh.0000278022.18702.22

Sellers, K., Solomon Fisher, J., Kuehnert, P., & Castrucci, B. (2021). *Meet the revised 10 Essential Public Health Services: Developed by the field, centering equity*. Retrieved October 30, 2024, from https://www.healthaffairs.org/content/forefront/meet-revised-10-essential-public-health-services-developed-field-centering-equity

Smith, G., Poteat-Godwin, A., Harrison, L. M., & Randolph, G. D. (2012). Applying Lean principles and

Kaizen rapid improvement events in public health practice. *Journal of Public Health Management & Practice, 18*(1), 52–54. https://doi.org/10.1097/PHH.0b013e31823f57c0

Spear, K., & Bowen, H. K. (1999). Decoding the DNA of the Toyota production system. *Harvard Business Review, 77*(5), 96–106.

Stone, D., & Davis, M. V. (2012). North Carolina Local Health Accreditation Program: Case 15. In C. P. Mc Laughlin, J. K. Johnson, & W. A. Sollecito (Eds.), *Implementing continuous quality improvement in health care: A global casebook*. Jones & Bartlett Learning.

Sullivan, K. (2022, October 5). *How the U.S. Virgin Islands is improving federal grants management*. Retrieved October 30, 2024, from https://www.astho.org/communications/blog/how-the-us-virgin-islands-is-improving-federal-grants-management/

Trust for America's Health. (2024). *The impact of chronic underfunding on America's public health system: Trends, risks, and recommendations*. https://www.tfah.org/wp-content/uploads/2024/08/2024-PublicHealthFunding-FINAL.pdf

Turning Point. (2006). *Welcome to Turning Point*. Retrieved January 29, 2010, from http://www.turningpointprogram.org

USAID ASSIST Project. (2020a). *USAID Applying Science to Strengthen and Improve Systems (ASSIST) Project. Final Report*. University Research Co., LLC (URC). Retrieved from https://www.urc-chs.com/wp-content/uploads/urc-usaid-assist-final-report-20-09-24.pdf

USAID ASSIST Project (2020b). *Improvement methods toolkit from the USAID ASSIST Project*. University Research Co., LLC (URC). Archived February 2, 2025, at https://web.archive.org/web/20250202080001/https://pdf.usaid.gov/pdf_docs/PA00WRQF.pdf

U.S. Department of Health and Human Services. (2008, August). *Consensus statement on quality in the public health system*. Retrieved from http://www.dhhs.gov

Winslow, C. E. A. (1920). The untilled field of public health. *Science, 51*(1306), 23–33. https://doi.org/10.1126/science.51.1306.23

WNC Health Network. (2024). *WNC healthy impact*. Retrieved from http://www.wnchealthyimpact.com/

CHAPTER 11

Assessing Quality at the Macro Level

Steve J. Meurer

CHAPTER OUTLINE

Introduction

There are four reasons why assessing quality in health care has proven to be challenging.

- The assessment of quality in health care is forever tied to the maturity of available data measuring the production of health care.
- Health care is complicated. After former Congressman Newt Gingrich, studied the American healthcare system, he said that health care was "100 times more complex than national security".
- The word quality means different things to different people.
- Data need to be transformed into information and then into insights for meaning to emerge.

Era of Counts and Word of Mouth

The earliest assessments of quality in health care were studies based on incidence. Two of the most notable of these occurred in the mid-1800s in England: Florence Nightingale's work to reduce soldiers' deaths in the Crimean War after determining that soiled, unwashed sheets were the reason for the infections causing deaths (McDonald, 2014) and John Snow determining that drinking water from the Broad Street pump was the leading cause of a cholera outbreak in London (Tulchinsky, 2018). These studies employed simple counts yet made powerful points leading to improvement in health conditions.

In the United States, the Flexner report in 1910 provided the first real attempt at assessing the quality of health care. The report was developed after Abraham Flexner visited a number of medical schools because of reports of high variability in the quality of medical education which corresponded with high variability in patient outcomes. This report established a scientific based model to educating physicians (Duffy, 2011). As a result of this report, **accreditation** of medical schools began as well as more mature record keeping in medical schools and hospitals.

Even as record keeping improved in the early 1900's, the complexity of health care and what was meant by quality became the leading reasons why assessment of health care was still poor. Unlike other industries, the interpretation of a quality outcome was highly subjective. In 1915, Dr. Earnest Codman proposed the end results idea, which required that patients be followed after being discharged from the hospital to determine whether they fully recovered. He was able to catalogue 123 errors in a study of 337 of his patients (Passaro & Organ, 1999). Dr. Codman used this study as an expose for the poor quality of the American Healthcare System, and stated that current healthcare leaders had "their heads in the sand". For this, he was dismissed from the Massachusetts General Hospital and the Harvard Medical School Alumni Association. This practice of following up with patients after discharge to see if they have fully recovered, while straightforward, still is not common practice.

As a result of the Flexner report and Codman's work (which was also highly supported by the Mayo brothers), the American College of Surgeons developed the first Minimum Standards of Hospitals in 1926. It was only one page and focused on the medical staff structure as well as a stronger push towards better capture of data (Wright, 2017). This document coincided with a number of clinical innovations that transformed the hospital from a place for people to go to when near death to a place for people to go to get healed. However, healthcare leaders continued for years to fail to own up to the variable outcomes and safety concerns in health care. Additional data being collected could always be disputed as incomplete or incorrect. Therefore, practitioners and leaders took advantage of the poor data and high complexity to choose the self-protective measures of patient volumes and word of mouth to assess the quality of their work.

Era of Accreditation

The Minimum Standards of Hospitals continued to expand into what became the next phase of assessment of quality in health care. Because data was still considered incomplete and unreliable enough to use, this phase of assessment was dominated by policies and procedures. The Joint Commission on Accreditation of Hospital Organizations (JCAHO), founded in 1950, became the assessor of quality in the American Healthcare System. JCAHO was not a government agency but was able to partner with the Centers for Medicare and Medicaid Services (CMS) so that hospitals could not be reimbursed without JCAHO accreditation. Because the healthcare system still had very immature data, JCAHO focused on Avedis Donabedian's work that detailed how uniform patient outcomes were a result of standard processes which flowed from a strong structure (Donabedian, 1966/2005) as illustrated in **Figure 11.1**. Healthcare outcomes data were immature during this era due to a number of factors, including lack of risk adjustment, difficulty in capturing usable data, and issues with standardized definitions of numerators and denominators. Therefore, comparisons between hospitals or even between time periods in the same hospital were useless because the differences had more to do with data weaknesses rather than clinical care. There were simply no apples-to-apples comparisons.

Until data became mature enough to be used in the 1990s (**Table 11.1**), JCAHO relied on policies and procedures to assess structure and process. Hospitals knew when they were going to be re-accredited by JCAHO, and the months prior became times to pay for additional hours from anyone who could

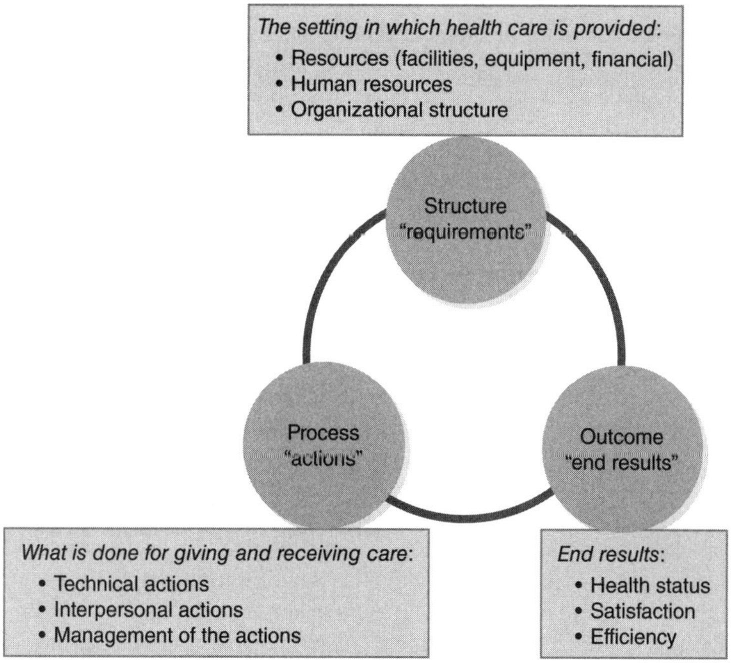

Figure 11.1 Structure-Process-Outcomes of the Donabedian Model

Table 11.1 Recent Evolution of Assessment of Quality in Health Care

	1990s	2000s	2010s	2020s
Prevailing Concept	Accreditation	The Balanced Scorecard	Big Data	Artificial Intelligence
Data	**Unusable** "The data is bad" & "The data was bad"	**Maturing** "The data is bad, but usable"	**Information** "Too much data & too little information"	**Insights** "Too much information & too little insight"
Quality Department Employees	Nurses	90s staff + Analysts and Change Agents	Physician leaders and analysts	Physician and nurse leaders and data scientists
Measuring Overall Quality	Prestige, Profitability & Word of Mouth	Safety Events, Rankings & Satisfaction	Movement to objectivity	Movement to accountability
Boards & Administrators	"We are a high quality organization!!.. Aren't we??"	"How do we become better?"	"HELP"	"We need to do better"

(continues)

Table 11.1 Recent Evolution of Assessment of Quality in Health Care *(continued)*

	1990s	2000s	2010s	2020s
Quality Metrics	Patient Satisfaction, Market Share, Operating Margin	Risk Adjusted metrics, AHRQ PSIs/QIs, HACs, Evidence-Based Medicine	Balanced metrics—quality, safety, operational, financial, satisfaction, & population health	Overall balanced metrics drill into to uncover insights

type over a certain number of words per minute to produce an updated set of policies and procedures. This updated set would end up on leaders' desks to review and sign. Then the leaders would ensure that employees read and understood them. Everything else was put on hold. The main task of quality departments was to prepare for JCAHO accreditation and then to ensure that all employees were where they were supposed to be during the JCAHO visit. In addition, the visit included tours to ensure the hospital and its employees were presentable. Hospitals would reduce clutter by loading equipment and boxes not in use onto large trucks which were parked out of eyesight of the JCAHO accreditors. The JCAHO team (typically a physician, nurse, and administrator) focused their tours inspecting refrigerator thermometers and storage areas; very little analysis of outcomes was conducted because they simply did not exist.

During the early part of the Era of Accreditation, quality and safety outcome data was not widely available. Along with the grade that was provided by JCAHO (a 0–100 scale), operating margin and market share were used to determine quality. The theory was that if patients continued to come back to the hospital, and the hospital was able to meet a positive operating margin, then they had to be a good hospital so long as their JCAHO score was greater than 90%. Very few hospitals received scores lower than 90%. If the hospital received greater than 95% on the JCAHO visit, and they had a greater than 10% increase in inpatients in the last year and a greater than 5% operating margin, they could consider themselves to be a great hospital.

A 2005 Washington Post article noted that 99% of inspected hospitals were accredited by the JCAHO with high scores, and that serious problems in the delivery of care were being overlooked or missed (Gaul, 2005). This article, along with a growing discontent from hospitals on the excessive time and energy that went into preparation for the accreditation, led JCAHO leaders to re-organize in 2007. They re-branded as The Joint Commission (TJC) and reduced the focus on policies and procedures. As data matured, they placed less emphasis on structure and more emphasis on a number of process measures that they developed in 2001 known simply as the core measures. The initial set of core measures focused on four clinical conditions—acute myocardial infarction, heart failure, pneumonia, and surgical site infection. These core measures became part of the ORYX program developed by CMS and JCAHO in the 1990s to integrate performance metrics in the accreditation process. These are updated yearly and can be found on The Joint Commission's website (https://www.jointcommission.org/en-us/accreditation/performance-measurement).

CMS worked closely with JCAHO to develop the core measures and these organizations made the capture of core measures mandatory for all hospitals in order to get reimbursement beginning in 2002. The capture of core measures and transfer to CMS and JCAHO in hospitals was labor intensive and involved hiring nurses to abstract data from the medical record. As the electronic medical record matured, CMS and TJC have now moved many of the core measures to electronic abstraction in order to reduce that labor burden. Core measures were the first comparative set of process measures and they dominated the assessment of quality and safety in hospitals for a number of years. Every year there were updates and changes and hospitals paid substantial attention to improving their

Table 11.2 Types of Accreditation in Hospitals and Health Systems

Type	Example	Measurement
Hospital	TJC	Structure and process standards and guidelines
	DNV	Risk-based approach focusing on continuous improvement and patient safety
Other Healthcare facilities	Skilled Nursing Facilities - CMS	Structure and process standards and guidelines
Department-Based	Laboratory - TJC	Structure and process standards and guidelines
	Laboratory - College of American Pathologists	Peer on-site inspections analyzing structure and process standards and guidelines
Specialty-Based	Trauma - American College of Surgeons	Optimal care of the injured patient based on the Orange Book
	Trauma – State Associations	

scores. Because of the labor needed for these, only a small sample of patient charts were abstracted which led to hospital leaders using low denominators as rationale for poor scores.

In 2008, Det Norske Veritas (DNV) took advantage of the criticisms that were being weighed on TJC to gain approval from CMS to become another option for hospital accreditation. They market their accreditation as having a clear framework for required compliance with a greater focus on continuous improvement and patient safety. Hospitals who had concerns with the time and resources they applied to accreditation now had an alternative that claimed to focus less on policies and procedures and more on risk assessment, improvement, and outcome metrics.

Accreditation has grown well beyond the hospital to now include healthcare sites such as behavioral health, rehabilitation, and skilled nursing facilities as well as departments and clinical conditions within the hospital such as laboratory, radiology, trauma, and cancer. **Table 11.2** provides some examples. Many of the department and clinical condition accreditations are conducted by the medical associations that were initially organized after the Flexner Report. It is now typical for larger U.S. hospitals to have 10 to 15 certificates of accreditation, and to use those to differentiate themselves from competitors.

In addition, a number of programs have been developed during this era to recognize excellence. The most notable of these is Nurse Magnet. While not mandatory, it has become the standard in recognizing and differentiating nursing practice in hospitals. Developed in 1990, Nurse Magnet designation, conducted by the American Nursing Credentialing Center (ANCC), designates organizations worldwide where nursing leaders successfully align their nursing strategic goals to improve the organization's patient outcomes.

Era of Assessment and Accountability

In 1988, Arnold Relman MD, then the editor of the New England Journal of Medicine, signaled data were becoming much more useful in the assessment of quality by stating that the Era of Assessment and Accountability was dawning (Relman, 1988). Dr. Relman stated this phase was finally pushing the American Healthcare System toward being more equitable, high quality and affordable. This dawning was propelled by four things:

- availability of data through the patient's bill;
- risk adjustment;

- the evolving change from paper to electronic records; and
- a series of publications that brought patient safety to the forefront.

Administrative Data

Since CMS began reimbursing hospitals for Americans over 65 years of age, the impoverished, and children in 1965, hospitals have had to produce and submit a bill for patients. Soon after 1965 it became common for other Americans to receive health coverage through the workplace. That health coverage was provided by a growing number of insurance companies. The patient bill is produced by individuals (coders) trained to analyze the patient's medical record and translate physician notes into diagnoses and procedural codes. These coders use the World Health Organization's International Classification of Diseases (ICD) system to determine the patient's main reason for the medical care as well as comorbid conditions and complications from the over 69,000 available diagnosis codes. The codes used for main reason for care determines which diagnostic related group (DRG) to place the patient which is the principal determination of reimbursement.

Since CMS moved from DRGs to MS-DRGs (medical surgical diagnostic related groups) in 2011, much more emphasis has been placed on capturing more diagnoses that could increase the severity of the patient. This is because there are levels in the MS-DRG system that result in higher reimbursement for more severe patients. In addition, CMS now mandates a present on admission (POA) status for each diagnosis. If a diagnosis is present on admission, it is considered a comorbid condition and reimbursement increases. If a diagnosis is not present on admission, it is considered a complication of care and reimbursement does not increase.

This patient-level billing information has become known as "**administrative data**" and has been the standard of assessing quality since it is available for all patients. Many clinicians have criticized the use of administrative data suggesting it is only useful for reimbursement purposes and does not completely capture the severity of patients. This argument may have been appropriate before the adoption of MS-DRGs when many fewer comorbid conditions were being captured. However, since that time databases and rankings that use administrative data have shown an increase in the number of diagnoses per case, which now is around 18 diagnoses per case on average. Contrast this with the average of 5 diagnoses per case that are provided by other countries that do not base their reimbursement on each patient but rather on a global budget of the patients seen in the previous year.

Comparative databases using administrative data have matured to the point where they can assist an organization in determining the changes that need to be made to improve performance. They are able to distinguish if performance is negatively affected by the hospital's documentation and coding practices, and suggest comorbid conditions that they are not capturing compared to other hospitals.

For example, a hospital determined that they were not capturing the ICD version 10 comorbid condition hyponatremia as much as a similar hospital in the same system. They used their clinical documentation specialists to compare medical records and determined that physicians in the low capture hospital were documenting "low sodium" for hyponatremia which the coders cannot use. These same clinical documentation specialists had hallway conversations with physicians to ask them to spell out hyponatremia on the medical record and improvement resulted which led to higher reimbursement. This also led to a more accurate severity of those patients, which became more and more important in the 1990s as **risk adjustment** for metrics became commonplace.

Risk Adjustment

You cannot assess quality in health care without comparisons. One may believe a JCAHO score of 87% is good because it is a solid B until it is recognized that 99% of hospitals received a score of 93 or better. Prior to the development and use of valid risk adjustment methods, hospitals would use the JCAHO score and outcome metrics like in-hospital mortality or length of stay

(LOS) comparisons to themselves over time to assess performance. Comparisons to other hospitals were difficult because it was understood that the large, urban academic medical center (AMC) were taking care of sicker patients which meant that they would see more deaths and longer LOS. Comparisons to other hospitals were always challenged as not being "apples to apples".

There were two lists of comorbid conditions that predicted greater severity developed in 1997 and 1998. These are the Charlson Comorbidity Index (CCI) and the Elixhauser Comorbidity Index (ECI), respectively. CCI included 19 chronic conditions (since shortened to 17) to predict 1-year mortality. The ECI has a longer list of chronic conditions at 30 or 31 (Sharma et al., 2021). Because the ECI is statistically superior and also predicts length of stay, adverse events, and hospital discharges, it has become the gold standard list of severity predictors. The risk adjustment used by CMS for their Stars ranking program utilizes the ECI list.

While risk adjustment has propelled assessment of quality in health care to the point of being able to differentiate hospitals in metrics like in-hospital mortality, readmissions, complications, and LOS, it can only adjust what data are captured. Since most of the available risk adjustment comes from administrative data, it only captures what is on the patient's bill. Patient acuity is multifactorial, and includes chronic conditions, demographics, and social determinants of health, not all of which can be captured reliably. Because of this, it is still important to compare only similarly sized hospitals and similar patients to each other. Risk adjustment allows for apples-to-apples comparisons. Comparing sepsis patients in a large AMC to other large AMCs ensures we are comparing red delicious apples to other red delicious apples.

A comparison will tell you if you are different. It does not tell you why you are different. It is important to remember that data without the ability to drill in and understand the why is useless. If a hospital is presented with a 1.1 observed to expected (o/e) mortality ratio (above 1 is worse than expected) and a comparison of another like hospital is 0.9, no action should be taken until they can drill in and determine why the difference occurs. There are two ways to improve a risk adjusted metric—lower the observed or increase the expected. The latter is a function of documentation and coding. The greater number of chronic conditions captured for a patient, the higher their expected value. The former could be a result of a number of factors, including higher LOS, more complications, or patients with more social determinants of health.

Figure 11.2 illustrates the process an organization might use to transforming data (mortality o/e = 1.1) into information that could identify a change needed to improve it. Without additional analysis and discussions, an organization's leadership may assume that they have a 1.1 mortality o/e because of poor clinical care. They would then

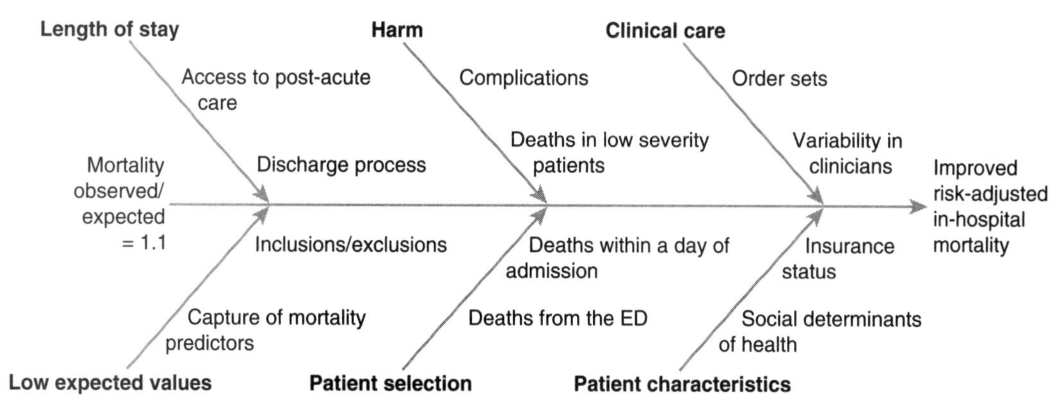

Figure 11.2 Fishbone of Possible Mortality Factors

focus all of their efforts on something like providing antibiotics to sepsis patients within an hour. However, this may not be a factor in improving this particular metric of risk-adjusted in-hospital mortality. Instead, it may be due to low capture rate of mortality predictors.

Too many hospitals react to poor quality results by discarding the data, pointing to the clinicians or trying to determine what care plan deficiency exists. This was the main reason for poor quality of care through the Era of Accreditation. As comparisons and risk adjustment became more robust, we realized that the difference between most hospitals is not due to poor clinicians or care plans, but on data factors like inclusions and exclusions or documentation and coding. Leading organizations in the myriad of rankings that exists realize this and place substantial attention on ensuring good data quality which will result in better rankings.

Risk adjustment shifted our focus in improvement from just clinical care to also paying attention to the quality of the data. For leading organizations, improvement involves both of these. During the Era of Accreditation, the term quality assurance was used which suggested that poor outcomes were due mostly to poor providers. As data matured with better risk adjustment, it became apparent that Donabedian had it correct back in the 1960s. Poor outcomes have as much to do with poor processes and poor structures than poor providers, which has led us to adopt the term quality improvement.

Clinical Data

Over the last 30 years, hospitals in the United States have converted from paper to electronic medical records which means that assessing quality in hospitals can now be performed using data from clinician's notes, and ancillary results. In contrast to administrative data that comes from the patient's bill, this data is called **clinical data** (see **Table 11.3**). While clinical data is preferable to the use of administrative data in assessing quality, it is still largely unstructured and difficult to extract from the EMR. EMRs were built for the purposes of getting data into the chart and not for getting data out of the chart.

A number of comparative databases, called registries, have been created that use data abstracted from the EMR, typically by trained nurses. While these registries are attempting to take the same path as core measures to develop and electronically link to retrieve the data they need, it still is labor and time intensive to get good

Table 11.3 Administrative vs Clinical Data

	Administrative Data	Clinical Data
Where do the data typically come from?	Patient's bill	Electronic medical record (EMR)
Main metrics derived from it	Mortality, length of stay, direct cost/patient, complications, readmissions	Diagnostic success, complications, patient biomarkers and comorbidities
Risk adjustment	Coded diagnoses and patient demographics	Lab values and other variables collected in the EMR
Best use case	Comparative benchmarking	Research
Strength	Inexpensive access and depth and breadth of data	Highly specific and accurate data
Weakness	Subject to variability and subjective nature of documentation and coding	Expensive to access in a usable manner for a broad number of patients and their entire patient experience

information. Because of this, registries will only get data on a subset of patients. Medical associations have developed registries for their own specialty, and they still only capture a subset of data points on a subset of patients in that specialty. For example, the American College of Surgeons (ACS) has developed a registry for trauma patients and one for surgical patients. In each case, abstractors only collect data on a sample of patients that are then fed into the registry, and they do not capture data for the entire stay of the patient. The ACS then provides quarterly comparative reports to subscribing hospitals. Because the ACS owns these registries, they will use their clinical members as the salesforce to sell the registries into hospitals.

While the clinicians prefer to use clinical data, its use is still limited due to the sampling. Therefore, most hospitals will use the administrative databases to populate their dashboards and then the registries as a way to drill further into opportunities. Registries do produce more research leading to clinical quality improvements. While registries are excellent at determining what drugs, tests, or other clinical interventions can improve patient care, administrative databases are best at determining which hospitals perform better on specific metrics.

Balanced Scorecard

It was during the Era of Assessment and Accountability, prompted by the maturity of administrative and clinical data, as well as publications such as *To Err is Human*, that most hospitals began to assess their performance using a **balanced scorecard** approach (Kaplan & Norton, 1992). The executives of an organization no longer relied on market share and financial performance. They were now discussing performance in a balanced manner, including metrics in finance, operations, quality, safety, and satisfaction. While the denominators and numerators, inclusions and exclusions may be different, most hospitals leadership teams were taking time every month or quarter to react to the metrics seen in **Table 11.4**. This also translated to the board room, where metrics were presented, analyzed, and discussed.

It is interesting to note that, as data matured, the reliance on core measures and accreditation to differentiate quality and safety performance in a hospital diminished. TJC continues to be a topic that is discussed, but now those discussions only coincide with their visits. This also changed the structure and makeup of quality departments in hospitals, which had been dominated by nurses well versed in accreditation. In the Era of Assessment and Accountability, there arose a demand for clinicians, administrators, and analysts with the following skills: curiosity, storytelling, understanding variation, healthcare proficiency, and problem solving. These are the skills necessary to create the changes that would lead to changing a red dot to a green dot on the balanced scorecard. At the same time, health care began to embrace two toolsets—improvement science methodologies and business

Table 11.4 Illustrative Balanced Scorecard For Hypothetical Organization

Domain	Metric	Current Value	Last Year Value	Compare Group Value
Finance	Cost/Patient	**$11,632**	$10,350	$9,301
	Expense/Patient	**$22,320**	$21,673	$19,550
Safety	Complications/Patient	**.043**	.044	.048
Quality	Risk-Adjusted Mortality	**.89**	.94	.96
	30-day Readmissions	**13.2%**	12.4%	11.6%
Operations	Risk-Adjusted LOS	**1.24**	1.13	.98
Patient Satisfaction	Would Recommend	**89%**	86%	85%

intelligence software. Improvement methodologies had been around in other industries for years, but with the balanced scorecard, health systems began to implement and train employees on Total Quality Management, Continuous Quality Improvement, Six Sigma, PDSA, and Lean. IT software companies began to see that balanced scorecards were being built on Excel and/or PowerPoint, so they developed much more sophisticated software like Tableau and Qlik to produce much more visibly appealing dashboards.

With all of this greater visibility into the performance of hospitals, you would think that we have moved into the Era of Improvement, but that has not been the case. Even recently the American Healthcare System has been plagued with flatlines in many of the major metrics on the balanced scorecard. One reason for the flat lines seen on **Figure 11.3** is that we have yet to go beyond believing the balanced scorecard is the end of the analytic exercise. Data are transformed to information, which is the balanced scorecard. However, more work needs to be done to transform information into insights. The balanced scorecard tells an organization that they are different in a key process indicator, while insights will tell that organization *why* they are different. It is the *why* that will determine the right action.

IT software companies may claim their software produces insights, but it is only through the interpretation of additional reports, and discussions with people involved that insights are gained. What we do too often in hospitals is to provide the executives and board with the balanced scorecard to react to rather than having someone present the balanced scorecard to the executives after insights are developed. For example, most hospitals who see they have a red dot in risk-adjusted in-hospital mortality of sepsis patients will immediately focus on improving antibiotic administration in a timely manner of newly detected sepsis patients, and then get frustrated when their success in antibiotic timing does not result in improved risk-adjusted in-hospital mortality. If they had drilled into their data, they may have found that their difference in risk-adjusted in-hospital mortality was because other hospitals are much better at discharging very sick sepsis patients to post-acute care so that they do not die in the hospital. While the patient still dies, they are doing so in a better environment for them and their families, and the hospital can fill that acute care bed with someone who needs it more.

To Err Is Human and Crossing the Quality Chasm

In November of 1999, the Institute of Medicine published *To Err is Human*, a book that used administrative data to suggest that 98,000 people die in hospitals every year from medical errors (IOM, Kohn L. T., Corrigan J. M., Donaldson M. S., 2000). This sentinel publication exposed the significant patient safety opportunity within the American Healthcare System. *To Err is Human* outlined structural and process changes that were needed to attack medical errors without pointing fingers at the clinicians, which harkened back to the Era of Accreditation.

This book set off a firestorm of debates within the American Healthcare System as well as within the general public because medical errors had largely been silenced for years. Only a few voices, like Ernest Codman in the early 1900s and Lucian Leape in the 1980s and 1990s, understood that medical errors accounted for more deaths in a year than workplace injuries. The debates typically revolved around the actual numbers of medical errors and the number of deaths. These debates initially stalled the improvement of medical errors and complications in health care, but there was no doubt that patient safety separated from quality as its own domain to be studied and to be used to assess and compare hospitals. Because of the factors discussed in this chapter, the American Healthcare System was widely thought to be the best healthcare system in the world. *To Err Is Human* challenged that assertion and the general public was first alerted to serious flaws in the provision of health care.

Widely known as the follow up publication to *To Err is Human*, The Institute of Medicine published *Crossing the Quality Chasm* in 2001. While its predecessor brought to life the reality of problems in quality and patient safety in the American Healthcare System, *Crossing the Quality*

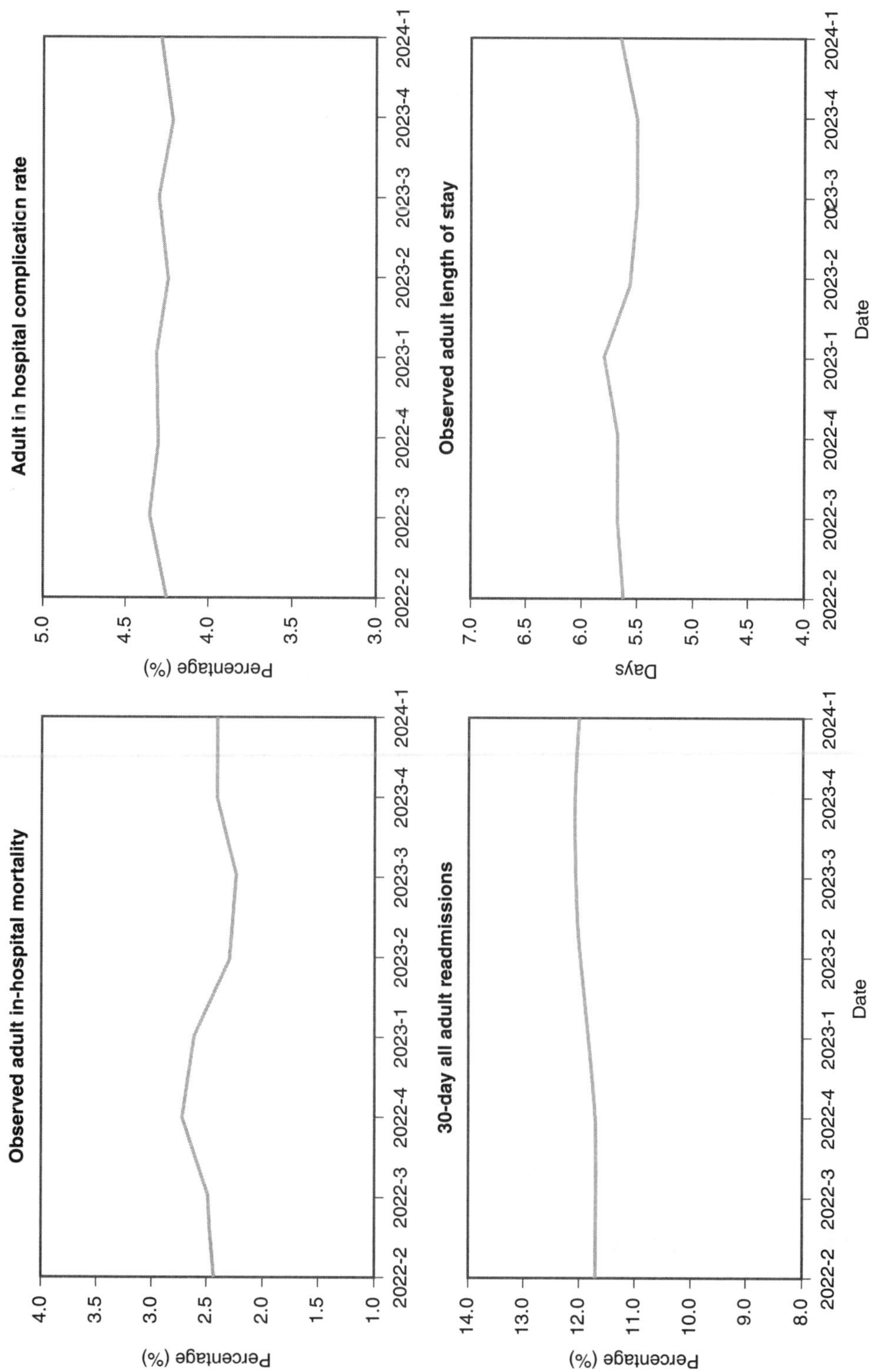

Figure 11.3 Trend Lines of 1,200 Hospitals from Vizient's Clinical Data Base

Data from Vizient, Inc. Clinical Data Base (2025).

Chasm provided a roadmap for fundamental change to a flawed system (IOM, 2001). The IOM suggested that health care today harms too frequently and routinely fails to deliver its potential benefits. *Crossing the Quality Chasm* came up with five macro agenda items needed to redesign health care. The agenda called for a commitment by all entities involved in care to a common purpose and six aims of care for health care improvement: safety, timeliness, equity, effectiveness, efficiency, and patient-centered (STEEEP). The agenda tasked the Department of Health and Human Services (DHS) to lead the transformation by identifying priority conditions with which to start and tasked DHS, academic centers, insurers and others to provide environments that facilitate and reward quality care. In addition, this publication laid out goals of improvement in quality and patient safety outcomes in the first 5 years. The Agency for Healthcare Research and Quality (AHRQ) created a set of patient safety (PSIs) and inpatient quality indicators (IQIs) from administrative data that have become the standard in assessment.

Because most of the response to these two publications in the first 5 years was disagreements around the numbers and how large of a chasm existed, the goals in improvement were not achieved. Also, the public began to push for more accountability in the American Healthcare System. In 2004 the Kaiser Family Foundation, AHRQ, and the Harvard School of Public Health conducted a national survey on the public's perception of quality and safety in health care. The findings were telling. Fifty-five percent stated that they were dissatisfied with the quality of care in the United States. This grew from 44% in 2000 (Kaiser & AHRQ, 2004).

Rankings and Assessments of Hospitals and the American Healthcare System

For the same reasons that prompted the use of balanced scorecards, hospitals have seen a proliferation of rankings and assessments since the 1990s. These are dependent upon available data and other information that can be received through surveys. At the hospital level, a few of these rankings and assessments are available to and widely used by the public. Notably, these include:

- **CMS Stars:** A yearly assessment using Medicare and Medicaid administrative data. This assessment has evolved from mainly comparisons of process core measures (e.g., aspirin to stroke patients with a certain time period) to now including mostly outcome measures, such as death rates and the AHRQ PSIs. In the CMS reports, hospitals receive one to five stars. The reports are available to the public online through a searchable database (https://www.medicare.gov/care-compare/resources/hospital/overall-star-rating).
- **US News:** A yearly listing of qualifying American Academic Medical Centers broken into an overall list of top hospitals, and a list of top hospitals in a number of specialties. This assessment includes structure, process, and outcome measures from available administrative and survey data. The majority of the list is determined by a select group of physician's subjective preferences on the hospitals they believe to be the best in their specialty.
- **Leapfrog:** A yearly assessment providing an A–F grade on patient safety. The grade is based on volumes that each hospital provides, outcomes metrics from available administrative data, and survey answers. The majority of the grade is based on the survey results, which include structure and process questions such as nurse/patient ratios.
- **Lown Index:** A yearly ranking providing an A–F grade. It is the first ranking to evaluate hospitals on their social responsibility, which includes metrics on health equity (e.g., uncompensated care and difference between executive and healthcare worker compensation) and value of care (avoiding overuse and cost efficiency) alongside traditional patient outcomes from available administrative data.

Because reimbursement in other countries is through a global budget, there is not nearly as much emphasis on capturing all of the comorbid conditions that are found on the patient's bill in the United States. Therefore, countries do not have the mature administrative data seen in the United States. Assessment of quality at the country level, therefore, cannot occur using the risk-adjusted, balanced scorecard process seen in American hospitals. Instead, agencies have used societal metrics to compare healthcare systems. Three examples with their metrics are listed below.

- **United Health Foundation**—Teen Suicide, Obesity, Low Birth Rate, Mental Distress
- **World Health System Facts**—Spending per capita + % of population covered = access, average life expectancy at birth, infant mortality rates, maternal mortality ratio
- **Commonwealth Fund**—Deaths from preventable and treatable causes, drug and alcohol overdose deaths, mental health issues

While the United States spends 35% more in health care per capita than the second highest country in the world, it ranks poorly in many of the societal outcomes. The United States justifies this uneven performance by claiming that our healthcare system is not set up to provide health. Instead, our hospitals, physicians, and nurses are providing medical care to patients that come to their facility. In addition, the poor societal metric outcomes that exist are because the United States has more mental and public health issues, including those metrics measured by the three agencies above. Whether it is class inequities, poorer eating habits, or greater pressure to achieve financial stability, the American Healthcare System contends that our outcomes would be the worst in the world if it were not for the excellence of the medical care we provide. However, that cannot be confirmed because of the lack of good, comparative data.

Critics around the world of the American Healthcare System will say that we have too much money, focus, and attention in providing medical care. They suggest that we should decrease resources to medical care and increase them to mental and public health issues. There has been research to shift the thinking about the American Healthcare System from a micro/meso-system focused on medical care to include the interplay with all of the embedded systems in health care (**Figure 11.4**) (Barach & Johnson, 2006) (Nelson, Batalden, et al., 2002). The challenge is that the American Healthcare System has become so big and entrenched that it cannot see a viable path to the provision of health without tremendous changes in the macro-system.

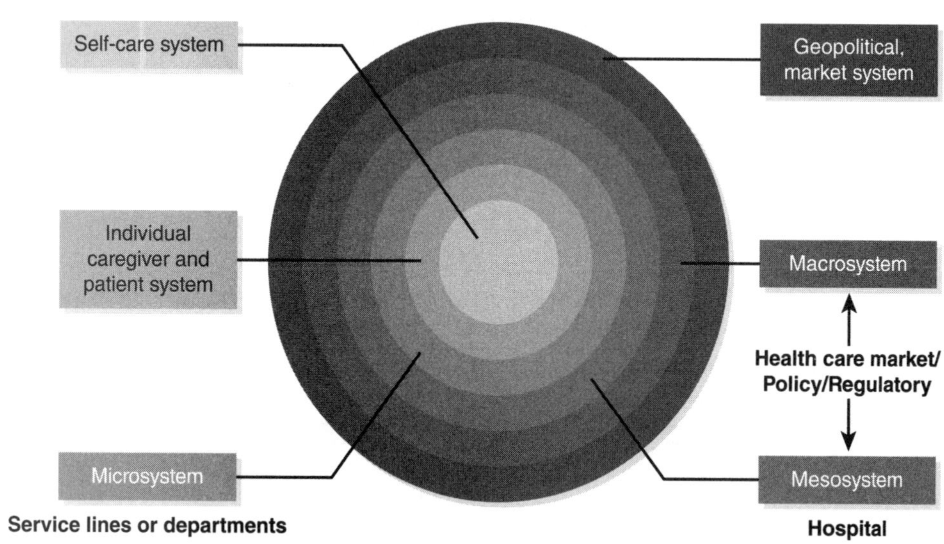

Figure 11.4 The Embedded Systems of Health Care

The Future of Assessment of Quality in Health Care

As data continues to mature, *Crossing the Quality Chasm's* STEEEP aims provide the vision of future balanced scorecards. The challenge is determining how best to measure each of the STEEEP components. **Table 11.5** provides a current metric and a future visionary metric for each aim. The future measurement of these aims will only get better as we combine the power of clinical data with the depth of administrative data. Even though proponents of registries suggest that clinical data should replace administrative data, it is better to not discount the breadth and depth of the coded data. In addition, one of the most exciting promises of artificial intelligence is in reducing the time of documentation and the cost of abstracting the record for ICD-10 diagnoses and procedures through the use of triggers in the electronic medical record. This promise opens up badly needed time for clinicians, and transforms coders into reviewers.

For example, one of the AHRQ PSI 03 captures pressure ulcers that occur in the hospital. The AHRQ definition is a stage III or IV pressure ulcer as a secondary diagnosis per 1,000 discharges among surgical or medical patients ages 18 years and older. Exclusions include: stays less than 3 days; cases with a principal stage III or IV pressure ulcer diagnosis; cases with a secondary diagnosis of stage III or IV pressure ulcer that is present on admission; obstetric cases; severe burns; exfoliative skin disorders. Today, the AHRQ software can determine if a PSI 03 occurs.

However, some hospitals will educate their physicians and coders on the importance of documenting that the pressure ulcer was present on admission, or they may have a slightly different interpretation of the difference between a stage II and III pressure ulcer. This leads to data quality issues when comparing PSI 03, because it introduces subjectivity into the assessment. The future of measuring complications is to use lab values or physician orders or voice notes to trigger more objectively whether a PSI 03 occurred. This is similar to what we have seen in core measures, where the abstracted measures based on administrative data have moved to electronic measures based more on clinical data.

Future assessment, undoubtedly, will also include assessment beyond the hospital to understanding whether a patient actually benefited from the care received. While this may seem like

Table 11.5 Current and Future Metrics for STEEEP Components

STEEEP Component	Current Metric	Future Metric
Safety	In-hospital complications from administrative data	Complications from healthcare found in the patient medical record that follows the patient after discharge
Timely	Antibiotic timing for newly diagnosed sepsis patients (episodic)	Percent of **all** care provided in a timely manner
Effective	Randomized controlled trials determine best practice	Artificial intelligence develops best practice
Efficient	Cost/patient based on ratio of cost to charge worksheet	Cost/patient based on a normalized actual cost of what is received
Equitable	Single studies of specific differences based on gender or race	EMR analytics signals inequitable care when it occurs
Patient-Centered	Patient experience	Patient-reported outcomes

a given, we all know of a friend or relative who did not recover from their ailment after a hospital stay. In the American Healthcare System, assessment of the ultimate outcome is not known because no feedback loop exists after the patient leaves the hospital. Many hospitals are following up with patients a day or two after discharge, but very few are employing Codman's end results idea to find out if the patient has fully recovered weeks or even months after the hospital stay. In the patient-centered aim of STEEEP, patient-reported outcome measures (PROMs) are being developed as surveys provided to a patient weeks and months after a procedure. These surveys employ both subjective and objective measures of whether the procedure successfully achieved the goals set forth initially by the patient and physician. PROMs, however, are not in widespread use by hospitals. Although they are encouraged, they are not mandatory from CMS like patient experience measures that evaluate the patient's hospital stay (CMS, 2026).

Finally, the future of assessment of quality in hospitals has to be more attuned to the main motive for benchmarking which is to motivate improvement in health care. Too many health systems want better ranks only to be used as a marketing tool. As mentioned under the balanced scorecard, hospitals and health systems must be able to develop skill in the data–information–knowledge–wisdom pyramid. Combining administrative with clinical data and artificial intelligence will expand the amount of data and information that will be available, but knowledge and wisdom can only result from data analysis and discussions that motivate change. This means that data without the ability to substantially drill into is useless. When CMS gives a hospital three stars, they will need to be able to not only understand which metrics they need to improve but why they fell short on that measure. While artificial intelligence may someday be able to point a hospital to that why, it will not be able to present it in a compelling way to motivate change. That will always fall to a person.

Key Concepts and Terms

Accreditation
Administrative data
Balanced scorecard
Clinical data
Risk adjustment

References

Barach, P., & Johnson, J. K. (2006). Understanding the complexity of redesigning care around the clinical microsystem. BMJ *Quality & Safety, 15*(Suppl 1), i10–i16. https://doi.org/10.1136/qshc.2005.015859

Donabedian, A. (2005). Evaluating the quality of medical care. *The Milbank Quarterly*, 83(4), 691–729. https://doi.org/10.1111/j.1468-0009.2005.00397.x. (Reprinted from "Evaluating the quality of medical care," 1966, *The Milbank Memorial Fund Quarterly, 44*(3, Part 2), 166–203.)

Duffy, T. P. (2011). The Flexner report—100 years later. *The Yale Journal of Biology and Medicine*, *84*(3), 269–276.

Centers for Medicare & Medicaid Services (CMS). Types of Measures – Patient Reported Outcome Measures. Accessed from, https://mmshub.cms.gov/about-quality/types/proms/overview, on 2/9/2026

Gaul, G. M. (2005, July 24). Accreditors blamed for overlooking problems. *The Washington Post*. https://www.washingtonpost.com/archive/politics/2005/07/25/accreditors-blamed-for-overlooking-problems/01cc8e09-0597-46e3-96fe-9055d2c7346c/

Institute of Medicine. (2001). *Crossing the quality chasm: A new health system for the 21st century*. National Academies Press. https://doi.org/10.17226/10027

The Joint Commission (2025). *ORYX® for Hospitals fact sheet*. Archived June 5, 2025, at https://web.archive.org/web/20250605204044/https://www.jointcommission.org/resources/news-and-multimedia/fact-sheets/facts-about-oryx-for-hospitals/

Kohn, L. T., Corrigan, J. M., & Donaldson, M. S. (Eds.). (2000). *To Err Is Human: Building a Safer Health System*. Committee on Quality of Health Care in America, Institute of Medicine. National Academies Press; 2000.

Kaiser Family Foundation & Agency for Healthcare Research and Quality. (2004). *National survey on consumers' experiences with patient safety and quality information: Survey summary and chartpack*. https://www.kff.org/wp

-content/uploads/2013/01/national-survey-on-consumers-experiences-with-patient-safety-and-quality-information-survey-summary-and-chartpack.pdf

Kaplan, R. S., & Norton, D. P. (1992). The balanced scorecard: Measures that drive performance." *Harvard Business Review, 70*(1), 71–79.

Nelson, E. C., Batalden, P. B., Huber, T. P., Mohr, J. J., Godfrey, M. M., Headrick, L. A., & Wasson, J. H. (2002). Microsystems in health care: Part 1. Learning from high-performing front-line clinical units. *The Joint Commission Journal on Quality Improvement, 28*(9), 472–493. https://doi.org/10.1016/s1070-3241(02)28051-7

Passaro, E., Jr., & Organ, C. H., Jr. (1999). Ernest A. Codman: The improper Bostonian. *Bulletin of the American College of Surgeons, 84*(1), 16–22.

Relman, A. S. (1988). Assessment and accountability. *The New England Journal of Medicine, 319*(18), 1220–1222. https://doi.org/10.1056/NEJM198811033191810

Sharma, N., Schwendimann, R., Endrich, O., Ausserhofer, D., & Simon, M. (2021). Comparing Charlson and Elixhauser comorbidity indices with different weightings to predict in-hospital mortality: An analysis of national inpatient data. *BMC Health Services Research, 21*(1), 13. https://doi.org/10.1186/s12913-020-05999-5

Tossaint-Schoenmakers, R., Versluis, A., Chavannes, N., Talboom-Kamp, E., & Kasteleyn, M. (2021). The challenge of integrating eHealth into health care: Systematic literature review of the Donabedian Model of Structure, Process, and Outcome. *Journal of Medical Internet Research, 23*(5), e27180. https://doi.org/10.2196/27180

Tulchinsky, T. (2018). John Snow, cholera, the Broad Street pump; waterborne diseases then and now. In Elsevier Press, *Case studies in public health* (pp. 77–99). https://doi.org/10.1016/B978-0-12-804571-8.00017-2

Wright, J. R., Jr. (2017). The American College of Surgeons, Minimum Standards for Hospitals, and the provision of high-quality laboratory services. *Archives of Pathology & Laboratory Medicine, 141*(5), 704–717. https://doi.org/10.5858/arpa.2016-0348-HP

CHAPTER 12

Your Role in Leading the Future of CQI in Health Care

Julie K. Johnson and Anna P. Schenck

CHAPTER OUTLINE

Introduction

Our vision for the sixth edition of *Continuous Quality Improvement in Health Care* was to provide a foundation for those interested in learning about CQI—a brief history of the field as well as some of the most relevant topics in improving quality and safety of health and health care. Additionally, we wanted to provide you with the necessary tools so you can join the ranks of those who are working to make things better. As we conclude this edition, we are reminded that many of the familiar challenges to quality care and patient safety persist. We have not solved all the problems, plus we face new and emerging challenges that make the future path uncertain. Academia, public health, and science have come under intense scrutiny, creating the need for more transparency and clearer communication to do our work. Uncertainty about the future isn't a comfortable position for anyone: learners who are embarking on a career, mid-career professionals looking to add QI skills to their repertoire, or senior professionals who are leading teams and organizations.

How can we anchor ourselves and our work during challenging times? Margaret Wheatley, in *Who Do You Choose to Be*, describes working with leaders who "created islands of sanity where good work still got done and where people enjoyed healthy relationships in the midst of chaotic conditions." (Wheatley, 2023).

What does the future hold for CQI in health care? While to a large extent the future is uncertain, there are foundational elements we believe will ground you and us as we continue our work. Even when things feel uncertain, Wheatley writes, there is so much we can do within our sphere of influence. "We can train ourselves to see clearly, to fully acknowledge this time in all its painful details. And then, wherever we are, whomever we are with, we can choose actions based on insight, compassion, and wisdom." (Wheatley, 2023, p. 59). The aim of this chapter is to create a road map for those who choose to step forward to lead the transformation of health care. We start with an overview of conceptual models and present three conceptual models that have helped guide our CQI work and research. We then turn to a discussion about leadership and circle back where we began in Chapter 1, with the premise "quality is local and personal." This premise contains the answer to the question, "Where do I start?"—you start locally and personally.

Conceptual Frameworks for Improving Care

As a research tool, conceptual frameworks help focus the research by providing a way to describe complex topics. Similarly, in CQI, a conceptual model can be useful to help frame your thinking and identify potential questions and measures. Simply put, if an element is important enough to be included on the conceptual model, that is a hint it is important enough for you to address in your research and CQI initiative.

Formally, a **conceptual framework** has been defined as a group of broadly defined and systematically organized concepts to provide a focus, a rationale, and a method for the integration and interpretation of information (Brady et al., 2020). In practice, a conceptual model provides a visual representation of what is possible to study through research or address through programs, practices, and policies.

Our suggestion is to choose a conceptual model that is useful for the task at hand. You don't have to always use the same conceptual model; some models are more useful for different tasks or at different times. There are three models we like and suggest you include in your toolbox. These models can be used in conjunction with other CQI tools you have learned about in this book, such as the PDSA cycle.

The Donabedian Model of Structure–Process–Outcome

An early framework that has been widely accepted is Donabedian's Structure-Process-Outcome (**Figure 12.1**), first described in 1966 (Donabedian, 1966/2005). It is also known as the **Donabedian model**. This model will resonate to those who are drawn to industrial quality improvement, for example, methods discussed in previous chapters by Shewhart and Deming, where there is an input of resources which go into the process or activities that create a set of outcomes.

The Socio-Ecological Model

For CQI to add value, have impact, and realize its potential, it will need to be managed at multiple levels. An ecological perspective provides

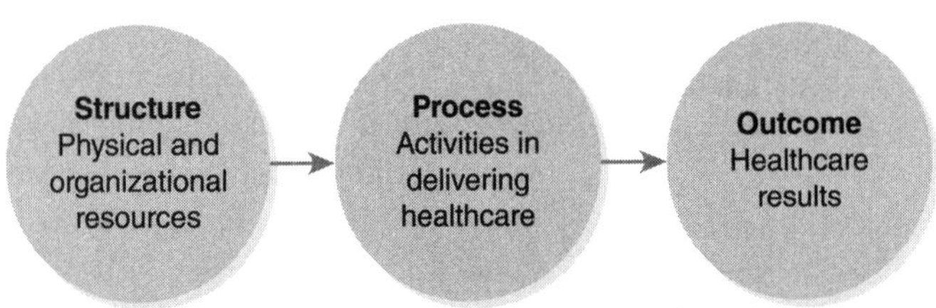

Figure 12.1 Donabedian's Structure–Process–Outcome Model

Data from Donabedian, A. (2005). Evaluating the quality of medical care. The *Milbank Quarterly, 83*(4), 691–729.

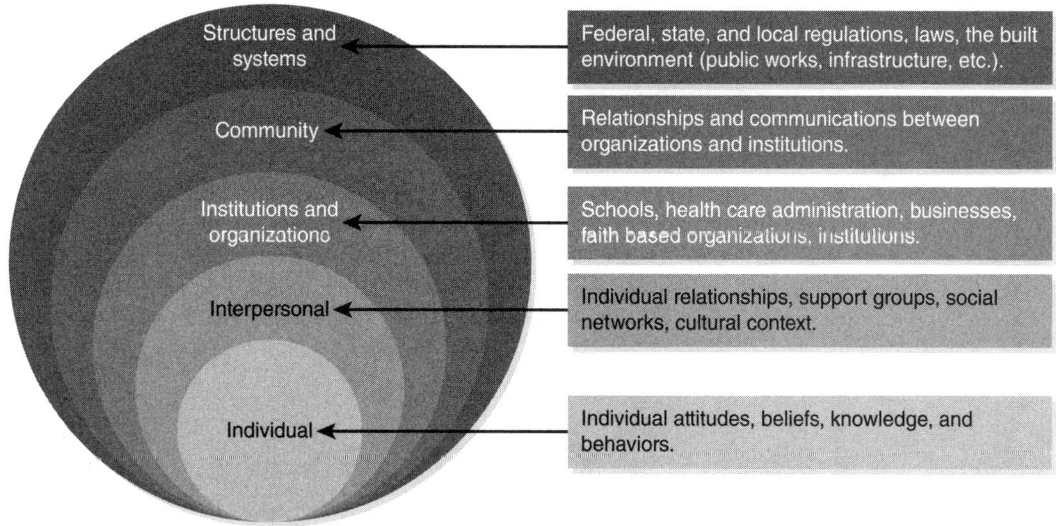

Figure 12.2 Socio-Ecological Model

Reproduced from Centers for Disease Control and Prevention. (2017, December 8). *Health equity resource for state practitioners addressing obesity disparities.* https://www.cdc.gov

a potential framework for thinking about CQI, because it acknowledges many contextual layers, such as the environment, organization, healthcare provider, family, and individual patient characteristics, directly or indirectly influencing a range of patient care outcomes. It also provides a model for breaking down the complexity into manageable components and identifying linkages and interdependencies to consider when making changes. This is sometimes known as the **socio-ecological model**. **Figure 12.2** illustrates the ecological perspective in public health.

The model shown in Figure 12.2 was developed by the public health profession, which has made great strides in quality improvement, spanning education and practice, in recent years and provides another model for accelerating CQI in health care. Much of the progress in CQI and public health was initiated with the release of a 2003 Institute of Medicine (IOM) report that "reviews the nation's public health capabilities and presents a comprehensive framework for how the government public health agencies, working with multiple partners from the public and private sectors as an intersectoral public health system, can better assure the health of communities" (IOM, 2003). The extension of this model to other sectors of health requires a conversion of terms, but not concepts; it is another example of cross-disciplinary thinking and interprofessional sharing of ideas.

The Model of the Domains of Quality for the New Era of Health

In *Crossing the Quality Chasm*, the Institute of Medicine (IOM) proposed six domains of quality in health care: person-centeredness, timeliness, efficiency, effectiveness, safety, and equity (IOM, 2001). The World Health Organization (WHO) added "Integrated" to the original list, as an important reminder of the need for continuity of health services across one's life course, as discussed in Chapter 1.

Lachman et al., (2021) proposed a conceptual model (**Figure 12.3**) that expands the IOM's original six domains of quality to include Ecology and Transparency (labeled Eco Friendly) and introduces the domains of "person-" and "kin-centered care" to emphasize the shared humanity of people involved in the interdependent work.

Figure 12.3 builds on the idea that person-centeredness is central to quality and

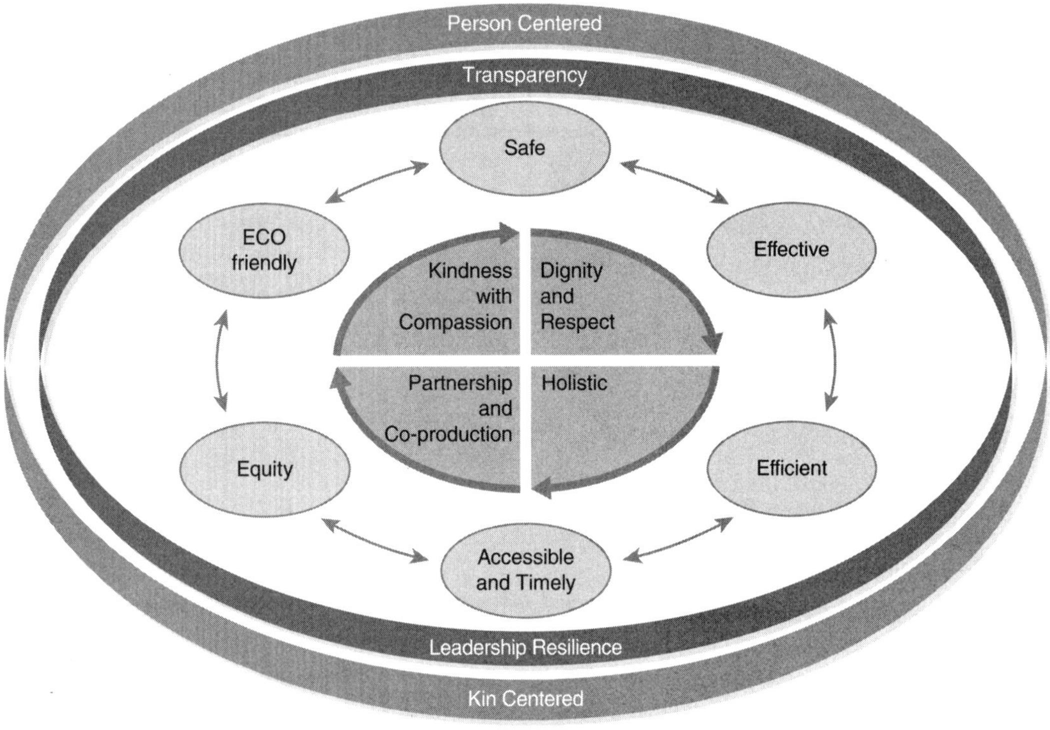

Figure 12.3 The Domains of Quality for the New Era of Health

illustrates that while it is a separate domain, it has an integral connection to all other domains.

When reviewing conceptual models, it's important to remember George Box, a British statistician who said, "All models are wrong, but some are useful." (Box, 1976) While Box was referring to statistical models, his comment is relevant for us as we look for conceptual models to support our CQI work and research. This is why we recommend you include several models in your toolbox and continually assess their usefulness. You may find it helpful to add context-specificity in your models.

Leaders Are Needed at All Levels

The role of leadership is recognized as fundamental to improving quality and safety because leaders enable connections between the aims and the design and testing of those improvements. Leadership has a critical role in setting a vision for change, or constancy of purpose (Deming, 1986) and shaping a culture that embraces quality and safety. Leadership is the first of seven Health Care Criteria for Performance Excellence for the Malcolm Baldrige National Quality Award. According to the Baldrige Performance Excellence Program (2026):

> An organization's senior leaders (administrative and health care provider leaders) should set directions and create a patient focus, clear and visible values, and high expectations. . . . Leaders should ensure the creation of strategies, systems, and methods for achieving excellence in health care, stimulating innovation, and building knowledge and capabilities.

Leadership roles for making decisions and guiding change must be afforded to people working in managerial or clinical roles, line staff, and field positions. Changes and decisions designed by people in offices apart from where the work is performed usually have limited effect. Their role should be limited to determining and communicating the broader environmental context in which local decision making takes place. For real innovation and improved performance, people working directly with problems and systems need to be empowered to be fully involved in designing and deciding how to improve processes and quality. These are the people on the sharp end of processes, who will experience intrinsic motivation to lead the transformations that are needed, including innovation and improvement.

Leading an organization committed to improving quality and adding value requires creating a "learning organization" that learns from within and formally seeks new ideas from outside as well, which are keys to the diffusion of CQI in health care (Berwick, 2003).

Leadership is not about applying a collection of tools and techniques to those being led; it involves integrating the learning disciplines throughout the organization—vision, values, and purpose; systems thinking; and mental models (Senge, 1990). Successful leaders motivate followers to contribute to the development of a shared vision, emphasizing the values of CQI, and demonstrating their personal commitment to achieving it. They "inspire" the vision throughout the organization. When defining leadership in the terms of creating a learning organization, the role of the leader is to take responsibility for learning, as a designer of the learning process, a steward of the vision, and a teacher by fostering the learning throughout the organization (Senge, 1990). In so doing, leaders ensure the development of an organizational culture that embraces change and improvement.

Leadership includes not only defining the vision but also living the vision and leading by example. Also important to note is leadership must occur at all levels within an organization, including scientific leaders, opinion leaders, and those who champion change ideas (Greenhalgh et al., 2005). These individuals may or may not have administrative leadership roles. As discussed earlier, education and training are the critical factors to ensure leadership in the future—and not merely for those at the top levels of an organization. If we want to establish leaders at all levels, we need leadership training at all levels. Leadership education is no longer confined to business schools, but is being expanded to the sciences, including medicine, nursing, and public health. This trend must continue. There has also been greater availability of leadership publications directed at the unique leadership challenges faced in academic medicine (Drake et al., 2023; Houpt et al., 2015; Viera & Kramer, 2016). Similarly, leadership programs and literature have expanded among other health disciplines directly involved in CQI; for example, biostatisticians (LaVange et al., 2012). These are only samples of broader initiatives that need to be replicated to encourage greater leadership development among a wide array of health professionals.

Leadership skills should not be limited to specific healthcare challenges but should emphasize aspects of leadership appropriate for leaders of CQI initiatives in health; for example, an emphasis on transformational leadership and the related broader topic of leading change (Daft, 2015; Kotter, 1996; Rowitz, 2009; Sapienza, 2004). Educational programs should address the predisposing, enabling, and reinforcing factors leading to higher quality, safer health care; for example, organizational dynamics and diffusion of innovation, and establishing a vision and culture to embrace change.

Quality Is Still Personal

If you read this textbook from start to finish you may be surprised to find we are ending where we started, pointing out that quality is local and personal. If you are new to quality improvement and wondering where to start, we suggest starting with a personal improvement project. If you are a seasoned health professional, we recommend starting with a personal improvement project. The underlying reason for this blanket recommendation is that improving quality is hard work and the best way to understand how hard it is before you ask people around you to engage in a quality improvement project, is to practice the tools and techniques you read about in previous chapters.

Conclusions

Our goal with the sixth edition of this text was to inspire students/readers to keep learning. While great progress has been made, we are sobered by the realization that much more needs to be done and sometimes good work is undone as political tides change. We find it fitting to conclude this chapter with words from Avedis Donabedian, one of the most well-recognized forefathers of quality in health care (Best & Neuhauser, 2004):

> Systems awareness and systems design are important for health professionals, but they are not enough. They are enabling mechanisms only. It is the ethical dimensions of individuals that are essential to a system's success. Ultimately, the secret of quality is love. You have to love your patient, you have to love your profession, you have to love your God. If you have love, you can then work backward to monitor and improve the system. (p. 472)

With Donabedian's words in mind, and with the future growth of CQI not an option but a necessity, we close this discussion with one further question, "Who are the future leaders in health care, and where are they from?" The answer is easy: They will come from us, our students, and our children.

Key Concepts and Terms

Conceptual framework
Donabedian model
Socio-ecological model

References

Baldrige Performance Excellence Program. (2023-2024). *Baldrige Excellence Framework (Health Care)*. National Institute of Standards and Technology. Available from, https://www.nist.gov/baldrige/publications/baldrige-excellence-framework/health-care. Accessed 2/10/2026.

Berwick, D. M. (2003). Disseminating innovations in health care. *Journal of the American Medical Association, 289(15)*, 1969–1975. https://doi.org/10.1001/jama.289.15.1969

Best, M., & Neuhauser, D. (2004). Avedis Donabedian: Father of quality assurance and poet. *BMJ Quality & Safety, 13*(6), 472–473. https://doi.org/10.1136/qshc.2004.012591

Box, George E. P. (1976). Science and statistics. *Journal of the American Statistical Association, 71*(356), 791–799. https://doi.org/10.1080/01621459.1976.10480949

Brady, S. S., Brubaker, L., Fok, C. S., Gahagan, S., Lewis, C. E., Lewis, J., Lowder, J. L., Nodora, J., Stapleton, A., Palmer, M. H., & Prevention of Lower Urinary Tract Symptoms (PLUS) Research Consortium. (2020). Development of conceptual models to guide public health research, practice, and policy: Synthesizing traditional and contemporary paradigms. *Health Promotion Practice, 21*(4), 510–524. https://doi.org/10.1177/1524839919890869

Daft, R. L. (2015). *The leadership experience* (6th ed.). Cengage Learning.

Deming, W. (1986). *Out of the crisis*. Massachusetts Institute of Technology, Center for Advanced Engineering Study.

Donabedian, A. (2005). Evaluating the quality of medical care. *The Milbank Quarterly, 83*(4), 691–729. https://doi.org/10.1111/j.1468-0009.2005.00397.x (Reprinted from "Evaluating the quality of medical care," 1966, *The Milbank Memorial Fund Quarterly, 44*(3, Part 2), 166–203.)

Drake, A. F., Sollecito, W. A., Horneffer, K. E., Martin, J. B., Westervelt, L. M., Murphy, B., Schenck, A. P., & Carter-Edwards, L. (2023). Building diverse leadership in an academic medical center: The ACCLAIM program. *Journal of the National Medical Association, 115*(2), 134–143.

Greenhalgh, T., Robert, G., Bate, P., Macfarlane, F., & Kyriakidou, O. (2005). *Diffusion of innovations in health service organisations: A systematic literature review*. Blackwell Publishing.

Houpt, J. L., Gilkey, R. W., & Ehringhaus, S. H. (2015). *Learning to lead in the academic medical center—A practical guide*. Springer.

Institute of Medicine (IOM). (2001). *Crossing the quality chasm: A new health system for the 21st century*. National Academies Press.

Institute of Medicine (IOM). (2003). *The future of the public's health in the 21st century*. National Academies Press. Retrieved from http://www.nationalacademies.org

Kotter, J. P. (1996). *Leading change*. Harvard Business School Press.

Lachman, P., Batalden, P., & Vanhaecht, K. (2021). A multidimensional quality model: An opportunity for patients, their kin, healthcare providers and professionals to coproduce health. *F1000Research, 9*, 1140. https://doi.org/10.12688/f1000research.26368.3

LaVange, L., Sollecito, W., Steffen, D., Evarts, L., & Kosorok, M. (2012, February 1). Preparing biostatisticians for leadership opportunities. *Amstat News*. http://magazine.amstat.org

Rowitz, L. (2009). *Public health leadership—Putting principles into practice* (2nd ed.). Aspen Publishers, Inc.

Sapienza, A. M. (2004). *Managing scientists—Leadership strategies in scientific research* (2nd ed.). Wiley-Liss, Inc.

Senge, P. (1990). *The fifth discipline*. Doubleday.

Viera, A. J., & Kramer, R. (2016). *Management and leadership skills for medical faculty—A practical handbook*. Springer.

Wheatley, M. J. (2023). *Who Do We Choose to Be?* (2nd ed.). Berrett-Koehler Publishers, Inc.

Glossary

A

acceptability Perception among implementation stakeholders (providers, consumers, managers) that a new treatment, service, or practice is agreeable, palatable, or satisfactory. Acceptability is a key implementation outcome.

accreditation An independent, external evaluation process where organizations prove they meet strict standards for quality and safety, ensuring high-performance patient care, better patient outcomes, and continuous improvement, often required by payors for reimbursement.

active listening The act of being attentive to what's communicated and then relaying that information to be understood, clarified, and create connection.

administrative data Information created during patient healthcare encounters to track service utilization, costs, and health outcomes and maintained by healthcare organizations, institutions, or government agencies to manage the administrative and financial aspects of healthcare services and improve quality of care delivery.

adoption The intent or decision to implement a new practice or innovation. Adoption is a key implementation outcome and is critical for translating research into practice.

aim statement A concise, time-specific, and measurable statement that guides the improvement process, answering "What are we trying to accomplish?". It defines the specific population, the magnitude of change, and a deadline for success, acting as a "north star" for projects.

appropriateness The perceived fit of the intervention for a specific setting. Appropriateness is a key implementation outcome.

B

balanced scorecard A set of measures that gives top managers a fast but comprehensive view of a business/organization. It includes financial measures that tell the results of actions already taken and complements the financial measures with operational measures on customer satisfaction, internal processes, and the organization's innovation and improvement activities—operational measures that are the drivers of future performance.

behavioral norms The unwritten, shared rules and expectations that guide acceptable conduct, interactions, and attitudes within a specific group, organization, or society.

blunt end Represents latent, system-wide factors that cause errors. In contrast with the "sharp end" (direct caregivers).

boundary spanners Combination of opinion leaders and champions that have influence across organizational and other boundaries.

C

cause-and-effect diagrams Also known as fishbone diagram or Ishikawa diagram. A visual tool to identify and display variation. Categories (causes) are typically labeled as people, methods, materials, and environment that contribute to the outcome (effect).

champion Individuals and/or team members who are advocates for the improvement initiative and have perseverance to fight both resistance and/or indifference to promote the acceptance of a new idea or to achieve project goals.

checklist A structured list of process activities, usually in a time-ordered sequence, that must be carried out by team members.

clinical data Information captured related to patient care activities, including clinician's notes and ancillary results.

clinical microsystem A small team of providers and staff providing care for a defined population of patients.

clinical risk management A systematic approach toward aligning the organizational culture, process, and structures that underpin effective management of potential opportunities and adverse events.

co-assessment First step in the coproduction cycle, which addresses the patient's current health status, whether prior treatments were effective, and if any changes are needed.

co-decision Second step in the coproduction cycle, which determines next steps based on the patient's goals, generally involving a comparison of options to facilitate "informed and preference-based choices."

co-delivery Fourth step in the coproduction cycle, which prompts service users and health professionals to reflect on both how the patient can contribute to their care and how a healthcare professional or clinical team can support the patient.

co-design Third step in the coproduction cycle, which creates a treatment or management plan that fits the patient's goals, context, and capabilities while minimizing treatment burden.

common cause variation Predictable variation that is inherently present in every process. Also known as *noise*.

compatibility How closely change ideas align with the existing culture and environment.

conceptual framework A group of broadly defined and systematically organized concepts to provide a focus, a rationale, and a tool for the integration and interpretation of information.

continuous quality improvement (CQI) The combined efforts of everyone—health care professionals, patients and their families, researchers, payers, planners and educators—to make changes that will lead to better patient outcomes (health), better system performance (care) and better professional development (learning)

control chart A time series plot of process measurements over time that includes three statistically computed lines: a center line, an upper control limit, and a lower control limit. Also known as a process behavior chart.

coproduction Health service users and health professionals working together to create, design, produce, deliver, assess, and evaluate the relationships and actions that contribute to the health of individuals and populations.

cost Money, resources, time, or effort needed to implement an intervention. Cost is a key implementation outcome.

culture The collection of individual and group values, attitudes, and practices that guide the behavior of group members.

Culture of Excellence A set of characteristics of healthcare organizations that ensure the highest quality and safety standards.

Culture of Health An action model developed by the Robert Wood Johnson Foundation to inform its decisions in awarding grants and develop strategic collaborations. Its goals include creating healthier and more equitable communities and transforming health and healthcare systems.

customer Anyone who has expectations regarding a process operation or outputs.

D

daily accountability Process of holding brief team meetings that involves people at all levels of an organization in checking whether the organization is on track for its goals, projects, and performance metrics.

data-to-decision cycle A systematic process in which data is transformed into information, facilitating the identification of improvement opportunities, which then leads to knowledge of how to redesign processes. The cycle finally results in decisions and actions for change and feedback regarding further improvements.

donabedian model First described in 1966, Avedis Donabedian's classic model for describing quality of care through a structure-process-outcome lens.

driver diagram Represents a theory of how changes can lead to improvements. It identifies an outcome of interest, the primary and secondary drivers of the outcome, and the change ideas.

E

ED boarding Phenomenon in which patients are admitted to a hospital yet are held in the emergency department (ED) due to a lack of availability of in-patient beds.

effective One of the Institute of Medicine STEEP dimensions of health care quality defined as providing services based on scientific evidence.

efficient One of the Institute of Medicine STEEP dimensions of health care quality defined as health care delivered in a manner that maximizes resource use and avoids waste.

equitable One of the Institute of Medicine STEEP dimensions of health care quality defined as quality of health care that does not differ in quality according to personal characteristics, such as gender, race, ethnicity, geographical location, or socioeconomic status.

evidence-based practice and management The selection of best health and management practices determined by scientific research, professional expertise, and consideration of internal experience.

F

Factory Physics A scientific framework that describes the laws that govern patient process flow.

feasibility The extent to which organizational resources, motivation, and capabilities can support the implementation of an intervention. Feasibility is a key implementation outcome.

fidelity The match between how an intervention is intended to be delivered and how it is actually delivered. Fidelity is a key implementation outcome.

flowchart Pictorial representation of the steps of a process in sequential order.

frequency chart A diagram of vertical bars representing the frequency of observations in specific categories.

G

gemba Japanese word meaning "the real place" where work is done; in manufacturing, the factory floor; in the clinical context, the operating room, the intensive care unit, or the emergency department.

Goods-dominant logic A way of thinking where goods are "the primary focus of economic exchange. In contrast to service-dominant logic."

H

health disparity Differences in health outcomes regardless of whether they were justly or unjustly imposed.

health equity State in which everyone has a fair and just opportunity to be as healthy as possible.

huddle board A visual management tool used during brief daily team meetings (huddles) to track progress, metrics, goals, and issues.

I

implementation A specified set of activities designed to put an activity or program into practice.

implementation determinants Factors that may affect the implementation outcomes in a particular context.

implementation drivers Key components of capacity and infrastructure that influence a program's success.

implementation outcomes The desired results of the implementation of interventions or change ideas arising from QI projects in an organization.

implementation science Scientific study of methods to promote the systematic uptake of research findings and other evidence-based practices into routine practice, and, hence, to improve the quality and effectiveness of health services and care.

implementation stages Process needed to plan and execute implementation of an intervention.

implementation strategies Implementation interventions to address the determinants that may impede or facilitate the achievement of the implementation—and ultimately the QI—outcomes.

improvement cycles Processes that ensure that the implementation is adapted to local contexts. Typically refers to PDSA cycles.

integrated Coordinated healthcare services across providers, settings, and time.

intrinsic motivation Engaging in an activity for its inherent satisfaction rather than for some separable consequence

L

leader standard work A structured, documented set of daily/weekly routines and tasks for managers and higher roles, applying Lean principles to leadership.

Lean Six Sigma (LSS) A process improvement methodology that combines Lean (identifying waste) and Six Sigma (quality/variation reduction), creating a powerful, complementary system.

Lean Management System (LMS) A management approach focused on maximizing customer value and minimizing waste due to non-value added activities.

learning organization An organization that proactively creates, acquires, and transfers knowledge and changes its behavior on the basis of new knowledge and insights.

localized improvement Improvement focused on addressing a specific problem or process within a defined unit or operational area. The term is used to distinguish between local improvement efforts and widespread improvement that results in organizational changes or process reengineering.

M

market The environment in which an organization operates including patient populations, competitors, regulatory conditions, and economic factors.

microsystem The smallest functional unit within a larger system where care is delivered and improvement activities occur.

muda Waste from activities that use resources but do not add value to the process. Muda can arise from activities that may be necessary (such as transporting products or materials) but do not add value to the process and those that are both unnecessary and do not add value (such as wait times or mistakes).

mura Waste from unevenness or variability in quality or costs, or inconsistency in workflow or demand. Mura may be manifest in resources needed for testing or inspection when quality is unpredictable.

muri Waste by excessive workload or overburdening of people, equipment, or systems.

N

near-miss An error that had the potential to cause injury or loss but did not either by chance or by timely intervention.

noise Variation that affects all outcomes of a process. It is also known as common cause variation. Noise is variation that is inherent in a stable process.

O

opinion leaders Individuals who influence the attitudes, beliefs, and behaviors of others within an organization due to their credibility, expertise, or social position.

organizational accidents Adverse events that occur as a result of systemic failures involving multiple organizational factors rather than isolated individual errors.

organizational culture Values, beliefs, norms, and behaviors shared in an organization that influence how work is performed and decisions are made.

organizational learning The process by which organizations actively seek to capture knowledge from experience, integrate it into systems and processes, and use it to improve performance throughout the organization.

outcomes The results of services, interventions, or processes.

P

P chart A type of control chart used to monitor the proportion or percentage of occurrences of a specific event over time.

Patient Flow Physics A scientific framework used to understand variability in patient flow in health care systems. It is used to identify and minimize bottlenecks and delays and improve efficiency.

Pareto diagram A special type of bar chart that displays categories of factors contributing to a problem in descending order of frequency to identify the most significant contributors.

penetration The degree of integration of an intervention into practice. Penetration is a key implementation outcome.

people-centered One of the Institute of Medicine STEEEP dimensions of health care quality defined as care that respects and responds to the needs, preferences, and values of patients and communities.

performance norms Explicit or implicit standards that define expected performance levels for individuals or teams.

Plan, Do, Study, Act (PDSA) cycle An iterative method for testing changes in real-world settings by planning an intervention, implementing it, studying the results, and refining the approach.

primary data Data collected specifically for the purpose of measurement, evaluation, or improvement.

process A series of actions or steps performed to achieve a specific outcome.

process behavior chart See control chart.

process reengineering A fundamental redesign of processes to improve performance.

psychological safety A belief by a team member that the work environment supports open communication, learning, and speaking up without fear of punishment.

public health The science and practice of improving population health through prevention, policy, education, and organized societal efforts.

Q

Quadruple Aim A framework that targets four goals: improved population health, enhanced patient experience, reduced costs, and improved work life of healthcare providers.

quality The degree to which healthcare services lead to desired health outcomes, result in positive patient experiences and are consistent with current professional knowledge.

Quality 1.0 The phase of quality where an organization is focused on inspection, compliance, and accreditation.

Quality 2.0 The phase of quality where an organization is focused on system-wide improvement using data, process redesign, and improvement science.

Quality 3.0 The phase of quality focusing on coproduction, population health, and integrated care.

quality assurance (QA) Activities focused on ensuring that performance meets established standards.

quality control (QC) QC is synonymous with inspection of products or other process outputs with the goal of determining which products should be rejected and/or reworked, often accompanied by counting the number of "defects."

quality improvement A systematic, data-guided approach to improving processes and outcomes.

Quintuple Aim An extension of the Quadruple Aim that includes advancing health equity, resulting in five aims: improving population health, enhancing patient experience, reducing costs, improving work life of healthcare providers, and advancing health equity.

R

risk The probability and potential impact of harm or an adverse outcome.

risk adjustment A statistical method to account for differences in patients based on their demographics and underlying health conditions used in health care to make comparisons across organizations, places and times more equitable. It is also used in payment models to ensure care provided to high acuity patients is compensated appropriately.

risk management The systematic identification, assessment, and mitigation of risks to an organization.

run chart A line graph that displays data over time, used to identify patterns.

S

safe One of the Institute of Medicine STEEEP dimensions of health care quality defined as care that minimizes harm.

safety culture An organizational culture that prioritizes safety at all levels.

sampling frame The population or source from which a sample is drawn.

secondary data Data collected for purposes other than use in quality, that can be repurposed and analyzed for quality. Commonly used examples include administrative data and payment data.

service-dominant logic A perspective that views service, rather than goods, as the primary source of value.

sharp end Personnel directly involved in patient care.

signals Data variation observed in a process chart indicating special cause variation. Signals result from variation that is not inherent in a process. They affect some but not all outcomes of a process.

Six Sigma A quality improvement methodology focused on reducing variation and defects.

social (and political) determinants of health The conditions in which people are born, grow, work, live, and age, and the wider set of forces and systems shaping the conditions of daily life.

socio-ecological model Developed by the public health profession to acknowledge contextual factors that influence patient outcomes.

special cause variation Sources of variation arising from specific, identifiable factors that affect some but not all outcomes of a process.

stakeholder Any individual or group with an interest or "stake" in an organization's activities.

STEEEP An organizing framework created by the Institute of Medicine representing essential dimensions of quality care: safe, timely, effective, efficient, equitable and patient centered.

structure The environment in which care is delivered. Structure can refer to facilities, organizational and administrative aspects of the care environment.

sustainability The extent to which an intervention is maintained over time. Sustainability is a key implementation outcome.

T

team norms Shared expectations guiding team behavior.

timely One of the Institute of Medicine STEEEP dimensions of healthcare defined as care that is delivered without unnecessary delays.

trialability The degree to which an intervention can be tested on a limited basis.

Triple Aim A framework focused on improving population health, patient experience, and cost efficiency. This aim has been expanded from its original form to include other outcomes (see Quadruple and Quintuple Aims).

U

usable interventions Interventions that are well defined, feasible, and implementable.

V

value chains standardized responses to commonly occurring needs in linked processes (e.g., cataract surgery).

value networks flexible responses to emergent needs.

value shop customized responses to particular needs.

visual controls Visual tools that communicate performance and process status.

VUT equation A mathematical calculating waiting time in a process based on variability, utilization, and time.

Index

Page numbers followed by *f*, *t*, and *b* indicate figures, tables and boxes, respectively.

A

B

C

D

E

F

G

H

Q

R

S

T

U